D1217342

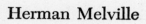

Herman Melville

THE MACMILLAN COMPANY
NEW YORK · BOSTON · CHICAGO
DALLAS · ATLANTA · SAN FRANCISCO

MACMILLAN AND CO., LIMITED
LONDON · BOMBAY · CALCUTTA
MADRAS · MELBOURNE

THE MACMILLAN COMPANY.
OF CANADA, LIMITED
TORONTO

Herman Melville

A Critical Study

by Richard Chase

1949 · THE MACMILLAN COMPANY · NEW YORK

Acknowledgment is hereby made for permission to quote material under
copyright: to Harcourt, Brace & Co. (*Trumpets of Jubilee* by Constance
Rourke, copyright, 1927; *American Humor* by Constance Rourke, copyright, 1931; *Lord Weary's Castle* by Robert Lowell, copyright, 1947) and
to W. W. Norton & Co. (*The Psychoanalytical Theory of the Neuroses* by
Otto Fenichel, copyright, 1945).

FOR FRANCES

Preface

My first purpose in writing this book is to set the works of Herman Melville before the reader in something like their full imperfect glory. My second purpose is to contribute a book on Melville to a movement which may be described (once again) as the new liberalism—that newly invigorated secular thought at the dark center of the twentieth century which, whatever our cultural wreckage and disappointment, now begins to ransom liberalism from the ruinous sellouts, failures, and defeats of the thirties. The new liberalism must justify its claims to superiority over the old liberalism. It must present a vision of life capable, by a continuous act of imaginative criticism, of avoiding the old mistakes: the facile ideas of progress and "social realism," the disinclination to examine human motives, the indulgence of wish-fulfilling rhetoric, the belief that historical reality is merely a question of economic or ethical values, the idea that literature should participate directly in the economic liberation of the masses, the equivocal relationship to communist totalitarianism and power politics. Translate all this back into the nineteenth century and you will see that these problems were also Melville's, and that his work was in its time just the continuous act of imaginative criticism which we now need to perform ourselves. I have the conviction that if our liberalism is serious about its new vision of life, if it has the necessary will to survive, it must come to terms with Herman Melville.

For Melville is one of our fathers. He stood opposed to the social pieties of transcendentalism very much as we must now oppose the progressive liberalism which was born fifteen or twenty years ago— and which now ventures into the perilous future unarmed by either passion or intellect, still marching toward the terrific unknown as confidently as if the unknown were only a well meaning "common man" extending his hand in brotherhood.

Now there is, of course, some semantic difficulty in using the words "liberal" and "progressive" to refer to certain kinds of contemporary thought and also to the thought of Melville and his time. Since Melville's day, these words have undergone various changes in connotation. As for the word "liberal," I use it literally and generally. It means a kind of thought which cherishes freedom and is free, free of dogma and absolutism; a kind of thought which is bounteous, in the sense that it is open-minded, skeptical, and humanist. Thus it is a large term, for one may remain a liberal and be more or less conservative in one's particular opinions, or more or less religious. But the word does denote a general kind of modern thought despite its historical vicissitudes, despite the different meanings it has acquired by being connected with, say, abolitionism or Stalinism. And in modern times liberalism has been repeatedly traduced in fundamentally the same way: by the pharisaism and power worship to which liberalism has itself been prone.

One may distinguish between "liberal" and "progressive." Melville was a liberal in questions of politics, morals, and religion. But he was a progressive only in a very limited sense of the word. To be sure, he wanted man to progress, to improve his lot; but he did not believe that progress was the principle of the universe or that man could do anything which would make progress inevitable —and he had a name for the pious and irresponsible progressive: he called him "the confidence man." Although Melville entertained larger social aspirations than his friend Hawthorne, he would have seen the truth in what Hawthorne wrote in his campaign biography of President Pierce: "There is no instance in all history of the human will and intellect having perfected any great moral reform by methods which it adapted to that end." Is this reactionary? Does it mean no progress is possible? We can hardly think so, for it simply states the truth that progress can be advanced only with difficulty and by indirection and a variety of means in a world timelessly imperfect.. As the well known dictum tells us, "Politics is the art of the possible." So is morality, and life itself. So is art.

In sloughing off a facile idea of progress, Melville accepted what that sloughing-off implied: a tragic view of life. No view of life can protect itself against the attritions of history if it cannot see man's lot as a tragedy—that is, if it cannot see that civilization, precious on any terms, is the fruit of human suffering and anguish, as well as of human joy. Melville thought of man's destiny in this way. And it is a true measure of the inadequacy of the progressive critics that they should have called him, on this score, "morbid," "pessimistic," and bemused by "metaphysical irrelevancies." Melville's work is an enormous cultural fact. It is one of the many facts we can no longer afford to ignore or misinterpret because they do violence to our bland hopes or our stances of moral rectitude.

I do not wish to present Melville as primarily a political thinker. I am interested in his views of personality, culture, art, and morals. And the great thing about his specifically political ideas is that they do not subsist in an ethical void; they are never cut off or abstracted from the full context of his thought. The relevance of Melville to our modern thinking is extensive and intricate. Melville knew many ways of seeking moral truth and he knew that moral truth must be sought in many ways. Mr. Lionel Trilling has suggested that genius is the ability to "counterattack nightmare," and we may be sure that the enemy which the moral intelligence counterattacks will not be reduced by marching single-file against only one of his redoubts. The counterattack must take various forms and be launched on a broad front—a fact which both the intelligent Communist and the intelligent conservative have understood more clearly than has the progressive.

Liberal-progressive thinking in America has been remarkable for the magnitude of the rejections it has made. Ahab himself was a progressive American. Where but in *Moby-Dick* shall we find such a terrifying picture of a man rejecting all connection with his family, his culture, his own sexuality even, expunging the colors from the rainbow, rejecting the stained imperfections of life for a vision of spotless purity and rectitude attainable only in death, drifting into the terrible future, jamming himself on, like a father turned into a raging child, toward a catastrophe which annihilates a whole world?

If the way of Ahab is death, that is because he sets himself up as a spiritual leader without being able to make himself the symbol of a culture. Melville's strong young heroes—the Jack Chases, Bulkingtons, and Ethan Allens—are preeminently culture heroes.

Let them be the test. They are Melville's "common man." They are men of epic size, great in heart, in sensibility, and in the quality of endurance; they are companions, storytellers, defenders of freedom, revolutionaries; their brotherhood with other men is open, frank, and based on the deepest ties of common humanity; they are, in their way, pure; but their purity is in their sensitiveness and in their longing for brotherhood and fatherhood; their purity is not the righteous monomania of Ahab. If it is true that one's liberalism stands or falls with one's image of the common man, can we any longer wish to apotheosize the common man of the contemporary liberal-progressive vision: this mindless, heartless, unsexed, and remote youth who stands—a dummy already dead and wonderful in his righteousness—in the midst of historical catastrophe?

2

In his *Essays in Criticism,* Matthew Arnold remarks that Byron lacked the "intellectual equipment" needed by a genuinely "supreme" modern writer. From the annotations in his copy of Arnold's book, we gather that Melville was anxious to know if he would be judged to have had the necessary "intellectual equipment." And well he might wonder! For his critics—progressive and nonprogressive—have in various ways denied him exactly what he was himself so jealous of having. When his reputation was salvaged from obscurity in the 1920's, Melville was pictured as a kind of primitive man—a natural or unconscious genius, as Van Wyck Brooks intimated—whose great creative powers, after *Moby-Dick,* were ruined by the callous indifference of the Gilded Age and by Melville's own temperament: his obscure, abiding neurosis and his ultimately subliterary, subintellectual talents. From the criticism of the twenties, we have inherited the partly true but finally misleading idea of Melville as a heroic failure, a baffled Titan or wounded Prometheus who could do no more than cry out with his agonized rhetoric and his mindless rage against the chains that bound him. Brooks pictures Melville as he did Mark Twain: as a frustrated genius who suffered and failed, not as a thinking and developing artist who achieved a series of imperfect successes. Brooks's theory of the "ordeal" of the American artist is still potent in literary criticism, and it still underestimates, because it cannot objectively see, the artist's works.

Melville studies after the twenties began to present a completer picture, partly by resuscitating the later works and trying to assess Melville's whole contribution in the light of these. Even so, the two later works which tell us most about Melville's mind—*The Confidence Man* and *Clarel*—were generally ignored or misunderstood. In the 1930's progressive writers like Granville Hicks brought Parrington's earlier strictures up to date and attacked Melville because he failed to "participate" and because the moral center of his thinking (which Hicks mistakenly supposed to be a doctrinal concern with evil) could not be immediately stated in economic terms. Do we not see in this attitude a disinclination or inability to perceive what was in fact a most crucial "participation" in American culture? In the 1940's two books—William Ellery Sedgwick's *Herman Melville* and F. O. Matthiessen's *American Renaissance*—added an unresolved religious strain to the earlier progressivism. And in this uneasy amalgam we see Melville in his later works modifying his earlier theological "titanism" and coming gradually to a "religious acceptance of life," apparently involving in *Billy Budd* an apotheosis of the common man as Christ.

The progressive critics have finally been unable to see one of the central intellectual facts about their author; namely, that he was a profound and prophetic critic of liberal-progressivism, that he demanded to be seen with a kind of awareness which the theoretical social orthodoxies of the 1930's automatically prohibited. This blind spot of the progressive critics could not help obscuring whole ranges of Melville's "intellectual equipment."

Those critics of the last twenty years who have not subscribed to the progressive doctrines—the Southern writers, the New Critics—have made no sustained effort to understand Melville. Those concerned with precise textual and structural analysis, with order and concentration, have seen only Melville's sometimes unruly emotions—emotions in excess of their occasions—or his vagueness or his lack of system. If the New Criticism applies itself to the task, however, it may determine the future of Melville studies. An intense verbal analysis might tell us much about *Moby-Dick*. It might give us the "Word" and form the "New Testament" of Melville criticism. On the whole I remain in the "Old Testament" and am interested in the man, the artist, his works, his idols, his myths, his gods, his laws, his history, his prophecies, and his morals.

Academic critics have been more aware of Melville's ideas. But they have generally been guilty of that common academic fallacy—the rationalist fallacy—which makes every artist into a would-be philosopher. Thus *Moby-Dick, Pierre,* and *The Confidence Man* are presented to us as philosophic quests for ultimate truth. This approach ignores the fact that for Melville, as for any artist, ideas have profound aesthetic value, that an artist's "position" is an aesthetic device or context which he uses in his art, besides being a set of explicit intellectual attitudes. A study of Melville's "intellectual equipment" cannot be conceived apart from a study of his art. And Melville was not so much interested in philosophical truth as in man and his culture.

Melville is still the least known of our great writers. Even people with wide literary knowledge are not likely to know very much about *Redburn* or *Pierre* or *The Confidence Man* or *Clarel,* to say nothing of *Cock-a-doodle-do* or *Jimmy Rose.* In this book I have tried to set the works of Melville before the reader and to ask: What do these works say within themselves and in relation to one another? and: What do they say to us in our time of troubles?

I have tried to be continually aware of the development of Melville's mind, from his birth to his death, in so far as his writings permit this and sketchy as the evidence on long periods of his life still is. My method, therefore, has been partly biographical, especially in the opening and closing pages; but, of course, the book is not primarily a biography. An artist's "intellectual equipment" is a complex armory—for Melville was eminently an "armed man" —of recurring and developing images, symbols, ideas, and moral attitudes; and these are what I am after.

It may be that my estimate of Melville as an artist is too high; I am sure that, as the professional practice of art goes, he belongs somewhat below Hawthorne and Henry James. But Melville had great qualities which Hawthorne and James lacked, qualities of pathos and lyricism and pity, of range and acceptance and courage.

One of Melville's persistent themes was the search for a father—

by which he meant not God but a cultural ideal, a great man in a great culture. Our effort to understand Melville ought to be a similar cultural quest.

The writing of this book has put me under many pleasant obligations. My greatest debt is to Mr. Lionel Trilling, from whom I have learned so much during the last ten years. Others who have been kind enough to read the manuscript of my book wholly or in part or with whom I have profitably discussed Melville are Mr. Robert Penn Warren, Mr. John Crowe Ransom, Mr. R. W. Flint, Mr. Leslie A. Fiedler, Mr. Quentin Anderson, Mr. Robert C. Waddell, Mr. Tyrus Hillway, and Mr. Howard P. Vincent. I wish also to thank my students at the Kenyon School of English who during the summer of 1948 taught me so many things about Melville. Among these, I wish especially to thank Mr. Howard S. Babb, Mr. Joseph M. Duffy, Jr., Mr. James B. Hall, Mr. Andrew Schiller, Mrs. Esther R. Solomon, and Miss Mary Wright.

I wish to express my gratitude to Professor Dorothy Bethurum of Connecticut College who so benevolently fostered the writing of this book.

I wish to thank Mrs. Eleanor Melville Metcalf for her gracious assistance and the officials of the Houghton Library at Harvard University for their courteous aid. And I am most grateful to Mr. Henry Allen Moe and the John Simon Guggenheim Memorial Foundation for the fellowship which, in 1947–1948, permitted me to write the bulk of this book.

R. C.

Columbia University

Contents

I
Portraits of the Young Man

Melville was born in New York City in 1819. His father, Allan Melville, was a well-to-do merchant and importer. The family was proud of its aristocratic heritage, Scotch-English on the father's side, Dutch on the mother's. In 1826 Allan Melville failed in business. In 1830 the impoverished family moved to Albany. In 1832 Allan Melville went mad and died. During the years between 1830 and 1837, Herman Melville was a student at Albany Academy and a clerk in his elder brother's store and in his maternal uncle's bank. In 1837 he shipped as a "boy" on a merchantman sailing between New York and Liverpool. This earliest voyage he described in *Redburn*. What Melville did between this voyage and 1841 is still mostly unknown, except that he taught school at Greenbush, New York, and Pittsfield, Massachusetts. In 1841 he shipped out of New Bedford on the whaling ship *Acushnet* on January 3. On July 9, 1842, he left the *Acushnet* as she lay in Nukuhiva Harbor in the Marquesas and lived for a time with a tribe of natives known as the Taipis. His adventures among the Taipis, real and imaginary, he described in *Typee*. Later in the year 1842 he sailed to Tahiti in an Australian whaler. In *Omoo* he described his sojourn in Tahiti. Still later in the same year he shipped out of Tahiti on a whaling cruise aboard the *Leviathan*. In 1843 Melville shipped aboard the U.S. frigate *United States* at Honolulu. He was discharged from the service at Boston in 1844, after a cruise around Cape Horn, which he described in *White-Jacket*.

In 1846 Melville published *Typee,* and in 1847, *Omoo*. In 1848 he married Elizabeth Shaw, daughter of the Chief Justice of Massachusetts, and set up housekeeping at 103 Fourth Avenue, New York. He became a member of the best literary circle in New York, which revolved more or less around the figure of Evert

Duyckinck, editor, publisher, and litterateur. In 1849 Melville published *Mardi,* an imaginary South Sea travel book. In the same year he published *Redburn.* In 1850 he published *White-Jacket* and moved to a farm known as "Arrowhead" in Pittsfield, Massachusetts, with his wife and first son, Malcolm. The family lived in Pittsfield until 1863.

To anyone studying Melville's work as a meaningful totality, the death of Melville's father will gradually appear to be the event with which one must begin. Melville's five early novels (as well as some of his later work) are, from this point of view, the record of a fatherless boy and young man painfully resurrecting his past and painfully learning about the world and reality. They are the record also of the discovery of the themes and symbols of the later work. In everything Melville wrote before *Moby-Dick,* spiritual autobiography is so closely interwoven with the discovery of theme and symbol that it has to be treated as a gallery of portraits of the young man. There is no definitive portrait. One must study the whole gallery of suggestive profiles and half-length pictures in order finally to discern the true features. And one often notices that in these pictures the young man assumes a relationship to an older man— an ambiguous figure who is sometimes a patriarchal hero and sometimes a satyr or a killer.

1

In *Mardi* we are told about the god Keevi, who "fell from a golden cloud, burying himself to the thighs in the earth, tearing up the soil all round." Also in *Mardi* we hear of the nimble god Roo. A long time ago Roo leapt down from the skies onto a mountain peak. Then, in three skips and a jump, he landed on the plain. He could never climb back, though with a strange infatuation he should dash himself on the rocks of the mountain.

Keevi and Roo are imaginative versions of South Sea divinities Melville had heard about in his travels or read about in a travel book. But in writing *Mardi,* Melville made them into mythical images of himself. Keevi and Roo are fallen gods, and the myth of the Fall was Melville's central idea about his own childhood. In Melville's mind the Fall had many aspects: it gave a meaning, sad and wonderful, to the social decline of the Melvilles after the father's failure in business; it gave meaning to Herman Melville's feeling of loss and bewilderment when his father's early death destroyed the mythical world of childhood and set Melville down abruptly and alone in the world of reality; it gave him a sense of being irretrievably involved in the real world; it gave him high ideals; and it made him suspect sometimes that all felicity was in the past. But finally, as we shall see, Melville was to arrive at the idea that progress, such as it is, generates itself out of the perpetual Fall of man.

As if consciously accepting the double heritage of Western man—the Hebraic-Christian heritage and the Greek heritage—Melville created two basic kinds of hero, one of whom may be called Ishmael and the other, Prometheus. Ishmael, cast out and disinherited by Abraham his father, and Prometheus, the Titan who fled from heaven to bring light to man and to suffer on earth in his behalf, are both heroes in the universal myth of the Fall.

In *Redburn, Typee,* and *White-Jacket* we find various portraits of the young man as Ishmael: the young man who enters upon life proudly but forlornly, who suffers much and learns much among the brutal realities of a merchant ship's forecastle, in a primitive Polynesian society, in the disciplined caste system of an American warship. Melville's early books describe the *education* of this proud, handsome, earnest, sensitive, and bereaved youth. They describe the emergence of an adult consciousness; they document the progress of a mind toward a moral awareness of the human situation.

Ishmael, seeking always for some human embodiment of the lost patrimony of nobility, splendor, and virtue, meets a various array of Promethean figures. In Melville's books there are two kinds of Prometheus, whom we shall call the true and the false. The false Prometheus betrays his humanity through some monstrous pride, some titanic quest for moral purity, some obsessed abdication from the natural ambiguities of life in quest of the absolute and the inviolable, or some moral treachery which involves his companions as well as himself in a final catastrophe. The true Prometheus is the hero whom Melville came to call "the Handsome Sailor." He is Prometheus, as we may say, in a state of becoming Oedipus. The ideal human hero must not be *only* the young Promethean revolutionary who battles against the old reactionary gods in order to liberate man and give him his creative intelligence. The ideal hero must also be Oedipus—the man who has accepted the full moral responsibility of his fallible humanity, the man who has suffered and grown wise in the leadership of his fellows, the man who has learned to embrace his father, his mother, and his children in the full knowledge of his human guilt and his human nobility and who, in doing so, makes himself the symbol of a culture formed in the rich magnitude of wisdom and love. The false Prometheus is he who rejects the psychological and cultural sustenance of life; the true Prometheus is he who accepts it.

The reader will note that Melville's Ishmael in one sense symbolizes Young America—the revolutionary nation, the bearer of light in the wilderness, in quest of its destiny; the Ishmael of the world seeking to become a "great nation" such as Abraham promised to his outcast son.

The novel called *Redburn* presents the first large-scale portrait of Melville's Ishmael.

2

At the age of seventeen, Wellingborough Redburn, impelled by "sad disappointments in several plans which I had sketched for my future life" and "the necessity of doing something for myself, united to a naturally roving disposition," left his mother's home up the Hudson and sailed for Liverpool on the merchant ship *Highlander*. His mind was full of shadowy reminiscences—of having visited the New York wharves with his father, now dead; of his father's descriptions of his own voyages to Europe: the mountain-high waves, the masts bending in a gale, the climb into the dome of St. Paul's in London. Redburn hoped that he would inspire people with wonder when he returned from his travels, as he himself had been inspired by his father and by a man he once saw who had visited stony Arabia. Other memories induced him to travel. He remembered some paintings his father had brought from Paris. One depicted a fishing boat with three red-capped, bewhiskered men hauling in a seine; in one corner of the picture was the fallen tower of a lighthouse. Another depicted three French men-of-war with castlelike decks fore and aft and turreted masts full of little men. Though he never noticed it, the number *3* had a mysterious significance for Redburn. And then there was a glass ship in a glass case which had belonged to Redburn's father. The interior of the ship was dark, and though one peered in at the portholes, one could not see what it contained. Redburn felt that if he could look inside he would find something wonderful, possibly gold. Often he felt an "insane desire" to smash the glass ship and get at the plunder. The ship would then be put on the mantelpiece out of reach. The name of the ship was *La Reine,* and Redburn was always giving her up for lost or foundered, for the glass waves ran high. As Redburn grew older, the ship began to fall into disrepair. The figurehead, a gallant warrior in a cocked hat, came loose and hung head-foremost into "the calamitous seas under the bows." Redburn's sisters told him that the warrior fell from his perch the day he left home to go to sea.

Wherever Redburn went he attracted attention and was scorned or laughed at. His impoverished family had fitted him out for his voyage as best they could. He wore a hunting jacket with gaudy brass buttons and he carried a rifle to be sold in New York so that he would have a little money. On the river boat he had only half enough money to pay the fare. A fat man stared at him insolently, and Redburn stared back fanatically until the fat man averted his gaze. Another passenger stared at him, and Redburn raised his unloaded gun and clicked the hammer, aiming at the man's left eye.

In New York, Redburn signed aboard the *Highlander* and bore the first of the sailors' interminable insults and crude jokes at his outlandish appearance, his genteel talk, and his aristocratic manner. Before sailing, he went ashore to sell the gun. He entered a shop over the entrance of which hung three balls; he was offered $3 for the gun but thought this was too little and departed. In another pawnshop he saw three old men standing in cages and looking out of three holes. Violently, Redburn pushed the gun through one of the holes but on being offered only $1, withdrew it, returned to the first shop he had visited, and sold the gun for $2.50.

Redburn's money was soon gone. The sailing was postponed, and he was hungry. He often felt sick, his soul was "sour," and the evil-smelling wharves nauseated him; he was filled with revulsion after drinking warm water from a glass just used by a Negro. He drank innumerable glasses of warm water.

As soon as Redburn boarded the *Highlander,* though he was "sick as death," the mate set him to cleaning out the longboat, which was used as a pigpen, and, for the first time, he was sent up the mainmast. As the men came aboard, Redburn was shocked at their profanity; the words they used filled him with "dreadful loathing." And he was outraged to see drunken sailors being carried aboard, for he was a member of the Juvenile Total Abstinence Association and the Anti-Smoking Society. He was tortured by superstitious foreboding when he was given the bunk of a sailor who, maddened with the delirium tremens, had rushed on deck and jumped overboard to his death.

Captain Riga, who Redburn had supposed was a sort of "father to his crew," repulsed him brutally when Redburn presumed to pay a social call on the quarter-deck. But everything foul and distasteful aboard the ship was centered for Redburn in the person of Jackson, an evil man who maintained an inscrutable ascendancy over the crew and who, gradually dying of tuberculosis and syphilis, was nothing but "the foul lees and dregs of a man." Jackson regarded Redburn with a bright, burning eye which bespoke pure malevolence and also homosexual lust, as Redburn dimly perceived. Redburn would be, as he soon saw, "a sort of Ishmael in the ship," taking what solace he could find in the beauty of the expansive sea, in thoughts of home, or in a copy of *The Wealth of Nations,* wherein, until he began to read, he hoped to discover some secret treasure, such as he had imagined to be hidden in the hold of the glass ship. But gradually Redburn learned to perform his duties and schooled himself to survive in an environment for which his father's descriptions of travel had in no way prepared him.

Redburn was determined to make a "filial pilgrimage" through Liverpool, using a guidebook called *The Picture of Liverpool,* which his father had used before him. The guidebook would be the "infallible clew" through the intricacies of the labyrinthine city, the very fact that his father had used the book proving its trustworthiness beyond question. His impression of his father's presence in the

city was so strong that he almost saw him in a crowd, entering a
street or turning a corner. Yet as he followed his father's walks
through the city, marked in pencil in the guidebook, he soon realized that the book did not correspond with the city. A castle described in the book was now a tavern. Riddough's Hotel, where
his father had stayed, had disappeared. And soon a light broke
upon Redburn which he had been trying hard not to see. The
guidebook was hopelessly outmoded. And he reflected sadly that
"the thing that had guided the father could not guide the son" and
that every age must make its own guidebooks. Redburn had learned
a bitter lesson, but he was no longer quite the sick boy who had
stepped aboard the *Highlander*.

On the return journey, Redburn knew that he had matured; he
could survive: he had been "rubbed, curried, and ground . . . in
the hopper of an evil fortune." As the ship approached Cape Cod,
Jackson, astride a yardarm, coughed up a mouthful of blood
which stained the mainsail, and then he plunged into the sea like
a diver. The foul old man, out of whom all humanity had been
blasted, was dead, and Redburn, whose name is apparently meant
to signify "the Promethean fire," lived on.

3

As the *Highlander* was about to leave Liverpool, three sailors,
apparently insensible with alcohol, were brought onto the ship by
crimps, who signed the men aboard and received their first month's
pay in advance. The drunks were taken below. After a few hours
two of them were able to go on deck, but the third remained in his
bunk in the dark recess under the bowsprit. It was assumed that
he was sick. Later a foul odor began to fill the forecastle, which
the sailors attributed to a dead rat probably hidden somewhere in
the hold. It was then discovered that the odor proceeded from the
sailor in the bunk, who was not drunk but dead, a corpse brought
aboard by the crimp. In the dark of the forecastle a yellow flame
was seen to hover at the mouth of the dead sailor, and then two
threads of greenish fire darted through the lips. Soon the whole
face was wreathed in curls of soft blue flame. The eyes were open
and fixed. The expression of the face was of grim defiance and

eternal death. It occurred to Redburn to call the dead sailor "Prometheus, blasted by fire on the rock."

4

Aboard the *Highlander* was a young man called Jack Blunt. He was a hypochondriac and took all sorts of pills. He feared that his hair was turning prematurely gray, and against this fate he had purchased two bottles of balm made by the same apothecary: Trafalgar Oil and Balm of Paradise. On the bottle of Trafalgar Oil was an engraving showing a gray-headed young man standing in his nightshirt in the middle of his chamber and applying the elixir with both eyes closed. On the bed beside him was a large bottle labeled Balm of Paradise. Jack Blunt had an astrological dream book by means of whose charts and tables he could interpret dreams and discover the secrets of futurity.

5

Harry Bolton, who became Redburn's friend in Liverpool, was a gay, pretty, effeminate English youth with a beautiful voice. He lived by gambling and by partly imaginary connections with the nobility. He was an orphan. His fortunes turning out badly in England, he decided to ship to America. He signed on the *Highlander*. He yearned to throw himself "into the unbounded bosom of some immaculate friend," and Redburn was that friend. Before sailing, he put on his best clothes, pasted a beard and a mustache on his face, and took Redburn to a London gambling den for a last do-or-die fling. To Redburn the gambling den seemed "like a bower in Babylon." It was another mysterious crypt which promised to contain an inward treasure. The walls of the sumptuous retreat were adorned with mythological paintings,

such pictures as the high-priests, for a bribe, showed to Alexander in the innermost shrine of the white temple in the Lybian oasis: such pictures as the pontiff of the sun strove to hide from Cortez, when, sword in hand, he burst open the sanctorum [*sic*] of the pyramid-fane at Cholula: such pictures as you may still see, perhaps, in the central alcove of the excavated mansion of Pansa, in Pompeii—in that part of it called by Varro *the hollow of the house* . . . such pictures as you might have beheld in an arched recess, leading from the left hand of the secret side-gallery of the temple of Aphrodite in Corinth.

In the middle of the room was a bust of a bald-headed, obscene old man who held one thin finger to his lips, his marble mouth trembling with secrets.

Aboard ship, Harry Bolton was as cruelly treated as Redburn had been. Occasionally, however, he was able to charm the sailors by singing his magic songs with a voice like Orpheus' lyre. In later years Redburn heard by chance of the final fate of Harry Bolton. He had signed on a whaling cruise and had been crushed to death between the ship and the ponderous body of a slaughtered whale.

6

The hero of *Typee* presumably suffered the same kind of alienation aboard his whaler as did Redburn aboard his merchantman. He found the crew mean-spirited and "dastardly." The captain was a vengeful "Lord of the Plank." The young hero and his companion, Toby, jumped ship in the Marquesas and fled inland. From then on the story describes another kind of alienation: the more pleasurable but more terrible alienation of one who was coddled and worshiped and at the same time inscrutably held prisoner by one's benefactors. Redburn was the young man who, though poignantly remembering the past, matured and began to accept the conditions of maturity. The young hero of *Typee* withdrew into the past, his anxieties and his pleasures were archaic, and he could finally break out of the prison of the past—his own past—only by a violent and tortured assertion of a nearly paralyzed will.

Having left the ship, the young hero and his companion fought their way into the mountainous interior of the island, painfully cutting a path through growths of yellow reeds, strong as steel rods, that thickly blocked their way. They scaled steep sunlit mountains by day and retreated into damp, wild glens by night. After much suffering from hunger and fatigue, they made a nightmarishly dangerous descent into a deep gorge which they hoped was Happar Valley and not Typee Valley—for though the Happars were rumored to be mild and friendly, the Typees were notorious for their cannibalism. As it happened, they made the wrong choice. But, surprisingly, the Typees turned out to be ostensibly as kind and temperate as possible.

The descent into the valley of Typee was a withdrawal from the world, and the valley was, for the young hero, a sanctuary containing unknown but enticing treasures. The chief enticement, which gives its character to the whole experience, was a mild, somnolent eroticism, tinged, however, with vague intimations of "frightful contingencies." The first human beings the hero saw in the valley were a naked boy and girl, the boy's arm placed fondly about the girl's shoulders.

The young hero, who had left a fatherless family at home, was accepted into a native family, with whom he lived during his four months' stay. The family consisted of Marheyo, the patriarch who had once been a splendid warrior and now tried to make the hero happy with an abundance of touchingly foolish deeds of kindness; Tinor, the affectionate matriarch who bustled about like a benevolently officious housewife; Kory-Kory, a bizarre but endlessly thoughtful young savage who was appointed to be the hero's constant attendant; and Fayaway, a beautiful girl with whom the hero soon fell in love. There were various other young men and women in the household, but the blood relationship of all of these people was equivocal: they were not said to be brothers and sisters or sons and daughters (beyond the explicit statement that Kory-Kory was the son of Marheyo).

At first the hero was painfully ill; he had a "mysterious malady" in his leg, presumably the result of an injury sustained in the long climb over the mountains. He was overcome by dark forebodings and a profound melancholy which he recognized as being far in excess of a natural response to his physical injury and for which, therefore, he could not account. The hero's low state of spirits and his paralysis of will were, however, justified by at least two outward circumstances: the Typees might yet prove to be cannibals, and Toby, who had fled over the mountains to summon help, might have met a violent end, or so, with a placid impenetrability, the natives vaguely hinted.

But on the whole the natives were gay and kindly. They ministered to the hero's needs, and Kory-Kory carried him around on his shoulders. His body was anointed every day by the young girls of the family, and soon he was able, with the help of Kory-Kory, to bathe with the girls in an idyllic lake set enchantingly in the midst of the valley and fed with fresh waters. Gradually the hero lost all sense of time and anxiety. He sank into a pleasantly hedonistic apathy. His leg improved and he began to enjoy a sort of passive happiness, a muted and continuous erotic ecstasy. Swimming with the girls, he dove under the water and playfully tried to pull them under. Fayaway, whose blue eyes and soft tawny skin enchanted him, became his constant companion. They bathed together; they lounged long hours together in a canoe paddled by Kory-Kory; or the young hero steered the canoe while Fayaway, having slipped off her mantle, unfurled it as a sail and stood gracefully in the center of the canoe, her straight body serving as a mast. He admired Fayaway; he admired the natives and their way of life, finding "the tranquillizing influences of beautiful scenery and the exhibition of human life under so novel and charming an aspect" a great consolation. And he admired himself; his own beloved image appealed to him with persistent eroticism. He came to feel that he was quite "the belle of the season, in the pride of her beauty and power"; and the charming, naïve natives, who reacted as surely as reflexes to his impulses, became less real external objects than extensions of his own personality. When he had first joined the household of Marheyo, Kory-Kory had insisted on feeding poi to the young hero with his own fingers. It was an appropriately symbolic act, for the hero, with a sad gaiety, was reliving his childhood in terms of the entrancingly fitting symbolic objects of which Typee Valley so expertly consisted.

But the sense of guilt and foreboding which the indulgences of his archaic emotions gave the hero could not be entirely avoided. They became sharply recrudescent when the natives insisted that he should be tattooed; it was a religious rite whose sanctions no one could do without. But Karky, the tattoo artist, with his slender instrument tipped with a shark's tooth and his small wooden mallet, aroused in the hero a deep revulsion, which proceeded far more from a fear that his body might be mutilated than from a realization that the pagan rite of tattooing would be sacrilege for a Christian. Shortly after meeting Karky, the pain in his leg returned so violently that he felt "unmanned." And this calamity was followed by the chance discovery that three tapa bundles which hung from the ridgepole of Marheyo's house contained three human heads, one of a white man, two of natives.

The hero's escape from Typee Valley was sudden and violent. An Australian whaler, in need of men, put a boat ashore, and with a terrible effort the hero limped down to the beach, eluded the hostile natives, taking advantage of a dispute among them as to whether he should be allowed to go or not, and leaving Marheyo, Kory-Kory, and Fayaway weeping in the surf, managed to fall exhausted into the boat.

In *Redburn* the young man, still a boy, learned to master the feelings aroused in him by hunger, discomfort, excrement, obscenity, cruelty, death, and alienation from his kind; and he began to see that somehow human life—personality and society—had to be based upon these things. It was an act of growing up. In *Typee* the young man performed a further act. With a great effort and much suffering, he withdrew into the recesses of his own infantile sexuality and then escaped to a higher level. He feared cannibalism in general; but specifically he feared castration. This was the real content of the nameless foreboding which he felt when he descended into Typee Valley and when he was about to escape. He did not feel this fear during the time when he was able to give himself over to the mild eroticism of the valley. To leave the archaic level of personality and civilization represented by Typee Valley was to face and suffer and overcome the fears which accompanied maturing sexuality. This figure, the hero suffering the fear of castration, became a common one in Melville's books. We can call him "the Maimed Man in the Glen"; and we shall discover him again in Ahab, in Pierre Glendinning (whose surname means "dweller in a glen"), in the "invalid Titan" of *The Confidence Man,* and in other of Melville's characters.

The hero's attachment to Fayaway cannot be regarded as a completely sexualized one. She remained a wraith of youthful erotic fantasies, as her name indicated. From the departing whaleboat the hero threw a bolt of colored cloth to Fayaway—an intolerably callous act, the reader thinks, until he begins to reflect that the young man, having taken his decisive step, now sincerely and perhaps correctly regarded Fayaway as a child or a wraith, not as a mature lover. It is by no means clear that the hero's act hurt Fayaway.

7

In *Mardi* there is mention of an imaginary author who wrote a book entitled *A Sojourn among the Anthropophagi, by One whose Hand was Eaten off at Tiffin among the Savages.*

8

The young man who had observed society in the forecastles of a merchantman and a whaler and who had seen the injustices of industrial civilization in Liverpool had begun to develop political ideas. Longing for the ideal society, where affairs are conducted with compassion and noble simplicity, he was very much impressed by the Typees. He compared Western civilization unfavorably with Typee Valley, and openly deplored the inevitable arrival of French military forces with their cruelty, corruption, and syphilis and the missionaries with their self-righteous hypocrisy. "Civilization," he decided, "does not engross all the virtues of humanity." The Typees

deal more kindly with each other, and are more humane, than many who study essays on virtue and benevolence, and who repeat every night that beautiful prayer breathed first by the lips of the divine and gentle Jesus. I will frankly declare that after passing a few weeks in this valley of the Marquesas, I formed a higher estimate of human nature than I had ever before entertained.

In Typee the young man found mild and dignified chiefs but no police and no courts of law. There was, to be sure, an extensive system of taboo, but it was seldom oppressive and did not interfere with the harmony of daily life. The natives generally conducted themselves according to an indwelling sense of virtue and honor which kept them free of the weight of social protocol and confusion. They were, in the best sense, "carefree." Eros, far from being the malign demon that often goads and worries civilized society, conspired harmoniously with the social institutions of Typee.

Still, as the young man realized, it was part of the process of growing up to force oneself to grow beyond the Typee society. There was an unintegrated part of Typee which its bland social institutions and its benevolence either ignored or could not control: cannibalism. And cannibalism might at any moment overturn and destroy Typee society. In Typee, Eros was an emasculated god and so was its political god; he was a god who remained a child, who was content to make his social arrangements at too low a level of maturity, a god who could not face, understand, and accept the tragic realities or the larger ecstasies of human life. The tendency of Western civilization was to take cognizance of these tragic realities and to try, at least, to arrange social institutions accordingly. And so the young man had to return to it, though he was so saddened at the thought of the undeniable advantages of Typee society.

As the author of *Mardi* intimated, "no past time is lost time." The past must be studied and understood, to keep it from playing on one its monstrous tricks of seduction. For those who could not understand their own past, or themselves as products of it, there was the danger that they would be betrayed into thinking that a reversion was really a standing in the present or a motion toward the future. In *Moby-Dick* the young man at the helm of the *Pequod* was to feel this danger one night when the crew was boiling blubber in the vats and the ship seemed to be "freighted with savages, and laden with fire, and burning a corpse, and plunging into the blackness of darkness." The young man succumbed to a momentary drowsiness and lost consciousness in an inexpressible dream. Then

starting from a brief, standing sleep, I was horribly conscious of something fatally wrong. The jaw-bone tiller smote my side, which leaned against it; in my ears was the low hum of sails just beginning to shake in the wind. . . . I could see no compass before me to steer by . . . Nothing seemed before me but a jet gloom, now and then made ghastly by flashes of redness. Uppermost was the impression, that whatever swift, rushing thing I stood on was not so much bound for any haven ahead as rushing from all havens astern.

The young man realized, with a "stark, bewildered feeling, as of death," that in his sleep he had turned around so that he faced

astern and that in letting go of the tiller he had almost brought
the ship up into the wind and capsized her. He had lost his bear-
ings, for, facing backward, he could not see the compass. Momentarily the relation of past, present, and future was confused. He
feared the present and the probably disastrous future; even more
he feared the past, under whose sudden influence he had turned
around and almost turned the little world of the *Pequod* with him:
he was gripped at this moment, as D. H. Lawrence says in his
study of *Moby-Dick,* with the "horror of reversion, of undoing."
In a later episode the same confusion of time is again symbolized:
the *Pequod's* compass is magnetically inverted during an electric
storm in the night, and the next morning finds the ship running
precisely opposite to the course that had been set for her.

Typee was Melville's most adequately symbolized study of the
past. But the memory of the past was not always accompanied
by horror. In a love poem, written in later times, Melville could
use such a wistful image as:

> I yearn, I yearn, reverting turn,
> My heart it streams in wake astern.

Again he could call himself and Ned Bunn (a mythical companion) "Typee-truants" who once as "pleasure-hunters broke loose"

> for our pantheistic ports:
> Marquesas and glenned isles that be
> Authentic Edens in a Pagan sea.

And with mildly sardonic wisdom he could indulge his nostalgia
for the "authentic Edens" and at the same time observe that
"Adam advances."

9

The implication of *Redburn* is that the young hero of the book
might have been like Harry Bolton had he not possessed certain
possibilities of knowledge, endurance, and growth. What the young
man might have been like had he been unable to escape the Valley
of Typee is intimated in the portrait of Donjalolo in *Mardi.* Donjalolo, the young king of Juam, was forced by an ancient taboo
to remain forever in Willamilla, a narrow defile in the mountains.

Before he had become king, while his father was still living, Donjalolo had been tempted to venture into the outer world. But just as he was about to set out on his travels, his father killed himself in order to keep Donjalolo in the valley. Thus the young king was doomed to live like his ancestors, "buried . . . forever in this fatal glen." He reacted to his fate by leading a riotous life, "wasting powers which might have compassed the noblest designs." He became "an effeminate Sardanapalus"; he was "universe-rounded" and "self-hugged"; he was "the red royal stone in an effeminate peach; the insphered sphere of spheres." Cut off from the world of outward, objective experience, he sent emissaries out of the glen to observe things and report to him. But when they examined, for example, a secret cave containing treasures, they came back with contradictory impressions of what they had seen, heard, or smelled.

Donjalolo fell victim to unaccountable vagaries: he believed himself haunted by the ghosts of his sires. He invented precious pleasures and niceties of sensuality. Seated on a "fair sedan" borne on the shoulders of thirty men, a "slender, enervate youth," he rested his anointed head on the bosom of a young girl. The pupils of his eyes were "as floating isles in the sea." His attendants fanned him with graceful plumes and blew incense under his nostrils to save him the effort of smoking. He started up in horror, thinking that he saw the ghost of one of his ancestors.

Donjalolo spent much of his time in two shaded temples, called the House of the Morning and the House of the Afternoon. The temples had the phallic gigantism of dream images. A well shaded path connected the House of the Morning, under the eastern cliff of the defile, with the House of the Afternoon, under the western cliff. The purpose of the temples was to shield Donjalolo from the oppressive energy of the tropical sun. As the sun moved from east to west, the pale prince repeated the transit on earth, in this manner "dodging day's luminary through life."

At night Donjalolo amused himself with his thirty wives. Each wife was named after one phase of the moon, and once each month each wife reigned as queen for the appropriate night. Donjalolo, we perceive, was wedded to Time. The symbols by which Donjalolo lived are the Glen, the House, Woman, Night, and Time.

The symbols of the existence he could not know, or that he feared to know, are the Mountain, the Sun, the Father, Light, and Space. In Melville's books the young man who cannot reconcile these antinomies is doomed to spiritual, moral, and aesthetic failure. The young man who can reconcile them is the true Promethean hero, the Handsome Sailor.

10

While the young man was a prisoner there, Typee Valley was visited by a native named Marnoo. He was about twenty-five years old but appeared already to have whole worlds of experience behind him. His body was strong and matchlessly symmetrical. He was just above average height. His elegant figure and his beard-less cheeks made him look like a Polynesian Apollo. His hair was a rich curling brown, and it twined about his temples and neck in small ringlets. On his back was tattooed a gracefully spreading tree, the trunk rising from the root of his spine. The natives treated him with awestruck reverence, admiring his powers of oratory and the brilliant fire which shot from his eyes. They listened to him as if he were a demigod or a prophet. He was *omoo,* a taboo *kanake*—that is, he was accorded the special privilege of travel-ing from valley to valley without being molested. Because of the perpetual mutual hostility among the tribes of the island, no one else could do this. His special sanctity and his ascendancy over others were generated by his physical and spiritual freedom: he could travel over the mountains and into the valleys; he had learned the language and the ways of the white man, and he could move freely between the white man's society and the native's. Marnoo is a first sketch of the true Prometheus, the heroic voy-ager Melville later called the Handsome Sailor.

11

As he had been in *Typee,* the young man at the beginning of *Mardi* was aboard a whaler, and, as in *Typee,* he jumped ship. It was as if he had temporarily to avoid the tremendous experi-ences recorded in *Moby-Dick* by leaving the whaler and seeking

out certain preliminary experiences. In *Mardi* the young man was
an ordinary seaman until he became involved in a momentous
event and then turned into the demigod Taji, who was said to
come from the golden shores of the sun in order to travel among
the islands of an imaginary ocean world called Mardi.

The momentous event took place at sea. Sailing in an open
boat, the young hero met a large native ceremonial canoe aboard
which were an old priest and his several sons. The priest "looked
old as the elderly hills." His eyes were "sunken, though bright";
and his head "was white as the summit of Mont Blanc." His brow
was wrinkled with characters bespeaking ancient mysteries. Aboard
the canoe was a tent, and the young hero learned that it contained
Yillah, a semidivine maiden, whom the priest and his sons intended
to sacrifice on a distant island. The young hero jumped aboard
the canoe, killed the old man with a cutlass, rescued Yillah, and
sailed off with her. He fell in love with Yillah, and they enjoyed
an ecstatic honeymoon, until she mysteriously disappeared. Yillah
had snow-white skin and eyes as blue as the firmament. She was,
in fact, an albino, of a type sometimes found in the South Seas.
The young man's pleasure in Yillah was taken at the expense of
his deep remorse at having killed the old priest. As he sailed
toward Mardi and made love to Yillah, he saw the old man's body
floating in the water. At the end of the book, the young hero
set out on his endless voyage in search of the lost Yillah, and the
green corpse of the priest struck against the prow of his boat.
Throughout his travels in Mardi, he was followed by the phantoms
of three of the priest's sons, who shot spectral arrows at him.

During his travels in Mardi, Taji met the figure of the old man
in other guises: as an "incognito" in a dark robe who stared at
him and Yillah with a single eye as terrifyingly as Jackson had
stared at Redburn; as Pani, a blind guide who promised that he
could lead pilgrims to their destinations but was himself guided
by a little boy; as Hivohitee the Pontiff, who dwelt in the top of
a tower like Zeus, in an atmosphere electric with spent thunderbolts, and who was invisible except for his necklace of hideous
jawbones.

In *Typee*, Fayaway had remained lovely, mild, and childlike.
But the young man in *Mardi*—no longer a child himself, but

Taji, a hero and a titan—could not imagine Yillah without connecting her with another female image. He had killed an old man
in order to rescue Yillah, and this act had changed his whole conception of woman. Henceforth woman would be not only Yillah,
the spotless love which took him back, as he said, to his own earliest experiences, but also Hautia. He was pursued through Mardi
by three female wraiths who threw flowers at him, symbolizing
"Love, Death, and Joy," and told him that the beautiful Hautia
awaited him on her magic isle. Hautia, Taji knew, threatened to
cripple and destroy him: she was the "vortex . . . deeper than
the sea." Yet he could not entirely separate the image of Yillah
from the image of Hautia, and finally he went to the magic island,
"wildly dreaming" to find Yillah and Hautia together. On the
magic island were two caves, the abodes of Hautia and Yillah.
Hautia's cave was an enchanted Babylon of doomed cities, made
of jewels and graceful columns lighted by gorgeous flambeaux.
Hautia told Taji that to dive with her into the crystal waters of
the cave was to find "Beauty, Health, Wealth, Long Life, and the
Last Lost Hope of man." Taji, however, would not dive. Instead he
plunged into Yillah's cave, found that it led to the open sea, and
set out in a boat on an impossible quest for guiltless love.

This rather absurdly symbolized situation—which Melville was
to treat more subtly in *Pierre*—suggests an important fact about
Melville. He could seldom picture a woman without terror. His
women seduce men from their manhood, turning them to stone
or ice, emasculating them, making them into titans, hermaphro-
dites, or children. Having murdered the old priest and having made
love to Yillah, Taji became, not a man like Oedipus with his
tragic sense of his own humanity, but a demon-driven titan committed to a finally suicidal quest for something he had lost without ever understanding. This something was symbolized by whiteness. Taji would never find his albino lover, but he sensed that
if he should, he would also find the secret of his relationship with
the old man whose head was white as Mont Blanc. Taji was fated
to lose his way in the emptiness between polarities he could not
reconcile: between the symbols associated with Yillah (Light,
Space, Consciousness, Mountain) and those associated with
Hautia (Dark, Time, Unconsciousness, Valley, or Cave).

In *Mardi* the young man was more directly concerned with politics and social idealism than he had been in *Typee*. Traveling through his imaginary world with four men of good will—a benevolent despot, a philosopher, a historian, and a Shelleylike poet—he reflected upon the social systems of the countries he visited. Sadly, Taji and his companions found themselves compelled to reject them all, even that of Vivenza (the United States). Finally they came to Serenia, a land whose only hero was Alma (Christ), a land which actually practiced Christian democracy, based upon the principles of the Declaration of Independence, the Bill of Rights, and the Sermon on the Mount. Serenia was the United States as it would be if it practiced its liberal democratic ideals. Serenia had a tranquil heaven, full of pensive, sad, birdlike angels who lived in Christian love. But perfect wisdom, the understanding of death and evil, belonged to God alone, not to men or angels. With the important exception of Taji, the world-weary voyagers were converted to the principles of Serenia and either remained there or returned to their own lands to spread the gospel. But Taji did not find Yillah in Serenia, and instead of staying there, sailed into "the endless sea." In *Typee* the hero's escape had been partly a protest against a kind of society not founded upon the whole personality of man. Taji's refusal to remain in Serenia implied the same criticism. The American ideal of liberal democracy was not actively or by intention bad; but passively it was. It was too mild, too wishful, too innocent. Serenia was not proof against history, which might put it at the mercy of the emotions it chose to ignore or repress. Nor could one believe in Serenia's bland and pensive heaven, which was not the heaven stormed by the cast-out Titans or the nimble god Roo. And Serenia's god might turn out (as he does in *The Confidence Man*) to be a dull little man in a white suit who looks wise but is afraid of dirt.

Taji's companions, in adopting the ideals of Serenia and its heaven, decided in effect to live in the future; and this, Taji reflected, was injurious if it meant ceasing to live in the past and the present. It was exhilarating, he thought, to cruise among celestial paradises and cities of the sun, "building our futurities," planting in universal space "cities of beryl and jasper." But such New

Jerusalems as there might be were "here and now." To live in the
ideal future was to "await the present," a present which would
never come. The young man had already come to see the necessity of accepting, in so far as one could, one's own past and of
trying to solve political and moral problems within the tensions
and polarities of life as people actually lived it. In other words,
the author of *Mardi* was already intellectually committed to a
naturalist and humanist view of things though as a social critic
he thought it his duty to point out the weaknesses of the American
liberal-democratic humanist ideal. Much of Melville's claim to critical intelligence must be based on his exercise of this attitude,
which he had adopted before he was thirty.

Taji's journey into the open sea was not entirely a mysterious
evasion of life or an act of madness; partly it was a flight to reality,
to that part of the human-emotional reality alienated by liberal
democracy. Taji was the hero later to be portrayed as Ahab and
Pierre. He was a titan, rather than a man, because of his intransigent devotion to the alienated passions. *His* way of life,
finally, is false. But through his suicidal career we discover the
values ignored by liberal democracy and so begin to attain a complete view of personality and culture. We watch him trying to live
beyond Serenia and its way of life with a desperate commitment
to this beyond-ness. And we conclude with Melville that we must
live, not *in* liberal democracy, nor *beyond* it, but both at the same
time. In Melville's books autobiography ends short of an identification of the author with Taji or Ahab or Pierre. These are beings
whom Melville, a larger man, has created. The assumption that
Melville himself was a suicidal, titanic figure involves a grievous
underestimation of him as artist and moralist.

12

The young man in *White-Jacket* was a polemicist who, with
a quiet and passionate assemblage of facts, denounced the American navy to the American people in the name of humanity and
democratic principles. He had shipped aboard a frigate felicitously
called the *United States* (Melville called it the *Neversink* in his
novel) and had seen with what perfection the navy had created

a way of life which ran counter to all civilizing influences. It was, in Melville's day, the perfection of life in the image of the military machine. And the fearful thing was not so much that five hundred men and a ship were so efficiently articulated into one death-dealing mechanism, but that this articulation represented to most of the men an admirable, or at least adequate, way of life, that, in short, there were ineradicable emotional needs in these American sailors which found fulfillment in the machinelike existence.

The young man quickly perceived that the exercise of justice aboard a man-of-war was impossible. The men were barbarously flogged after only the most summary inquiry by the captain: the captain was more interested in preserving the system of flogging than in learning to what extent alleged miscreants merited punishment. Captain Claret, not by any means a completely contemptible man, was nevertheless usually fuzzy-minded with wine and was not, in crises, a competent sailor, wine or no wine. Some of his officers were obviously incompetents; some were cruel and effeminate; some were small-minded and timeserving. On the other hand the crew were men of rather lower moral level than the population at large. The rigid stratifications of rank and the immutable protocol of the ship, while in many ways correcting human incompetence, offered subtle modes of expression for the worst impulses of both officers and crew; and the young man was "sickened" by the complex and interacting "irritabilities, jealousies, and cabals, the spiteful detractions and animosities that lurked far down and clung to the very kelson of the ship." Like the painter instructed by Jove to portray Medusa, the young polemicist felt his soul sink at the thought of what he had portrayed. And he found no easy solution. It was not simply that the officers were abnormally malicious or the crew abnormally vicious. Evil was organic with the kind of man-of-war society which had to exist as long as the navy had to exist. At the end of his polemic, White-Jacket wrote: "Oh, shipmates and world-mates, all round! We the people suffer many abuses. Our gun-deck is full of complaints. In vain from Lieutenants do we appeal to the Captain; in vain—while on board our world-frigate—to the indefinite Navy Commissioners so far out of sight aloft." Such appeals might bring about a measure of justice even aboard a man-of-war if the man-of-war society adopted in so far as possible the principles of republican government. But this was by no means the whole solution. "Yet the worst of our evils we blindly inflict upon ourselves; our officers cannot remove them, even if they would. From the last ills no being can save another; therein each man must be his own savior." Not to take this responsibility would finally be to "train our murderous guns inboard," a prediction which helps to explain Melville's deep distress at the Civil War. The young polemicist's hatred of the American man-of-war society was clearly the complement of his profound belief that the Americans were, as he said, the chosen people and political Messiah of modern times, the advance guard bearing the ark of liberty into the wilderness.

13

Aboard the frigate, White-Jacket met Jack Chase, the great-minded and great-bodied captain of the maintop. Jack Chase (to whom Melville dedicated *Billy Budd* at the end of his life) was a prototype of what Melville envisioned as the full, heroic Promethean-Oedipean personality. Chase was born a Briton, but for Melville he was the heroic American.

When White-Jacket was sent to serve in the maintop, he was immediately taken with his commander. Jack Chase was tall and well knit, with a clear open eye, a broad brow, and a nut-brown beard. His chest was broad as a bulkhead, his nose aquiline. He was frank, bluff, hearty, and gallant. He was a teller of stories, a man of strong animal appetites who drank liberally, and a man who never lost his native dignity. He was a sort of oracle to whom sailors from all over the ship came with disputes or questions about obscure points in the technique of sailing. He was easy, free, and eloquent. He believed that he had that in his head which under different circumstances might have made him a Homer. He was a devotee of poetry and, sitting in the maintop, he would regale White-Jacket with recitations from Scott, Byron, Shakespeare, and Camoëns or, "stretching his bold hand over the sea," would compose an impromptu song of greeting to Aurora. It occurred to White-Jacket that Jack Chase must be of noble blood; possibly he was a "by-blow of some British Admiral of the Blue."

Like Marnoo, Jack Chase was taboo, in the sense that he was exempt from some of the restrictions custom placed on ordinary men. At one time he had deserted the frigate to fight on the side of a republican revolutionary movement in Peru and had been welcomed back by Captain Claret, without punishment.

Jack Chase was the young man as Promethean hero. But he was widely experienced in the world, and he had an air of aristocracy, authority, and final dignity. It was a mark of White-Jacket's gradual liberation from his attachment to his own dead father that in moments of emotion he could call Jack Chase his "sire."

14

The young man still sought for new symbols of his own past and his growth out of the past. Since there was no pea jacket for him aboard the frigate, he wore a crudely contrived white linen surtout. He had become an adequate sailor and knew now how to preserve himself from the cruelty of the men. But still he was alienated, and the white jacket became the mark of his alienation. He knew that in some way the white jacket was dangerous to him; he feared it might be his shroud and, in fact, it nearly was. Repeatedly he asked for paint so that he could both make the jacket waterpoof and change its color; and getting no paint, he tried to clean the deck with his jacket in order to besmirch its whiteness. As they neared home, he tried to sell the jacket at a ship's auction. But still the white jacket clung to him. The jacket became of even less use to him than it had been at first, because to protect himself against the pickpockets among the crew he had to sew up all the pockets, as if they had been "closets, crypts, and cabinets" containing valuables.

Two events of the voyage held special significance for White-Jacket: the passage around Cape Horn and the stopover at Rio de Janeiro. Passing the dangerous cape was indeed like descending into a horn, as Orpheus, Ulysses, or Dante had descended into hell. Passing the cape was a spiritual experience which might be generalized on. For every young man at some point faced an encounter with "the Spirit of the Cape," a "Jezebel," a "wilful, capricious jade that must be courted and coaxed into complaisance." This experience was a withdrawal into a night of storms which one must endure in the transit from the Pacific to the Atlantic, from one phase of life to another. White-Jacket hoped that no boy, unprepared for such a spiritual transit, would have to pass the cape, for he would almost surely founder. In the Atlantic they encountered a freezing cold calm which lasted for several days. Then came a gale which threatened to wreck the ship and made the ship's bell toll wildly in the night, filling White-Jacket with an indescribable horror. But the frigate came through, and White-Jacket was overjoyed at the thought of a safe trip home.

The stopover in the harbor of Rio de Janeiro was a time of erotic fantasies and of one brief erotic holiday when the crew was grudgingly given twenty-four hours' shore leave. Here it occurred to White-Jacket that his jacket was like the shirt of Nessus. The myth recounts that Hercules married Dejaneira (a name apparently identified by White-Jacket with "Rio de Janeiro"). The couple approached a flooded river, which Dejaneira could not cross. Nessus, a centaur, offered to carry her across, to which Hercules agreed. But Nessus tried to assault Dejaneira and for this was shot by Hercules with an arrow. The dying Nessus gave Dejaneira some of his blood, saying that she could always make Hercules love her by smearing it on his garment. Later Hercules fell in love with Iole, and to win him back Dejaneira smeared some of the blood on his robe. But the blood contained an evil charm and the robe clung irremovably to Hercules, burning his flesh unendurably. Hercules made a pyre, placed himself on it, and, inducing the father of Philoctetes to light the flame, his mortal part was consumed. We may perhaps surmise that the significance of this story for White-Jacket was that the whiteness of his own jacket was smeared with the blood of past sins and that if he was to escape the fate of Hercules, he must end his thralldom to it.

The white jacket had come to symbolize the mystery of the young man's paternity. Whiteness was the color he had come to associate with the moral immaculateness of his dead father. He had now reached the point where he could understand that his father must share the guilt of all human beings. To realize that his father had been anything but perfectly pure was an ordeal, was to recognize the bloodstains on the white image. But the recognition made it possible for him to be rid of the jacket. Having fallen from his own state of innocence, the young man could admit that his father had fallen too, and this was a step toward maturity and freedom. The fate of father and son, as of Hercules and Nessus, had now become clearer. They had loved the same woman, and a murder had been committed over her. Their common guilt was the reason why the son could now escape the father, and it also made possible their atonement.

White-Jacket's fall from innocence is symbolized by his memorable fall from the yardarm. It was like falling from a cross, as he said; it was like falling from the cross of St. Paul's (one of his father's stories of travel, we recall from *Redburn,* was of ascending into the dome of St. Paul's); it was like the fall of Lucifer (who in Melville signifies Prometheus rather than Satan) "from the well-spring of morning down to the Phlegethon of night." The description of White-Jacket's fall must be quoted at length:

The ship gave a plunge in the sudden swells of the calm sea, and pitching me still further over the yard, threw the heavy skirts of my jacket right over my head, completely muffling me. Somehow I thought it was the sail that had flapped and under that impression, threw up my hands to drag it from my head, relying upon the sail itself to support me meanwhile. Just then the ship gave another sudden jerk, and head-foremost, I pitched from the yard. I knew where I was, from the rush of the air by my ears, but all else was a nightmare. A bloody film was before my eyes, through which, ghost-like, passed and re-passed my father, mother and sisters. An unutterable nausea oppressed me; I was conscious of gasping; there seemed no breath in my body. It was over one hundred feet that I fell—down, down, with lungs collapsed as in death. Ten thousand pounds of shot seemed tied to my head, as the irresistible law of gravitation dragged me, head-foremost and straight as a die, toward the infallible center of this terraqueous globe. All I had seen, and read, and heard, and all I had thought and felt in my life, seemed intensified in one fixed idea in my soul. But dense as this idea was it was made up of atoms. Having fallen from the projecting yard-arm end, I was conscious of a collected satisfaction in feeling, that I should not be dashed to the deck, but would sink into the speechless profound of the sea.

With the bloody, blind film before my eyes, there was a still stranger

hum in my head, as if a hornet were there; and I thought to myself,
Great God! this is Death! Yet these thoughts were un-mixed with
alarm. Like frost-work that flashes and shifts its scared hues in the
sun, all my braided, blended emotions were in themselves icy cold
and calm.

So protracted did my fall seem that I can even now recall the feeling of wondering how much longer it would be ere all was over and
I struck. Time seemed to stand still, and all the worlds seemed poised
on their poles as I fell, soul-becalmed, through the eddying whirl and
swirl of the maelstrom air. . . .

As I gushed into the sea, a thunder-boom sounded in my ear; my
soul seemed flying from my mouth. The feeling of death flooded over
me with the billows. The blow from the sea must have turned me, so
that I sank almost feet-foremost through a soft, seething foamy lull.
Some current seemed hurrying me away; in a trance I yielded and sank
deeper down with a glide. Purple and pathless was the deep calm now
around me, flecked by summer lightnings in an azure afar. The horrible
nausea was gone; the bloody, blind film turned a pale green; I wondered whether I was yet dead, or still dying. But of a sudden some
fashionless form brushed my side—some inert, soiled fish of the sea;
the thrill of being alive again tingled in my nerves, and the strong
shunning of death shocked me through.

For one instant an agonizing revulsion came over me as I found
myself utterly sinking. Next moment the force of my fall was ex-
pended; and there I hung, vibrating in the mid-deep. What wild sounds
then rang in my ear! One was a soft moaning, as of low waves on the
beach; the other wild and heartlessly jubilant, as of the sea in the
height of a tempest. Oh soul! thou then heardest life and death: as he
who stands upon the Corinthian shore hears both the Ionian and the
Aegean waves. The life-and-death poise soon passed; and then I slowly
found myself ascending and caught a dim glimmering of light. .

Quicker and quicker I mounted; till at last I bounded up like a
buoy, and my whole head was bathed in the blessed air.

In this remarkable passage, at the end of the book which immediately preceded *Moby-Dick*, the young man finally found himself
able to symbolize, in the completed form of art, his own past and
his understanding and acceptance of it. His fall from innocence
was a second birth. He emerged from his deep plunge with something like the full consciousness of himself and his world which
the young man has when he definitively achieves the vision of the

artist. He would no longer be tyrannized by his past. The young man, floating in the water, struggled to remove his jacket, which threatened to pull him under again. But he tore if off and it sank into the sea.

15

White-Jacket served aboard the frigate as a maintopman. At the foot of the mainmast there often sat an old sailor known as the mainmastman. He sat there "in the evening of life, and at the close of day" as "old Abraham sat at the door of his tent, biding his time to die." The image reminds us that the various portraits of the young man in Melville's early novels constitute a portrait of Ishmael. As in the biblical story, Melville's Ishmael wandered over the earth searching for the elusive birthright he had lost, hunting, while he turned his hand against every man and lived in the wilderness as an archer, for the nation that Abraham had promised to make for him. In *Moby-Dick,* Ishmael is the consciousness which observes and understands the events recorded by the story. In the early novels Melville had traced the path by which the infant orphan Ishmael developed into this consciousness, a consciousness which, no longer held prisoner by the lost father, was free to search for (among other things) the meaning and value of paternity as it bears upon morals, politics, and art.

16

Melville was a great and profound man and his myth about himself is a magnificent one. But this should not keep us from seeing that his writings are characterized by a basically simple, or at least unobscure, realism and that the symbols which illustrate and define the myth are also basically simple. Sometimes the myth itself seems a little homespun or ramshackle, a contrivance put together out of odds and ends by an ingenious American in order to meet an emergency. Perhaps that is why Melville's myth tends to laugh at itself, as American mythology in general does.

The myth has two central themes: the Fall and the Search, the Search for what was lost in the Fall or for the earthly and possible substitutes for what was lost. The idea of the Fall was Melville's instinctive image of his own fate and the fate of his family. The Melvilles and the Gansevoorts (the mother's family) had been proud, aristocratic, and successful Americans. They had been squires, soldiers, merchants, professional men, staunch patriots in the Revolution and builders of the New World. To be born, an aspiring youth might think, constituted a Fall in itself, a leaping down from a golden cloud and an irredeemable engrossment of oneself in earth—buried to the thighs like the god Keevi. But to watch one's father go mad and die after having failed in business and having ruined the family fortune was to be given fearfully tangible evidence that one's instinctive sense of disaster and loss was well founded and was in fact the one real truth about life. And certainly there was much corroborative evidence for such an idea in the Greek and Hebrew and even the Polynesian myths: this much the amateur traveler and student of comparative mythology might easily see. The myth of the Fall seemed to be also an American myth, a so-far undefined legend of the Promethean nation which had revolted and fled from the high tyranny of British rule, an Ishmaelite nation cast out by Europe to wander in the wilderness, a nation betrayed by the Old World as a father might betray a son, forcing him to revolt and seek his own fortune but leaving him, too, with a patriarchal ideal which he must seek out and make his own in his own terms.

In *Mardi,* Melville had begun to think of the American destiny against the background of world history, and this became a theme which he pondered throughout his life. He worked out in *Mardi* a mythical language strangely similar to Toynbee's account of the growth of civilizations. America became for Melville the Prometheus of the West—the Titan whose momentous creative act had been his revolt against Zeus. The Promethean American is the hope of the world's peoples. In him is the divine creative *élan,* with its promise of endurance, growth, and fructifying civilization. But the revolt of Prometheus is in the past, and, as Melville pictures him, he is now the suffering hero, persecuted by a heavenly father who seeks to impose a stasis upon the universe, who seeks to reestablish the stagnant reactionism which the revolutionary *élan* of Prometheus had once smashed. The question Melville asks is: Will

America turn out to be the true Prometheus who successfully opposes the will of Zeus, redeems Zeus with the Promethean creativity, and so leads man along the path of growth toward a higher culture? or will America turn out to be a false Prometheus who in his suffering becomes, like Zeus himself, a blind and self-destructive tyrant? *

When Taji and his companions land in the northern part of Vivenza (that is, the United States), they are immediately pleased with the passionate and manly republicanism which seems to prevail there, for the inhabitants greet with wild elation each new report of revolution in Europe. (The time is presumably 1848.) The travelers are "refreshed" and filled with sensations of promise for the future as they survey the inhabitants and their green fields and groves, from which the "dew of the first morning" seems hardly to have vanished. Yet they soon learn that some Americans are sad in the midst of elation; for these Americans feel that the victorious republicanism of the day is really a new tyranny in disguise. "Some victories," they warn, "revert to the vanquished."

Soon the travelers reach a "great valley, whose inhabitants were more than commonly inflated with the ardor of the times." As they watch, a prophetic scroll is read to the populace by "a fiery youth mounted upon the shoulders of an old man, his sire"—Prometheus and Zeus. "The grand error of your nation," announces the fiery youth reading the scroll, is this: "the conceit that Mardi [the world] is now in the last scene of the last act of her drama; and that all preceding events were designed to bring about the catastrophe you now believe to be at hand—a universal and permanent Republic." This is followed by a discourse on the historical process of maturation and decay, with references to the rise and fall of Rome—the substance of which is that a civilization is doomed if it is not continuously self-regenerating. America is fortunate to be still so young, so fiery, and so generous. Yet look to the future,

* Certainly at the present moment Prometheus is engaged in redeeming Zeus, but whether this is a genuine redemption and atonement of the son with the father or simply an infusion of Marshall Plan money and "Americanism" is an open question. It is still very much Melville's question: Are we Prometheus or just another Zeus? I am one degree more inclined than the Wallacite liberals to think that we are still Prometheus, Melville's Prometheus, not Wallace's "common-man" Prometheus, that self-mortifying waif whose only real emotion is the fear that nobody loves him.

warns the prophetic scroll: the "bold boy is transformed. His eyes open not as of yore; his heart is shut up like a vise. . . . The maxims once trampled under foot are now printed on his front; and he who hated oppressors is become an oppressor himself."

The historical tragedy described in the anonymous tract is what Toynbee calls the "reversal of roles." This is the fate which overtakes a nation which has made a creative response to a challenge (such as the combined challenge British tyranny and a hostile environment presented to America in its early days) but by that very feat has become reactionary, and so is unable to meet the fresh challenges which threaten to inhibit its growth. What Toynbee calls "the nemesis of creativity" is precisely the fate which Melville feared would prove to be the fate of the United States. "Throughout all eternity," Melville writes, "the parts of the past are but the parts of the future reversed"—which is simply to say that the revolutionary Prometheus may turn into Zeus the tyrant.

The search for Prometheus, the question of who and what he may be, how much of human emotion and intelligence his personality encompasses, is a fundamental part of Melville's myth. Melville delineates a kind of Prometheus complex as the source of emotional and intellectual values. The "Prometheus complex" and the Oedipus complex have much in common, and Melville's vision of life makes use of many specifically Oedipean themes: the fear of castration (symbolized by cannibalism, decapitation, the injured leg, the horror of women), homoeroticism, narcissism, incest, and parricide. Ultimately, as we have noticed, Melville's vision seeks to delineate a Promethean king-hero who is less like our usual conception of Prometheus than he is like the Oedipus of Sophocles. Most of Melville's protagonists are Prometheus-like men shown in the act of failing to become the American Oedipus—that fully moral, fully wise, and fully tragic American who in Melville's books always strides just beyond the horizon, just beyond our ken. Melville does not give us a complete portrait of this American hero—how could any American writer do this in our time and our society?—being able only to symbolize him and to show what he is not, to call him the Handsome Sailor, and to communicate to us the awe with which, since he is the central symbol of a possible American culture and of humanity, we must regard him.

Melville's cultural-historical myth, then, includes an abode of the Gods and the fathers: Zeus or Jehovah, the "fiery father" whom Ahab defies or the "Commissioners" invoked by White-Jacket. And these heavenly fathers have their representatives on earth: the tyrants such as the kings of Europe and England, and the "Lords of the Plank" in the American marine, the Captain Rigas and the Captain Clarets; the humane patriarchs such as the Founding Fathers of the United States, and the old seamen or Abrahams of the fleet. In *Redburn,* Melville had seen one of the instruments by which the tyrant god entrenches himself on earth; cutthroat capitalism and exploitation of man by man. In *Typee* and *Omoo* he had seen another of these instruments: imperialism. And in *White-Jacket* he had seen a third: militarism.

The brutal and immoral Western civilization of the nineteenth century is the adult level of the fallen world of Melville's myth. The preadult level is the Circe's Isle, or fallen Eden, represented by Typee Valley—an archaic level of existence which wears the mask of childhood and innocence but is really guilty of terrible crimes and which in its devious way traps unwary young voyagers: the young hero of *Typee*; Harry Bolton, the homosexual youth whose life was ground out in the violent, exploitative machinery of the whaling industry; Jack Blunt, the regressive hypochondriac; Donjalolo, the father-haunted narcissist and exquisite; and the unfortunate young man whose hand was eaten off at tiffin among the savages. The young hero of Melville's myth must come to terms with Typee Valley in order to prepare himself to make his way in opposition to the high capitalist-military civilization. In psychological language, he must revert to his own childhood in order both to make the experiences of his childhood a possession of his adult life and to be free from them. The figures of the myth who, like Harry Bolton and Donjalolo, never escape their own childhood are unable to cope with the conditions of civilized life. Those who are not imprisoned by their childhood but who nevertheless possess the freedom, spontaneity, vitality, and myth-making imagination of childhood—like Marnoo and Jack Chase—are the most mature and admirable figures in Melville's myth. And those who commit themselves to the violent, suicidal drives of the high civilization and grow less and less capable of possessing their own childhood—

however much they themselves may be possessed by childish ideals —are the self-destructive titans and wreckers of the world, the Tajis, the Ahabs, and the Pierres.

In Melville's myth there are these cultural possibilities: Typee, capitalist-military civilization (the man-of-war world), Serenia, and the culture symbolized by Marnoo and Jack Chase. The culture of Marnoo and Jack Chase is based on the ideals of brotherhood and fatherhood, the democratic virtues of freedom and humanitarianism and the aristocratic virtues of order, authority, art, and heroism. Serenia is a neutralized utopia, an unresolved amalgam of Typee and the capitalist-military civilization. The society of Marnoo and Jack Chase is the only one in the myth which accepts the full tragic implications of its humanity. Serenia, like Typee and the capitalist-military civilization, does not know or will not admit that it is part of a fallen world. It believes in its own innocence. By rejecting the darker and more violent ranges of human nature, by unmanning itself, in short, it throws itself upon the dubious mercies of history. Serenia is the mythical prototype of that self-lacerating dream of the American liberal-progressive mind, the mild and infantile utopia of the "common man," whose dangers Melville was concerned to warn us against.

Such, in brief, are the persons and places of Melville's historical-cultural myth, a myth of suffering and regression, of emergence and creativity, of tyranny and revolution, of authority and submission, of innocence and guilt, of masculine love, love of brother and of father. Feminine love is the missing quantity. Melville tries to make it a part of the myth, but it remains the remote, cold, uncreated part. Fayaway is the child love, the pre-Oedipean "crush." She is real enough at this childish level. But nothing could be more unreal than the mythical woman when she becomes a bride.

Melville was married in 1848, and *Mardi*, the book in which we meet Yillah and Hautia, appeared in 1849. Surely Elizabeth Shaw has found her mythical transfigurations in these airy images. Yillah's symbolic whiteness connects her with the mythical image of the father and explains what she stands for. She is the pure or ideal love, the love who disappears after the bridal because Taji cannot keep her, as an ideal, in a world in which he has to kill the father to capture her in the first place. Marrying her as an ideal,

Taji is committing incest, since the ideal woman is his mother or sister. Having taken Yillah as his bride without a recognition and acceptance of his guilt, the young hero of *Mardi* finds that he has lost her and that she has cast a dark shadow over him—Hautia, or the sexual woman. The sister, ideal love, has become the wife, sexual love. Melville's "myth of the Bridegroom" * implies that the young man must accept the conditions of guilt and darkness and mindless passion symbolized by Hautia before he can recapture Yillah. Hautia is that part of Yillah which the immature—that is to say, the unredeemed—hero is unable to accept. Seeing his weakness, Yillah flees from him. But we must notice that Melville is the master of his myth; he is not mastered by it. Taji does not know that ideal love can be achieved only by an acceptance of the conditions of guilty love; Melville does know it.

The plot of Melville's historical-cultural myth is that experience continuously presents itself to the young man as partaking of an innocent and unfallen nature. The hero is tested, that is, by encounters with masked experience. When he unmasks experience, he succeeds in taking one step further in self-education, in the discovery of reality. But sometimes he fails. Taji, for example, unmasks Serenia but he fails to unmask Yillah, fails, in other words, to see that Yillah *is* Hautia. The young hero unmasks Typee Valley, finding behind its innocence the crime of cannibalism, and so is able to move on to higher levels of cultural possibility; but Donjalolo, unable to see any moral implications in his regressive hedonism, remains a prisoner of Willamilla. And Ahab—his is the purest insanity, for he rejects the conditions of life so fanatically and for so long that reality *is* for him the mask, which is what he finally calls the white whale. And behind the mask there is Nothing. The mask itself is Nothing; it is pure, neutral whiteness or death.

The discovery of reality is the precondition, and the acceptance of reality is, perhaps, the whole condition of the atonement of the young man with the gods and the fathers from whose estate he has fallen.

This, then, is the somewhat less than cogent mythical world in which Ishmael wanders. He seeks to become the complete Prome-

---

* I am indebted here to a brilliant unpublished essay by Mary Wright, called "The Blonde Woman in Hawthorne and Melville."

thean-Oedipean man, in whom father and son are reconciled—the true hero who has discovered and accepted human life and hence cannot be misled by the man-of-war, capitalist-military way of life, the primitive Typee way of life, or the unresolved liberal-progressive utopian way of life represented by Serenia.

Given this mythical world, what symbols might be adduced to represent and illustrate it if our mythmaker be a man of surging and somewhat disorganized nineteenth century romantic impulses tempered with a darkly tragic view, a man of imperfect education, a man living in an emergent and still undefined culture in which there was almost no traditional art of fiction? The idea of the Fall implies two sets of opposed or polar symbols, since the crude necessity is to be able to symbolize Up and Down. The mythical abode of the gods and the fathers from which the young hero has fallen has the symbolic qualities of the father, and the earthbound world of the fallen hero has the symbolic qualities of the son (the son as Ishmael or Prometheus in their purely passive and suffering roles: Ishmael as Consciousness and Prometheus as creative culture-hero function *between* the polarities). The symbolic qualities of the father are, let us say, height, strength, wealth, authority, majesty, and intellect. The symbols Melville uses for these qualities are commonly *Light, Space, Mountain, Tower, Fire, Phallus, Life.* The son is the father bereft of all his positive qualities. He is passive, withdrawn, vacillating, effeminate, impotent, and miserable. Thus the other set of symbols is: *Dark, Time, Valley, Cave, Stone, Castration, Death.*

These symbolic polarities are contained (with one or two specific exceptions such as Tower and Cave) in Melville's first book, *Typee.* In other words, he had his characteristic symbols before he ever set pen seriously to paper. The hazardous and painful descent of Toby and the hero into the Valley of Typee symbolizes the Fall, a descent from the sunlit *mountain* peaks into the recesses of the *valley,* from *light* to *dark,* from the upper *spaces* to a life measured by the anxiety of *time* and process and suspense and ambiguity (or by its absence), from the creative *fire* of the sun to a withdrawn existence characterized by the massive inertia of *stone* idols and temples (fire in Typee Valley can be kindled only with the greatest difficulty, as Melville tells us), from a brutal Western civilization which exalts the violence and exploitativeness of the *father* (for it was the whaling ship *Acushnet,* or *Pequod,* that the young hero had just left) to a primitive utopia of the *infantile* and effeminate impulses, from the *phallic* level of life to the *prephallic,* and so on.

These symbols, deriving from the myth of the Fall, remain Melville's primary symbols throughout his work, from *Typee* to *Billy Budd.* But Ishmael's mythical Search must go on within the symbolic polar extremities, since it is his destiny, in so far as he becomes the true hero, to reconcile them, to achieve the atonement. There must be, then, a dialectical continuity between the poles. Melville found such a dialectic in the idea of withdrawal and return, though he did not use those terms at first. In *Moby-Dick* he speaks of Father Mapple's "spiritual withdrawal," a retreat from the outer world into the meditative and recessive reaches of the mind in preparation for the great sermon he is about to preach. But by the time he wrote *Clarel* (published in 1876), Melville was frequently using the terms "withdraw" and "return." In that poem he asks: "Returns each thing that may withdraw?" And he answers:

> The schools of blue-fish years desert
> Our sounds and shores—but they revert;
> The ship returns on her long tack:
> The bones of Theseus are brought back:
> A comet shall resume its path
> Though three millenniums go.

Melville is speaking here of a spiritual transit which takes place between the polar symbols discussed above. The first set of symbols represents the return; the second set, the withdrawal.*

* Melville's Promethean-American dialectics needed only the elegant scholarship of Professor Toynbee to make them exactly like Toynbee's account of "Withdrawal-and-Return." As Toynbee uses this idea, it is a "rhythm"—the passage of the ego from the objective world into the unconscious and back into the outer world. The whole process of life, the process of human history and of every genuinely creative act, moves through this cyclical rhythm. As a spiritual transit it is only the highest manifestation of the basic rhythms of the universe: the alternation of day and night, of death and life, the change of the seasons, the cycle of vegetation. The transit is not necessarily productive in the higher forms of life. It succeeds only when the organism emerges on the returning beat of the rhythm transfigured by the spiritual illumination of the journey and in possession of revived potency. Withdrawal and return is symbolized by a great many mythical themes. To name a few: the folk heroes who are beheaded or otherwise injured and magically restored, the death and rebirth of the savior-gods (Christ, Attis, Adonis, Osiris), the retirement of youths at puberty, the banishment and return of heroes like Oedipus.

Melville's idea of withdrawal and return is a complex and far-reaching concept. But it is in no sense esoteric. On the contrary, it is a simple and even brutal piece of spiritual realism, as natural as the primary facts of life. It might even be argued that withdrawal and return *are* the primary facts of life, since whatever the condition of life in the universe, it is either withdrawing or returning. Melville is only presenting us with the idea that man succeeds in his high destiny when he can ally himself with the creative rhythms of the universe and fails when he cannot. The idea is of course common in nineteenth century thought, though it seldom achieves the magnificent and uncompromising realism it achieves in Melville.

Withdrawal has at least three related meanings in Melville's myth. It signifies the spiritual ordeal of the fallen son; his suffering in the dark reaches of the soul; his preparation for the creative emergence or return (Ishmael wandering in the wilderness, preparing himself for the great nation which has been promised him; Prometheus on the rock, suffering and waiting for the time when his example will regenerate Zeus and ensure the cultural progress of mankind). It signifies the post-revolutionary spiritual ordeal of America, the Ishmael or Prometheus among nations. And it signifies the general condition of the modern world, which Melville conceives as having withdrawn (or fallen) from a former state of health, power, and heroism into a wasteland and as trying to return. (This is the explicit subject matter of *Clarel.*) Without making theological commitments, Melville was often in the state of mind to which Christian thinkers refer when they tell us that in modern times we are in the desolate hours between Good Friday and Easter Sunday.

Ishmael's search for the secret of his paternity is his attempt to "return." He must first accept the withdrawal in its full horror. He must make a whole system of choices of behavior, accepting the conditions of life they imply, attempting to reconcile them. This is an earthly task. There can be no titanic storming of the heavens, since that is suicide. Ishmael—the American—can succeed if, generously coveting the lost paternal values of intelligence, authority, art, and heroism, he realizes that he can return to them only by accepting his human involvement in the filial values, an involve-

ment which allows him to leaven the paternal ideal, to force the
paternal ideal to rid itself of violence, power worship, and
reaction.

Surely Melville was profoundly correct and prophetic in his
judgment of our society. The cultural anthropologists are only the
latest observers to tell us of our unconscious but systematic "rejection of the father" and all the values he stands for. Since early
revolutionary times, we have conspired to reduce the stature of
manhood and heroism, to make it impossible, by setting up cultural
taboos, that an American should present himself as in the complete
sense a man. We have been, and still are, a regressive, a "withdrawn" culture, living by predominantly feminine ethics and systematically carving the paternal virtues out of our national personality. Our democratic ideals have destroyed both the father and
the mother as shaping cultural forces. The father we reduce to an
impotent dependence on the mother and children. We rejoice in
ridiculing him, as Hawthorne shows us in the terrible concluding
scene of the tar-and-feathering of the old man in the story called
My Kinsman, Major Molineux. The mother image we dissect into
two contraries, unconsciously admitting our unworthy ambivalence.
For most of us the American woman, because we have forced upon
her by default so much power and influence, is either the untouch-
able pure ideal or she is the murderer, the engulfing vortex—as she
was for Melville's Taji and Pierre.

The hope that our country can put childish things aside is the
hope that, in Melville's language, it will be able to "return." As it
is, we are ruined by our own perpetual and unredeemable sonhood.
This is the compelling significance of the quip that America is a
nation of children, a vast and plushy nursery. So America is pictured in Melville's *Pierre,* as later it was to be pictured in *The Great
Gatsby* and *The Sun Also Rises.*

Without making exact equivalents, let us call the filial polar values (discussed above) "democracy," or "democratic socialism."
And let us call the paternal values by the obvious name, "patri-
archy." It is clear that Melville advocates a reconciliation of these
polar values, a redemption of each by the other. Melville's most
decisive criticism of American society was that on the left and on
the right, among the abolitionists and transcendentalists and among

the capitalists, it was in danger of destroying itself by surrendering to bland and harmless-looking icons of the "withdrawal." He feared that Americans were abandoning the Promethean spirit of adventure and creativity which would see it through the arduous transits between the extremities of human experience and were idolizing instead the spirit of "confidence." The "confidence man," at once a capitalist and a reformer of capitalism, played it safe; he took it easy. He refused to recognize any of the spiritual extremities of life. He thought the idea of Fatherhood was illiberal. (It has since been called a fascist idea.) He idolized the least admirable virtues of sonhood, impotence, harmlessness, neutrality. He never saw the extremities of experience—which are always implied, whether admittedly or not, in any moral position one may take—and hence he was at the mercy of these extremities. And so was the nation to which he skillfully sold his ideals. The confidence man was what is now called "just a confused liberal." But he was anything but harmless. In a world full of evil, his potentiality was all for evil. "You are the moderate man, the inveterate understrapper of the wicked man," as a frontiersman remarks to the confidence man in Melville's great satire. "You may be used for wrong, but you are useless for right." Melville does not mean to imply that one should be *im*moderate, but only that one should not be neutral, that one should not "unman" oneself (to use one of Melville's key words) by failing to recognize and accept the full meaning of life and to make choices among the possibilities life offers. Melville's polar symbols represent aesthetic and philosophic orders of discourse. But they are also the ultimate moral and cultural symbols in relation to which one must make choices of action. Like every other organism, man is fated to move between the polar symbols with the cyclical rhythms of universal life. There are two general possibilities. One may make a surface commitment to life's rhythms, ignoring the idea of man's fallen nature and betraying the search for the secret of his paternity—that is, one may "unman" oneself; or one may make the ultimate wager that to withdraw into the subterranean places of the soul is to see not death, but "God's foot on the treadle of the loom" and is to pass not into madness, but into the upper regions of human strength and human vision; to return, that is, and to possess the full humanity which is one's birthright.

To put it in simpler language, a man may evade his own humanity or he may recognize and accept the sonhood and the fatherhood implicit *in* his humanity. Again, a man may be either a false hero or a true hero.

As we should expect, there are three kinds of false hero: those who withdraw but cannot return from their archaic level of life (Donjalolo, Harry Bolton, Pip in *Moby-Dick*), those who cannot withdraw in any other way than by committing suicide (Taji, Ahab, Pierre), and those who deny that withdrawal and return has any real meaning at all (the Serenians, the confidence man). And there is one kind of true hero: the Promethean-Oedipean culture hero who is like Prometheus because he seeks the regeneration of the heavenly father and atonement with him, and like Oedipus because he has accepted the full knowledge and guilt of his sonhood and the full responsibility of his fatherhood. No humane culture can have any other image of perfection, any other hero, than the one Melville presents in his portrait of Marnoo, Jack Chase, and, in later books, Bulkington and Ethan Allen.

The reader will by this time have noticed many elements of Christian thought in Melville's myth and will perhaps have wondered why Christ has not entered into my account of Melville's idea of heroism. But Melville identifies Christ with strength and kingship only in portraying Ahab; elsewhere he always identifies Christ with the weak, the passive, and the hermaphrodite. Yet Melville was far from unmindful of his Christian heritage. On the contrary, Christ was such a massive and moving image in Melville's mind that it had to remain on the whole unuttered and implicit. He was too close to it and too personally responsible for it. Greek, Jewish, and Polynesian myths he could see objectively, and he could therefore use them for artistic and moral purposes. Anyone who tries to study Melville as a Christian will have to deal largely with the unconscious, ineffable Melville.

If, in the realm of Western myth, Melville's Ishmael is the younger brother of Isaac, he is also, in the realm of the Western novel, the younger brother of Pierre Bezuhov in *War and Peace,* of little Pip in *Great Expectations,* of all the young men of uncertain parentage whom the European novelists have represented as coming from obscure regions of the country to learn about society and to take part in it. Ishmael's elder brothers have an easier task, for the society they seek is already established; they have but to learn what it is and to seek their fortunes in it. But Ishmael, like his American counterparts in Hawthorne—Robin in *My Kinsman, Major Molineux,* Dominicus Pike in *Mr. Higginbotham's Catastrophe,* the writer in *The Seven Vagabonds,* Holgrave in *The House of the Seven Gables*—has the preliminary task of seeking for society itself, for it is by no means clear what it is or even whether it exists. In the books before *Moby-Dick* we see Ishmael leaving the primitive condition of man and trying to discover Western civilization: Redburn leaves the family home up the Hudson and makes his "filial pilgrimage" to Liverpool; the young man flees from Typee Valley and boards a whaler and then a warship; later we see Pierre leaving the agrarian bowers of the family estate and settling in a colony of intellectuals in New York, and Israel Potter leaving his Berkshire forests for London, the City of Man.

The theme of Melville's first five books is the education of the young man. It is difficult to overestimate the act of intellect which permitted Melville to create this mythical construction (philosophically inchoate as it may sometimes be) and to give it such unavoidable moral solidity. It would be a great act in any time or culture. But we must remember the "masterless commotion" (a phrase describing the sea in *Moby-Dick*) of the culture Melville lived in, the absence of stability and tradition, the perpetual cultural failures and the undefined and abortive cultural successes. Melville's myth of the young man was not unalloyed art. But the importance of Melville's example is prodigious. Culturally, we have little advantage over Melville, except our sophistication. We still do not know who we are or what society we live in. We may know *more* about these things than Melville did. But in so far as we are Americans, we are Ishmael, and we cannot afford to evade the responsibility of recapitulating in our art and our morals Ishmael's difficult self-education. We are all Ishmael; but without Ishmael's education, we become not Bulkington, the democratic hero, but Ahab, the exploiter whose exploitation is all of himself and his fellows; or Pip, the negro cabin boy, whose personality breaks down in the midst of the destructive enterprise and who goes mad; or, like the confidence man, the Laodicean liberal-progressive, an intellectual whose sweet voice denies the possibility or misrepresents the exigencies of Ishmael's education.

Melville's myth of the young man was a distinctly American myth. Yet the emergence of Ishmael as Consciousness had occurred within the framework of Western civilization. He had educated himself in Liverpool, in European colonies, on an Australian (as well as an American) whaler. We have the sense in Melville's first five books of an evasion according to plan, partly unconscious, partly conscious, of the definitive statement about American culture. Melville's experiences on the whaling ship *Acushnet* had perhaps been so momentous that they could not be written about until other things had been written about first. The abyss which lies between *White-Jacket* (1850) and *Moby-Dick* (1851) is one of the most enormous in the history of letters. *Moby-Dick* might have been, like *White-Jacket,* only a realistic narrative of a voyage, with certain implicit and undeveloped mythical references. But it *was* the single epic statement about America. The rereading of Shakespeare while *Moby-Dick* was in progress no doubt kindled Melville's mind to the possibilities of tragic action, as Charles Olson maintains in his *Call Me Ishmael*. But Melville's genius, as we see it in *Moby-Dick,* cannot be something that happened overnight. One piece of evidence for this is that *Typee,* the first book, is more symbolically complete and profound than the books between it and *Moby-Dick*. Out of the necessity of his own development, Melville seems deliberately to have avoided large-scale symbolic writing after *Typee,* or to have tried it only in the realm of rather heavily facetious fancy, as in *Mardi*. He admits as much by making the early books an account of the emergence of Ishmael's consciousness: Ishmael can have no complete mythical or epic grasp of himself and his culture while he is still imperfectly conscious. The fall of White-Jacket from the yardarm and his emergence from the depths of the sea was the announcement that now Ishmael could rescue from his unconscious mind all the terrific and loving images of cultural action which had been deposited there. To write an epic in this late day and in this undefined culture must be in part a willed and personal and self-generative act. The myth of the young man had delineated the author who was to perform the act. Now, if ever, an epic could be written.

II

Light in the Morning

I should say that Ahab is as much the American of his time as was Homer's Odysseus the Greek of his time or Joyce's Leopold Bloom the Jew of his time. He is the American cultural image: the captain of industry and of his soul; the exploiter of nature who severs his own attachment to nature and exploits himself out of existence; the good progressive American; the master of the most beautifully contrived machine of his time; the builder of new worlds whose ultimate spiritual superficiality drives him first to assume an uneasy kingship and a blind, destructive motive of revenge, and then gradually reduces him to a pure, abstract fury on whose inhuman power he rides off into eternity, leaving nothing behind but disaster for the races of the world and an ambiguous memory of the American flair which accompanied the disaster and was the only hint of moral meaning or of solace for the future or for the dead at the bottom of the Pacific. This much, and much more, of the epic hero of *Moby-Dick* was given to Melville by the folk tales and legends of New England and the frontier. But Melville was not Homer, not having Homer's rich mythical material. He had to generate much of the myth as he went along; he had to exploit foreign mythologies and to adduce and re-create the very folk tales he was at the same time transmuting into epic. Thus Melville constructs Ahab out of many myths and many men.

Ahab is a primitive magician who tries to coerce man and the universe by compulsive ritual; and again like the magicians, he insults and castigates his god. He is the *shaman,* that is, the religious leader (common among certain tribes of American Indians) who cuts himself off from society to undergo his private ordeal, through which he attains some of the knowledge and power of the gods. The *shaman* is usually deeply neurotic and sometimes epileptic— the savior with the neurosis. Again, Ahab is the culture hero (though a false one) who kills the monsters, making man's life possible.

But Ahab also resembles an even more momentous mythical
being: Christ. Were he not so committed to his "monomaniac"
pursuit of the whale, Ahab might have been the source of genial
spirits and reviving life. He is "stricken" and "blasted," says Captain Peleg, but "Ahab has his humanities." And in the beautiful
chapter called "The Symphony," Ahab, overcome for a moment
by the insinuating feminine vitalities of the Pacific air, is seen to
shed a tear into the sea, a tear of compassion for the suffering in
the universe. "Nor did all the Pacific contain such wealth," Melville says, "as that one wee drop." The memory of the true Savior
remains, though obscurely, in Ahab's personality; he works out his
fated failure within the ghostly scaffolding of the Savior's career
on earth. Like the Savior, Ahab is preceded by a prophet; namely,
the demented Elijah, who so persistently importunes Ishmael and
Queequeg with his divinations shortly before the *Pequod* sets sail.
Indeed, Ahab speaks of *himself* as a prophet. "Now then," he says,
addressing himself, "be the prophet and the fulfiller one." Again,
we are told that Ahab sleeps "with clenched hands, and wakes with
his own bloody nails in his palms." The pun is unavoidable. But
there is this difference between Ahab and Christ: these are Ahab's
own nails. He is not a sacrifice; he is a suicide.

In his poem on Melville, W. H. Auden says of Ahab that "the
rare ambiguous monster . . . had maimed his sex." And indeed
in the fall of the year—some time, that is, before Christmas, when
the *Pequod* sailed—Ahab, like the divine hero Adonis, suffered a
"seemingly inexplicable, unimaginable casualty." He was found
lying on the ground, "his ivory limb having been so violently displaced that it had stakewise smitten him and all but pierced his
groin." Like the savior-heroes, Ahab withdrew from the world
after being wounded. Only when the *Pequod* left Nantucket behind
and began to feel the springlike breath of the south did Ahab
return to the world to perform his fated task. Like a resurrected
savior he stepped from his cabin, in which he had been "invisibly
enshrined," a "supreme lord" in his "sacred retreat." The ordeal
Ahab suffered in his spiritual transit of withdrawal and return left
him a transfigured being. When he came on deck, "as if, when the
ship had sailed from home, nothing but the dead wintry bleakness
of the sea had . . . kept him so secluded," his appearance absolutely appalled Ishmael, who had been watching the afterdecks for

some time with "foreboding shivers." As Ahab finally stood at the taffrail on his "barbaric white leg," he looked "like a man cut away from the stake, when the fire has overrunningly wasted all the limbs without consuming them, or taking away one particle of their compacted aged robustness." Ahab stood before the crew, says Melville, "with a crucifixion in his face; in all the nameless regal overbearing dignity of some mighty woe." Ahab was in appearance, if not in reality, the Savior. For apparently he had returned to mankind from his ordeal, having acquired the new insight, the new sense of dedication, the new sanctity necessary for the accomplishment of his task.

But Ahab's is the Promethean task, and as the *Pequod* searches for Moby-Dick, Ahab becomes more and more the Promethean type of hero. Modern classical scholars suppose that Prometheus was a fire-god; and so Melville considers him. In *Mardi,* Taji was described as a demigod from the sun. And in the same book Melville exclaims that it is to the sun that "we Prometheuses" must go for our source of fire. By "fire" he means the creative principle: in the same passage he speaks of "the All-Plastic Power" which pervades the universe. And he warns that "only perpetual Vestal tending" will keep the fire alive in man. For fire is a double principle: it can create and it can destroy; and without perpetual tending, the act of creation becomes itself an act of destruction.

Ahab has learned this lesson well. And, like Prometheus, he is the possessor of a secret which God, whom he addresses as "my fiery father," does not know. In the tortured and difficult chapter called "The Candles," Ahab hurls his challenge at God, who has laid His "burning finger" on the *Pequod* as it sails through an electric storm. To the corposants which light up the masts like three candles and to the lightning itself, Ahab shouts:

I know that of me which thou knowest not of thyself, oh, thou omnipotent. . . . Through thee, thy flaming self, my scorched eyes do dimly see it. Oh, thou foundling fire, thou hermit immemorial, thou too hast thy incommunicable riddle, thy unparticipated grief. Here again with haughty agony, I read my sire. Leap! leap up, and lick the sky! I leap with thee; I burn with thee; would fain be welded with thee; defyingly I worship thee!

Like Prometheus, Ahab "reads his sire" better than his sire can read himself. Ahab's secret, as we shall see, is the knowledge that creation becomes a destruction when the Promethean *élan* is allowed to become mechanical or to degenerate into force.

As the *Pequod* sails on toward the whale, ship and crew becoming more and more like objectifications of the will of the "monomaniac" commander, Ahab perceives the strange dualism of mechanicalness and creativity in the ship's carpenter. The carpenter has so far descended in the scale of life that he is little more than an extension of his own technique. He "was a pure manipulator . . ." writes Melville,

yet this omnitooled, open-and-shut carpenter, was, after all, no mere machine of an automaton. If he did not have a common soul in him, he had a subtle something that somehow anomalously did its duty. . . . And this it was, this same unaccountable, cunning life-principle in him; this it was, that kept him a great part of the time soliloquizing; but only like an unreasoning wheel, which also hummingly soliloquizes.

In the fire, too, Melville discerns the paradox of creativeness and mechanicalness. We recall that in the reversion scene, when Ishmael in horror suddenly finds himself facing astern, he had been gazing into the flaming tryworks just as he lost consciousness. As Ishmael regains control of himself and the ship, Melville exclaims, "believe not the artificial fire, when its redness makes all things look ghastly." Wait, he says, for "the natural sun . . . the only true lamp—all others are but liars!" And later, as the crew looks forward to the third and final lowering of the boats against Moby-Dick, the following interchange occurs:

Ahab: D'ye feel brave men, brave?
Stubb: As fearless fire.
Ahab: And as mechanical.

Ahab knows that his fiery father, though in fatal control of the *Pequod,* is transcended by a greater power from which the fiery father derives whatever of creativeness he has. Again we hear the suffering Prometheus who taunts Zeus: "there is some unsuffusing thing beyond thee, thou clear spirit, to whom all thy eternity is but time, all thy creativeness mechanical." This transcendent power Ahab calls the "sweet mother." She is the *personality* that lives in and despite the world machine, the human *élan* which survives in the iron mill of the universe and which asserts the possible existence of the human soul within the process of history or among the "sheer naked slidings of the elements," as D. H. Lawrence says in his essay on *Moby-Dick*. Sometimes the sweet mother comes to Ahab, though he believes that ultimately he is committed to the mechanico-apocalyptic aspect of the divine fire. "Come in thy lowest form of love," he can sometimes say, "and I will kneel and kiss thee." At these times, he is able to defy the annihilating god with the only weapon which can conquer him—the assertion of humanness. "In the midst of the personified impersonal, a personality stands here." Yet his premonition tells him that the act of defiance will finally rob him of personality, will turn out to be the act of suicide—that where the true Prometheus succeeded, Ahab, the false Prometheus, will fail.

The idea of the false Prometheus often occurs to Ahab. In the ship's carpenter and blacksmith he sees the false Prometheus made doubly terrifying by his almost hallucinatory awareness of an apotheosis looming up behind him. In the scene where the carpenter and the blacksmith are at work on a new whalebone leg for Ahab, the carpenter asks Ahab whether or not it is true that "a dismasted man never entirely loses the feeling of his old spar, but it will still be pricking him at times." It is true, says Ahab; and the following dialogue ensues:

Ahab: Look, put thy live leg here in the place where mine once was; so, now, here is only one distinct leg to the eye, yet two to the soul. Where thou feelest tingling life; there, exactly there, there to a hair, do I. Is't a riddle?

Carpenter: I should humbly call it a poser, sir.

Ahab: Hist, then. How dost thou know that some entire, living, thinking thing may not be invisibly and uninterpenetratingly standing precisely where thou now standest; aye, and standing there in thy spite? In thy most solitary hours, then dost thou not fear eavesdroppers?

We can make an algebraic equation out of what Ahab is thinking: The carpenter's leg is to Ahab's whalebone leg as the true, the creative, the life-giving Prometheus is to the carpenter. As the *Pequod* sails to its doom, the titanic "Eavesdropper" walks the deck, promising success against the Annihilator of personality. But

aboard the *Pequod* this tranfigured Creator meets an antagonist
who is not to be overcome: Ahab transfigured into the mechanical
man. Tell the blacksmith, he commands, "to forge a pair of steel
shoulder-blades; there's a pedlar aboard with a crushing pack."
And addressing the blacksmith ironically as "Prometheus," he
says:

I'll order a complete man after a desirable pattern. Imprimis, fifty
feet high in his socks; then, chest modelled after the Thames Tunnel;
then, legs with roots to 'em, to stay in one place; then, arms three feet
through at the wrist; no heart at all, brass forehead, and about a quarter
of an acre of fine brains; and let me see—shall I order eyes to see
outwards? No, but put a skylight on top of his head to illuminate
inwards.

As Ahab stands on deck, his ivory leg stuck into its accustomed
hole in the plank, the mechanical man rises up behind him; and
the ship and its terrified crew are his.

The predicament of Ahab as Prometheus is, in certain senses,
the Puritan predicament; and his failure is the Puritan failure.
Having cut himself off from society, having become in his "radical
protestantism" (to use Sedgwick's phrase *) an "individualist,"
Ahab turns in upon himself and eats away his own vitality. "For a
long time now," says Melville, "the circus-running sun has raced in
his fiery ring, and needs no sustenance but what's in himself. So
Ahab." Like Hawthorne's Ethan Brand, that other custodian of
the fire, Ahab is the victim of a disintegrating personality, a personality in which the mind driven by the will has cut itself off from
the heart. The furious amoral intellect is like the destructive
lightning Ahab challenges in "The Candles": "I own thy speechless,
placeless power; but to the last gasp of my earthquake life will
dispute its unconditional, unintegral mastery in me." As Melville
says, when Ahab had

yielded up all his thoughts and fancies to his one supreme purpose,
that purpose, by its own sheer inveteracy of will, forced itself against
gods and devils into a kind of self-assumed, independent being of its
own. Nay, could grimly live and burn, while the common vitality to
which it was conjoined, fled horror-stricken from the unbidden and

* *Herman Melville: The Tragedy of Mind*, 1944.

unfathered birth. . . . God help thee, old man, thy thoughts have created a creature in thee; and he whose intense thinking thus makes him a Prometheus; a vulture feeds upon his heart forever; that vulture the very creature he creates.

When we are trying to account for the extraordinary preeminence of *Moby-Dick* among the author's works, it will help to remember that Ahab is the one fully objectified character who is both the father and the son. He is both the savior-god who addresses his fiery father and the patriarch with forty years of whaling behind him who lords it over his awestruck men like a sultan. Since for Melville much of the excitement and mystery of the world came out of the tensions set up by the father-son relationship, the great feat for him was to create a single character in whom this relationship was brought into concentration under pressure. Once Melville had conceived and created Ahab, the story of the disintegration of his personality, symbolizing, as it does, the primeval and universal father-son relationship, could not fail to be a spectacle that was unique in its magnificence and its evocation of pity and wonder. What was needed to complete the picture was a compelling, external symbol of the father.

2

Moby-Dick is God incarnate in the whale. In Babbalanja's journey to heaven, described in *Mardi,* Melville had already symbolized the ineffable by its whiteness. In heaven, Babbalanja is told, "one note of laughter . . . might start some white and silent world." And as Ishmael decides to go to sea in a whaler, he senses the awful mystery of the white god: "the great floodgates of the wonder-world swung open, and in the wild conceits that swayed me to my purpose, two and two there floated into my soul, endless processions of the whale, and, midmost of them all, one grand hooded phantom, like a snow hill in the air." Like an overpowering dream image, "the grand god" will "reveal himself" to Ishmael as he flings his majestic body out of the Pacific when he is about to sound. As we look at the head of the decapitated whale, we see the image of the "big, white god" to whom Pip, the negro cabin boy, prays. And as Melville tells us, "in the great Sperm Whale, this high and mighty god-like dignity inherent in the brow is so immensely amplified, that gazing on it, in that full front view, you feel the Deity and the dread powers more forcibly than in beholding any other object in living nature."

In the chapter on "The Whiteness of the Whale," Melville compares Moby-Dick with other animal deities. Moby-Dick is like Zeus, who made himself incarnate in a snowy-white bull. There is in him the pure lascivious beauty of the mythic beast. "A gentle joyousness," writes Melville, "a mighty mildness of repose in swiftness, invested the gliding whale. Not the white bull Jupiter swimming away with ravished Europa clinging to his graceful horns; his lovely leering eyes sideways intent upon the maid; with smooth, bewitching fleetness, rippling straight for the nuptial bower in Crete; not Jove, not that great majesty supreme! did surpass the glorified White Whale as he so divinely swam." Or again, Moby-Dick is like the sacred White Dog which was sacrificed by the Iroquois at their midwinter festival. Or he is like the white polar bear or those "transcendent horrors," the white sharks of the tropics. He is like the Ancient Mariner's albatross, or the legendary White Steed which the Plains Indians held in reverence and awe.

As we watch the whale swimming over the surface of the Pacific, we feel aesthetic intuitions of the beauty of God:

> How nobly it raises our conceit of the mighty, misty monster, to behold him solemnly sailing through a calm, tropical sea; his vast, mild head overhung by a canopy of vapor, engendered by his incommunicable contemplations, and that vapor—as you sometimes see it— glorified by a rainbow, as if Heaven itself had put its seal upon his thoughts. For, d'ye see, rainbows do not visit the clear air; they only irradiate vapor. And so, through all the thick mists of the dim doubts of my mind, divine intuitions now and then shoot.

In the calm of aesthetic contemplation, the terrifying whiteness of the whale is broken into the rainbow of its component colors and we see the inward reality revealed objectively by the aesthetic intuition. But when the terror of the whale rushes upon us, the revelations of conscious art will again be obscured, the rainbow which art has shown us will be swallowed up in the massive whiteness, art will collapse into nature, and God will descend into the mechanical brute to renew His war against man.

The inscrutable secrecy, the profound wisdom of God are in Moby-Dick. "Of all divers, thou hast dived the deepest," says Ahab.

That head upon which the upper sun now gleams has moved amid this world's foundations. Where unrecorded names and navies rust, and untold hopes and anchors rot; where in her murderous hold, this frigate earth is ballasted with bones of millions of the drowned; there, in that awful waterland, there was thy most familiar home. Thou hast been where bell or diver never went; hast slept by many a sailor's side, where sleepless mothers would give their lives to lay them down. . . . O head! thou hast seen enough to split the planets and make an infidel of Abraham, and not a syllable is thine!

The horror, too, of God as tyrant and annihilator is in *Moby-Dick*. When the whale strikes the bows of the *Pequod* like a battering ram, Ahab cries that the ship is a "god-bullied hull." The Old Testament has taught Melville that God is fearful. In his *Journal up the Straits* he describes Jehovah as a "terrible mixture of the cunning and awful." And beholding the parched and stony landscape of Palestine, he asks: "Is the desolation of the land the result of the fatal embrace of the Deity? Hapless are the favorites of Heaven."

Imagining an American Olympus, Melville says that if we ever people our naked, overbearing heaven with divinities, if we "lure back to their birthright the merry May-day gods of old; and livingly enthrone them again in the now egotistical sky; in the now unhaunted hill; then be sure, exalted to Jove's high seat, the great Sperm Whale shall lord it."

3

God attempts to defeat the heroic defender of man by forcing him into the pattern of the beast or the machine. The hero attempts to escape this fate and to preserve the *élan* of human intelligence, creativeness, and adaptability. The human *élan* is the one weapon which can defeat the tyrant God; it is the one attribute God Himself needs if He is to keep His throne.

Melville is often fascinated by the flux of animal life through the various evanescent forms it assumes. The indifference of the lower species of this "wolfish world" to life and death, to all values, he finds appalling. "Consider the subtleness of the sea," he says,

how its most dreaded creatures glide under water, unapparent for the most part, and treacherously hidden beneath the loveliest tints of azure. Consider also the devilish brilliance and beauty of many of its most remorseless tribes, as the dainty and embellished shape of the many species of sharks. Consider, once more, the universal cannibalism of the sea; all whose creatures prey upon each other, carrying on eternal war since the world began.

Or again, when a whale has been brought alongside the *Pequod,* schools of sharks assemble for the feast. Two sailors are detailed to keep the corpse free and they carry on "an incessant murdering of the sharks" with their whaling spades. But still the sharks come on. "They viciously snapped, not only at each other's disembowelments, but like flexible bows, bent round, and bit their own; till those entrails seemed swallowed over and over again by the same mouth, to be oppositely voided by the gaping wound." Later, when the whale has been beheaded and stripped of his "blanket" of blubber, the carcass is cut loose and allowed to drift astern.

The peeled white body of the beheaded whale flashes like a marble sepulchre; though changed in hue, it has not perceptibly lost anything in bulk. It is still colossal. Slowly it moves more and more away, the water round it torn and splashed by the insatiate sharks, and the air above vexed with rapacious flights of screaming fowls, whose beaks are like so many insulting poniards in the whale. The vast white headless phantom floats further and further from the ship; and every rod that it so floats, what seem square roods of sharks and cubic roods of fowls, augment the murderous din. For hours and hours from the almost stationary ship that hideous sight is seen. Beneath the unclouded and mild azure sky, upon the fair face of the pleasant sea, wafted by the joyous breezes, that great mass of death floats on and on, till lost in infinite perspectives. . . . There's a most doleful and mocking funeral! The sea-vultures all in pious mourning, the air-sharks all punctiliously in black or speckled. In life but few of them would have helped the whale, I ween, if peradventure he had needed it; but upon the banquet of his funeral they most piously do pounce. Oh, horrible vulturism of earth from which not the mightiest whale is free.

The great whale, too, lives by "vulturism." His murderous jaw, his mighty tail, at once so subtle and so violent, seem to be motivated by an impersonal malice before which all preeminently human values must go down to destruction. When man is faced with the reckless flux of the universal process, he seems a helpless misfit, an epiphenomenon, a temporary mistake of nature which the flux will in good time amend. Prometheus faces this vision of life when, as he lies chained to the rock, the vulture eats out his vitals. Ahab faces it as he feels his own vitals being eaten away by the sharkish onslaught of his own implacable will. Prometheus survives the torture of the nightmare world with which Zeus has confronted him. But the ordeal is too great for Ahab. He is forced by the too formidable challenge of Moby-Dick to give ground. He opposes the whale, not as a man, but as a beast. He has been forced to assume the nature of his enemy. Stubb, the second mate, unconsciously puts his finger on Ahab's failure. To Flask, the third mate, he says: "A white whale—did ye mark that, man? Look ye—there's something special in the wind. Stand by for it, Flask. Ahab has that that's bloody on his mind."

The towering, mindless head of the White Whale, the immense hulk driven instinctively through the oceans remind us that Moby-Dick is a machine; and he is a machine out of human control. In his violent motions we seem to see the mechanism of the universe, innocent of all human intelligence and feeling. As Lawrence says, Melville was "spellbound by the strange slidings and collidings of Matter." Here we find another reason (though we have mentioned it before) for the failure of Ahab. In order to combat Moby-Dick, when like an ocean-going *deus ex machina* he appears at the end of the drama, Ahab himself becomes a machine. Like Taji in *Mardi,* he rushes on, "fixed as fate," a somnambulist "fast-frozen" in a "horrid dream." "The path to my fixed purpose is laid with iron rails, whereon my soul is grooved to run," cries Ahab. All the creative human emotions, "joy and sorrow, hope and fear, seemed ground to finest dust, and powdered . . . in the clamped mortar of Ahab's iron soul." The crew, too, is frozen into inflexibility: "like machines they dumbly moved about the deck." Ahab sees clearly enough the cumulative "unmanning" of himself and his crew.

Ahab is an old man, the aging American titan. In his youth he

could determine his own course of action; he could direct his creative zest toward what goals he wished. But the great accomplishments of his youth themselves gave birth to his own ensuing destructiveness. "When thou wast young, thou girdedst thyself, and
walkedst whither thou wouldest; but when thou shalt be old . . .
another shall gird thee, and carry thee whither thou wouldest not."
The "nemesis of creativity" of which Toynbee speaks has overtaken
Ahab. He is no longer the true Prometheus, but the false; he is
no longer Christ, but Caesar; he is no longer Orpheus, whose subtle
lute led men out of their primitive stasis into the motion of growth,
but the tyrant captain. No longer can he oppose the divine Tyrant
with the only weapon which can defeat Him; for now Ahab must
play the game of the Tyrant.

Here we have come close to Melville's central idea of tragedy,
which, I should say, is the self-defeat of leadership. In the chapter
called "The Specksnyder," he tells us that "Captain Ahab was by
no means unobservant of the paramount forms and usages of
the sea." And he continues thus:

Nor, perhaps, will it fail to be eventually perceived, that behind
those forms and usages, as it were, he sometimes masked himself;
incidentally making use of them for other and more private ends than
they were legitimately intended to subserve. That certain sultanism of
his brain, which had otherwise in a good degree remained unmani-
fested; through those forms that same sultanism became incarnate in
an irresistible dictatorship. For be a man's intellectual superiority what
it will, it can never assume the practical available supremacy over other
men, without the aid of some sort of external arts and entrenchments,
always, in themselves, more or less paltry and base. This it is that for
ever keeps God's true princes of the Empire from the world's hustings;
and leaves the highest honors that this air can give, to those men who
become famous more through their infinite inferiority to the choice
hidden handful of the Divine Inert, than through their undoubted
superiority over the dead level of the mass. . . . Nor will the tragic
dramatist who would depict moral indomitableness in its fullest sweep
and direct swing, ever forget a hint incidentally so important in his
art, as the one now alluded to.

Tragedy, then, is the degeneration of the potential hero, "mystically illumined" by his withdrawal from the world and by his

spiritual ordeal, into the sultan who leads his followers to destruction instead of leading them along the path of civilization.

Melville was, finally, not a religious man in the sense of making ultimate commitments to God or Church. I have called him a "naturalist," and "humanist," and so, in a large sense of these words, he was. But he felt uneasily that he must go along with religion part way, at least to the extent of using its terminology and concepts and believing in them as an artist, prophet, and moralist, if not as a theologian or an anchorite. Religious terminology allowed him to deal with what I have called "the alienated passions," that range of emotion which extends to the comprehension of social-historical tragedy and spiritual failure, realms of experience which remain opaque to less imaginative views of life.

4

Ahab's doomed voyage is symbolically opposed by three of the crew: Starbuck, Pip, and Bulkington. Starbuck's eyes, Melville tells us, were "lighted up with the stubbornness of life." And Ahab realizes that his first mate is his strongest potential enemy aboard the *Pequod* (Melville having seen fit to let Bulkington lie dormant). In the mate there is a spiritual attachment to life which is always threatening to elude Ahab's machinery of dictatorship. "Starbuck's body and Starbuck's coerced will were Ahab's, so long as Ahab kept his magnet in Starbuck's brain; still he knew that for all this the chief mate, in his soul, abhorred his captain's quest, and could he, would joyfully disintegrate himself from it, or even frustrate it." Starbuck is well aware of the crucial issue between him and Ahab. He knows that Ahab is the nemesis which creative life itself creates; as he muses at dusk by the mainmast, he hears the crew at revelry in the forecastle and cries: "Methinks it pictures life. Foremost through the sparkling sea shoots on the gay embattled, bantering bow, but only to drag dark Ahab after it, where he broods within his sternward cabin, builded over the dead water of the wake. . . . Oh, life! 'tis now that I do feel the latent sorrow in thee!" And Starbuck knows that he has already been undone by the "horrible old man." "My soul is more than matched; she's overmanned." But he resolves to take the only

course he can, to cling blindly to "the soft feeling of the human."
"Stand by me," he cries, "hold me, bind me, O ye blessed influences!"

Only once does Starbuck gain ascendancy over Ahab, and it is
only for a moment. In the chapter called "The Symphony," the
enchanted feminine air of a fair Pacific day summons up for one
last time all of Ahab's "humanities," as he stands at the rail, "lifting his splintered helmet of a brow to the fair girl's forehead of
heaven," as the "immortal infancy and innocency of the azure"
play about the "burnt-out crater of his brain." Starbuck is drawn
to Ahab at this moment, for "he seemed to hear in his own true
heart the measureless sobbing that stole out of the center of the
serenity around." "Close!" cries Ahab, "stand close to me, Starbuck; let me look into a human eye; it is better than to gaze into
sea or sky; better than to gaze upon God. By the green land; by
the bright hearthstone! this is the magic glass, man." Yet against
the genial greenness of the land which he sees in Starbuck's eyes,
against "all natural lovings and longings" Ahab is bound to "keep
pushing, and crowding, and jamming" himself on to the end. He
cannot think of the land without bringing death to it:

"it is a mild, mild wind, and a mild looking sky; and the air smells now,
as if it blew from a far-away meadow; they have been making hay
somewhere under the slopes of the Andes, Starbuck, and the mowers
are sleeping under the new-mown hay. Sleeping? Aye, toil we how we
may, we all sleep at last on the field. Sleep? Aye, and rust amid greenness; as last year's scythes flung down, and left in the half-cut swaths—
Starbuck!"

But the chief mate has stolen away, pale with horror and despair.

Little Pip, the negro cabin boy, jumps from the whaleboat as it
approaches the whale; he alone definitively secedes from the destructive enterprise. And for this he is called a "coward" aboard
the *Pequod;* but he is called a "hero" in heaven. Pip is "very
bright" with the "pleasant, genial, jolly brightness peculiar to his
tribe." He loves life with a fine, free relish. He is the only one
aboard who proves no match for "the panic-striking business in
which he had somehow unaccountably become entrapped." He is
driven mad by the terror of floating alone in the sea, and after the
Pequod finally picks him up, he goes about the deck "an idiot."

He believes that he has died, that Pip's bones welter in the sea. Yet his idiocy is an illumination. He walks the deck like a resurrected spirit. He was "not drowned entirely," says Melville.

Rather carried down to wondrous depths, where strange shapes of the unwarped primal world glided to and fro before his passive eyes; and the miser-merman, Wisdom, revealed his hoarded heaps. . . . He saw God's foot upon the treadle of the loom, and spoke it, and therefore his shipmates called him mad. So man's insanity is heaven's sense; and wandering from all mortal reason, man comes at last to that celestial thought, which, to reason, is absurd and frantic; and weal and woe, feels then uncompromised, indifferent as his God.

Pip's withdrawal from the world has been more successful than Ahab's; he has been able to deliver himself over to his spiritual illumination as Ahab has not, though Ahab, the mechanical titan with his forehead of brass and his shoulder blades of steel, has a window which faces heaven out of the top of his head. "Now, then, Pip, we'll talk this over," says Ahab; "I do suck most wondrous philosophies from thee! Some unknown conduits from the unknown worlds must empty into thee!" When Ahab realizes Pip's superiority over him, he cries: "Thou touchest my inmost centre, boy; thou art tied to me by cords woven of my heart-strings." To the crew he warns, "hands off that holiness." And Ahab installs Pip in his cabin, as the *Pequod* drives nearer and nearer the whale upwind.

As Ahab is about to leave his cabin, at last to encounter Moby-Dick, Pip pleads to be allowed to go with him. But no, says Ahab, "thou shalt sit here in my own screwed chair; another screw to it, thou must be." And the reason he gives for thus banishing Pip from the deck is that there is that in Pip "which I feel too curing to my malady," there is that which makes "Ahab's purpose keel up in him." In these last glimpses Melville gives us of Pip, he seems to be not so much an individual as an allegorical figure representing that part of Ahab's personality which Ahab has repressed, the part which longs to be one with the "Divine Inert." When Ahab has gone on deck, Pip goes to the place where Ahab last stood: "here he this instant stood; I stand in his air,—but I'm alone." Pip then sits in Ahab's chair: "Here, then, I'll seat me, against the transom, in the ship's full middle, all her keel and her three masts before me." Then Pip imagines himself a kind of mock king or admiral at a last supper. The real lord of the plank is heard above, his ivory foot tapping steadily on the deck. In the cabin Pip swaggeringly entertains rows of imaginary captains and lieutenants at table.

What happens to Bulkington, the heroic figure who stands at the helm on that Christmas night when the *Pequod* "thrust her vindictive bows into the cold malicious waves," and who fills Ishmael with such fear and "sympathetic awe"? He had seen Bulkington for the first time at the Spouter-Inn in New Bedford and had been struck by his appearance.

He stood full six feet in height, with noble shoulders, and a chest like a coffer-dam. I have seldom seen such brawn in a man. His face was deeply brown and burnt, making his white teeth dazzling by the contrast; while in the deep shadows of his eyes floated some reminiscences that did not seem to give him much joy. His voice at once announced that he was a Southerner, and from his fine stature, I thought he must be one of those tall mountaineers from the Alleganian Ridge in Virginia. When the revelry of his companions had mounted to its height, this man slipped away unobserved, and I saw no more of him till he became my comrade on the sea. In a few minutes, however, he was missed by his shipmates, and being, it seems, for some reason a huge favorite with them, they raised a cry of Bulkington! Bulkington! where's Bulkington? and darted out of the house in pursuit of him.

After this, we hear of the hero only once, and that is in a "six-inch chapter" which Melville says is Bulkington's "stoneless grave." But before we lose sight of him entirely, we are told that he is the restless kind of seaman who never remains for long on shore, but ships out on one long perilous voyage after another. He seems to have made the most successful kind of adjustment to the conflicting claims of land and "landlessness," the claim of the port—"safety, comfort, hearthstone, supper, warm blankets, friends, all that's kind to our mortalities"—and the claim of the sea, where the "soul" makes its "intrepid effort" to keep its "open independence." He knows the danger with which the land threatens the ship when she is driven into the lee; and he knows the danger to be encountered when the ship "seeks all the lashed sea's landlessness again." Yet he lives successfully in the discomfort of the dilemma. He is able to reconcile the "humanities" with the domineering mind which seeks "mortally intolerable truth" without destroying either one. He is the true Promethean hero. Whatever the future may hold, his success is assured: "Take heart, take heart, O Bulkington! Bear thee grimly, demi-god! Up from the spray of thy ocean-perishing—straight up, leaps thy apotheosis!"

Bulkington is the champion of Man. As we have noted, he is like Jack Chase, maintopman on the frigate *United States*. (It is fitting that Prometheus should be maintopman of the *United States*.) Bulkington disappears from *Moby-Dick* because if he had been more a part of the story it would have been inevitable that he should do what Starbuck can only try to do: oppose the command of Ahab and save the ship. But there is another reason why we do not see more of Bulkington. Melville himself does not see much of him. We know that he is a Promethean figure, who can save man from catastrophe and lead him safely through the creative rhythms which constitute growth, just as Bulkington's career is run to the rhythm of his repeated passages to sea and back to land again. But Bulkington eludes exact description. He is the stuff and energy of personality in the act of setting forth toward fulfillment. To employ the image of withdrawal and return, we see Bulkington just as he emerges on the returning beat—just as he is setting forth to sea. We know, too, of his ultimate setting forth, his apotheosis. We know that he is the hope of the world because he is the heroic American—the Handsome Sailor, as Melville calls this heroic figure in *Billy Budd*. He is the titanic body of America (as the word "Bulkington" suggests) stirring out of the uncreated night and passing ponderously into motion and consciousness.

5

Like an "unfathered birth," like a monstrous mockery of Bulkington, Ahab drives the ivory-tusked *Pequod* on toward the White Whale. And Ishmael watches and watches for the moment of catastrophe when the stricken old man, with unspeakably poignant tenderness and unimaginable violence, finally turns suicide and murderer. Like dream images, other American ships pass through the dark clarity of Ishmael's spell. There is the *Town-Ho*, a whaling ship lorded over by Radney the first mate, who, like Ahab, is an outlaw and a warlike man. The *Town-Ho, vis à vis* Moby-Dick, is hopeless and unredeemed. Aboard the *Pequod,* Ahab still retains in his soul some of the Orphean music which induces men to obey, though, flourishing his fiery harpoon at the crew, he uses the threat of force. But there is no Orphean music and no Ishmael aboard the *Town-Ho.* A small world in herself, she is near to total disintegration, for there is a deadly mutiny aboard and only flogging to quell it, whereas Ahab is able to frustrate the potential mutiny of Starbuck by his spiritual ascendancy. When the *Town-Ho* meets the whale, the outcome is quick and decisive. Radney makes a brave assault, even beaching his boat on Moby-Dick's back. But he is washed overboard and is last seen clamped in the huge malicious jaw—the victim of a black, chaotic "bundling into eternity."

The *Bachelor* sails by the *Pequod,* jaunty, gay, carefree. She has evaded the whale; and her captain, in reply to Ahab's stern request for news of Moby-Dick, says, "only heard of him; but don't believe in him at all." For the *Bachelor* the whale hunt is ended. Every cask is full to the brim, and in "gay holiday apparel" she is sailing for Nantucket, the gentle isle which Starbuck remembers. Three men at the masthead of the *Bachelor* wear long red streamers on their hats; her trypots have been fitted with the stomach skin of a whale to make enormous drums, on which the crew beats out a "barbarian sound," while on the quarter-deck the mates and harpooners dance "with the olive-hued girls who had eloped with them from the Polynesian Isles." The primitive rhythms of Typee recede into the distance as the *Bachelor* passes the *Pequod* and as Ahab's crew looks after her "with grave, lingering glances." Nantucket, too, calls out of the past with a softening nostalgia, which even Ahab cannot easily shrug off. As he watches the *Bachelor* sink under the horizon, he fingers a small glass of Nantucket sand which he has brought with him.

If the *Bachelor* represents America sailing off evasively toward an archaic utopia, the *Jeroboam* is America seeking with equal evasiveness a futurist utopia. The command of the *Jeroboam* has fallen into the hands of a member of the crew, a Shaker zealot who has proclaimed himself the archangel Gabriel. "He was a small, short, youngish man, sprinkled all over his face with freckles, and wearing redundant yellow hair. A long-skirted, cabalistically-cut coat of a faded walnut tinge enveloped him; the overlapping sleeves of which were rolled up on his wrists. A deep, settled, fanatic delirium was in his eyes." Melville tells us that Gabriel "had been originally nurtured among the crazy society of Neskyeuna Shakers" (that is, Niskayuna, north of Albany, where Mother Ann, the Shakers' female Christ, set up her first community). Gabriel is a false god, the god out of the machine; for, as Melville tells us, in the Shakers' "cracked, secret meetings" he had "several times descended from heaven by way of a trap-door, announcing the speedy opening of the seventh vial, which he carried in his vest-pocket." Under the impression that the Shaker millennium is at hand and that he is its prophet, Gabriel publishes a manifesto, once the ship is at sea, proclaiming himself "the deliverer of the isles of the sea and the vicar-general of all Oceanica." Most of the crew aboard the *Jereboam* regard Gabriel as sacred and sometimes even worship him as a deity. Gabriel has announced that the White Whale is the Shaker god incarnate and has issued warnings about the terrible vengeance to be visited upon the ship if it molests the whale. Only Macey, the first mate, and a small number of sailors have been hardy enough to ignore Gabriel's prophecies and lower a boat for Moby-Dick. But Gabriel has seemed to be justified, for with his violent tail Moby-Dick has sent Macey hurtling through the air to a watery death. When Gabriel perceives that Ahab is determined to kill the whale, he fills the air with maniacal prophecies of doom and denunciations of the blasphemy of all who would do battle with his god. The *Pequod* sails on, pursued by the hysterical imprecations of this futurist savior who is determined to evade the ordeal altogether.

6

But these other ships represent only the vulgar errors of American culture. Though dangerous and ill fated, they are the passing daydreams of our experience. The *Town-Ho* is a dream of the sheer, brutal exploitation of nature and man, the dream of big business, the frontier, and the pragmatic present. The *Bachelor* is a dream of comfort, opulence, bachelorhood, flags, progress, dancing girls, and a safe home-coming, the dream of little business, the city, and one's lost childhood. The *Jeroboam* is a dream of utopia, a society uncultured and unhistoried, of a female Christ and a hermaphrodite god, of spiritualism, celibacy, old age, and bonuses for all, the dream of the wayward reformer, the small town, and the world of tomorrow.

These are also the daydreams of Ahab. Ahab is the essential American, and these daydreams are all born of his essential nightmare. That nightmare is *rejection, abdication*—the sheering away of the emotive context from the will and the intelligence, as the encompassing flesh is sheered away from the body of the great whale and his white carcase set adrift like a sepulcher which floats away and merges with the "infinite perspectives" of the empty sea. The White Whale does not represent evil, as is usually said. As a divinity, he is an exceedingly complex being. Yet the question of what Moby-Dick represents can be answered very simply. He represents purity, the purity of an inviolable spiritual rectitude which, since it cannot be discovered among the imperfections of life, must be sought in death. Ahab's purpose is to die in one final heraldic gesture of righteousness—pure, meaningless, inhuman, violent. All the terrific action of his career is directed toward this ultimate stasis, this perfect objectification of his own inner image of self-destruction in which all of life freezes into the representation of death, in which, finally, all the colors of the rainbow disappear into the whiteness of the whale.

Ahab's "purpose," as Melville says, is an "unfathered birth" from which "common vitality" flees horror-stricken. Ahab is himself unfathered, and that is why Starbuck is horror-stricken by him. As we have noticed, the image of the father was for Melville an image of culture—the sort of culture distantly symbolized by the humanity of Bulkington. Ahab's quest is for his father; yet his quest can only be the evil aftereffect of a great rejection. Ahab can accept no earthly, no human father. He can love only that abstract father, that "fiery father," who speaks to him from the lightning. He can love only the ageless purity of Moby-Dick, the spotless, eternal whiteness which, though it has felt the irons of many hunters, still remains inviolate. He can love only those images of the father which represent pure power—power, that is, set free from the fallible responsibilities of human morals and emotions.

And because Ahab is unfathered, he cannot be a father. Ishmael may wonder if Ahab will turn out to be a "father to his crew," as Redburn had wondered about Captain Riga. Starbuck may wish that his majestic captain would look upon him with "all natural lovings and longings." But neither Ishmael, consciously searching for his mythical destiny, nor Starbuck, the good and loving mediocre citizen, can be anything but repulsed and terrified by this "horrible old man." The *Pequod,* therefore, can be no civilization, such as Ishmael seeks in its full mythical meaning and Starbuck longs for with his natural affections and sense of justice. It can be only an anarchy planned in the likeness of a machine, contrived with American technical skill, driven forward by a ruthless and mindless bravery which, though it is embellished with a touching hint of swagger, is totally devoted—since no other ideals seem to be natural or workable—to self-destruction in the name of purity.

And Ahab is also the most wonderful and fateful figure yet imagined by an American writer. We must see him in his downright childish simplicity. But we must also see him in his magnificent complexity; for in so far as we allow him to betray the manhood of Bulkington, he is the heir of all the ages—and so Melville correctly pictures the soul of Ahab as the contested battleground of the gods, saviors, and heroes of the Western world. Pity poor Ishmael, who watches with such rapt fascination as Ahab jams himself on toward the catastrophe which will blot out all of time in one disastrous act. There is a magnificent felicity in the final image of *Moby-Dick*—this purifying act of annihilation which, it may be, recalls from the dim past some awful white nakedness of flesh that blotted out the mind and petrified the hapless beholder and which, with a tender lyricism, translates this fierce encounter into a symbolic smash-up of the American world. The sky-hawk sinks with the ship, nailed to the mainmast and wrapped in a pennant, where the already submerged arm of the American Indian Tashtego transfixes him with a hammer. The American ship, with the tribes and complexions of the world aboard, thus meets its doom. And the very flag undulates through the final scene: the red of Tashtego's pennant; the whiteness of the whale; the roofless blue

of the Pacific spaces. And then, nothing is left save the whiteness
of Death in its appalling domesticity with Space. But the heraldic
tableau is broken and by some obscure saving grace the resurrected life wills to set the world in motion again. Ishmael floats
on the coffin-lifebuoy, a lost American brooding over the vast and
timeless sea.

7

The images of world-historical tragedy have the power to excite
us. Yet they are monsters of abstraction, which, if they are not to
remain monsters, require a context of fact and fantasy. Melville
discovered this context, inevitably, in American folklore. His early
novels do not show much awareness that the folk spirit might be
useful to literary expression, though, as we shall see, the young
hero of these books was in fact a folk figure. Melville's realization of the literary availability of American folklore contributed
markedly to his extraordinary success in *Moby-Dick*. *Moby-Dick*
was the product of several discoveries which, taken together, constitute a truly remarkable visionary conversion. Among these discoveries was the realization that the whaling voyage offered a
perfect "objective correlative" for his parable, the emergence in
Melville's mind of Ishmael as consciousness and mask, his redis-
covery of Shakespeare, and his discovery that the folk spirit could
be made into literary experience.

One recurring defect of Melville criticism is the picture of Melville setting himself determinedly against the American grain.
Though it has been customary to say that *Moby-Dick* is in one way
or another an American epic, still, it is maintained, the work of
Melville as a whole shows him as first a critic of American culture
and then as a discouraged and beaten fugitive from his own times,
hiding himself in the obscurity of the long years which Raymond
Weaver, Melville's first biographer, described by such terms as
"The Great Refusal" and "The Long Quietus." This attitude has
beclouded the fact that Melville's work has a strong ground swell
of folklore, whose rhythms ebb and flow through his work as a
whole, and especially through *Moby-Dick, The Confidence Man,*
and *Israel Potter*. (In studying Melville's interest in folklore, it is

significant that he was acquainted with the life of Israel Potter as early as 1849—before he wrote *Moby-Dick*.) Melville deplored many of the forms American culture was taking in his time: the decay of the spirit of freedom and humanitarianism; the whole enormous shell game of American commerce and American infantile uplift progressivism and cash-value philanthropy which concerned him in his later works. Melville deplored everything in the social scene that betrayed intelligence and the full understanding of, and sympathy with, human personality. As a critic he was often against the American temper. But, as Constance Rourke has written, Melville also moved *with* the American temper. My purpose in trying to corroborate this statement (beyond the brief sketch of Melville in Constance Rourke's *American Humor*) is to show the extent of Melville's commitment to American culture and the consequent urgency of his attacks upon it. It is another case of hating the weaknesses most in what one most loves.

To recognize the native mode in *Moby-Dick* is to feel the texture of the fabric whose pattern is the allegory of historical tragedy, to grasp the psychological quality of the superhuman persons of the drama, to perceive the Space with which Time collides and upon which it begets Destiny, to sense the Promethean fact through which God operates.

8

The American folk hero who emerged in the 1830's and 1840's in oral story and in popular almanacs, magazines, newspapers, and drama was a variegated mixture of two basic figures: the Yankee peddler and the backwoodsman of the West. He incorporated the shrewd, humorous, combination commercial man, mystic, and trickster—the New Englander—with the hunter, pioneer, civilizer, killer, and megalomaniac of the Western border. The new composite folk hero retained the penchant for yarn-spinning, practical joking, and theatrical self-assertion which had characterized both figures. Melville himself had affinities with this folk hero. He was part New England both by ancestry and by temperament. By temperament alone he was a Westerner. By predilection he was much more a Westerner than a New Englander: he tended to be

free, expansive, sensual, heroic, and though partly Puritan himself,
deeply anti-Puritan. When in *Mardi* he speaks of the fearful rapier
of the Pacific swordfish, he says, not that it is as incisive as Yankee
wit or as murderous as the musket of a Minute Man, but that it is
as deadly as the rifle of Davy Crockett. And Bulkington, that most
awe-inspiring of Handsome Sailors, is no New Englander but a
mountaineer from Virginia. In describing Ethan Allen in *Israel
Potter,* Melville wrote:

> Though born in New England, he exhibited no trace of her char-
> acter. He was frank, bluff, companionable as a Pagan, convivial as a
> Roman, hearty as a harvest. His spirit was essentially Western; and
> herein is his peculiar Americanism; for the Western spirit is, or will yet
> be (for no other is, or can be), the true American one.

And these words apply as well to *Moby-Dick* as to Ethan Allen,
despite its strong Yankee traits, despite the evasive, humorous
twang of Captain Peleg, who meets Ishmael's question, "Is this the
Captain of the Pequod?" by asking another question: "Supposing
it be the Captain of the Pequod what dost thou want of him?"—
and despite the punning, Bible-quoting fleecer, Captain Bildad,
who bids the *Pequod* good-by with: "Don't whale it too much a'
Lord's days, men; but don't miss a fair chance either, that's rejecting Heaven's good gifts."

In his writing Melville is frequently conscious of the two original
folk figures. There are repeated references to Yankee peddlers,
Yankee preachers, Yankee farmers, Yankee soldiers, sailors, and
philosophers and to Western hunters and mountaineers—to Crockett, Kit Carson, Lewis and Clark, Logan the Indian hero, to plains-
men, canallers, and lakemen. In his travels he had met Americans
of all kinds and had swapped stories with them, a native pastime
at which, as Mrs. Hawthorne testifies, Melville was a master. During the voyage on the frigate *United States,* as Melville tells us in
White-Jacket, he met men from the backwoods. And he met New
Englanders like Williams, "a thorough-going Yankee from Maine,
who had been both a peddler and a pedagogue in his day"—Williams, who was "honest, acute, witty, full of mirth and good humor,
a laughing philosopher." He had closely observed the purser's
steward, who acted as auctioneer aboard the frigate and who combined many Western traits with Yankee traits.

Like many young Americans of his class, he had at various times assumed the most opposite functions for a livelihood, turning from one to the other with all the facility of a light-hearted, clever adventurer. He had been a clerk in a steamer on the Mississippi River; an auctioneer in Ohio; a stock actor in the Olympic Theater in New York; and now he was a purser's steward in the navy. In the course of this diversified career his natural wit and waggery had been highly spiced, and everyway improved; and he had acquired the last and most difficult art of the joker, the art of lengthening his own face while widening those of his hearers, preserving the utmost solemnity while setting them all in a roar. He was quite a favorite with the sailors, which, in a good degree, was owing to his humor; but likewise to his off-hand, irresistible, romantic theatrical manner of addressing them.

For whatever reasons—rusticity and naïveté, fear of death in the wilderness or boredom in the towns, the guilt of the raper, or simply the desire to prick absurdly inflated self-pretensions—the American folk spirit has been humorous. Melville, we must remember, was a humorous writer, as well as a lyric and epic writer. In *Mardi* the humor is often uncomfortably hearty, jovial, and broad. In *Moby-Dick* it is lyrical and heroic; it expresses itself in a subtly flowing stream of fantasy, alternately gay, grim, festive, erotic, regretful, and sad. In *The Confidence Man* it is spare, light-footed, buoyant, and savage. In many mythologies the Promethean culture-hero easily modulates into the comic demigod whom the anthropologists call "the trickster." This is true of American mythology, both Indian and white. The Yankee peddler and the Crockettlike backwoods hero, who merge in the figure of Uncle Sam, are as much comic Prometheuses as the sly bear and rabbit magicians of the Indians.

Melville's novels from *Typee* to *Moby-Dick* are tales told by an elusive figure who observes the action, reflects upon it, and soliloquizes. The taleteller emerges in his full development in *Moby-Dick,* though even here he remains obscure, mythical, and not completely human. The soliloquizer is Ishmael, the outcast of whom the Lord declared that "he will be a wild man." From *Moby-Dick,* with certain retrospective glances at the earlier books, we can sketch out something of Ishmael's peculiarly American character. He is the New England spirit partly Westernized. In Ishmael, Melville created a literary-mythical version of the American folk hero who, in all his rudeness and native vigor, was appearing in the popular literature of the day. Sam Slick, the creation of the humorist Thomas Chandler Haliburton, was the type. Sam Slick had been a clock peddler up and down the Eastern states and into Canada. As the frontier was gradually opened up, he had aspired westward. He had been a steamboatman on the Mississippi and a fur trader for the Astors in the Northwest. Like many folk heroes—Crockett himself—he answered the restless westward urge by sailing over the Pacific, far beyond the bounds of the land. The theme of the castaway among cannibals, which Melville used in *Typee,* and the theme of the sailor ensnared by a Polynesian Circe, as in *Mardi,* were well known in American folklore. For example, in the *People's Comic Almanac* appeared the saga of Jack Bolin, an American sailor who was kidnaped by two mermaids one day while strolling along the shore of the Wangfo Islands. Davy Crockett (*Crockett Almanac,* 1854) was said to have been wrecked off the Sandwich Islands. After swimming for several days and fighting off the sharks, he landed among the cannibals. He was made prisoner, but overhearing several "cannibalesses" as they prepared to cook him, he burst free of his bonds, killed the cannibalesses with a spear, and escaped. And in a manner reminiscent of Taji's experience in *Mardi,* Crockett had visited a mysterious underwater cave in the Pacific Isles and had dived for pearls off the coast of Japan.

Sam Slick possessed a great variety of talents and went quickly and restlessly from occupation to occupation, making the changes with great aplomb. It was an American characteristic to make a change whenever one felt oneself "growing grim around the mouth," as Ishmael said. Ishmael had made many changes; at the beginning of *Moby-Dick* he is changing from schoolmaster to sailor, and he finds the transition "a keen one" which "requires a strong decoction of Seneca and the Stoics to enable you to grin and bear it." It was a keen transition, too, from thoughts of the classic philosophers to the American idiom, "grin and bear it," but a transition often made by American Ishmaels. But if Ishmael, an intellectual, found changes sometimes hard to make, the folk ideal was more cavalier. Colonel Crockett wrote of himself:

It is certainly a very curious phase of American and especially of western character, which is exhibited in the ease and promptness with which the colonel passes from one act of the singular drama of his life to another. Yesterday, a rough bear-hunter, today, a member of the legislature, tomorrow, about to become a member of Congress. . . . Such sudden and successful advances in life are scarcely seen except in our own country.

Sam Slick had collected art in Italy, outwitted the law in France, and gone to England on a diplomatic mission. Melville himself was to collect art in Italy, and his Israel Potter was to be sent from England to France on a diplomatic mission on behalf of American interests. Sam Slick had hunted whales in the Pacific. Like the Ishmaels of Melville's early novels, he was a connoisseur of strong liquors and could hold his share. Like Melville's confidence man, Sam Slick claimed to have a special knowledge of "simples" which would cure practically all known ailments. Like Israel Potter, Sam Slick had been a farmer and a trapper. Like the Ishmael who wrote *Mardi,* he was accustomed to make a somewhat self-conscious parade of his historical and biblical learning. Like the castaway of *Typee,* he had acquired outlandish lore from foreign maidens. Like Ishmael in *Moby-Dick* and like Israel Potter, he could dance a competent jig. He was a taleteller, a liar, a flirt, a preacher of steadfast morality, and an enemy of every kind of cant and hypocrisy. Sam Slick was a sort of poor-man's Ishmael, a proletarian cousin of the soliloquizer of *Moby-Dick,* who, though he was an intellectual and an aristocrat by birth, ran no poor second in the variety of his pursuits and attainments. For Ishmael was not only schoolmaster and whaleman: he was also a stonemason, "a great digger of ditches, canals and wells, wine-vaults, cellars, and cisterns of all sorts," a merchant seaman, a moralist, a philosopher who swayed high in the spars above the Pacific with Plato in his head, a scientist who pretended to write an original work on the natural history of whales, a traveler who had discoursed with the king of the Arsacides, and a man whose best friend was a cannibal.

The metaphors which Ishmael uses and the tall tales he tells are comic mythology. The great metaphors of the book are metamorphoses. A whale transformed by nature into an albino is further transformed by the story into a god. The heroes of the story are transformed into titans, beasts, or machines. A whaling cruise is transformed into an allegory of the destiny of the world. The central tall tale is the yarn about the fabulous White Whale and the heroes who pursue him through a strange world of fact and fancy. The epical metaphors are supported and also given relief by innumerable incidental comic similes. Very often these similes transform men into animals and back again in a brief flight of fantasy. Ishmael jumps from spar to spar "like a grasshopper in a May meadow"; the befrosted and icicled crew of a newly landed whaler bursts into an inn like "an eruption of bears from Labrador"; Ishmael eats so much fish chowder that he feels as though fishbones must come through his clothes; in his cabin "Ahab presided like a mute, maned sea-lion on the white coral beach, surrounded by his war-like but still deferential cubs"; Ahab roars with "his old lion voice"; when Ahab pledges the crew to hunt the White Whale, "he stood for an instant searchingly eyeing every man of his crew. But those wild eyes met his as the bloodshot eyes of prairie wolves meet the eye of their leader, ere he rushes on at their head on the trail of the bison; but, alas! only to fall into the hidden snare of the Indian"—a metaphor which transforms the larger allegory of the book into the language of grim frontier humor; again, Ahab is said to have "lived in the world, as the last of the Grisly Bears lived in settled Missouri." These many quick references to animals are usually intended to heighten the sense of strength, size, or ferocity. Sometimes, however, it works the other way and for a moment the whole enterprise seems a hoax, as when Flask is said to have been of the opinion that "the wondrous whale was but a species of magnified mouse." The animal-man simile was a favorite device of American humor. Crockett proclaimed himself "an entire zoological institute": he was "shaggy as a bear, wolfish about the head, active as a cougar," and he could "grin like a hyena." One of Melville's strongest adjectives is "wolfish," and he entitles a significant chapter of *Moby-Dick* "The Hyena."

Subordinate to the large fable of *Moby-Dick,* there are a number of legends and tall tales, sometimes merely referred to, sometimes not much more than metaphors, once carried out fully in the story of the whaler *Town-Ho* and the grim battle between

Radney and Steelkilt. These tall tales can be divided loosely into four kinds: (1) simple exaggeration of size, strength, or ferocity; (2) supernatural or magical tales; (3) whimsy which brings out the sheer impracticalness and fancifulness of human activity; and (4) tales which suddenly upset the laws of nature.

1) We are told, for example, of the jawbone of a whale that was so big a coach might drive under it. We are told that in New Bedford, fathers give whales for dowers to their daughters. Certain old authors have maintained that the sperm whale is "so incredibly ferocious as continually to be athirst for human blood." The crew of the *Pequod* one day beholds a monstrous white squid, so large that it seems to fill the whole horizon and to loom far above the sea into the heavens. We are told of whales alleged to have been eight hundred feet long. (To keep the proper perspective, we might note that Moby-Dick was perhaps eighty feet long.) We are told of a whale so powerful that he could plow a canal through Panama.

2) Some people have thought, says Melville, that the sperm whale is immortal. The beautiful girls of Salem, it is said, breathe such musk that "their sailor sweethearts smell them miles off shore." As the *Pequod* pursues Moby-Dick, it follows for several nights a strange "spirit spout" which looms up dead ahead and appears to be the spout of some chimerical, taunting, mythical whale. In the realm of pure fantasy is the vision of the "Titanic circus-rider" whom Ishmael imagines to be riding the backs of the whales which swim around him as he sits in the whaleboat at the center of the school.

3) Some of the pleasantest of American tall-tale fantasy is that which envisions a beguiled impracticalness. Speaking of Nantucket, Melville writes: "Some gamesome wights will tell you that they have to plant weeds there, they don't grow naturally; that they import Canada thistles . . . that pieces of wood in Nantucket are carried about like bits of the true cross in Rome." Again, we hear that Nantucketers wear quicksand shoes, like Lapland snowshoes, to keep from sinking in the sand. We are told that when the Nantucketers first went to sea to hunt whales, they took along a load of cobblestones, which they threw at the whales in order to judge when they were close enough to venture throwing a har-

poon. We even hear of a whale who could spout hot or cold water at will.

4) The breach of the laws of nature could not fail to excite and amuse a people who took much of their character from the frontier The hallucination of the sudden upset of the verities of gravity, mass, dimension, or form provides that element of terror from which most American humor gets its force. A grotesque humor is elicited by the story of a monster which was half man and half whale. This is an analogue of the common saying that Davy Crockett or some other Western hero was half horse, half alligator, and half man, a saying which adds an enticing transfiguration to the violation of the law of wholes and parts. More purely whimsical, but still containing the brief flirtation with horror and madness, is the reference in *Moby-Dick* to the great whale so pictured by Hogarth that he seems to draw only one inch of water; or the reference to the rumor that the White Whale was capable of being in two places at the same time. These jokes are akin to those found in the almanacs of Melville's day. For example, in the *Crockett Awl-Man-Axe* for 1839 appears the story of "a certain gentleman who being subject to the occasional absence of mind, one evening lit a candle, and instead of going to bed walked down his own throat." Again, *"The height of folly"* is said to be "Being so tall that you are obliged to climb a ladder to shave yourself."

Constance Rourke has pointed out that the American folk mind is, if anything, impractical, visionary, given to endless fantasy. This does not mean that fact and practicality have no place. It means rather that the direction of the folk mind is always away from fact. American myth and story is a special amalgam of fact and fantasy. Its peculiarity resides in its surface reliance on fact, while underneath the story wanders at large in fantasy. This pretense to fact and practicality of American folk literature helps to explain why the preponderance of fantasy has often escaped notice. How easy, after all, it is for an Ahab to lead his crew off on a fantastic hunt after a nearly mythical beast. Starbuck may warn that an old man's blasphemous vengeance won't fetch as much in the Nantucket market as a hold full of whale oil. But when Ahab shouts, "Nantucket market! Hoot!" the sailors listen to him and not to Starbuck. And so a whole crew of practical, money-grubbing

Americans delivers itself over to the magical trance of Ahab's ascendancy. Still, paradoxically, the *Pequod* goes about the business of killing ordinary whales and filling the oil casks. But within the magic world of the book, practical pursuits are less real than the fantasy of the supreme hunt after the myth.

The soliloquist of *Moby-Dick* speaks in the style required by the basic relation between fact and fantasy in American folk art. Ishmael is nearly omnipresent in the book. The reader shares experiences with him in varying degrees of immediacy; we understand some of his emotions; we hear all of his story; but he remains elusive and impersonal. He is a nearly blank mask, not a specifically comic or tragic one. As Constance Rourke points out, this has been the characteristic of American storytellers from the earliest times; for the mask has been useful to Americans. "In a primitive world crowded with pitfalls," writes Miss Rourke, "the unchanging, unaverted countenance had been a safeguard, preventing revelations of surprise, anger, or dismay. The mask had otherwise become habitual among the older Puritans as their more expressive or risible feelings were sunk beneath the surface." And the mask was useful for less compelling purposes: the Yankee peddler had used it to sell his victim a clock or a story or an opinion.

On the stage of the 1830's and 1840's, the performer was likely to adjust his face to the requirements of the mask. From behind the mask issued the principal entertainment of the evening. For dramatic entertainment came to be mostly the monologue of one actor, the dramatic action, if any, sometimes interrupting the speaker. The listener might perceive two voices in this curious monologue: the ostensible voice, pitched high and drawling in slow-running rhythms, and an inner voice, taking masked cognizance of the wonderful and the strange. It is precisely the method of *Moby-Dick*. The book is a monologue told through a mask, Ishmael; the mask is an abstraction from the full richness of American folk experience—it is the consciousness of that experience. The outward voice speaks more often and more explicitly; it describes objectively and states facts; it gives us the whole science of whaling and tells the story. Combining subtly with the inner voice of fantasy, it creates the larger metaphors and the allegory and the hundreds of incidental supporting figures of speech. Sometimes the outer voice breaks off entirely, and we hear the inner voice spinning out its fantasy as if it were reflecting on what the monologuist had been saying. Thus, after the persons of the drama have been introduced and the long spiel on "cetology," at once science and sales talk, has been run through, there is a sudden silence, broken, however, by the reverie of Ishmael on the masthead. The reverie begins with the sensuous feeling for space and size: "There you stand, a hundred feet above the silent decks, striding along the deep as if the masts were gigantic stilts, while beneath you and between your legs, as it were, swim the hugest monsters of the sea. . . . There you stand, lost in the infinite series of the sea, with nothing ruffled but the waves. The tranced ship indolently rolls; the drowzy trade winds blow; everything resolves you into languor." The fantasy becomes more meditative: "lulled into such an opium-like listlessness of vacant, unconscious reverie is this absent-minded youth by the blending cadence of the waves with thoughts, that at last he loses his identity; takes the mystic ocean at his feet for the visible image of that deep, blue, bottomless soul pervading mankind and nature." Then there is the sudden sensation of horror: "slip your hold at all, and your identity comes back in horror. Over Descartian vortices you hover. And perhaps, at mid-day, in the fairest weather, with one half-throttled shriek you drop through that transparent air into the summer sea." The outer voice quickly takes over and the story proceeds. But repeatedly the outer voice falls silent and the underlying fantasy is allowed to emerge: the discourse has the rhythmic beat of withdrawal and return. We hear the inner fantasy in the dream of Fate and Free Will described in the chapter called "The Mat-Maker." After the description of how a whale is killed and stripped of blubber comes the grim fantasy of "The Funeral," soliloquizing on the monstrous carcase cut adrift from the ship and floating on the sea. In "The Sphinx" there is a sudden imaginative plunge into the "awful water-land" at the earth's foundations. After more cetology, an encounter between Ahab and Starbuck, and the sickness of Queequeg, comes "The Pacific," in which the fantasy opens out into the enchanted spaces of the sea, into a sense of primeval wonder, freshness, and light, dissolving all the values of time into one contemporaneous moment of serene utopian vision.

To any meditative Magian rover, this serene Pacific, once beheld, must ever after be the sea of his adoption. It rolls the mid-most waters of the world, the Indian Ocean and Atlantic being but its arms. The same waves wash the moles of the new-built California towns, but yesterday planted by the recentest race of men, and lave the faded but still gorgeous skirts of Asiatic lands, older than Abraham; while all between float milky-ways of coral isles, and low-lying, endless, unknown Archipelagoes, and impenetrable Japans. Thus this mysterious, divine Pacific zones the world's bulk about.

Later there is the wonderfully tender erotic fantasy of "The Symphony," broken off by the final tense rise in pitch as the outer voice recounts the tremendous three days of the chase.

Breaking through both voices of the soliloquy is the dramatic action itself, for dramatic action of course demands an objectivity inconsistent with soliloquy. The taleteller stands aside while the persons of the drama perform their parts, parts which are frequently written in stage-drama form. But the separateness of the objective drama is no unbridged gulf. The drama breaks through the surface, but the sources of its energy and meaning are the sources of the soliloquy. And even on the surface the dramatic action sometimes merges with the soliloquy, so that in a chapter like "The Dying Whale" Ahab speaks with a voice indistinguishable from that of Ishmael. The persons of the drama, furthermore, stem from the folk personality of which Ishmael is the general mask. When Melville came to write *The Confidence Man,* he called it a "Masquerade." *Moby-Dick* was also a masquerade.

9

In the 1840's Phineas T. Barnum emerged as the master showman of his day. His long, hard training as an editor, storekeeper, and lottery promoter in Connecticut and as a traveling showman who had worked his way up and down the Midwest and through the South had taught him what it was that appealed to the Americans of his time. They had developed a taste for the exotic and the strange, a reverence for violence and size, a hankering for monstrosities, abortions, and morbidities. The entertainment which offered these things must be presented, not as fairy tale or myth, but as science and education. And the upshot of the entertainment must be, not a sense of wonder and excitement, but a reassurance that no wonders really existed, none more wonderful, at any rate, than grotesque or pitiable mistakes of nature. In other words, the entertainment must be a hoax, in spite of the scientific presentation and in spite of the genuine wonder and excitement which the entertainment might momentarily provide. The Barnum method was very much in keeping with the technique of the tall-tale teller of the West and the sales talk of the Yankee peddler: the dead-pan presentation of facts, the air of authenticity, the apparent unawareness of anything fantastic or strange or fabulous in what one was saying. The long American tradition of practical joking found verbal expression in storytelling and sales talk, for often both listener and talker were tacitly conscious that a hoax was being perpetrated. Barnum became the great master of the hoax.

Barnum began his successes by installing himself in Scudder's Museum in New York in the 1840's. As the proprietor of a museum he was respectable; the Puritans of all denominations could at that time still run circuses and traveling shows out of town with their moral denunciations. In a museum, people would expect to find science. And Barnum knew exactly what they wanted. As a physiological specimen he exhibited Joice Heth, an ancient, shriveled negress who was 161 years old and had been the nurse of George Washington. After an outburst of awe-inspiring, erotic advertising, Barnum exhibited a genuine Feejee mermaid, which turned out to be, as Constance Rourke describes it in her *Trumpets of Jubilee,* a "tiny wizened relic of fin and skin, varnish and bone, forever contorted into a posture of agony." Besides the mermaid, the eager thousands might behold other scientific specimens, such as the *Ornithorhyncus,* the paddle-tail snake, and certain monsters adorned with names from Greek mythology, like the *Proteus anguinus.* Barnum advertised a "free buffalo hunt" to be held in Hoboken, and when the buffaloes turned out to be timid yearlings who trotted off and huddled in a corner while a "buffalo hunter" stood around in Western costume, the crowd "roared with mirth, roared at its own predicament, and went good-naturedly home, demanding to know the perpetrator of so excellent a hoax," for Barnum, as he often did, had conducted this venture anonymously. Barnum exhibited Colonel Frémont's "wooly horse," a combination elephant, deer, horse, buffalo, camel, and sheep. He exhibited giants, fat boys, albinos, Indians, and Chinese, as well as a "live Yankee." He exhibited the famous Tom Thumb, in whom the whole American illusion of size and strength was reversed, the greatest hoax of all. He exhibited four Feejee cannibals and induced the king of the Sandwich Islands to visit New York. He had two "white whales" sent to New York, one fifteen feet long and the other twenty feet long, and kept them in a large glass tank. And he produced a hippopotamus which he called "the Sweating Behemoth of the Scriptures," thus contradicting Melville's contention that the biblical Behemoth was a sperm whale.

Moby-Dick, it does the book no disservice to admit it, is a literary-scientific extravaganza with very clear affinities to Barnum's showmanship.* The fact that the tale winds up in anything but a hoax does not invalidate the relationship. Indeed, that is Melville's point: it looks like a hoax, but woe to him who allows himself the comfortable belief that it *is* a hoax. Blandly Barnum offered the following apology for his methods: "I should hope that a little clap-trap occasionally, in the way of transparencies, exaggerated

---

* After writing these pages, I discovered that Melville wrote in 1847 a series of nearly unknown humorous sketches in which he parodies Barnum's advertising style and gulls him generally. The sketches were called "Authentic Anecdotes of 'Old Zack'" and purported to be letters written from General Zachary Taylor's Mexican War headquarters. They were published in a short-lived magazine called *Yankee Doodle*. (See article by Luther Stearns Mansfield, *American Literature*, IX.)

The level of Melville's humor on this occasion is pretty low: General Taylor is so insensitive to bodily pain that he does not feel a tack mischievously placed in his saddle. On dismounting, however, a considerable section of the general's pants is torn away and the general, though impervious to pain, is overcome with mortification. A proclamation demanding the capture of the miscreant is issued and the War Department is consulted. Phineas T. Barnum asks for the torn pants, so that he may exhibit them in his museum, and Melville draws up a draft of the advertising placard:

Prodigious Excitement ! ! ! ! !
OLD   ZACK'S   PANTS ! !
Great Sights at the American Museum ! ! ! !
Old Rough and Ready!
Uptown Emptied of its Inhabitants!
Tom Thumb Floored!

In other sketches Melville represented Peter Tamberlane B———, i.e., Barnum, as asking for a shell from which Taylor had pulled a burning fuse, a pie plate which had fallen on Taylor's head, and finally for the right to exhibit the general himself in a cage.

pictures, and puffing advertisements, might find an offset in the wilderness of wonderful, instructive, and amusing realities." He was voicing the sentiments of the author who slyly remarked: "In behalf of the dignity of whaling, I would fain advance naught but unsubstantiated facts. But after embattling his facts, an advocate who should wholly suppress a not unreasonable surmise, which might tell eloquently upon his cause—such an advocate, would he not be blameworthy?" (Melville then proceeds to maintain that the oil used in anointing the heads of the kings of England at coronations is sperm oil.)

At the beginning of *Moby-Dick,* the whole extravaganza which Ishmael is about to conduct is said to be a "performance" stage-managed by Fate and heralded in a celestial combination headline-and-advertisement appearing in "the grand programme of Providence." It was to be "a sort of brief interlude and solo between more extensive performances":

> *Grand Contested Election for the Presidency*
> *of the United States*
> WHALING VOYAGE BY ONE ISHMAEL
> BLOODY BATTLE IN AFGHANISTAN

The spectator would behold all kinds of instructive curiosities: "Feegeeans, Tongatabooarrs, Erromangoans, Pannangians, and Brighggians." And he would behold the feature attraction: an albino whale with a deformed back, "a portentous and mysterious monster," the most marvelous of "all the attending marvels of a thousand Patagonian sights and sounds"—the albino whale, the most awe-inspiring monster imaginable, than which the albino man is only less awe-inspiring.

What is it that in the Albino man so peculiarly repels and often shocks the eye, so that sometimes he is loathed by his own kith and kin! It is that whiteness which invests him, a thing expressed by the name he bears. The Albino is as well made as other men—has no substantive deformity—and yet this mere aspect of all-pervading whiteness makes him more strangely hideous than the ugliest abortion.

At its lower levels, *Moby-Dick* is pure showmanship of the peculiarly American kind, science tacitly tending toward the fabulous, normality subtly misshaping itself into monstrosity, fact covertly throwing off images of itself and creating an elusive world of fantasy. Even Audubon had amused himself by hoaxing a foreign naturalist with imaginary species of birds and fish.

An undercurrent of humorous hoaxing runs through *Moby-Dick*. The dialogue between the proprietor of the Spouter-Inn and Ishmael, for example, is the speech of the familiar comic encounter between the humorous, whittling Yankee and the greenhorn. The inflated syntax and the exaggeration of the simulated emotions are in keeping with the atmosphere of this popular situation. Ishmael is questioning the landlord about his prospective bedmate, Queequeg.

"Landlord!" said I, "what sort of a chap is he—does he always keep such late hours?" It was now hard upon twelve o'clock.

The landlord chuckled again with his lean chuckle, and seemed to be mightily tickled at something beyond my comprehension. "No," he answered, "generally he's an early bird. . . . But tonight he went out a peddling, you see, and I don't see what on airth keeps him so late, unless, may be, he can't sell his head."

"Can't sell his head?—What sort of a bamboozingly story is this you are telling me?" getting into a towering rage. "Do you pretend to say, landlord, that this harpooner is actually engaged this blessed Saturday night, or rather Sunday morning, in peddling his head around this town?"

"That's precisely it," said the landlord, "and I told him he couldn't sell it here, the market's overstocked."

"With what?" shouted I.

"With heads to be sure; ain't there too many heads in the world?"

"I tell you what it is, landlord," said I, quite calmly, "you'd better stop spinning that yarn to me—I'm not green."

After some more of this give and take, with several crude puns, and a restatement of the whole situation by Ishmael, such as might happen in a humorous stage dialogue, comes the hoax. It appears that the head the harpooner is trying to sell is a "balmed New Zealand head (great curios, you know)" and that the harpooner had been peddling four of them, "strung on a string, for all the airth like a string of inions." To the modern taste this kind of of humor seems intolerable on several counts. No doubt Melville was trying faithfully to reproduce the tone and language of the humor of his time and was able to do so with a certain amount of objectivity. Still, he had a weakness himself for this sort of thing, a fact which helps to account for the awkward verbiage and clumsy emotions into which his literary style sometimes degenerates.

Presumably one of the reasons for the popularity of the practical joke in America was the danger of life in the early days. Often a practical joke artificially creates a situation which appears dangerous, horrible, or uncanny and then disperses the sensation of terror with the sudden revelation that the whole thing is a hoax. It is the exercise of what Freud called "anxiety"—the imaginative creation of danger, a psychic exercise designed to reduce the stature of real danger or to keep the senses alert against real danger; this has always been one of the main functions of myth. The tension of anxiety is relieved by the upshot of the practical joke, just as it is by the dénouement of story and myth. It is not surprising that amid the dangers of the whale hunt the idea of the practical joke should occur very urgently to Ishmael. In the chapter called "The Hyena," Melville wrote:

There are certain queer times and occasions in this strange mixed affair we call life when a man takes the whole universe for a vast practical joke, though the wit thereof he but dimly discerns, and more than suspects that the joke is at nobody's expense but his own. However, nothing dispirits, and nothing seems worth while disputing. He bolts down all events, all creeds, and beliefs, and persuasions, all hard things visible and invisible. . . . And as for small difficulties and worryings, prospects of sudden disaster, peril of life and limb; all these, and death itself, seem to be only sly, good-natured hits, and jolly punches in the side bestowed by the unseen and unaccountable old joker. That odd sort of wayward mood I am speaking of comes over a man only in some time of extreme tribulation; it comes in the very midst of his earnestness, so that what just before might have seemed to him a thing most momentous, now seems but a part of the general joke. There is nothing like the perils of whaling to breed this free and easy sort of genial desperado philosophy; and with it I now regarded this whole voyage of the Pequod, and the great White Whale its object.

A white whale was, after all, an improbable and even a comic beast. A great, unwieldy, insentient mass of blubber, probably more mottled than white, he was a buffoon, with no face, his eyes, a third of the way back toward his tail, looking out at the world in opposite directions so that the contemptible brain sunk somewhere in the ponderous protoplasm beheld a ridiculous multiverse, made of two mutually exclusive worlds. He was a sluggish and confused monster who, despite his speed and strength, would allow a whaleboat virtually to beach itself on his back, a creature so insensitive to danger that he would stop to copulate in the very waters where the deadly harpooners were taking aim. He was a very tun of guts and gigantic cask of oil whom men lanced, bled, butchered, and cast away to the sharks and birds, an awkward satyr whose six-foot phallus was joked upon by mere men and skinned to make cassocks for blubber-cutters. The White Whale, for a moment at least, was the greatest of all hoaxes, of whom Stubb might sing:

> Oh! jolly is the gale,
> And a joker is the whale. . . .

Yet Moby-Dick is no hoax, or rather, the emotions and ideas he excites are no hoax. Looking back after one hundred years, we perceive a certain unity in American culture which embraces the kinds of thought and feeling represented by Barnum's scientific museum and Melville's *Moby-Dick*. Yet the difference is that most important of all differences: the one between art and other forms of organizing experience. Barnum's use of the peculiarly American amalgam of fact and fantasy served in effect to affirm that the high and difficult emotions of wonder and exaltation did not really exist or did not need to be taken seriously, for he always dispersed troublesome phantoms by the hoax, which came upon the stage like a *deus ex machina* to wind up the play. He had realized, as all successful commercial dealers in popular culture have after him, that the timid emotions of Philistia and the *Lumpenproletariat* were the ones which, by and large, the American people wanted and would pay for. The violence, megalomania, and exoticism of his advertising, the echo of life in a new, wild land, serve only to emphasize the tameness of the emotions aroused by that which was advertised. The commercial classes were willing to be the most abject kind of dupe if only they were given in return the comfortable sense of having mastered and destroyed every high or fierce emotion. It was the great American con game which Melville was to examine in *The Confidence Man*. But *Moby-Dick* uses the folk

spirit differently. If there is a hoax, it is directed against those who
are looking for a hoax. Like any work of art, it is uncompromising
in its emotions and its intellectual quality. It is as resolutely against
the American grain as it is resolutely with it.

10

Certain of the characters in *Moby-Dick* are combinations of the
scientific curio and the folk hero. Queequeg would do well enough
in a side show, a hideous savage, the son of a cannibal king: "Such
a face! It was of a dark, purplish, yellow color, here and there
struck over with large blackish-looking squares." And he worshiped "a curious little deformed image with a hunch on its back,
and exactly the color of a three days' old Congo baby." These
outlandish qualities merge with heroic attainments of the folk-tale
variety. Queequeg eats nothing but steaks, rare ones. He shaves
with his harpoon. He is a noble fellow, "George Washington can-
nibalistically developed." He throws an insolent youth bodily into
the air, and later saves him from the sea, after single-handedly
capturing a murderously swinging mainsail boom which had burst
loose in a squall. An uncanny marksman, he tosses his harpoon
jauntily over the head of Captain Bildad and hits a minute drop
of tar floating far away in the water. The other harpooners,
the American Indian Tashtego and the Negro Daggoo, are also
creatures of folklore: of prodigious strength, they are imposing in
their native dignity and devoted to the spirit of the hunt. Two minor
characters direct the reader's attention to the supernatural, the
realm of the miraculous which had become part of the American
experience: Gabriel, the Shaker zealot, reminding us of the hidden
Powers of Light and Darkness, of the spiritual heights and depths
of madness, of utopian visions at once a part of, and different
from, the general tendency of American life; and Elijah, the Yankee
whose shrewdness and wit are transmuted into the prophetic inspiration of the oracle.

11

Of the two most obviously humorous characters on board the
Pequod—Stubb, the second mate, and Flask, the third mate—

Flask is the more easily described. We do not see much of him, and what we do see is perhaps all there is. Something of a frontier type of screamer, Flask is compounded of simple ingredients: ruthlessness, pugnacity, mindless but unfailing gaiety. He has an "ignorant, unconscious fearlessness" which makes him a "little waggish in the matter of whales" and allows him to take a whaling voyage around Cape Horn as no more than a three-year joke. His size befits his comic personality, for among oversized whale hunters and large-scale events, Flask must make his way as a little man. "Truly vivacious, tumultuous, ostentatious little Flask," perching on the gigantic shoulders of Daggoo to spy whales from a rocking boat, he reverses the direction of the usual comic situation. We cannot be sure: either Flask wears no mask, or behind his mask there is nothing to behold.

But Stubb is more fully drawn and more complicated. Full of immense and highly vocal self-esteem, he too is a screamer. The only virtues in his world are strength, speed, size, power, and a careless, ruthless humor. Stubb does his screaming as he sets out in command of his whaleboat, boasting that he has been known to lower for whales from a leaking ship in a gale off Cape Horn. "Every keel a sun-beam! Hurrah!" he roars as the oarsmen begin to pull. "Here we go like three tin kettles at the tail of a mad cougar!" And he drives the men on with a ritual chant, varying strangely from outright ruthless threats delivered with fanatic zeal to bitter sarcasm thinly hidden by an apparent easygoing, humorous, off-hand, gentle concern for the well-being of the oarsmen, which he would voice between affected yawns even as the terrible whale was being harpooned. "Stubb is one of those humorists," says Melville, "whose jollity is sometimes so curiously ambiguous." And with his simple, humorous ambiguity, he cut a gaudy swath through "a world of grave peddlers, all bowed to the ground with their packs." The ambiguity of Stubb's humor stems from the ironic incommensurability of his gaiety with the horror of the adversary he is up against. In a business which at any time might suddenly mean the "speechlessly quick chaotic bundling a man into Eternity," Stubb defies all dangers with his inadequate challenge, ambiguously composed of affected boredom and humorous screaming. It is one of the atti-

tudes of the hunter and it has become a part of the American spirit.
Stubb himself sees clearly enough why this attitude should exist:
"Here's a carcase," he muses. "I know not all that may be coming,
but be it what it will, I'll go to it laughing. Such a waggish leering
as lurks in all your horribles! I feel funny. Fa, la! lirra, skirra! . . .
a laugh's the wisest, easiest answer to all that's queer." In himself
this humorous American in a world of terrors is an attractive
figure. But the figure is not entirely human, and he embodies,
furthermore, certain reprehensible qualities: callousness, nihilism,
sadism. These qualities in Stubb come out in his dealings with
people of other races; in these he is insensitive, cruel, overbearing.

References to negroes in ante-bellum popular humor were likely
to be incredibly callous. The humorous simile which referred to
bears, possums, and other "varmints" was often extended to include
the negro. Ben Hardin, astride the rampaging whale, hangs on
"like death to a dead niggar." Mike Fink (whom of the well known
folk heroes Stubb most resembles) was famous for having demon-
strated his marksmanship by skinning "a nigger's heel" at one
hundred yards. We see something of Stubb's sadism in the scene
between him and old Fleece, the *Pequod's* negro cook. His tone
and language are in the popular mode, as he bedevils the old man
with contradictory commands and ambiguous complaints about the
whale steak the cook has prepared for him. Calling the cook back
again and again after half-appearing to dismiss him, he complains
that the steak is too well done, it is too tender, it has to be tough
to be good, and so on. Endlessly repeating the insulting word
"cook" in that form of direct address which characterized the
humor of the time (and which Melville himself apparently regarded
as delectably funny), he forces the negro to deliver a sermon to the
sharks which are busy tearing at the carcase of the whale tethered
alongside, berating them for their noisy voraciousness. This the
negro does in a but too obviously humorous dialect: "Fellow-
critters: I'se ordered here to say dat you must stop dat dam noise
dare. You hear? Stop dat dam smackin' ob de lip! Massa Stubb
say dat you can fill your dam bellies up to de hatchings, but by
Gor! you must stop dat dam racket!" Repeatedly the resentful cook
is forced to continue his mock sermon before Stubb relents and
sends him limping away, shouting after him, "Whaleballs for break-

fast—don't forget." No doubt the scene is unpleasant enough. But it has the relevance of cultural fact.

The encounter between the canny American and the gullible, foolish, or effete European was standard comic fare in Melville's time. And Stubb appropriately dominates the scenes in which the *Pequod* meets the French ship *Rosebud* and the German ship *Jungfrau*. The captain of the French ship is a somewhat delicate dandy —small, slight, dark, and wearing a red velvet vest. In matters of whaling he is strangely guileless. A Guernsey man, acting as interpreter, serves as the mask for Stubb's humor. The *Rosebud* has captured a diseased whale which, tied alongside, emits a prodigious bad odor. The Guernsey man, convinced that the carcase will infect the ship with a plague, wants the whale cut loose and abandoned. In English, Stubbs utters such dead-pan insults as: "Tell him that now I have eyed him carefully, I'm quite certain that he's no more fit to command a whale-ship than a St. Jago monkey. In fact, tell him from me he's a baboon." Pretending to translate, the Guernsey man argues the captain into cutting the whale loose. The captain, under the impression that he has had a cordial interview and grateful to the Yankee for his kindness, gives the necessary orders. As the *Rosebud* sails over the horizon, Stubb leaps aboard the diseased carcase and, after the necessary excavations with a whaling spade, scoops out handfuls of the priceless ambergris which he had surmised would be found in the body.

The German ship *Jungfrau* furnishes scarcely less fun for Stubb, as, approaching within hailing distance, the German lowers a boat to come begging for a kettle of whale oil to light his lamps, a humorous anomaly in the whale fishery and one which provides a ribald joke; for the *Jungfrau*, being innocent of sperm, is a virgin indeed. As the German sailors sheepishly borrow oil, whales are sighted by both ships. In an instant American boats are vying with German boats to see who shall get the prize, Stubb entertaining the "Yarman" with his savage American "screaming." Soon the American harpooners have cast their harpoons straight over a German boat, have fastened to the whale, and are off on "a Nantucket sleigh-ride" as the whale drags them over the sea. The German ship provides a final bit of amusement when she spies spouts in the distance and, leaving the *Pequod,* sets out after them. The Amer-

icans, however, easily discern that though the spouts look almost
exactly like those of the sperm whale, they are actually being made
by the worthless finback. Americans were acutely aware of adverse
European criticism of their rude manners and their innocence. The
innocent American being outwitted or patronized by the worldly
European was of course a well known fictional image on both sides
of the Atlantic; it was an image which Melville himself used
seriously in *Benito Cereno* and humorously in *Israel Potter*. It was
natural enough that especially in comic literature figures like Stubb
should turn the tables on the worldly European.

12

As we shall have occasion to note again in considering *The
Confidence Man*, another favorite motif of American humor was
the revenge of the frontiersman upon the New Englander. Very
often the encounter was between a rough and ready Westerner
and a Yankee peddler whose sly tricks the Westerner dealt with
by means of unmistakably boisterous physical action. In the interpolated story of the *Town-Ho*, the basic situation receives epic
treatment. It is a brilliant, cruel story in which Melville pictures
with consummate artistry the pure hatred of man for man. The
antagonists are the stubborn, malicious Nantucketer, Radney, first
mate of the *Town-Ho*, and one of the sailors, Steelkilt, a Lakeman
from the West. The main events of the story are a terrific fight
between Radney and Steelkilt, the herding of Steelkilt and his
mutinous accomplices into the forecastle, the defection of Steelkilt's fellow mutineers, the final death of Radney in pursuit of
Moby-Dick, and the eventual escape of Steelkilt to parts unknown.
The character of Steelkilt stirs Melville to tropes of epic praise of
the Western lakes and rivers and the men who live on them. Steelkilt is very much like the Ethan Allen of *Israel Potter*. He is "a tall
and noble animal with a head like a Roman, and a flowing golden
beard like the tasseled housings of your last viceroy's snorting
charger; and a brain and a heart and a soul in him . . . which
had made Steelkilt Charlemagne, had he been born son to Charlemagne's father." Like Radney himself, but in nobler dimensions,
this "backwoods seaman, fresh from the latitudes of buckhorn

handled Bowie-knives," is "vengeful and full of social quarrel."
"This Lakeman in the land-locked heart of our America," Melville
writes in a truly inspired expatiation through the magic spaces of
the West,

had yet been nurtured by all those agrarian free-booting impressions
popularly connected with the open ocean. For in their interflowing
aggregate those grand fresh-water seas of ours—Erie, and Ontario, and
Huron, and Superior, and Michigan—possess an ocean-like expansive-
ness, with many of the ocean's noblest traits, with many of its rimmed
varieties of races and climes. They contain round archipelagoes of
romantic isles, even as the Polynesian waters do . . . they have heard
the fleet thunderings of naval victories; at intervals they yield their
beaches to wild barbarians, whose red-painted faces flash from out
their peltry wigwams; for leagues are flanked by ancient and unentered
forests where the gaunt pines stand like serried lines of kings in Gothic
genealogies; those same woods harboring wild Afric beasts of prey,
and silken creatures whose exported furs give robes to Tartar Emperors; they mirror the paved capitals of Buffalo and Cleveland, as well
as Winebago villages; they float alike the full-rigged merchant ship, the
armed cruiser of the State, the steamer, and the beech canoe; they are
swept by Borean and dismasting blasts as direful as any that lash the
salted wave; they know what shipwrecks are. . . .

Though many have tried, it remains true that besides Melville,
only Whitman has been able to write with the genuine epic breadth
which encompasses the American scene and with the penetrating
depth of sympathy which exposes the American character. It is not
the only mode of self-comprehension, but it is one of the great ones.

13

In discussing Melville's style, writers like Matthiessen, Sedgwick,
and Olson have pointed out several influences: chiefly, Shakespeare, Sir Thomas Browne, and the Bible. It is clear by now that
whatever may be said for or against Melville's style, he was a consciously "literary" writer, not, as used to be said, an unlettered or
"natural" genius. Henry James, it could once be said, was a
"literary" writer, whereas Melville was simply a great talent with no
special professional sense of his medium. We can now see that Melville was fully as "literary" as James, if by "literary" we mean

conscious of style (which is not to imply that Melville is the equal of James as a stylist).

Melville had other models of style besides the great English authors. One of these was the popular American rhetoric and oratory of his own time. And whereas this accounts for much of what one objects to in Melville's prose—its occasional clumsiness, its purposeless inflation, its vagueness, its jargon—it also accounts for many of his most felicitous passages. A glance at such a story as *The Obedient Wife,* written in 1840 by an anonymous author for the popular New York journal *Spirit of the Times,* will demonstrate how dependent Melville sometimes was on this sort of prose:

There is an old story of a man who had married a young lady, and who had a friend somewhat skeptical as to the obedient tendency of the wife's disposition, much to the dissatisfaction of the Benedick, who strongly asserted, and warmly asseverated, that his will was law, and that she never by any chance disobeyed any wish or injunction of his.
"Have you ever tried her in that respect?" said his friend.

There are long passages in Melville which sound just like this. It is, of course, very consciously literary. The writer feels that he would be less literary if he wrote "who had a friend somewhat skeptical of his wife's obedience" instead of "somewhat skeptical as to the obedient tendency of his wife's disposition." It is a genuine low-Melvillian trick; and so is the delicious reference to the "Benedick," the toying with "asserted" and "asseverated," and the magniloquent humor of "Have you ever tried her *in that respect?*" The following passage, also from the *Spirit of the Times,* might easily have been written by him who tells the story of *Typee* or *Omoo* or *Mardi.*

When we got up and rubbed our eyes, to our great disappointment we found that neither day nor wind would suit for *"Snipe Shooting",* so we sat down to our salt shad and our rye coffee, as disconsolate as Israel's maids of yore beside Babylon's waters. Looking out on the glittering expanse of Shinnecock Bay, we gazed with feelings of envy on the clam-men at anchor in their graceful whaleboats, who never knew the *ennui* arising from want of occupation, and were now engaged in destroying the happiness of many a bivalve's family circle with their merciless rakes. . . . After dinner,—a repetition of our morning's enticing fare,—we sat down to enjoy a quiet smoke. "Pooh! Pish! Psha!" muttered L——, a stately old bachelor.

"Damn the day," exclaimed B——, who was an irascible ditto, not reflecting for a moment that Providence would be unwilling to increase the torrid state of the air by adding the hyper-temperature of the infernal regions. As for myself I don't exactly remember what I did, but I believe I ejected a mouthful of smoke and whistled.

Truly Ishmaelian is the philosophical humorist who here ejects his mouthful of smoke. The writer of this passage is a very literary writer, highly conscious of his allusions, careful to use a French word, proud of saying "the hyper-temperature of the infernal regions." He is jocular, reflective, acutely conscious of words. Carefully he constructs a mask of rhetoric and places it between the reader and that which is being described, hiding or merely obscuring the truth behind his featureless style. Probably he is not aware that his style *is* featureless, that what he takes to be a rich humorous-serious involution of phrase is really, much of it, blank and meaningless jargon.

There arose in this country in the 1830's and 1840's a most violent spirit of magniloquence. Oratory was one of the accomplishments of the folk hero. "I can outspeak any man," was one of Crockett's boasts. An orotund native oratory, full of bombast, humorous mythology, and rough Americanisms, emerged, as if by necessity, to express the tumultuous feelings of the people. This oratorical language, which could be heard in various forms in tall talk, in congressional addresses, in sermons and written literature, had its effect on Melville, as did the milder humorous jargon we have glanced at above. As H. L. Mencken observes, the native rhetoric had its influence on Whitman and Mark Twain (he does not mention Melville), helping to set them apart from the conventional writers of the time, who looked back to the style of Addison and Johnson. The distinction must have been brought home to Melville in the 1850's, when he began to send short stories to literary magazines; one editor, distressed by Melville's style, suggested that he try to emulate Addison.

The following, from Mark Twain's *Life on the Mississippi*, will demonstrate the style in its more purely egomaniac mode:

Whoo—oop: I'm the old original, iron-jawed, brass-mounted, copper-

bellied corpse-maker from the wilds of Arkansas! Look at me! I'm the
man they call Sudden Death and General Desolation! Sired by a hurri-
cane, dam'd by an earthquake, half-brother to the cholera, nearly
related to the small-pox on the mother's side! Look at me!

If this was an expression of the Manifest Destiny of the folk personality, its political-historical counterpart could be heard in the
House of Representatives, in such speeches as the following:

MR. SPEAKER: When I take my eyes and throw them over the vast expanse of this expansive country: when I see how the yeast of freedom
has caused it to rise in the scale of civilization and extension on every
side; when I see it growing, swelling, roaring, like a spring freshet—
when I see all *this,* I cannot resist the idea, Sir, that the day will come
when this great nation, like a young schoolboy, will burst its straps,
and become entirely too big for its boots.

Sir, we want *elbow-room*—the continent—the *whole* continent—and
nothing *but* the continent! And we will have it! Then shall Uncle Sam,
placing his hat upon the Canadas, rest his right arm on the Oregon
and California coast, his left on the eastern sea-board, and whittle away
the British power, while reposing his leg, like a freeman, upon Cape
Horn! Sir, the day *will*—the day *must* come!

These words of "General Buncombe" have their counterparts in
Melville's books, though Melville is never so vulgar a phraseologist
as the General. The feeling of power, openness, space, and freedom
is the central emotion in many of Melville's best passages, and as
any reader of *Moby-Dick* will know, Melville purges the mood of
exaltation of all vulgarities, of mere power worship, muscle-flexing,
or intoxication with the *mystique* of force and space. About such
a piece of oratory as the one quoted above, he would have been of
two minds: he would have deplored the jingoism and the mindlessness of the sentiments; but at the same time he would have felt
a deep sympathy with the speaker. In *Mardi* he had satirized just
such an orator. In that book he represents his travelers as stopping
off in Washington to visit the Senate. They hear a speech by a
senator from the West. Roaring like a wild beast and smiting his
hip with one hand and his head with the other, the speaker proceeds
thus (I substitute real names for Melville's mythical ones):

I have said it! the thunder is flashing, the lightning is crashing!
already there's an earthquake in England! Full soon will the King dis-

cover that his diabolical machinations against this ineffable land must soon come to naught. Who dare not declare that we are not invincible? I repeat it, we are. Ha! ha! The audacious King must bite the dust! . . . Ha! ha! I grow hoarse; but would mine were a voice like the wild bull's . . . that I might be heard from one end of this great and gorgeous land to its farthest zenith; ay, to the uttermost diameter of its circumference.

The felicity of Melville's parody indicates clearly enough that he was aware of the false and dangerous emotions lying beneath this kind of oratory—despite the fact that he was himself not entirely proof against the oratorical mood. This kind of "screaming" caused him many doubts about the American future and convinced him that America might be throwing away all the opportunities of its wonderful youth even as it enthusiastically celebrated its own new-found confidence. He saw two aspects of the American spirit. He feared, on the one hand, that America would never be more than the "braggadocio" of the world. He hoped, on the other hand, that America was like "St. John, feeding on locusts and honey, and with prophetic voice, crying to the nations from the wilderness." Both of these possibilities he detected in the rough and fulsome cadences of American speech.

In *Moby-Dick* the language of the screamer is transmuted, when Melville is at his best, into an exalted apostrophe to power, space, and freedom. The mood is at once lyric in its poignancy and epic in the large nobility of its vision. The mood is not brutal or blind or chaotic or megalomaniac. It is serene and joyful, with the serenity and joy which follow upon the sense of great power controlled and great violence purged. It is the mood expressed by Father Mapple at the end of his sermon (which is itself perhaps the high point of American oratory):

Delight is to him—a far, far upward and inward delight—who against the proud gods and commodores of this earth, ever stands forth his own inexorable self. Delight is to him whose strong arms yet support him, when the ship of this base, treacherous world has gone down beneath him. Delight is to him who gives no quarter in the truth and kills, burns, and destroys all sin though he pluck it out from under the robes of Senators and Judges.

The style of *Moby-Dick* is a rhythm of three basic styles: the

style of fact, the style of oratorical celebration of fact, the style of
meditation moving toward mysticism. A passage from the chapter
called "Nantucket" will document this:

What wonder that these Nantucketers, born on a beach, should take
to the sea for a livelihood! They first caught crabs and quohogs in the
sand; grown bolder, they waded out with nets for mackerel; more experienced, they pushed off in boats and captured cod;

these are facts; but gradually the reader's attention is led away
from fact toward a vision of size and power; the speech becomes
metaphorical; the field of observation opens out:

and at last, launching a navy of great ships on the sea, explored this
watery world; put an incessant belt of circumnavigations around it;
peeped in at Bering's Straits; and in all seasons and all oceans declared
everlasting war with the mightiest animated mass that has survived the
flood; most monstrous and most mountainous! That Himmalehan, salt-
sea Mastodon, clothed with such portentousness of unconscious power,
that his very panics are more to be dreaded than his most fearless and
malicious assaults!

Note the quality of the images. The "incessant belt of circumnavigations" for size, and for the cyclical route of the voyager;
"peeped in" for vision; "the flood," one of Melville's favorite symbols for the primal sense of power and space; "Himmalehan,"
image of the mountain; the "Mastodon" with his "portentousness
of unconscious power," a phallic, imperial, and masculine image.
As the rhythm of the style turned upward and outward into
space, Melville would have had the sensations he expressed in
another chapter: "One often hears of writers that rise and swell
with their subject, though it may seem but an ordinary one. How
then with me, writing of this Leviathan? Unconsciously my chirog-
raphy expands into placard capitals. Give me a condor's quill!
Give me Vesuvius' crater for an inkstand! Friends, hold my arms!"
And, then, Melville writing in full possession of his power, there
follows the celebration of the Nantucketers:

And thus have these naked Nantucketers, these sea hermits, issuing
from their ant-hill in the sea, overrun and conquered the watery world
like so many Alexanders parcelling out among them the Atlantic,
Pacific, and Indian oceans, as the three pirate powers did Poland. Let

America add Mexico to Texas, and pile Cuba upon Canada; let the English overswarm all India, and hang out their blazing banner from the sun; two thirds of this terraqueous globe are the Nantucketer's. For the sea is his; he owns it, as Emperors own empires; other seamen having but a right of way through it. . . . *There* lies his home; *there* lies his business, which a Noah's flood would not interrupt, though it overwhelmed all the millions in China. He lives on the sea as prairie cocks in the prairie; he hides among the waves, he climbs them as chamois hunters climb the Alps.

The "hermits, issuing from their ant-hill" give us an image of the "return" to the world after a "withdrawal." The "blazing banner," the sun—the sun under which the conquerors and patriarchs, the "naked Nantucketers," divide the oceans among them. The active forces here are all masculine; the feminine quantities are acted *upon*. Not far under the surface is a metaphor expressing the primeval scene of capture and division of the spoils. The whalemen are the rapers of the world. The "prairie" gives us another image of space, reminding us that the Pacific is an extension of the American land frontier. "He hides among the waves" we may read "he withdraws into the trough, the valley"; then, hunting the elusive game, he "climbs the Alps"—that is, he returns.

The style there modulates toward reflection and quiet:

For years he knows not the land; so that when he comes to it at last, it smells like another world, more strangely than the moon would to an Earthsman.

In these words there is an abrupt sense of loss, of the need to turn back. The celestial symbol is now the moon, a feminine symbol. The faculty of sensation now invoked is smell; the inward, possessive, animal sense now replaces the projective, aspiring, and conquering one.

And then the introversion, with a reminder that a brutal power surges under the peaceful surface of meditation as it does under the delight of the oratorical mood.

With the landless gull, that at sunset folds her wings and is rocked to sleep between the billows; so at nightfall, the Nantucketer, out of sight of land, furls his sails, and lays him to his rest, while under his very pillow rush herds of walruses and whales.

Again the idea of loss: the "land*less* gull." Notice also that the style is here recapitulating the Fall; two words help to accomplish it: "sun*set*" and "night*fall*." The feeling of a downward motion out of space is invoked, and the sensation of inwardness: the folded wings, the furled sails, the female gull asleep in the trough of the waves. The kinaesthetic sense of horizontality and relaxation is achieved by "lays him to his rest"; and the passage leaves us with the idea of femininity, sleep, and dream; a dream, it may be, of time and the process of nature, the eternal, recapitulant rush of walruses and whales.

Melville's epic style is a rhythm which flows through a life cycle, embodying itself in the appropriate images. At the beginning of the above description of the Nantucketers, we have the style emerging from a context of fact. In the middle of the passage, the style has opened out into the full moon of light and space. The energy, the flight, of the day declines into the myth and fantasy of the afternoon, which in turn modulates into darkness, toward sleep and dream. The first style is a neutral statement of fact. The images of the second style, the mood of oratory, are those we have identified with the return (though they do not all overtly occur in the present passage): Light, Space, Mountain, Tower, Fire, Father, Phallus, Life. The images of the third style, the withdrawal, are: Dark, Time, Valley, Cave, Stone, Son and Mother, Castration, Death. (We might notice here that the sea and the land do not appear as symbolic constants in Melville's books. They have different symbolic meanings in different contexts.)

14

Ahab is a highly conscious literary creation. And yet much of what he does and says would have been familar to those Americans of Melville's time who had no literary learning but who instinctively felt the values of folklore. There is even a folklore version of the Promethean hero who sets the frozen universe in motion and controls the sun-god. Crockett himself easily became Prometheus, as we see from the *Crockett Almanac* of 1854:

One January morning it was so all screwen cold that the forest trees were stiff and they couldn't shake, and the very daybreak froze fast as it was trying to dawn. The tinder box in my cabin would no more ketch fire than a sunk raft at the bottom of the sea. Well, seein' daylight war so far behind time I thought creation war in a fair way for freezen fast: so, thinks I, I must strike a little fire from my fingers, light my pipe, and travel out a few leagues, and see about it. Then I brought my knuckles together like two thunderclouds, but the sparks froze up before I could begin to collect 'em, so I walked out, whistlin' "Fire in the mountains!" as I went along in three double quick time. Well, arter I had walked about twenty miles up the Peak o' Day and Daybreak Hill I soon discovered what war the matter. The airth had actually friz fast on her axes, and couldn't turn around, the sun had got jammed between two cakes o' ice under the wheels, an' thar he had been shinin' and workin' to get loose till he friz fast in his own cold sweat. C-r-e-a-t-i-o-n! thought I, this ar the toughest sort of suspension, an' it mustn't be endured. Somethin' must be done, or human creation is done for. It war then so ante-luvian an' premature cold that my upper and lower teeth and tongue war all collapsed together as tight as a friz oyster; but I took a fresh twenty-pound bear off my back that I'd picked up on my road, and beat the animal agin the ice till the hot ile began to walk out on him at all sides. I then took and held him over the airth's axes an' squeezed him till I'd thawed 'em loose, poured over a ton on't over the sun's face, give the airth's cog-wheel one kick backward till I got the sun loose—whistled "Push along, keep movin'!" an' in about fifteen seconds the airth gave a grunt an' began movin'. The sun walked up beautiful, salutin' me with sich a wind o' gratitude that it made me sneeze. I lit my pipe by the blaze o' his topknot, shouldered my bear, an' walked home, introducin' people to the fresh daylight with a piece of sunrise in my pocket.

Crockett's rude motto: "Be sure you're right, then go ahead," clearly bespeaks what Melville thought of as the Promethean *élan* of the civilizer, the energy which would save mankind from the static sun-god or save the sun-god from himself by forcing him to break through the perfection of his own indolent stasis and to move onward. But where Crockett succeeded, Ahab was destined to become himself a part of the frozen universal machinery.

There is something of the "screamer" or the "ring-tailed roarer" in Ahab. We hear the same note of blind defiance when Ahab, deliberately grasping the lightning-rod chains, shouts his challenge to the electric storm as we do in the jauntier tones of the frontier hero's boast that he could tame a streak of lightning as easily as

he could a stallion and that, as a cure for lovesickness, he was
accustomed to swallow thunderbolts. The unreasoning rage of
Ahab against Moby-Dick had its frontier counterpart in the reckless destruction of the wilderness and its creatures which often went
far beyond the needs of security. "Long exile from Christendom
and civilization," Melville wrote, "inevitably restores a man to that
condition in which God placed him, *i. e.*, what is called savagery.
Your true whale-hunter is as much a savage as an Iroquois." The
"splintered heart and maddened hand . . . turned against the wolfish world" might become as much a way of life for the frontiers-
man-killer as it did for Ahab, no matter how much the Starbucks
of the new country might denounce the mad hunt as a work of
blasphemy against God's bounteous world.

There were many legends in the West concerning strange beasts
encountered in the woods: jet-black coursers, fabulous mountain
lions, and white steeds (which Melville himself mentions in "The
Whiteness of the Whale"). Often these mythical beasts cast a spell
over the hunter. The story of the enchanted hunter is told by Constance Rourke: At sunset a Kentucky woodsman suddenly noticed
that the streams were running in the wrong direction, shadows
were falling the wrong way, and the woodsman's own shadow
"traveled around him like the marker on a sun dial, though much
faster." The spell could be relaxed only by Indian incantations
and the appearance of a snow-white fawn. Such a spell descends
upon the *Pequod* at the moment when Ishmael falls into a trance
and nearly turns the ship around and during the episode of the
magically turned compasses. The end of *Moby-Dick*, too, recalls
themes from the folk tales. Ahab, pulled into the sea by Moby-
Dick, shared the fate of a hero called High-Chin Bob, who roped
a mountain lion and rode off into eternity with the stricken and
rampaging beast. And the tale of the ship rammed by a whale was
known outside the factual accounts such as Owen Chase's account
of the *Essex*, which Melville had read.

But there is a profounder similarity between Ahab and the folk
heroes, a similarity with crucial implications in any estimate of
American art and culture. The folk hero, writes Constance Rourke,
stepped with one bound "out of a darkness which seems antediluvian." He had no history, had been through no tangible process

of maturation, he was disinherited by whoever had begot and borne him, and his parents had vanished. He was, in short, Ishmael in search of his paternity. Lacking a knowable natural-human genesis, he was not quite human himself or quite of this world. "He was seldom deeply involved in situations," writes Miss Rourke; "even his native background was meagerly drawn. . . . Though he talked increasingly his monologues still never brimmed over into personal revelation. He was drawn with ample color and circumstance, yet he was not wholly a person. His mask, so simply and blankly worn, had closed down without a crack or a seam to show a glimpse of the human creature underneath." It is true of Ahab, the masked old man of whose past we have only shadowy details. He has been whaling for forty years; he has lost a leg; he has, we are told, "his humanities"; there are vague references to a girl-wife whom he married in his old age. Much of the wonder of *Moby-Dick*, as Charles Olson has said, comes from its antediluvian mood. In the Asiatic countries, wrote Melville, we still see "much of the ghostly aboriginalness of earth's primal generations, when the memory of the first man was a distinct recollection, and all men, his descendants, unknowing whence he came, eyed each other as real phantoms, and asked of the sun and the moon why they were created and to what end." To have no history is to have no humanity, to be a "phantom." Whatever is "grand" in Ahab, as Melville admits, "must needs be plucked at from the skies, and dived for in the deep and featured in the unbodied air." Phantoms are undeniably "real," as Melville says. And one can produce profoundly human works of art using phantoms for characters—Starbuck is, after all, the only *homme moyen sensuel* in *Moby-Dick*. (His name indicates this; it is a common one in Nantucket; and the other characters all have biblical or barbarian or comic names.) When Starbuck is on the point of openly mutinying, he becomes the center of the story. He is a human being with human emotions, an instinctive attachment to life, and poignant regret for what he has lost. He is Man ready to destroy the Phantoms. But he fails, and the central figure is Ahab once again, the central sun of a doomed phantom world.

Melville knew instinctively as well as intellectually this deep flaw in American culture. The American personality was uncon-

ditioned, only imperfectly human. The wealth of present experience
in which this personality found itself was wonderful, rich, and
exciting, but finally meaningless by itself. Melville's books therefore present the symbolic figure of Ishmael, seeking for his own
humanity, looking from present to past for the revelation of his
paternity, hunting for the form and substance of his own being,
contesting with God and Nature the right to refuse the revelation.
Space, that obsessive image of the American, is psychologically
the Void—the Void of personality, experience, and consciousness
which have been neutralized or emasculated. There are many symbols of this Void in Melville's books: the whiteness of the whale,
the rainbow turned white, the pure emptiness behind the mask,
the "sheer vacancy" of the world of Bartleby the Scrivener—even,
in *The Encantadas,* the vacant lot. The inhuman horror of space
and emptiness fascinated Melville, and it is what drags his characters off center, away from full humanity toward the unmanned
—the humanly voided—condition of the titan, the beast, the
machine, or the child. The American failure, he showed, was the
sterilizing of the human core of personality. Melville's fictional
heroes, searching for the secret of their paternity and their selfhood, seek to rehumanize and reprinciple the Void.

As we have noted, Melville thought that the hope of America
was to be found in the spirit of the West. Yet the West is an ambiguous image. It symbolizes vigor, accomplishment, nobility, mag-
nanimity, but it is also the home of the setting sun and the abode
of the dead. In *Mardi,* Melville envisioned stars and suns, mankind
and all human empires, streaming westward, toward the "beacon
by which the universe is steered." In the Pacific, too, all of life
streamed out toward the West. As Ahab says, watching the dying
whale:

"He turns and turns him to it,—how slowly, but how steadfastly,
his homage-rendering and invoking brow, with his last dying motions.
He too worships fire; most faithful, broad, baronial vassal of the sun!—
Oh that these too-favoring eyes should see these too-favoring sights.
Look! here, far water-locked; beyond all hum of human weal or woe;
in these most candid and impartial seas, where to traditions no rocks
furnish tablets, where for long Chinese ages, the billows have still rolled
on speechless and unspoken to, as stars that shine upon the Niger's
unknown source; here, too, life dies sun-wards full of faith."

In the West, Ahab saw the secret of his own doom, saw that he was betraying the spirit of life to be found there and giving himself over to the spirit of death. "Time was," he says, "when as the sunrise nobly spurred me, so the sunset soothed. No more. This lovely light, it lights not me; all loveliness is anguish to me, since I can ne'er enjoy. Gifted with the high perception, I lack the low, enjoying power; damned, most subtly and malignantly! damned in the midst of Paradise! Good night—Good night!" It was Melville's most bitter, suspicious fear for the American that before his career had fairly got started in his wonderful country he might suddenly turn out to be damned in Paradise. If so, the reason would be clear: the superhuman struggle toward civilization would have abstracted man from his own emotions. To be damned is to be unmanned, to become the Mask, the Idea, the Will, the Titan.

In *Moby-Dick* a great man allows himself to be unmanned by the lure of God. The White Whale is for Ahab the mask which affirms, because of its horror and beauty, that all human, natural, and divine reality is concealed behind the masks of appearance. The tremendous mass of the sperm whale, propelled with such resources of power, has no face. The whale's head is a "dead, blind wall," as Ishmael observes; an inscrutable, menacing blankness. Replying to Starbuck, who tries to dissuade Ahab from his obsessed hunt, Ahab says: "All visible objects, man, are but as pasteboard masks. But in each event—in the living act, the undoubted deed—there, some unknown but still reasoning thing puts forth the moulding of its features from behind the unreasoning mask. If man will strike, strike through the mask! How can the prisoner reach outside except by thrusting through the wall? To me the White Whale is that wall, shoved near to me." The pursuit of the White Whale forces the hunter more and more into an inhuman, unnatural world where there is no reality but the mirage of shifting, mocking masks. It is this world which above all Starbuck fears and hates, knowing that there can be no commitment to life in such a world, no leavening of the superhuman will with human emotions. To Starbuck, the White Whale, though wondrous and terrible, is, finally, a dumb brute; and that is the fact which he will not abandon. For Starbuck it is blasphemous to strike a dumb brute with Ahab's kind of insane vengeance, a

blasphemy against nature and man. This basic difference between
Ahab and Starbuck is far more than a simple difference in philosophy. Their instinctive disagreement about the whale is a psychological and cultural difference.

As patriots we may enjoy with Melville his excursions into
American folklore. It was, for him, a healthy impulse. Like Ahab,
he was gifted with the high perception; without it *Moby-Dick*
would lack the over-all structure of its universal-historical allegory.
Yet underneath the high perception, supporting and nourishing
it, Melville knew there must be a low enjoying power. This he
sought and found in the folk spirit of his country. As Constance
Rourke writes, beneath the mask the variegated folk hero was "a
symbol of triumph, of adaptability, or irrepressible life—of many
qualities needed to induce confidence and self-possession among
a new and unamalgamated people." In the folk spirit, as none
knew better than Melville, there was much which was destructive
of its own better self. But in it he sought and found the "humanities" which Ahab had in but far too small a quantity. To have
"confidence" Melville knew to be vital for his countrymen, which
helps to explain the bitterness of his denunciation, in *The Confidence Man*, of the various forms of false confidence discernible
in the American character. Most important, he knew that the
American quest must be to come into possession of the human
self. It is selfhood from which his false heroes flee in their disastrous
abdications.

15

Moby-Dick is an American epic; so far it seems to be *the* American epic. An epic is the response of a poet to the body of received
and implicit myth which his culture bequeaths to him. The myth
his society bequeathed to Homer was a good deal more complete,
more established, more complex, more elegant than the myth
Melville's culture bequeathed to him. It is fortunate that Melville
had the American knack of exploitation, which allowed him to
find more in the folk myths of his country than one might have
thought was there and which allowed him to pluck all manner of

curiosities and mythical odds and ends out of the world's store. The pack of the peddler contained a weird array of wares.

But there *is* a received and implicit myth in *Moby-Dick*. The high perception makes it into the universal allegory; the low enjoying power establishes it as the folk foundation. This myth is capitalism. *Moby-Dick* remains intransigently a story of the whaling industry; a hymn to the technical skill of the heroes and the marvelous perfection of their machine and to the majesty of what they appropriate from the sea—the sheer weight, mass, wealth, power, and beauty of the whale's body; a saga of the exploitation of nature and man for profit or for righteousness (for our American capitalism has had spiritual motives and spiritual weaknesses and strengths never imagined by Marx). There is no doubt that the voyage is an industrial enterprise bossed by Ahab, the nineteenth century type of the manager of an absentee-owned plant. All the facts are there: the wage of the sailor, the occupational hazards, the deployment of personnel in the field, the precautions to be taken and the risks to be calculated in each operation, the nature and care of the various kinds of equipment—all the intricate parts and economy of the machine which reduced the whale by a series of lovingly described processes to the useful oil in the casks.* Almost every process included the possibility that a man might be killed; if so, his death was at once the murder of an industrial worker and the ritual sacrifice of a hero.

The hunt for the White Whale is anything but an abandonment of the capitalist myth. Ahab may hoot at the Nantucket market, but he never hoots at capitalism. Quite the contrary, he accepts its full disastrous implications. Ahab is the epic transmutation of the American free enterpriser, and the White Whale is the transmutation of the implicit spiritual meaning of free enterprise. The meaning is clear: the American who exploits nature soon learns to pursue a mysterious and dangerous ideal, and this pursuit transforms him into the likeness of what he pursues. Ahab was once a child and then a man. He was injured in line of duty by the enterprise of which he was a part. A suffering man, he became dedicated. "Unmanned," he became through an abortive and illusory

* At this point I am indebted to an enlightening unpublished essay by Mr. James Hall.

transfiguration a titan, a savior. Into his ken swam the obsessive White Whale, and pursuing him, the titan was transformed into his likeness—into the beast, the machine, and the purity of death.

"I try all things," says Melville in *Moby-Dick*. "I achieve what I can." His plight as an epic writer was less desperate than his words might imply, for he did not have to invent the central epic theme. That was given to him by his culture; he had merely to recognize it, though that was no doubt difficult enough. What he had to do was adduce the body of supporting mythology, clothe the skeleton with flesh and the habiliments of style. For this purpose "all things" were grist for the mill—jokes, puns, dances, ceremonies, side shows, catalogues, scientific discourses, orations, meditations, confessions, sermons, tall tales, redactions of Old World mythologies, and literary conventions. Much more so than the Homeric epic, *Moby-Dick* remains the willed, self-generating, and idiosyncratic act of a partly lost and un-cultured man. But this is the typical act of the American genius.

III

The Ruined Tower

Melville was writing with furious energy in the first three years (1850–1852) after his removal with his wife and son from New York to "Arrowhead" in Pittsfield. *Pierre*, published in August of 1852, appeared less than one year after *Moby-Dick*. Melville wrote relentlessly, and the strain of producing *Pierre*, together with the probable sense of having failed in this novel to do his best and the suspicion that people were not going to see what there was of good in it, severely taxed his health. This we can detect in the tone of *Pierre* itself; its author seems to be writing himself into the ground. But *Moby-Dick* and *Pierre* are two of his major efforts. This and the fact that Melville turned so quickly from one to the other makes us wonder about the thematic relationship between them.

Moby-Dick is a record of the creative mind in the ecstasy of accomplishment and the serenity of success—a record of the mind appropriating men, gods, and nature with the full, open vision and energy of the spiritual return. *Pierre* is the record of a mind in the act of withdrawal: we seem to see the events of this book through the mouth of a dark cave into which we are slowly retreating; at the end it is as though we had turned our faces to the inner wall of this Platonic cave (a city jail, as it turns out), beholding only the shadows of reality. The cave image is used repeatedly in *Pierre*, as, for example, when the author says, "I shall follow the endless winding way—the flowing river in the cave of man; careless whither I be led, reckless where I land." The mood and texture of the two novels are as different as light and dark. The governing images shift from Space to Time, from the open air and the sky and the sea to the glen, from folk figures to psychologized characters (which are in turn mythicized), from Society to the Family.

2

When we first meet him, Pierre Glendinning is a proud and noble youth. He is the scion of an ancient Dutch and British-American family. He lives with his mother on the family acres, Saddle Meadows. The only real sorrow he has known has been the early death of his father, who died when Pierre was twelve and whom his youthful emotions have canonized into a god of stainless purity. There is a "romantic filial love" between Pierre and his mother; they are accustomed, to the embarrassment of the reader, to call each other "brother" and "sister." Mrs. Glendinning is a handsome woman and has retained much of the charm of her youth: "Litheness had not completely uncoiled itself from her waist." She has a "triumphant maternal pride," and "in the clear-cut lineaments and noble air of her son" she sees "her own graces strangely translated into the opposite sex." In his mother's possessiveness, Pierre is one day to see something sinister, but meanwhile, "in the playfulness of their unclouded love," mother and son "flow freely and lightsomely . . . on the pure joined current of life."

Like Taji, in *Mardi*, Pierre is torn between two women who symbolize two aspects of the mother. He is in love with Lucy Tartan, a pure and beautiful girl, whom in the natural course of events he is expected to marry. Their relationship is fresh and idyllic as the book opens and as we accompany them one June morning on a lighthearted excursion into the countryside. The morning is made gay with Pierre's "young, manly tenor" and Lucy's "girlish treble," as they say such things to each other as: "With kisses I will suck thy secret from thy cheek" and "Ah! Thou too ardent and impetuous Pierre!" But on this very morning the blight begins to appear to the surprised and confused hero. Intimations of the dark side of life, of sin and guilt, creep into the young lover's soul even as he pledges himself eternally Lucy's. The mystical face of a phantom appears to him, the face of a "mysterious girl." And he knows only that she brings "grief" and is a "self-willed guest." He feels that he may never again know "Joy" and that if he is deprived of joy, he will find "cause for deadly feuds with things invisible." But then the face disappears, and "Pierre is Joy's and Life's again."

The mystical face, we soon discover, has a real counterpart. The mysterious girl proves to be Isabel, Pierre's half-sister, the illegitimate daughter of his father. He first sees her at a sewing circle which he visits with his mother. The girl shrieks and faints away; for she knows that Pierre is her brother, though Pierre does not know until she later sends him a note that she is his sister. Isabel's face, recalling to him "a thousand forms of bygone times and many an old legendary family scene," almost "unmans" him with its "wonderfulness." For a time—before Isabel's note confirms his presentiments—Pierre is able to preserve his "Joy" against the phantom face. Yet more and more "the old original mystic tyranny would steal upon him; the long, dark locks of mournful hair would fall upon his soul, and trail their wonderful melancholy along with them; the two full, steady, overbrimming eyes of loveliness and anguish would converge their magic rays, till he felt them kindling he could not tell what mysterious fires in the heart at which they aimed."

As the face of the mysterious girl gradually summons Pierre to his "life-revolution," his mother grows obscurely menacing. She watches Pierre and Lucy together and smiles with satisfaction; for she is satisfied that Lucy is weak of will and can never really take Pierre away from her. Lucy is no more than the bright, seductive bait which will lead Pierre irrevocably into his mother's snare. Later Mary Glendinning, with "the proud, double-arches of the bright breastplate of her bosom," will loom "high up and towering and all-forbidding" before her son, like Semiramis herself—the divine queen-harlot and great mother of Babylon with all her bizarre panoply and her "infinite Haughtiness." *

Finally Pierre receives the fateful note from Isabel. He is on his way to visit Lucy when a hooded messenger puts the letter in his hand: Truth must be faced at last; Pierre is Isabel's own beloved brother; he must fly to her lest she perish; no more can she bear being an outcast; Pierre must ignore the "heartless usages and fashions of a banded world" and respond to the "unquenchable yearnings" of Isabel's heart. He will find her at the farm where she

* In Chap. CLXXXI of *Mardi*, Melville had imagined a supper given by Pluto in the Lower Regions. Among the guests is "Semiramis eating bon-bons with Bloody Mary." It is a supper splendid enough to make "Babylon nod her towers."

works; he must come tomorrow at nightfall. The words, blotted
with tears, are confirmation of what Pierre had already dimly
seen: that the phantom face had announced his Fate. Like Ahab,
Pierre will do battle with a monster: "Thou Black Knight, that
with visor down, thus confrontest me and mockest me; lo! I strike
through thy helm, and will see thy face, be it Gorgon!—Let me
go, ye fond affections; all piety leave me; I will be impious. . . .
From all idols I tear all veils."

Pierre commits himself so immediately and tumultuously to
Isabel's welfare, knowing that it means the end of everything he
has cherished—his relation to his mother, his engagement to Lucy,
his desire to be the noblest of the Glendinnings—that we feel he
must be harboring some unconscious malaise. And as the book
proceeds, this is confirmed by the self-destroying eagerness of
Pierre to take upon his shoulders all the woe and evil of the world.
We feel that he is determined to destroy his malaise by destroying
himself. Significantly, Melville thinks it necessary to explain why
his hero acts so ineluctably to "so small a note." Why is Pierre
"insecure"? And Melville tells us that it is because the revelation
has besmirched Pierre's god, his father. In "the fresh-foliaged
heart" of Pierre, we are told, there stands the "one-pillared temple
of his moral life; as in some beautiful Gothic oratories, one central
pillar, trunk-like, upholds the roof." In the shrine is "the perfect
marble form of his departed father; without blemish, unclouded,
snow-white, and serene."

Pierre's thoughts about his father are ambivalent, and they are
symbolized by two portraits in the possession of the family—one,
Mrs. Glendinning's favorite, showing him as a tranquil and substantial middle-aged man; the other, painted, so a maiden aunt
tells Pierre, while Mr. Glendinning was befriending a beautiful
French refugee (the mother of Isabel, as Pierre later learns),
showing him as "a brisk, unentangled, young bachelor, gaily rang-
ing up and down the world." The second portrait has been given
to Pierre by his maiden aunt and he has hung it in his study or
"closet." Isabel's note has sent him stalking insanely through the
countryside. But long after midnight he returns to his closet and,
like a Gothic hero in a tower, sits before the portrait and broods
at the awful paralysis it seems to impose on him. And then, moved

by "an irresistible impulse," he turns the face of the portrait to the wall and cries, "I will no longer have a father!" Indeed, he will be an orphan, for he knows that there will be an abrupt alienation from his mother as soon as she learns that he is determined to forsake Lucy for Isabel. He is "driven out an infant Ishmael into the desert, with no maternal Hagar to accompany and comfort him."

In the first interviews between Pierre and Isabel, we are faced with some of those long passages of bad writing * which make Melville's novel so striking a mixture of clumsiness and magnificence. As a piece of narrative the scene is preposterous. The silence of the dark farmhouse is broken only by the sighs and cryptic symbolism of the conversation between brother and sister and by the scarifying sound of the footsteps of Delly, a ruined maiden, who paces the floor above in the extremity of her anguish. Pierre is overwhelmed by "the death-like beauty" of Isabel's face as she looks at him and with "the wild musicalness" of her voice murmurs, "I know not where to begin to speak to thee, Pierre; and yet my soul o'erbrims." Her mind is an unearthly confusion of fantasy and fact; her past a dream of miasma and reality. As she tells her story, her mind occasionally goes blank, and then she says, "Bring me the guitar!"—and the autobiography continues in the form of music. The sounds are "pendulous like glittering icicles from the corners of the room" as Isabel utters a mysterious chant consisting of the words "mystery" and "Isabel."

Encouraged by Pierre to "go on with thy too touching tale," Isabel concludes her story. Her earliest recollections are of a far place over the sea ("perhaps France") where she lived with an old

* In *Pierre*, Melville admits that his young hero writes carelessly (for indeed Pierre does turn out to be a writer), and I think we may take this as a self-confession. The proofs of Pierre's book, we are told, "were replete with errors; but preoccupied by the thronging and undiluted, pure imaginings of things, he became impatient of such minute, gnat-like torments; he randomly corrected the worst, and let the rest go; jeering with himself at the rich harvest thus furnished to the entomological critics."

There is scarcely one of Melville's novels which would not benefit by verbal revision. Most readers, one imagines, would be glad to exchange some of the pure imaginings for a careful rewording of such troublesome phrases as the following: "Long, I, shrinking, sideways turned to meet it, but could not"; "Her thawed form sloped sidelong into the air"; "I could surmise; but what are surmises worth? Oh, Pierre, better, a million times, and far sweeter are mysteries than surmises: though the mystery be unfathomable, it is still the unfathomableness of fulness"; or "Abashed, smote down, I, quaking, upward gazed."

man and an old woman and a frightful cat in a drafty house in the forest. Then there was a sea voyage, and she went to live in a huge house full of strange people, some of whom "grew as savages and outrageous, and were dragged below by dumb-like men into deep places" from which came dismal sounds, "groans and clanking fallings, as of iron in straw." Now and then some men came to the house with a coffin, which they pushed in through the window and then pushed out again and went away. Once she saw "a robust but squalid and distorted man" * tied with long cords, four of which were held by "many ignorant-looking men who with a lash drove the wild squalid being . . . toward the house." Then she heard "hand-clappings, shrieks, howls, laughter, blessings, prayers, oaths, hymns, and all audible confusions issuing from all the chambers of the house."

Finally, she was taken from this house to another house, smaller, pleasanter, and inhabited by a different kind of people. Here a fine gentleman visited her and whispered that he was her "father." He was called by a noble-sounding name, "Glendinning."

Isabel explains that she got her guitar from a peddler, who had got it from a servant of a great estate near where she lived. She had always been known simply as Bell, but in the guitar she had found inscribed the name "Isabel." She had concluded in a moment of mystic illumination that *her* name was Isabel and that the guitar had belonged to her mother. She indicates to Pierre that the guitar is her mother-symbol, after prefacing this revelation by saying: "I am called woman and thou, man, Pierre. . . . Why should I not speak out to thee? There is no sex in our immaculateness." To the mute, wild music of the guitar, she breathes the words "mother, mother, mother." Then, kneeling on the floor and completely concealed by "her dark tent of hair," which undulates "like a tract of phosphorescent mid-night sea," she strokes the guitar and again utters the magic words. "Almost deprived of his consciousness," Pierre feels that he is in "the vestibule of some awful shrine . . . softly illuminated by the mild heat-lightnings and ground-lightnings." And he worships at the shrine of the great mother as he had worshiped at the one-pillared temple of the father.

* Melville's father, we recall, went mad before he died.

Pierre goes to tell Lucy that his duty is to abide eternally with Isabel. She is already prostrated by Pierre's unaccountable neglect. Pierre finds her "decked in snow-white and pale of cheek"; and sitting by her bed, he says, "thou indeed art fitted for the altar; but not that one of which thy fond heart did dream:—so fair a victim!" Pierre then announces that he is "married," and Lucy falls over in a swoon. A "terror-smitten maid" enters and cries, "Monster! incomprehensible fiend! depart! See! She dies at the sight of thee— begone!" And Pierre walks heavily away. Still resolved to "cross the Rubicon," he goes to his mother. In an anguished scene he tells her that he is "married," whereupon she bids him seek "other lodgment and other table than this house supplies." Pierre looks about him "with idiot eyes," and staggering dumbly from the house he trips over the threshold and falls flat on his face—"jeeringly hurled from beneath his own ancestral roof." As Melville writes later in the book, describing his hero at work on his hopelessly ambitious novel, "Now cruel father and mother have both let go his hand, and the little soul-toddler, now you shall hear his shriek and his wail, and often his fall."

When Pierre sees Isabel again, he experiences "a terrible self-revelation": his own incestuous love for her. They will flee to the city, passing themselves off as man and wife. Back in the local hotel where Pierre's belongings have been sent, he finds the portrait of his father, with its maddeningly ambiguous smile. Pierre declares that "it shall not live"; and in a kind of ecstatic ritual, he burns the portrait. "So now I will serve thee," he says. "Though that solidity of which thou art the unsolid duplicate hath long gone to its hideous churchyard account . . . yet will I now a second time see thy obsequies performed, and by now burning thee, urn thee in the great vase of air!" Having performed this ceremony, Pierre has a new sense of freedom, a new sense that his will is his own.

It becomes clear that two of the main themes of *Pierre* are incest and parricide—incest which actually occurs between Isabel and Pierre, and imaginary incest and parricide which occur in Pierre's unconscious mind and determine the course of his life. This Melville tells us most explicitly by means of a little symbolic pantomime near the end of the book. We find Pierre, Lucy, and Isabel in an art gallery. Pierre and Isabel pause before a painting

marked "Stranger's Head by an Unknown Hand"; they are agitated
by the resemblance to their common father of the "dark, comely,
youthful man's head" with its ambiguous smile. Directly across the
gallery the innocent Lucy pauses before the "sweetest, most touching, but most awful of all feminine heads"—Beatrice Cenci. Hers
is a "double-hooded" face, says Melville; her face is hooded by
"the black crepe of the two most horrible sins . . . possible to
civilized humanity—incest and parricide."

Pierre, Isabel, and Delly leave Saddle Meadows in a coach and
finally arrive in New York. The reaction of the bewildered travelers
to the big city is straight out of the commercial fiction of the day,
whose values Melville sometimes accepted wholesale in writing
Pierre. When Delly observes timorously that the paving blocks
seem harder than the greensward of Saddle Meadows, Pierre replies that they are the hearts of dead citizens. And he adds that
"milk dropped from the milkman's can in December freezes not
more quickly on those stones than does snow-white innocence, if
in poverty it chance to fall in these streets."

Pierre has previously sent a letter to his city cousin, Glendinning
Stanly, requesting that he and Isabel be allowed to install themselves in an unoccupied house which Glen owns. But arriving at
the house, they find it dark and securely locked. Pierre decides to
seek out his cousin and demand the reason for this inhospitality.
He leaves Isabel and Delly in a police station and walks hurriedly
through the streets toward his cousin's house, though not hurriedly enough to miss "the person of a wonderfully, beautifully-
featured girl; scarlet-cheeked; glaringly arrayed, and of a figure all
natural grace but unnatural vivacity," who makes Pierre exclaim,
"My God! the town's first welcome to youth!" At his cousin's
house, Pierre bursts in upon a very exclusive gathering. He confronts Glen and demands an explanation. But Glen, having heard
of Pierre's activities, has turned against him. Through his monocle
he examines Pierre, says that he doesn't know him, and returns to
a conversation with a lady named Clara concerning a certain *"chef
d'œuvre"* in the Louvre. Pierre retreats in a rage, and on reaching
the police station, finds Isabel and Delly engulfed in a brawling
company of wastrels, the entire population of a disorderly house

just raided by the police. Spying Isabel "struggling from the delirious arms of a half-clad, reeling whiskerando," Pierre fells the villain, and the three exiles escape into the night—solitary, friendless, and oppressed by the stony fastnesses of the American Babylon.

At this point, two-thirds of the way through the book, Melville tells us that Pierre is a writer and that he has already made a reputation for himself with certain frivolous sonnets and essays. This is of course preposterous, for nothing we have been told about Pierre has prepared us for this revelation. But a writer Pierre now is, and he is determined to write a great book. With his two companions, he establishes himself in a Bohemian section of the city, inhabited by painters, writers, teachers, and political refugees from Europe. They find lodgings in certain buildings once belonging to a church; the intellectuals who live here call themselves "the Apostles," since the church had been known as "the Church of the Apostles." In his unheated room the young hero sits through the fall and winter, his fingers numb, his fevered breath visible in the cold air, writing with gigantic zeal. He learns that his mother has gone insane and died. Lucy, still faithful and thinking only of Pierre, arrives at the Church of the Apostles, preceded by her easel and trunk. There are now three awestruck girls to watch with ever growing apprehension the suicidal fanaticism with which the frantic author, wasting away with the effort, writes down his thoughts.

A nightmarish vision overtakes Pierre one day as he writes. He sees a mountain which stands near the ancestral manor. It was named the Mount of Titans, by a "disappointed bard." The crowning precipice is a "cunning purple" and the lower slopes, covered with amaranth, are the "glittering white" of "snow" and "sterileness." At the foot of the inaccessible summit lie monstrous stones, "sphinx-like shapes thrown off from the rocky steep," among which is the image of Enceladus the Titan. "Writhing from out the imprisoning earth," he turns "his unconquerable front toward that majestic mount eternally in vain assailed by him." Defiantly, he looks up at the precipice, where once he dwelt before his catastrophic Fall, his bull-like neck, his mighty chest, his mutilated shoulders struggling against the shackles of the earth. Then the heaven-

assaulting Titan, "American Enceladus," tears himself loose and
flings himself once again upon "the precipice's unresounding wall."
And the battered, petrified face of Enceladus changes into the face
of Pierre.

Titanism is the offspring of incest: so Pierre reflects as he wakes
from his trance. As Enceladus was born of incest, so Pierre is transformed into a Titan, so his mood becomes "mixed, uncertain,
heaven-aspiring, but still not wholly earth-emancipated." And the
Titan "precipitated" in Pierre will still "seek to regain his paternal
birthright even by fierce escalade." The disinherited son is a "vulnerable god," struggling out of the earth in which his stony loins
are sunk, seeking atonement with the Father, goaded on by an
"ever-encroaching appetite for God."

Pierre's great book is, of course, a failure; the young author is
trying to write on a plane beyond his experience and capabilities.
Tortured by this failure and by an intensifying sense of guilt, he
is brought near to madness by an insulting letter from Glen Stanly
and Frederic Tartan, Lucy's brother, who have appointed themselves Lucy's unwanted protectors. Pierre takes two pistols from
the drawer of an Apostle, crying as he does so: "Ha! what wondrous tools Prometheus used who knows? but more wondrous
these, that in an instant can unmake the topmost three-score-and-
ten of all Prometheus' makings." Pierre will kill with the mechanical fire. He totters into the street "thronged with haughty-
rolling carriages and proud-rustling promenaders, both men and
women." Fate brings him face to face with Glen; the pedestrians
fall back "in a ring of panics." And crying " 'Tis speechless sweet
to murder thee!" Pierre shoots his cousin.

In his prison cell the two girls are allowed to visit Pierre, and as
Isabel wails, "My brother, oh my brother . . . thy sister hath
murdered thee," Lucy "shrinks up like a scroll" and falls dead at
Pierre's feet. Pierre then snatches a secret vial from Isabel's bosom:
"in thy breasts life for infants lodgeth not, but death-milk for thee
and me." They drink and expire on the floor, the long black hair
of Isabel covering Pierre.

Pierre dies the last of the Glendinnings. But out of the final
mystery and confusion of the book—as Ahab looking over the
side of the boat beholds the White Whale rising dimly through the

water—there emerges the marble-white, one-pillared monument to his father which Pierre has enshrined in his soul. Pierre's search is for atonement, for his paternity, for his lost birthright of wisdom, power, order, intelligence, and the authoritative mythical connection between himself and the world. It is a search for his own selfhood. To the masks of *Moby-Dick, Pierre* adds two more to bedevil the Ishmaelite exile: the mother and the infantile son. A false Prometheus like Ahab, Pierre ends his life with violence, murder, and suicide. But whereas Ahab dies a sultanic Prometheus, wrathful and overwhelmingly majestic, Pierre dies like a stricken hermaphrodite, chained to his Promethean stone, writhing his soft limbs and screaming with a childish rage at his ambiguous father.

3

In *Pierre*, Melville tried to write a psychological novel of character and fate, perhaps somewhat under the influence of Hawthorne, with whom he had become acquainted in the early 1850's. (It is the premise of psychologists that, art being in some sense an act of aggression, the artist has feelings of fear, alienation, and guilt after he has completed a work. Is this why both Hawthorne and Melville turned directly from their greatest works, *The Scarlet Letter* and *Moby-Dick,* to the writing of *The House of the Seven Gables* and *Pierre,* both of which are concerned with the Orestean conception of inherited guilt and both of which present young Ishmaelite heroes who live among outcasts and Bohemians?) But Melville was a good deal less capable than Hawthorne of writing such a "novelistic" novel. Only the framework and possibility of such a novel are to be found in *Pierre*.

My contention is that Melville wanted to write a novelist's novel but that he saw that he was failing to do so and then summoned a complicated symbolic construction to the rescue. I do not mean that *Pierre* may not have had its symbolic values from the earliest conception, but only that the extraordinary array of symbols and myths which Melville rather desperately adduces as he goes along has very much the appearance of the straw for which the drowning man grasps. In writing *Pierre,* Melville became a sort of drastic and flamboyant Joyce. As in *Ulysses* and *Finnegans Wake,* the

characters of *Pierre* embody the *élan* of myth and the mana of
magic. Like Joyce's books, *Pierre* has a universal allegory, based
on family relationships and the search for the father, which is
often connected with the narrative by means of puns. There is a
kind of half attempt to make Pierre a portmanteau character, like
Leopold Bloom or Humphrey Chimpden Earwicker. Great writers,
says Melville in a chapter of the *The Confidence Man* in which he
defends his right to create composite characters, must be allowed
to present the human spirit in all the richness of its real and
mythical resources, to picture "the last complications of that spirit
which is affirmed by its Creator to be fearfully and wonderfully
made." The writer who creates composite characters, even though
they have contradictory traits, is no more producing an impossible
monster (says Melville) than is nature when she creates flying
squirrels and duck-billed beavers.

   Pierre is a multiple personality. He is Ishmael, he is Hamlet, he
is even Memnon, "the dewy, royal boy" who died miserably
beneath the walls of Troy. Pierre, we learn, is accustomed to
retreat to a monstrous rock formation he has discovered in the
woods. (This "balancing rock" is to be seen near Melville's Pittsfield home.) Pierre thinks of it as his "Terror Stone" or "Memnon
Stone," for its shape, as it crouches on its "colossal haunches," is
reminiscent of Memnon's dolorous monument. In the myth of
Memnon, says Melville, there lies "an unsummed world of grief,"
in which "we find embodied the Hamletism of the antique world;
the Hamletism of three thousand years ago: 'The flower of virtue
cropped by a too rare mischance.' " Like the young hero of *Redburn*, Ishmael, Memnon, and Hamlet live in two worlds, the world
of the father and the world of the son. But the two basic mythical
images of Pierre's personality are Prometheus and Christ.

   In the following pages, it may frequently occur to the reader to
ask: How conscious was Melville of the symbolism which is being
attributed to him? No doubt this must in many cases be a matter
of speculation. But it seems to me that *Pierre* is Melville's most
contrived book, that here he is trying to make systematic and
explicit use of his typical symbols (see Chapter I). The Melvillian
symbols enter into *Moby-Dick* in great force. But there they are
marvelously implicit and integrated into the whole work. In *Pierre*

they are continually showing through, so to speak; they tend to stand out clearly and statically and to have an intellectually associative relation to the whole work rather than an artistically achieved relation. There can be no doubt that Melville was consciously *trying* to set up a symbolic and allegorical structure: the names he chooses for his characters make that an unarguable point. In what follows, I try to discuss only those symbolic constructions which are (1) obviously conscious contrivances and (2) the kind of contrivances which have an obvious relation to the whole book and seem to be the expectable products of Melville's mind as one understands it from his whole work. The dividing line between the conscious and the unconscious is, of course, not always clear. *Pierre* is not the systematically conscious production which Joyce might have made of it. But my contention is that *Pierre* is very much more a Joycean art work than has hitherto been established.

4

Like Ahab, Pierre is the vessel of the Promethean fire. He is "stone," charged "with the fire of all divineness"; he is the human clay, transfigured into a Titan by "caloric . . . the great universal producer and vivifier."

Isabel, or Bell, as she is also called, is Darkness. Her name signifies several things: beauty (that is, *belle*); Baal, the god of sun and fire; * and, simply, bell.

Melville makes it clear that Lucy is Light in more than name. Almost invariably Pierre visits her in the morning, just as he almost invariably visits Isabel at night. Lucy is "radiant," she "shines," she is "a visible semblance of the heavens," she has a "bright glance," she is the "summer lightning" that fills Pierre with the "sweet shocks" of "ethereal delights." "Delight" is the word most frequently used to describe Pierre's feeling for Lucy; their chat is "lightsome"; and when Pierre tells Isabel about Lucy, he "enlightens" her. Lucy says that she can "tear herself into ten trillion pieces," assuming perhaps the ethereal brilliance of Zeus' golden

* The traditional, dictionary definition of "Isabel" is "oath of Baal," and this is doubtless the one Melville knew. Certainly Melville connected "Isabel" with "Jezebel" (Hebrew: *Izebel*), the dark and depraved queen of King Ahab. Melville probably knew Baal as a sun-god.

shower of atoms which, as Melville says, poured down on both Danaë and Lucy.

Melville's novel assumes a new coherence when we recognize the allegorical presence of Lucy in many passages which, without her, seem commonplace or meaningless. For instance, when Pierre seeks through the dark New York street for a light in the window of the stone house he has expected Glen to have ready for him, he is, on the allegorical level, the human clay seeking the vivifying fire. Again, "Lucy" shines from the druggist's window, illuminating the harlot who accosts Pierre. As we have noticed, Lucy is one aspect of Mrs. Glendinning; she illuminates the human clay of her prospective mother-in-law. Mary Glendinning "evenly glowed like a vase which, internally illuminated, gives no outward sign of the lighting flame, but seems to shine by the very virtue of the exquisite marble itself." Isabel represents Darkness; but her eyes glow with Lucy's fire, though it is dimmed and made mysterious in the dark. Isabel's eyes shine like the will-o'-the-wisp or like the balefires which burn in honor of Baal on rural heaths or hearthstones.

Lucy's mother, we are told in a satirical passage, is a "match-maker"; and Melville is perfectly aware that this may be taken as a pun to mean a "Lucifer match-maker." Mrs. Tartan has made the two matches which furnish light in the novel, so Melville seems to be thinking: Lucy is a "Lucifer match," and the match between Lucy and Pierre is part of the central theme of the book. In another passage Pierre thinks of himself as Pluto carrying his Lucy-Proserpine into the realms of dark. Later, when his mother compares him with Lucifer, we are to translate: "he who carries Lucy into Hell."

Shortly after Pierre thinks of himself as Pluto, he receives the note from Isabel which does indeed presage a dark doom for Lucy. But just before he receives the note, there is a beautiful tableau in which we see Lucy for the last time in her original brilliance. She appears to Pierre and his mother in what amounts to a mystic vision. It is evening and "the setting sun, streaming through the window, bathed her whole form in golden loveliness and light." She disappears into the sinking sun, leaving Pierre to reflect that "I am of heavy earth, and she of airy light."

At one level of meaning, the action in *Pierre* takes place in one

day. It is morning as the novel opens and evening as it closes.
Lucy is Pierre's companion during the brief morning. But she is
obscured by the smoke of Pierre's volcanic emotions (Pierre, as we
shall see, sometimes represents the earth in space) and by the
storm clouds of his spiritual trial, and Pierre turns to Isabel. Only
just before dusk does Lucy reenter the scene, enlightening the
world briefly but failing to redeem it from the darkness into which
it has plunged. Lucy goes through the transit of withdrawal and
return. As she says in her letter to Pierre announcing her intention
to come to New York, she has been in "a long, long swoon" during
which "heaven" was "preparing me for the superhuman office," the
office of bringing the light of love to Pierre. Heaven, she writes,
"was wholly estranging me from this earth, even while I yet lingered
in it; was fitting me for a celestial mission in terrestrial elements."
When she arrives, Pierre and Isabel perceive her "wonderful
strength in . . . wonderful sweetness." Her face is transfigured
with a brilliant, supernatural whiteness. Her presence conveys a
"shock" to Pierre and Isabel. Aware that Lucy is the possessor of
the divine creative *élan*, Pierre and Isabel experience what Melville
in his essay on Hawthorne called a "shock of recognition." Lucy
is the symbol of the Promethean fire, which she contains as does
the hollow reed in which Prometheus is said to have carried the
fire from Heaven. Like Prometheus, she has found the secret of
subduing the violence of the old God—"sustained she was by those
high powers of immortal Love, that once siding with the weakest
reed which the utmost tempest tosses; then that utmost tempest
shall be broken down before the irresistible resistings of that
weakest reed." In her spiritual transit Lucy has learned to live with
God, as Prometheus does and as Pierre fails to do. Prometheus is
the true light-carrier, the true Lucifer; Pierre is the false.

The attempt of Lucy to redeem Pierre is symbolized by her
painting. Lucy's last name is Tartan—that is, Scotch plaid, a cloth
in which we see unambiguous colors, the colors of the painter's
palette. In his utmost desperation Pierre bursts in upon her and
finds her at work on a portrait of himself, which has proceeded only
as far as a sketch of the skeleton. "Dead embers of departed fires
lie by thee, thou pale girl," he cries; "with dead embers thou seekest
to relume the flame of all extinguished love." The "dead embers,"

we perceive, are the charcoal sticks Lucy is using in her symbolic re-creation of Pierre.*

If Lucy symbolizes one pole of the transit of withdrawal and return, Isabel symbolizes the other. Pierre first sees Isabel at night; she is dressed in "modest black." Thinking of Isabel on a later night, Pierre wonders "if this night which now wraps my soul" is "genuine as that which now wraps this half of the world." If it is, he will have "a choice quarrel" with the "Black Knight, that with visor down, thus confrontest me, and mockest at me." The pun is apt, and tremendously ironical. To Pierre the Black Knight is "Fate"; but the reader knows that the Black Knight is Pierre under the domination of Isabel.

Isabel is the "night of Chaos and Doom"; periodically she comes to the world as a reminder of the uncreated universe. She is the "clog from Chaos" who drags the world back into the womb of Old Night. On the allegorical level, Pierre's first meeting with Isabel represents the first night in the life of the created earth, the first of an infinite number of partial withdrawals to the original state of things. Isabel lives in what Pierre calls "the dream-house of the earth"; earth dreams of the universe, the womb from which it came. (We recall that, unlike Pierre and Lucy, Isabel is in one house or another practically throughout the book.) Her early life, as she tells it to Pierre, is associated in her mind with three houses. The first is a "desolate old house in a desolate, round, open space" among deeply wooded mountains. It is a dark, ruinous, drafty building, with nailed-up windows and empty, doorless rooms. Every hearthstone (the Promethean symbol) has "one long crack through it." The proprietors of this universal house are a primordial patriarch and matriarch who come and go like evanescent dream images. Sometimes the old man leaves the house early in the morning and comes back through the trees at night, as if he were the sun. He may be the Creator, for he has "earthy crumbs" in his

* *The Divine Comedy* is a great favorite with Pierre; and it may be that Melville took Lucy's name and some of her characteristics from Dante's patron saint, Lucia. In *The Divine Comedy* St. Lucia seems to represent "illuminating grace" or "cooperative grace." She is a part of the light-symbolism in Dante's poem. As Lucy is urged upon Pierre by Mary Glendinning, so Lucia is sent to Dante by the Blessed Virgin as a guide and consolation. It may be significant that St. Lucia is the patron of the myopic and the blind, and that, as we learn from Melville's letters of 1851–1852, he was suffering from serious eyestrain at that time.

beard. The second house is also in a large round space, and it has three treelike sticks on which men climb up and down. It is, in short, a ship. And if we follow the Freudian analogy, Isabel's voyage over the waters represents birth, as the first house represented prenatal existence. The third house which Isabel describes is an insane asylum. Night is born to dwell in Hell with Chaos and Madness, as Day is born to dwell in Heaven with Order and Reason.

Isabel's account of her own history is full of dream imagery, which Melville handles admirably. Her thoughts are never far removed from the unconscious. As she rehearses her autobiography for Pierre, she repeatedly lapses beneath the threshold and is able to summon speech forth again only by the strummings of her guitar.

Again, Isabel (or Bell) represents Sound, as Lucy represents Sight. Isabel is a bell. Whenever we *hear* anything in the novel, we hear Isabel; whenever we *see* anything, we see Lucy. Realizing this, we detect a note of irony in such apparently meaningless scenes as the one in which Mrs. Glendinning, angry with her son for having taken up with an as yet unknown woman, says, "Pierre, Pierre! Shall I touch the bell?" Pierre answers, "Mother, stay!" and then, "yes, do." Ostensibly she is merely ringing the bell to summon the family butler. Symbolically, she is invoking the spirit of Isabel and summoning Time, the destroyer, as it turns out, of both her son and herself. For the butler's name is Dates. Melville is conscientious about using appropriate auditory images when writing of Isabel (her voice "peals") and appropriate visual ones when writing of Lucy.

Given the conventions of his day, Melville had to keep Isabel relatively bodiless, stating only by indirection that there was sexual intercourse between her and Pierre. Delly Ulver is apparently meant to lend biological substance to the story. An ordinary farm girl who has had an illegitimate child, she goes wherever Isabel goes, the body of the dark woman, as Isabel is the spirit. Her name is certainly suggestive of female sexuality.

Finally, Isabel, whom Pierre sometimes sees only as a beautiful but terrible face with a "basilisk" eye and surrounded by her strange black hair, is Medusa, who turns the young hero to stone. The symbol of the creative Pierre is the stone touched by fire—

the hearthstone which is the only part of the family mansion he leaves regretfully, the hot bricks on which he rests his feet as he composes his novel in the cold room. The symbol of the destructive Pierre is the inert stone, within which the rhythms of life cannot operate. Metaphorically, Melville reduces Isabel and Lucy to stone as Pierre leaves them on his way to shoot Glen: Isabel "sits petrified in her chair" and Lucy is "marble."

But Pierre represents not only stone in general, but *a* stone in space—that is, the earth. Pierre and his mother "wheel in one orbit of joy," Pierre "revolves in the troubled orbit of his book" or he "revolves" through his "phases," and when he goes forth to shoot Glen he says, "Here I step out before the drawn-up worlds in widest space." Again, Lucy forecasts her own "migration from this heavy earth," as she begins to fear that some unknown force is drawing Pierre from her. And when Pierre decides that he must be Isabel's, Melville tells his hero that "all brightness hath gone from thy hills, and all peace from thy plains." There is a titan in Pierre who writhes under the Mount Etna of the soul and blows his volcanic breath through the mountain. When Pierre goes through his "life revolution," the "melted lava . . . rolled down his soul, and left so deep a deposit of desolation that all his subsequent endeavors never restored the original temples to the soil, nor all his culture completely revived its buried bloom."

The central trope which Melville made into the larger allegory of *Pierre* occurs in his essay on Hawthorne. Commenting on the strange mixture of gay intelligence and humor with the sense of sin and tragedy which he found in *Mosses from an Old Manse,* Melville wrote, "spite of all the Indian Summer sunlight on the hither side of Hawthorne's soul, the other side—like the dark half of the physical sphere—is shrouded in blackness ten times black." Pierre *is* this physical sphere; and Lucy and Isabel are the Day and Night which encompass him.

Melville apparently means us to take Glendinning Stanly, Pierre's cousin, to be Pierre's other self. He is about Pierre's age; like Pierre he is an only son and was still a child when his father died. Glen is a suitor for Lucy's hand. As Pierre grows more and more desperate and suicidal, he becomes confused about this own identity, since he is unable to believe in himself as a creative human being, as a writer, or as a man of moral principle. At the end of the book he is haunted with the idea that Glen is "the finest part of Pierre, without any of Pierre's shame." Sometimes Glen seems to be almost his "personal duplicate" or the dead Pierre "brought back to life." Glen is only one of the images which make existence for Pierre unbearably hallucinatory, the more so because the image is Pierre's own. Etymologically, we perceive, Pierre Glendinning and Glendinning Stanly are the same name, since "Stanly" comes from a Germanic word for "stone" and "Pierre" comes from a Greek work meaning the same.

The element of narcissism is often apparent in Melville's books, which should not surprise us in an author who sometimes attributes homosexuality (the relation between Ishmael and Queequeg) and infantilism (Pierre and Billy Budd) to his heroes. With the exception of Lucy, all the important characters in *Pierre* are members of Pierre's family, and even Lucy comes to New York as his "cousin." Mrs. Glendinning, we are told, bears a striking physical resemblance to her son. Isabel is his own flesh. Glen is his alter ego. The "little toddler's" raging demand upon others is that they function as parts of himself. It is the infant who, in Melville's resonant phrase, "dabbles in the vomit of his loathed identity." On another level, the earth's desire is that all men return to dust. The deaths of Pierre's father and mother, of Lucy, of Isabel, of Glen, are planetary castastrophes involved in earth's general suicide.

The narcissist's misrepresentation of objective reality is, of course, not an enrichment but an impoverishment. Psychologically, *Pierre* is the story of a human being with comprehensive emotive possibilities who gradually sloughs off everything except his own insanely ideal will. The characters from whom Pierre gradually separates himself represent emotive qualities in himself. In this connection we have Lucy as spiritual light or intelligence, Isabel as unconscious emotion, Pierre's father as the principle of paternity, his mother as pride and convention, Delly Ulver as physical passion, and Charlie Millthorpe (the boyhood friend Pierre meets in New York) as rebelliousness, idealism, and the kindliness of the heart.

If we read it as realistic fiction or as melodrama, the conclusion of *Pierre* seems painfully artificial and unconvincing. But it is something else again when we have understood the allegory and the tropes which give it substance. In the jail where Pierre lan-

guishes, the turnkey is confronted by Lucy's brother and a childhood friend of Pierre's. The turnkey mutters to himself that he
will let them both into the cell at once: "Kill 'em both with one
stone," he says. But we see that the phrase has a multiple reference,
for it also refers to Pierre, the stone which kills Lucy and Isabel.
The phrase apparently occurred to the turnkey after Fred Tartan
had said that he had been to the murderer's rooms but that "both
birds were flown." Lucy is here presented in her allegorical guise:
"Hath any angel swept adown and lighted in your granite hell?"
asks Fred Tartan. And he repeats the pun on "light" when he cries
a moment later, "Lucy! A light! a light!—Lucy!"

This concluding scene takes place at sundown, and as Pierre
watches the last gleams of the sun fading from the granite walls
of his cell, we perceive that Melville is symbolizing the tragedy of
his hero, from whom the divine fire is finally passing. We are
reminded of the chapter in *Moby-Dick* called "The Dying Whale,"
where Melville describes the whale turning his head to the setting
sun and where we read that "life dies sunwards full of faith." And
then Melville exclaims, "But see! no sooner dead than death whirls
round the corpse." And so, as Lucy dies with the dying sun, Pierre
turns to Isabel, who covers him with her black hair.

In 1855 Melville published a short story called *The Bell-Tower*,
in which he further developed some of the imagery of *Pierre*. The
central images of this story are the stone tower (Pierre) and the
bell (Isabel) which proves too heavy for it. As the story opens we
are invited to imagine a vast dark body lying upon a plain. It is
the mossy remains of the ruined tower which had been built in the
Renaissance by a newly rich Italian state. The designer was a
foundling who became the master "mechanician" Bannadonna.
When Bannadonna's "Titanic tower" has risen three hundred feet *
above the plain, he triumphantly puts the "climax stone" in place,

---

* *Pierre* invites many questionably occult readings. The porter who brings
Lucy's easel and trunks to Pierre's rooms at the Apostles announces himself as
No. 2151. Is this a reference to some apocalyptic coming 300 years after the
writing of *Pierre*?

"Bannadonna" is a resonant word. Does it refer to a man who is "banned" by
a maiden, "donna"? Isabel takes the name of Banford from the family she is
living with when Pierre meets her. Is there a distant echo in the mechanician's
name of "belladonna," the natural poison known as deadly nightshade? Isabel,
the "bell maiden," is such a poison to Pierre.

as the sound of music rises from the celebrating crowds below.
Two great bells are cast and hoisted to the summit: the clock bell
and the "state bell." Bannadonna then works in secret on a device
for striking the hours. It is a wonderful "automaton," and though
Bannadonna carefully keeps it hidden in a dark cloak, two state
officials see enough of it—it seems almost to walk and breathe—so
that they suspect it is alive. Visiting the belfry where Bannadonna
is at work, they spy an earthen cup and are terrified at the thought
that this may be the drinking cup of some "brazen statue, or, perhaps still worse" hiding under the cloak. This wonderful machine
Bannadonna calls Haman, apparently after the tyrant in the Book
of Esther who ordered Mordecai to be hanged but was later himself
hanged on the gallows he had prepared for Mordecai. Taken
naïvely, the name suggests "half man"—and, of course, Herman.
Haman, we learn, is only a prototype of a mechanical slave of all
trades which Bannadonna hopes some day to perfect.

The clock bell is decorated with female figures representing the
hours; they are called Una, Dua, and so forth. Una is the emblem
which proclaims the presence of Isabel. The officials are frightened
by the uncanny expression of her "unchanging face." Her smile
seems "a fatal one." As the officials descend for the last time before
the first ringing of the bell—which is to take place on the following
day at one o'clock—they hear a noise above, which they imagine
to be the footfall of the automaton. They are reminded by
Una of the prophetess Deborah and the story of Jael, who took
Sisera into her tent and drove a nail through his head as he
slept.

The next day the crowds gather around the tower and await the
tolling of the bell at one o'clock. Instead they hear "a dull mangled
sound." Rushing to the belfry, the officials find the bloody body
of Bannadonna entangled in the arms of the dragonish mechanism,
which has crushed his head between its hammerfist and the bell;
for Bannadonna, entranced by the enigmatic face of Una, has been
struck by the mechanism. An arquebus is sent up from below and
the automaton is shot. That night the bell is secretly dragged to
the beach and sunk at sea. The officials decree a state funeral for
the mechanician. As the bier is carried into the cathedral, the
great state bell is tolled. But it makes a "broken and disastrous

sound," and then the bell falls from its moorings and plunges into the earth within the foundations of the tower. The bell, we learn, had one flaw in it, caused by some drops of blood which got into the amalgam when Bannadonna struck and killed one of the casters, who during the casting had shrunk back in fear of the molten metal. The bell is hoisted back in place. But one year after the tower's completion, the tower is ruined by an earthquake.

As Melville tells us, Bannadonna's weakness is that "he stooped to conquer"—stooped, that is, beneath the level of existence at which human personality must live. He took machinery for miracle; he took "Prometheus . . . for machinist." Furthermore, he made violence a part of his creative method. In other words, his faults are those of Ahab and Pierre. The idea of a mechanical bell ringer had come to Bannadonna as, from a distance, he had once watched some human bell ringers at work. "Perched on a great mast or spire," says Melville, "the human figure, viewed from below, undergoes such a reduction in its apparent size, as to obliterate its intelligent features. It evinces no personality. Instead of bespeaking volition, its gestures rather resemble the automatic ones of the arms of a telegraph [that is, a semaphore]." Bannadonna, it would seem, always looks at man from a vantage point which is either too close or too far away. Studying the miasmal face of Una, he is struck by the machine. Studying the bell ringers at a distance, he sees them as automatons. He has "banned" Lucy, by whom we judge Space, and has turned to Isabel, by whom we judge Time. In a larger sense Lucy *is* Space. She is the medium, the measurement, the future possibility of earth in its celestial transit. She is the dimension of clarity, intelligence, and aspiration. Isabel represents Time and the dark processes of growth, maturation, and decay. For Pierre, Isabel is the "ruination of Temples." As Melville says in *Mardi*, Time seizes and spoils the column and the capital: "the proud stone that stood among the clouds, Time left abased beneath the soil." Like Donjalolo, who longs for the unattainable Space beyond the narrow walls of his valley kingdom, Pierre is disastrously wedded to Time.

The tower and the bell are common sexual symbols. But in the dreamlike conclusion of Melville's story the imagery is more startling. It is a dream of castration. As the pallbearers carry Bannadonna's bier into the cathedral, where he will be committed to God the Father, the belfry is "groined" (an architectural term which Melville uses as a pun) and the bell falls. The sexual symbolism of "bells" is plain. Like Ahab, Bannadonna has laid himself open to the vengeance of the Father. Like Pierre, he is unmanned by the entrancements of a dark woman.*

5

Reading and rereading *Pierre*, we find that its meanings proliferate and its texture becomes rich. As Melville wrote, his mind rather desperately reached out beyond the factual-human level of the story, seeking larger frames of discourse in an effort to unify his novel on several levels at once. But whereas the larger meanings of a book like Joyce's *Ulysses* are readily available because presented to us in created form, the larger meanings of *Pierre* are for the most part less immediately clear. The *emotive equivalent* of meaning is easily felt throughout; but to grasp and name Melville's meaning is something we must finally do by inference and suggestion. Melville himself invented the best word one can think of to describe *Pierre*: in *Mardi* Babbalanja tells a story and, being chided for its obscurity, he tells his listeners that the story is a "polysensuum." If one of the main themes of this "polysensuum" is Pierre as Prometheus, the other is Pierre as Christ.

Moby-Dick is Old Testament in mood: it has the primeval mood of Genesis and the savage, heroic action of the historical books. Also it is full of Old Testament prophecy. As Nathalia Wright has pointed out, one can almost trace the development of Jewish prophecy in Melville's novel from such soothsayers as the Indian Tistig and the mad sailor Elijah through the interpreter or spokesman of Jehovah (Father Mapple) to the apocalyptic foreteller (the Shaker zealot, Gabriel). In *Pierre* we find the spirit of

* The psychoanalysts tell us that blindness is associated in the unconscious mind with castration—cf. the expiatory self-blinding of Oedipus. In *Pierre*, Melville attributes his own severe eyestrain to his young hero. Symbolically, the meaning may be that Pierre can be castrated (blinded) by Isabel (dark) or saved from castration by Lucy (light). Again we recall that St. Lucia was the patron of the blind.

the Gospels and a continuation of the prophetic spirit in the form of revelation. Mr. Quentin Anderson has indicated in an important essay on Henry James (*Kenyon Review,* autumn, 1946) that *The Ambassadors, The Wings of the Dove,* and *The Golden Bowl* may be taken as a symbolic trilogy using the themes (respectively) of the Old Testament, the New Testament, and Revelation. That Melville should have done something of the same thing in *Moby-Dick* and *Pierre* is of great literary-historical interest. (*Typee,* of course, had pictured a South Seas Eden. In that first vision of the world, the topography of the island had merged symbolically with the form of the human body; and Typee Valley was a pleasant garden which, however, the specter of guilt forced the young Adam to leave.)

Embarking on his spiritual ordeal, Pierre (whose mother is named Mary) is possessed of "the Christ-like feeling." He has been "impregnated" with "high enthusiasms"; in his soul there stirs an "incipient offspring"; thus, says Melville, "in the Enthusiast to Duty, the heaven-begotten Christ is born." Pierre becomes "a fool of virtue," because he tries to live in This World according to the principles of the Other World, and the effort brings him to destruction. In the coach which takes him to New York, he finds a pamphlet written by one Plotinus Plinlimmon, which sets forth the idea of the two worlds. "There is a certain most rare order of souls," writes Plinlimmon, "which if carefully carried in the body will almost always and everywhere give Heaven's own Truth." This Truth the author compares with the chronometrical time of Greenwich as opposed to the horological time of the rest of the world. Horological time, he says, is as much out of step with chronometrical time as is the morality of the mundane world with the morality of Heaven. The "rare order of souls" live in the horological world in accordance with chronometrical time. As he reads the pamphlet over and over again, Pierre feels "a great interest awakened in him"; yet he never consciously comprehends "the profound intent of the writer." Later, seeing Plinlimmon in New York (he lives at the Church of the Apostles), Pierre tries to obtain another copy of the pamphlet, but is never able to get one. Melville tells us that as Pierre searches for the pamphlet, he bears on his person the very copy he had read on the coach, for it has slipped into the lining of his coat, where it remains until Pierre's death. And Melville asks,

"Could he likewise have carried about with him in his mind the thorough understanding of the book, and yet not be aware that he understood it?" If Pierre does not grasp the full meaning of Christ, he is nevertheless a naïve and unconscious Christ himself. An "earnest, loving youth," he had experienced an "intense self-absorption into that greatest real miracle of all religions, the Sermon on the Mount." The young hero dies a victim of the faulty ways of This World, and, dying, he is attended by his Mary and his Mary Magdalene. In the Scriptures, Christ is sometimes referred to as a "stone." ("The stone which the builders rejected, the same is become the head of the corner," Matthew 21:42.)

But the Apocalypse has had a greater influence on *Pierre* than the Gospels. The word "revelation" is frequently used: the great discoveries consequent upon the appearance of Isabel are described as Pierre's "wonderful vital world-revelation." Like the visionary who wrote "I am Alpha and Omega, the beginning and the ending, saith the Lord," and who beheld that "which is, and which was, and which is to come," Melville assumes the large prophetic mood. "Before miserable men . . . all the ages of the world pass as in a manacled procession," he writes. Elsewhere we read that "in the times to come, there must be—as in the present times, and in the times gone by—some splendid men, and some transcendent women." Or again: "We lived before, and shall live again; and . . . we hope for a fairer world than this to come." Throughout *Pierre* there is the recurrent feeling of approaching disaster: Lucy and Pierre pause in their joyful lovemaking as if awaiting an "earthquake" or some other "terrible commotion." And to Pierre the world seems dressed for "final rites," even as he makes love to Lucy on a bright June morning. More or less random verbal references repeatedly remind us of the Book of Revelation. Of his mother, Pierre wonders "in what galleries of conjecture, among what horrible haunting toads and scorpions, would such a revelation lead her?" And we recall St. John's symbolic chastisements of the Beast with scorpions and locusts. (One of the roads leading to Saddle Meadows is called "Locust Lane.") Pierre's maiden aunt, who adored his father, is appropriately named "Dorothea." And "Ned," the name of Delly Ulver's seducer, reminds us of Satan.

The zeal against idolatry which the Apocalypse takes over from the Old Testament prophets leaves its mark on *Pierre*. Often it is simply a matter of metaphor, as when Pierre wonders if he is not baser than brass or harder and colder than ice. The ineffectual and too respectable Reverend Mr. Falsgrave is symbolized by the word "silver." The literary contents of the wooden chest Pierre takes with him to New York are said to be "silver" and "gold." But Melville makes a larger use of the idolatry theme by the implication that Isabel brings ruin upon Pierre because she makes him an idol— turns him to stone, that is. The gradual translation of human life into inert matter which *Pierre* describes was a theme of the Old Testament writers, especially the writer of Ecclesiastes, who feared, with Pierre, that the events of this world have the strength of brass in contrast to which faith and philosophy are as thin as air and that, finally, despite all human desire, the world is only a monstrous idol to mechanical necessity.

Pierre is written in the mood as well as the metaphor of the biblical Apocalypse: the writer has intuitive and sometimes actually hallucinatory visions; he writes as a seer to whom truth has been revealed; he has a messianic sense of urgency and intimations of catastrophe; he has a strong animus against idolaters, apostates, and Laodiceans; he writes on a cosmic, world-historical scale.

The characters of Melville's Apocalypse and their biblical equivalents may be listed as follows: Pierre is Christ, but he also has something of the character of the seer and magian, Daniel, who, like Pierre, was, as Melville says, "God's indignant ambassador" to Babylon. Glen is Antichrist. Pierre's mother is History or Society, the old, established, conventional, unredeemed Jewish church. The Reverend Mr. Falsgrave is the Laodicean church. Lucy is the New Jerusalem. Isabel is Babylon. Although God is symbolized by Pierre's father (as we see him in the portrait showing him as a middle-aged man) and although Satan is symbolized by Ned and also by Pierre's father (the young man we see in the other portrait), these cosmic antagonists, so important in St. John, are largely missing from *Pierre*. God is dead and is only a recurrent memory, as he tends to be in Ecclesiastes, and Satan is an elusive power obscurely entering many souls. And the messianic hope for the return of the Redeemer is missing in Melville.

We have seen that Pierre is to be identified with the Christ of the

Gospels. He is also, as his relation to the other figures of the story makes clear, the Christ of Revelation. This is symbolized, I take it, by an occult passage near the beginning of the book. Pierre takes Lucy for a ride in an old family phaeton, sixty years old. It is drawn by two colts, each six years old. The name of the family groom is "Christopher," which refers to the fact that the phaeton "bears Christ." The age of the phaeton, handed down from Pierre's revolutionary ancestors, was (in 1851) approximately the age of the United States. The numerals involved in this situation seem to refer to the Beast of the Apocalypse, whose "number" was "Six hundred threescore and six"; 666. The implication is that the conventional, aristocratic tradition of the Glendinnings in America may turn out to be as much the Beast as did Rome, a thought which surely constitutes one of the more remarkable "ambiguities" of Melville's novel.

Pierre becomes a prophet, a "master of the magicians," as does Daniel * in his captivity. As he rides out into the countryside with Lucy, Pierre "seemed a youthful Magian, and almost a mountebank. . . . Chaldaic improvisations burst from him." To Pierre, who associates trees—especially pine trees—with Isabel, the woods seem "Babylonian." And in these woods he had had the first vision of the face, a "basilisk" face with "steady, flaming" eyes. Like Daniel, Pierre is an alien in the places where his visions come to him. Instinctively he and Lucy "fly to the plain" (that is, Saddle Meadows) after Pierre has seen the face. The plain they regard as a haven of life and joy. (I would conjecture that "the plain" in *Pierre,* a symbol of space and freedom, somewhat tangentially represents the United States—the native home from which Pierre wanders to Babylon.) New York, at least, is Babylon. One of the first things Pierre sees there is the "scarlet-cheeked" harlot. (In one of his letters Melville half jocularly refers to "the Babylonish brick-kiln" of New York.) And when Pierre is established at the Apostles, he is again, I take it, compared with Daniel: "there he sits, a strange exotic, transplanted from the delectable alcoves of the old manorial mansion," looking out over "the desolate hanging

* In 1859 Melville wrote an amusing poem to a New York friend named Daniel Shepherd. Punning on both names, Melville invites Shepherd to come to Pittsfield and to interpret a dream he has had, as the biblical Daniel interpreted the dreams of Nebuchadnezzar.

wildernesses of tiles, shingles, and tin" of the "modern Babylon-
ians." The account of Pierre's new experiences, as Melville says,
is the account of a young and immature soul "ushered into the full,
secret, eternally inviolable Sanhedrim, where the Poetic Magi discuss . . . the Alpha and Omega of the Universe." And aware of
his vast new experiences, Pierre cries, "I will gospelize the world
anew, and show them deeper secrets than the Apocalypse!"

As the career of Daniel symbolizes the spiritual progress of
Israel, so Pierre symbolizes that of America. As a chapter title intimates, Pierre is "young America." He is "intended by nature" to
be a "rare and original development." Yet even before he reaches
maturity, we see the "blessing pass from him as did the divine
blessing from the Hebrews." The blessing is the knowledge of "the
most mighty of Nature's laws . . . that out of Death she brings
Life." This law seemed to Melville to apply especially to the American spirit and American culture. The passing of the blessing is symbolized when Pierre burns the "mementos and the monuments of
the past" which he has kept in an old chest: letters, locks of hair,
flowers, and, above all, the portrait of his father. Burning his
mementos, Pierre proclaims himself free of the past and ready to be
"his ever-present self." But the fact is that he has cut himself off
from life and destroyed the possibility of achieving manhood. For-
getting the intricate relation of death to life and past to present, he
finds in his mementos death and decay "and nothing more." The
chest appears to be only "Love's museum." The blessing has irrevocably departed when Pierre, about to burn his father's portrait,
asks: "How can lifelessness be fit memorial of life?" Here Pierre
becomes unequivocally the false hero; for it is of the essence of the
spiritual triumph of the true hero that he knows the relationship
between lifelessness and life.

A minor theme of *Pierre* is the theme of the keys. As in Joyce's
Ulysses, the keys are those of St. Peter, whose name Melville's hero
bears. The key symbolizes the secret of Pierre's paternity. In his
earlier portrait, Pierre's father wears a seal and a key on his watch
chain, and these Pierre's mother has kept in a drawer since her husband's death. Seeking to open the chest containing his father's portrait, Pierre cries, "The key! the key!" But the chest has been
forwarded to him without the key, making it necessary for Pierre

to force it open with the fireplace tongs. Since presumably this symbolizes the attempt to learn a secret through violence rather than wisdom or insight, Pierre feels that it is an unlucky move, that "it bodes ill." Later the key comes to symbolize the secret of Pierre's selfhood. In his distraction Pierre hands the porter who brings Lucy's effects to the apartment a key instead of a tip. Taking it back, he says: "Well, you at least shall not have the thing that unlocks me." The keys to the Kingdom of Heaven, if he could find them, would discover to Pierre his father and himself.

The bottomless pit of the Apocalypse becomes in *Pierre* a purely psychological symbol, signifying the unsounded depths of man's personality. Pierre stands on the verge of "the bottomless gulf" of his "guilt." When he hears that Lucy is coming to New York, he is momentarily joyful and exalted; but then "he sank utterly down from her, as in a bottomless gulf, and ran shuddering through hideous galleries of despair, in pursuit of some vague white shape, and lo! . . . Isabel stood mutely . . . before him." Again, the bottomless pit is the abyss over which the artist floats when he is "entirely transplanted into a new and wonderful element of Beauty and Power." The intimation is that Pierre, unprepared to be so transplanted when he begins writing his book, will be engulfed in the depths of his own soul. The abode of the Devil, Melville is saying, and the spawning place of all demonic horrors, is man's own unconscious.

We have noted in what ways Pierre's cousin Glen is at once his double and his opposite. He is like the Antichrist of the New Testament, the impostor of whom it was prophesied that he would come to earth to establish the reign of Satan, "Babylon," and the Beast. The relation of Pierre to Glen is curiously symbolized by the ardent letters they wrote to each other as youths: they were in the habit of writing "crosswise . . . with red ink upon black." That is, they wrote a page of horizontal black lines of script and then superimposed vertical red lines.

Glen, we remember, is described as "Europeanized." The "thousand nameless fascinations of the . . . brilliant paradises of France and Italy" have had their "seductive influence" on him. And when Pierre visits Glen in New York and finds his cousin discussing a statue to be seen in the Louvre, he feels that Glen is like a count or a duke. In this aspect of Melville's symbolism, Europe becomes a part of that state of depravity which he calls Babylon. Isabel, too, has sailed from Europe, and her mother was French, supposedly a French noblewoman. Like Jezebel before her, she seduces a chosen people with the blandishments of an old, corrupt culture. It was to be left to Henry James to elaborate upon the international situation which Melville sketches in bold biblical images in *Pierre*.

Mrs. Glendinning in her role as History has reached her state of perfection (false though it is) by giving birth to Pierre (America) and making him her one true lover. Other nations woo her: she has "a train of infatuated suitors," but she is true to her own son. Approaching the fruition and goal of Time, she "flows" with Pierre on "the current of life." (Dates, or Time, we recall, is their servant.) She is "not far from her grand climacteric," which, as a piece of symbolism, means that she is about to achieve the perfection of Society, though, as Pierre is to discover, the Society she represents is false, being decreed by convention and false aristocratic standards. Glowing evenly like an internally lighted marble vase, as Melville says, she is the image of a perfection which will finally be achieved when the light emerges from the vase, when History finally creates the perfect Society in the person of her son. Pierre, we remember, looks so much like his mother that he seems to be the same person translated into a different sex. History, the feminine, creative process, finds its final issue in Society, the masculine, formal construct. History is ready to die into Society, for once the light emerges from the vase, the vase will be merely inert stone. It is the role of the hero, however, to overcome all such false stases, and Pierre, impelled by his having taken up a moral position incompatible with conventional Society, smashes the vase. "When Pierre thought of the touchstone of his immense strait applied to [his mother's] spirit, he felt profoundly assured that she would crumble into nothing before it." This figure of speech seems to refer to Daniel's interpretation of Nebuchadnezzar's dream of the image of the successive world empires—an image of gold and silver and brass and iron and clay which was smashed by "a stone cut out without hands." The unavoidable ambiguity of this phrase compels us to remember Pierre's vision of Enceladus, the armless stone image. And the biblical passage describing the smashing of the idol must have had a special significance for Melville: the pieces of the idol "became like chaff of the summer threshing floors; and the wind carried them away, and no place was found for them: and the stone that smote the image became a great mountain, and filled the whole earth."

The vase image of Pierre's mother, symbolizing History nearing its "climacteric," suggests that in Mrs. Glendinning there are two possibilities for Pierre. We have noted that Lucy and Isabel are two aspects of Mrs. Glendinning. The light, with its promise of emerging from the vase, is a promise that History will bequeath to Pierre (America) the New Jerusalem. Seen in this aspect, Mrs. Glendinning is the Bride promised to Christ in Revelation. She reminds Pierre of "the sweet dreams of those religious enthusiasts who paint to us a Paradise to come, when etherealized from all drosses and stains, the holiest passion of man shall unite all kindreds and climes in one circle of pure and unimpairable delight." But on the other hand, if through a spiritual failure the light should be extinguished, the vase would bequeath to Pierre its dark, hollow inwardness—that is, Isabel. Pierre, smashing the vase, is in fact bequeathed a host of torturing ambiguities which in the end he cannot master. In biblical imagery Mrs. Glendinning represents the Jewish church, symbolized on the one hand as the Bride of Christ and on the other hand as the backsliding, haughty Daughter of Zion chided by the Prophets for moral corruption.

The Reverend Mr. Falsgrave, who lets Pierre down on every spiritual and moral question and who is not "too warm" like Pierre nor "too cold" like Mrs. Glendinning, clearly stands for the church at Laodicea. The Laodicean church in every age submits itself to conventional Society, and Mr. Falsgrave has several times sought the hand of the handsome widow of Saddle Meadows, who, though she is fond of him, will not marry him.

Lucy is the incarnation of the New Jerusalem. She is repeatedly described as an angel coming down from heaven. She "belongs to the regions of infinite day." From "unknown climes" she "comes floating into sight, all symmetry and radiance." Announcing "I am coming, I am coming," she promises Pierre a "bridal" when they meet in "the pure realms of God's final blessedness," safe from the "ever-marring world." She comes as if her body "were the temple of God," giving token of "vision and intelligence." To Melville, as to St. John, the New Jerusalem is symbolized by Space and Light. The city "lieth foursquare, and the length is as large as the breadth: and he measured the city with the reed, twelve thousand furlongs. The length and the breadth and the height of it are equal. . . . And the city had no need of the sun, neither of the moon, to shine in it: for the glory of God did lighten it, and the Lamb is the light thereof." (As we have noted, Lucy is once referred to as the reed containing the Promethean fire. In Melville's biblical allegory, she becomes the reed which measures the New Jerusalem).

When Pierre first visits Isabel, he finds her in a red farmhouse by a dark lake, which he approaches through the woods. She sings her strange chant: "Mystery! Mystery! Mystery of Isabel!" Later she gives him a drink (presumably wine) from a cup. This is Melville's version of St. John's dream of the whore whom, after being carried through the wilderness, he saw sitting upon many waters on a scarlet colored beast, holding a golden cup full of abominations and bearing on her forehead the words "MYSTERY, BABYLON THE GREAT, THE MOTHER OF HARLOTS AND ABOMINATIONS OF THE EARTH." Near the end of the book, Isabel, who Pierre fears may be a "world-syren," is suddenly filled with "spiritual awe" and involuntarily throws herself at the feet of Lucy when she hears an unaccountable "jarring" of her guitar. Isabel, or Bell, as we have noted, symbolizes Sound, and this apocalyptic note struck on the guitar seems to speak to her of the final events of the world and the Day of Judgment, when, as Babylon, she will be overthrown in favor of the New Jerusalem. That Melville may connect the name Bell with Bel, the Babylonian deity, as well as with "Baal," is at least hinted by a passage in *Clarel* where four "voices" chant,

> Earth shall be moved, the nations groan
> At the jar of Bel and Babylon
> In din of overthrow.

It may be noted, too, that Jezebel is mentioned in Revelation as the false prophetess who has misled the church at Thyatira with her knowledge of "deep things."

There are three cultural levels in Melville's vision of world-historical destiny as we find it in *Pierre*. The first is Religion. The second can be called Conventional Society and is represented by Pierre's mother, Lucy's mother, Glen Stanly (European-culture-in-America), and Frederic Tartan (the military element in society; as one might expect from the author of *White-Jacket,* Frederic Tartan is a naval officer). The third cultural level is Bohemia. When Pierre, Isabel, and Delly go to New York, we recall, they take up quarters in a building which was once a church but is now the living quarters of assorted impoverished intellectuals. This Bohemian society, Melville seems to be saying, has inherited not only the buildings of a once flourishing church, but also its spiritual and moral functions: it is the duty of the secular intelligentsia to furnish the leadership once furnished by religion. Pierre, the savior hero, is also the writer. Lucy is a painter and Isabel a musician. The apocalyptic religious theme is matched by a secular one. For as the "zealous conservatives and devotees of morals" who "keep a wary eye on the old church" know, the intelligentsia has its own vision of the social revolution to come. Plinlimmon, who also lives at the Apostles, is the secular version of Falsgrave: a Laodicean apostate of the intellectuals.

It is certainly clear from what happens in *Pierre* that Melville saw no salvation in Conventional Society. Salvation must come either from religion or from the secular intelligentsia, or from a combination of both. The proletariat, as a level of culture, does not exist in *Pierre.* Delly simply represents physical passion. Charlie Millthorpe, a proletarian intellectual, is again mere emotion, "all heart, and no head." The porters, grooms, and carriage drivers of the novel are either comic oafs or surly clods.

The American cultural fate which Melville feared may be deduced from the dénouement of *Pierre,* which leaves America in the hands of Mrs. Tartan, who has taken Mrs. Glendinning's place as Society; Frederic Tartan, the military man; Glen Stanly; and the Laodicean apostates, Falsgrave and Plinlimmon. The only probable emotions and intellectual endeavor thus become those which protect wealth and position with force; and Falsgrave and Plinlimmon—apostate liberals—can always be counted on to make even these emotions seem harmless.

Pierre describes the death of Society. At a deeper level it de-

scribes the death of the body. There is much celebration of the
body and of vitality in *Moby-Dick,* often sublimated in the ana-
tomical description of the whale or projected into descriptions of
the ship or the natural surroundings. The opening of *Pierre* also
celebrates bodily vigor, Pierre's athleticism and animality being
insisted upon. Despite the violent action with which *Pierre* ends,
there is an elegiac undercurrent expressing in quieter poetic terms
the dissolution of life. The passage at the end of Ecclesiastes, which
certainly moved Melville deeply, seems to have had its influence
on *Pierre.*

In the day when the keepers of the house shall tremble, and the
strong men shall bow themselves, and the grinders cease because they
are few, and those that look out of the windows be darkened,
   And the doors shall be shut in the streets, when the sound of the
grinding is low, and he shall rise up at the voice of the bird, and all
the daughters of musick shall be brought low;
   Also when they shall be afraid of that which is high, and fears shall
be in the way, and the almond tree shall flourish, and the grasshopper
shall be a burden, and desire shall fail: because man goeth to his long
home, and the mourners go about the streets:
   Or ever the silver cord be loosed, or the golden bowl be broken, or
the pitcher be broken at the fountain, or the wheel broken at the
cistern.
   Then shall the dust return to the earth as it was: and the spirit shall
return unto God who gave it.

Referring to Ecclesiastes, Melville wrote to Hawthorne in 1851:
"I read Solomon more and more, and every time see deeper and
deeper and unspeakable meanings in him. . . . It seems to me
now that Solomon was the truest man who ever wrote." "Solomon's" underkeyed apocalypse symbolizes the dying of a society,
but also of the human body—if we equate the "grinders" with
teeth, the "windows" with eyes, the "daughters of musick" with
hearing, and so on. This gives the passage a specific as well as a
general relation to *Pierre,* if we remember that Pierre bows himself
and returns to dust (Stone), and that Lucy (Sight) and Isabel
(Sound) die with Pierre. Perhaps at less conscious levels there are
other relationships. For example, we are not "afraid of that which
is high" (the Tower) while Lucy lives; desire does not fail while

Isabel lives; Lucy may be the silver cord, Isabel the golden bowl, Mrs. Glendinning the pitcher, the cycles of history the wheel, Pierre the body which contains these symbolic organs.

Melville's "New Testament" and "Apocalypse" end without the hope of a Redeemer. At the end of *Pierre,* Melville returns to an Old Testament view of things, not to Genesis and Kings and the tremendous primeval creative forces he invoked in *Moby-Dick,* but to "Wisdom." Still, to embrace Wisdom is not an act of despair or self-annihilation. Pierre is a suicide but Melville is not.

It is an impressive measure of Melville's greatness that even so imperfect a book as *Pierre* should be so constructive an act. We have noted that the polar extremes of Melville's set of symbolic values are Light, Space, Father, Mountain, Tower, Fire, Phallus, on the one hand, and on the other, Dark, Time, Son and Mother, Valley, Cave, Stone, Castration. We have suggested that these represent the extremes of attitude and behavior out of the tensions of which the true hero learns to evolve consciousness and morality. The true hero commits himself to the rhythms of life and achieves a creative mobility among extremes. The false hero is he who cannot achieve this mobility but commits himself, not to the tensions and harmonies within extremes, but to the extremes themselves. The false hero, in other words, is false because he tries to derive consciousness and morality from absolute values. In *Pierre* we have the statement that when the extremes of human experience become immobile absolutes, they must be annihilated; and we have the statement that the act of making absolutes and taking them for final truth is the act of an adolescent mind.

In *Pierre,* Melville returned to his earlier myth of the education of the young man and his "myth of the Bridegroom." In *Mardi* it had been intimated that Taji could never become the complete and responsible man—the Oedipean man—because he had tried to possess himself of ideal love (Yillah) without being able to accept guilty or sexual love (Hautia). The same situation occurs in *Pierre.* For though Pierre gives himself over to Isabel, he is never able to admit that Lucy is anything but ideal love, the spotless sister. Actually, Lucy, as we finally see her, is as large as life itself, and Isabel is only her dark and guilty side—as we perceive when we learn that Lucy is the true Promethean spirit, that she contains within her soul the full possibilities of withdrawal and return. Pierre, still unable to admit his father's guilt and his own, is driven to what we may call the "sin of idolatry." This is the sin of reducing the vital and the moving to the condition of the absolute, the dead, and the inert. The redemption of the bridegroom—that is, his final maturity —would have been achieved through Lucy if Pierre could have accepted her as wife, and not simply as sister and mother. But Pierre is horrified by Lucy's sexuality and by the inevitable idea that the bridegroom, in marrying the ideal (one's sister or mother), is committing incest. He must therefore artificially dissociate incestuous sexuality from Lucy. But this is to rob her of her humanity, to make her first an angelic ideal and then a stone idol, a corpse on the prison floor. This is the momentous sin, the first act of the madness of the false hero as bridegroom. For after this first act, he becomes irrevocably a child, himself the stone idol with which he will smash the whole world.

The fact is that the majestic consciousness of the creator of *Moby-Dick* was an ill founded eminence, and if, for Melville, consciousness and maturity were to endure, a prodigious retrenchment had to be made. The theme of the madness of the unfathered son had to be returned to and displaced into the repository of art. *Pierre* was this displacement. In no sense is *Pierre* the product of an insane man, as used to be said. On the contrary, it is the product of a great intelligence in the act of affirming its maturity by disburdening itself of a great insanity. We can measure the enduring richness and solidity of this mind by the acuteness with which it seeks out **and** the relentlessness with which it purges all that destroys vital consciousness. *Pierre*, like *Moby-Dick*, is an affirmation of the survival of consciousness.

Every notable act of mind implies the act of withdrawal and return—a regression, such as is so fully described in *Pierre*; a recognition and acceptance of the dark side of life; an emergence. Every work of art is the product of a mind disburdening itself of its own potential insanity. In *Hamlet*, Shakespeare found it necessary to displace the madness of the unfathered son, as in the *Eumenides* Aeschylus had done. Melville's theme is universal. And yet is not *Pierre* a peculiarly American book—the deepest and most searching fictional treatment of our national adolescence? Adolescence is almost an American invention, and the uniqueness of *Pierre* among the great works on the same subject is its close cultural reference. *Pierre* is more American than *Hamlet* is English or the *Eumenides* Greek. And among American books there is no more vivid portrait of the young man, the bridegroom whose marriage is the threshold of the adult world but who cannot pass over this threshold because his ideals are inveterately the ideals of childhood. The ideals are admirable in themselves; they must not be abandoned but revised (like Redburn's map of Liverpool). Pierre's inviolate ideals are the indisputable symbol of "young America's" inability to bear the psychic and moral burden of being fully human. The American must venture a great deal, and he may win much or lose all. Our culture, as Pierre found out, seems almost to have been contrived to put the burden of humanity wholly on the shoulders of the individual. In firmer cultures institutions tend to support and enhance human maturity; but our American institutions often seem calculated to make maturity impossible. So Pierre discovered, turning in vain to his own upper class, to the church, to the city, to the intelligentsia of the left. Pierre ventured more than Hamlet, and lost more. The final momentous act of the Renaissance prince was to kill Laertes, his friend. But Pierre kills Fortinbras—that is, Glendinning Stanly, the image of Pierre himself, but with the power, authority, and endurance which Pierre fatally lacked.* Pierre destroys not only the regressive image of "young America," but also the very qualities most needed in "young America's" peculiar plight.

There is a sense of strong personal urgency in *Pierre*—a sense, indeed, of apocalypse. And there is also a sense of strong cultural urgency, of definitive cultural statement. The critics of Melville,

---

* For this point I am indebted to "The Blonde Woman in Hawthorne and Melville" by Mary Wright. Miss Wright also makes the following comment: "The Orestes theme, which applies particularly to the transfiguration of Lucy and the murder of Stanly, is an addition to the Oedipus theme at the point where Pierre has killed his mother and the sexual image of his father for the sake of his sister and is pursued by Tartan and Stanly. Pierre has brought about the death of his real mother, and, by becoming inhuman, the death of her two projections, Lucy and Isabel, who are now only supernatural symbols, Good and Bad Angels. Like Orestes, he was led to matricide by the desire to defend his father's honor. The transfigured Lucy becomes Apollo, contending with the pursuing Eumenides; but even though she has sought out Pierre in an attempt to save him she is powerless before the intensity of Pierre's will."

many of them writing from the point of view of the older liberalism of the 1920's and 1930's, have not taken *Pierre* seriously enough, either as art or as cultural document. Each generation of American criticism likes to assume that at last America has come of age—exactly the assumption which makes us uneasy about such a book as *Pierre*, pointing out to us, as it does, the enormous difficulties to be encountered in coming of age. Surely, we have no right to explain away Melville's book as a muddle or as morally out of date. *Pierre* is not merely a curiosity, a nineteenth century *Hamlet* vitiated by romantic Gothicism and obscure philosophizing, if not actual insanity. Melville believed that American thought, both on the left and on the right, was regressive. (The obstinate tendency of all Americans to characterize their thinking as *pro*gressive is probably a good sign that he was correct.) He saw that our liberal-democratic thought was perfectly capable of disarming us in our struggle for personal and cultural fulfillment. He saw the self-destructive qualities which weaken our liberal democracy and reduce the well meaning idealist to the sheer existential sickness, so that he "dabbles in the vomit of his loathed identity." Until we have constructed a culture in which our Pierres can survive and be fruitful, we must, as liberals with hopes for the future, continuously come to terms with Melville's novel. Pierre's madness is our own as no other is.

At the end of *Pierre*, Melville has reached a point where he might ask, in the words of Robert Lowell,

> What can the dove of Jesus give
> You now but wisdom, exile?

The significant tendency of Melville's writing between *Pierre* and *Billy Budd*—in general indicating the tone of his thought during nearly forty years of his life—is a tendency to write of man as man, rather than as titan, god, or child. As was the case with Rammon (a somewhat shadowy autobiographical character Melville sketched in a late fragment of prose), exile, neglect, and personal catastrophe "confirmed him in his natural bias for a life with men." *Pierre* had acted as a painful but purifying bath of acid, and Melville, having plunged furiously through it, found that his vision had been purged, not so much of the titanic power and beauty of *Moby-Dick*, as of the residual monstrosity and insanity of this titanism as it had appeared in *Pierre*. Melville had reached out in *Pierre*, as we have seen, for two hierarchical images: Christ and Prometheus. He had not found a believable Christ, for after Ahab he could imagine Christ only as a beautiful, hermaphrodite youth. At the beginning of *The Confidence Man*, there is a striking image of a restively sleeping Christ. And indeed Christ was for Melville a kind of sleeping though unquiet shade—a Presence as real and as unrecognized as Plinlimmon's pamphlet in the lining of Pierre's coat—during the long years of his life between the early fifties and, say, 1888.

But Prometheus survives Pierre, a scaled-down, a humanized demigod who, though he can still be identified with the godlike Ethan Allen of *Israel Potter*, finds his completest expression in the eminently human character of Rolfe in *Clarel*. *Pierre* and the unhappy reception it got from the public could not have been better contrived to ensure the exile of the author. The wisdom of the exile would now consist in his study of man. But exile also has its illusions. (As Melville was to write in *Rammon*, "isolation is the mother of illusion.") And these were to find a startling expression in the book of Melville's old age, *Billy Budd*, in which the sleeping Christ was to awaken. Meanwhile Melville wrote short stories—in which Herman Melville took stock of Herman Melville.

IV

Vines and Roses

The period of Melville's life between 1852 and 1856—between *Pierre* and the trip to the Near East—was a time of uncertain health and uncertain literary accomplishment. Melville was often in low spirits and complained of sciatica and eyestrain. The biographical evidence suggests that when Melville's family arranged to have him examined by Dr. Oliver Wendell Holmes, a summer neighbor at Pittsfield, one of their objects was to find out if Herman was going mad, as his father had before him. Having left New York in 1850, Melville had in effect renounced literary fame and the possibility of continued popularity. Once the well known and well feted author of adventure stories, he had become the generally misunderstood and even reviled author of *Moby-Dick* and *Pierre*. Though never actually impoverished, he was constantly in need of money. He had been trying to get a consular position, but without success. The writer whose only portrayal of the sex act was to be an allegory depicting the female body as a horrible engine had become the father of two sons and two daughters by 1855. The man who had lived among cannibals and loved such great, hearty pagan giants as Jack Chase now lived in a busy, genteel domestic circle, including, off and on, his mother and his sisters.

The writings of this period unmistakably indicate Melville's nervous instability and his deep unhappiness, and I should want to be the last to underestimate or shrug off what one must think of as "the ordeal of Herman Melville," this saddened genius who by 1852 had entered upon his shadowed years. Still, it is misleading to assume that after 1852 Melville was plunged into impotent despair, blind cynicism, and "morbidity." It has too often and too easily been assumed that since Melville himself was poor, unhappy, and unhealthy after 1852, and especially during the 1853–1856 period, everything he wrote was injured by excessive introspection and pessimism. On the contrary, a look at such writings as *The Lightning-Rod Man, The Tartarus of Maids, Bartleby the Scrivener, Benito Cereno, The Fiddler, Jimmy Rose, I and My Chimney, Israel Potter, The Confidence Man,* and *The Encantadas* gives us the impression of a man carefully probing new areas of experience and seeking out new styles. Most of the short stories have faults of taste and conception, but *Benito Cereno* is surely one of the best of short stories, *Israel Potter* is a superior light novel, and *The Confidence Man* is a striking achievement of the moral intelligence, and a work, furthermore, which conditions our final idea of Melville more deeply than any single book except *Moby-Dick.* The point to be stressed about these stories is that they show the author seeking out new kinds of wisdom, which involve an acceptance of some of the things in life Ahab and Pierre had too madly transcended. These stories are the product of a mind which always knew but now knows with a sharper poignancy than before that life must be understood and lived in lower worlds of ecstasy than those through which Ahab and Pierre stalk with such disastrous *éclat.* This humanist truth is, after all, the secret of Prometheus.

The short stories of 1853–1856 may be subdivided as follows: those which investigate the possibilities of the complete withdrawal of the personality from life (*Bartleby* and *Benito Cereno*), those which deal with certain kinds of emotional catastrophe which may defeat the artist (*The Tartarus of Maids, Cock-a-Doodle-Doo,* and also *Bartleby*), and those which deal with the possibilities of a return to the world at lower but more stable levels of being (*The Lightning-Rod Man, I and My Chimney, Jimmy Rose,* and *The Fiddler*).

1

Like Holmes's *Elsie Venner, Bartleby* is a study of schizophrenia; *Benito Cereno* is a study of a man on whom withdrawal is enforced against his will by external events. On the scale of personality, Bartleby and Benito Cereno are, with little Pip, among those whom in *Moby-Dick* Melville called the "Divine Inert"— divine because of their saintly passivity and because they have taken the first step in the spiritual transit of the creative hero; inert because they remain below the threshold and are unable to pass into the motion of leadership or creativity.

Bartleby is a starkly simple tale told with great economy of metaphor and symbol, for Melville is preeminently interested in simplicity—a kind of simplicity at once nakedly tragic and wistfully comic. The story is relieved of the clashing commotion and weight of *Moby-Dick* and *Pierre* largely because the central figure has no will. *Moby-Dick* and *Pierre* take their inner dynamism from compulsively violent assertions of will, building up slowly to an apocalyptic crescendo; *Bartleby* proceeds in reverse, toward a gradually encroaching silence. The mood and even the method of Melville's story remind one of Kafka's *The Trial*, the haunted inwardness of Kafka's Joseph K. *vis à vis* the bank where he works and the elusive but all-powerful bureaucracy which condemns him to death corresponding with the situation of Bartleby *vis à vis* the lawyer's office and the authorities who finally jail him. But the comparison cannot be pressed too far, for though Melville shares Kafka's interest in guilt and the weird futility of reason, he attempts, unlike Kafka, to beatify his hero.

The story is told by Bartleby's employer, a corporation lawyer with offices in Wall Street. A prudent, methodical, and successful man, the lawyer is also liberal according to his lights and kind-hearted. One day he hires Bartleby as a copyist: "In answer to my advertisement, a motionless young man one morning stood upon my office threshold, the door being open, for it was summer. I can see the figure now—pallidly neat, pitiably respectable, incurably forlorn!" At first Bartleby works with devoted application, as if he had long been deprived of the joy of copying. Yet there is no joy in his exertions; he writes "silently, palely, mechanically." The lawyer soon has occasion to ask Bartleby to assist him in a proof-reading task, and Bartleby answers with what from then on is nearly the sum of his communication with other human beings: "I would prefer not to." He gives this answer to whatever request his employer may make, if it involves anything but copying. The lawyer is alternately enraged and filled with a reverence which keeps him from taking the forceful measures he would ordinarily take against a recalcitrant employee.

Bartleby gradually recedes into himself, participating less and

less in the activity of the office. The straight line of his gradual
recession is very cleverly emphasized by a sort of counterpoint of
mania and depression in the other two employees of the lawyer.
One of them is always quiet, subdued, and efficient in the morning,
but in the afternoon gets drunk, spills ink on his copy, and grows
noisy and belligerent. The other has chronic indigestion and is
irritable and quarrelsome in the morning but by afternoon is calm
and cooperative.

Finally Bartleby refuses to do any more copying: he would
prefer to do no work at all. Sitting or standing in silence behind
the screen which separates his desk from the rest of the office, he
stares endlessly through the window at the pure and awful void of a
blank brick wall. Coming to the office one Sunday morning, the
lawyer discovers that Bartleby never leaves the premises; the office
boy brings him food, and he sleeps in the office. Though he tries
both reason and threats, the lawyer is unable to handle the situation. Bartleby meets every advance with passive resistance. The
lawyer is wonderfully touched and disconcerted by Bartleby's
"great stillness." He had never imagined such intolerable loneli-
ness: ". . . his solitude, how horrible! Think of it. Of a Sunday,
Wall Street is deserted as Petra; and every night of every day it is
an emptiness. This building too, which of week-days hums with
industry and life, at nightfall echoes with sheer vacancy, and all
through Sunday is forlorn. And here Bartleby makes his home."
The "sheer vacancy" of Bartleby's world horrifies and nonpluses
the lawyer. To be confronted with a being who dwells in such a
world is to be overcome with the "hopelessness of remedying"
such "excessive and organic ill." Bartleby seems to be so much the
"victim of innate and incurable disorder" that ordinary human feelings are incapable of touching him. His disorder transforms him
into a saint, and the lawyer is aware that Bartleby exercises a
"wondrous ascendancy" over him. The lawyer's fellow feeling of
pity, which he now sees is irrelevant to the situation, is replaced by
a sense of dedication to a duty which runs entirely contrary to all
the moral principles of the modern commercial metropolis. He will
go on protecting Bartleby. "I penetrate to the predestined purpose
of my life," he says. "I am content. Others may have loftier parts
to enact; but my mission in this world, Bartleby, is to furnish you

with office room for such period as you may see fit to remain."
Bartleby is safe with his employer as long as the lawyer can act the
part of dedicated man. But he must go on functioning as a part of
organized society, and this is finally what makes his protection of
Bartleby impossible. The decisive break comes when the lawyer,
having failed to move Bartleby out of his office, moves his whole
establishment to a different building. This act dramatizes the moral
ambiguity of the story, for it occurs to us that though we think of
Bartleby as withdrawing from the American financial society, it is
also true that that society is withdrawing from him.

Bartleby remains in the building after his employer has moved.
He lurks in the corridors; he sleeps in the doorway; he "prefers"
to do nothing else. Finally he is imprisoned in the Tombs. His
employer comes to see that he gets what privileges can be arranged
for him. He finds Bartleby dead, lying in the prison yard with his
head on the cold stones. Like an unborn child, he is "strangely
huddled . . . with his knees drawn up." Peering out of the narrow
prison windows are "the eyes of murderers and thieves." "Eh!—
He's asleep, ain't he?" asks a functionary. "With kings and counsel-
lors," answers the lawyer.

Madman and saint, clown and savior, Bartleby sleeps like an
infant Christ in the midst of the City of Man, as hopelessly alienated from that city as it is from him. Melville's story is a kind of
epigraph to *Moby-Dick* and *Pierre*, in which the figure of Christ is
separated from the sultanic titanism of Ahab and the young heroism of Pierre, finally becoming a silent, withdrawn memory of a
beautiful Innocence which is indistinguishable from "excessive and
organic ill."

The short stories of this period of Melville's life are personal
and introspective. Melville was thinking of himself as an artist and
trying to understand the artist's relation to his society. Bearing this
in mind and on the internal evidence of the story, there seems no
doubt that Melville was consciously writing a parable of the artist
in *Bartleby the Scrivener*. The story is subtitled, *A Story of Wall
Street*. Bartleby is a scrivener—that is, a writer. He insists on writing only when moved to do so. Faced by the injunction of capitalist
society that he write on demand, he refuses to compromise, and
rather than write on demand writes not at all, devoting his energies

to the task of surviving in his own way and on his own intransigent terms. The strained and complex relationship between Bartleby and the lawyer may have certain similarities to the relationship between Melville and his father-in-law, also a lawyer, who helped the Melville family finance itself while Melville went on writing instead of getting a job.

The other scriveners, Turkey and Nippers, represent what we might now call "middle-brow" culture. They have sold out to the commercial interests and suffer from the occupational diseases of the compromised artist in a commercial society—neurosis, alcoholism, and ulcers. Their depressions and manias are equally unproductive of first-rate work, and they maintain a grudging and suspicious attitude toward Bartleby, their acknowledged superior as a scrivener—the attitude of the uneasy middle-brow toward the genuine artist.

It was rumored that Bartleby had been "a subordinate clerk in the Dead Letter Office." That is, Melville, while he was still writing salable adventure stories and before his own intransigence began, with *Moby-Dick*, had been a minor practitioner in the moribund profession of letters. But he had lost his audience and these early writings were as dead as modern literature as a whole seemed to be. Bartleby had suddenly been removed from the Dead Letter Office "by a change of administration." "When I think over this rumor," writes the lawyer, "I cannot adequately express the emotions which seize me." No wonder, if this "change of administration" is a reference to the spiritual wager which removed Melville from New York to Pittsfield in order that he might start on the great work of his life. The last words of the story are, "On errands of life, these letters speed to death." For Melville, literature was life; ideally *Bartleby* should have been able to convey its message of love and vitality to the readers who awaited it. But there were no such readers—at least none such as might rescue Melville's fiction from the death he accurately predicted for it. "Ah Bartleby! Ah humanity!" The artist and the rest of mankind seemed to be fatally sundered.

But there is a profounder level of symbolic meaning in *Bartleby the Scrivener*. Melville identifies himself partly with the lawyer. For example, when the lawyer describes himself complacently as "one of those unambitious lawyers who never addresses a jury, or in any way draws down public applause," the lawyer's complacency is certainly an irony, for Melville himself was by no means complacent about his lack of public applause. The lawyer tells us that he once had a lucrative position but lost it unexpectedly and along with it the income he expected would be lifelong—a reference presumably to the paying audience Melville commanded with his early books and then lost. And surely the lawyer's "original business—that of a conveyancer and title hunter, and drawer-up of recondite documents of all sorts" is a facetious reference to Melville's own business.

The author of *Moby-Dick* was a successful artist, a man of power, intelligence, and authority. By comparison the author of *Pierre* was a weak, regressive, dark-souled, and earth-minded man. After 1853, Melville's images of himself were still related to these grander images, but they were drastically scaled down. In *Bartleby* and in *Benito Cereno* we find Melville identifying himself with two figures. The first is the upper-middle-class Anglo-Saxon American, sound in moral principle, mediocre in spiritual development, a successful and respectable citizen. There can be no doubt that the qualities represented by the lawyer in *Bartleby* and by Captain Delano in *Benito Cereno* were a substantial part of Melville's own personality. After all, he was a successful family man and a customs inspector for nearly twenty years. The second figure, the spiritual man, is Bartleby and Benito Cereno. However complete we may think Melville's self-identification with Bartleby is or ought to be, we must see that Melville also identifies himself with the bourgeois American gentleman. Melville, we perceive, did not share that sentimental view of the artist's personality which pictures the artist only as a suffering and alienated and innocent being. At this deepest symbolic level of the story, Melville is as much the lawyer, the man of action, aggression, and authority, as he is Bartleby. This is to say, Melville is as much the father as the son. For we have indeed once more come upon Melville's central theme: the relationship between the father and the son and their failure or success in achieving the atonement, in redeeming each other. In *Bartleby* and *Benito Cereno* the son dies without bringing spiritual illumination to the father, and the father lives on unredeemed, but with the strength and authority which he did not know how to bequeath to the son. The situation occurs again in *Billy Budd*, though in such an obscure representation that the book testifies only to the fact that finally Melville could not deal with the father-son relationship without being so deeply moved that, for the son at least, his emotions could find no clear or controlling symbols.

But we must remember that the Melville who wrote *Bartleby* and *Benito Cereno*, and even *Billy Budd*, was an authoritative and efficient artist. The symbolic war between the father and the son does not by any means fully characterize the mind of Melville—it was the madness his mind, in order to remain a continuing economy, had repeatedly to shed into its fictions.

The story of Benito Cereno is based on a chapter of the *Voyages and Travels* of Amasa Delano, a New England sailing captain who published his book in 1817; but as Harold H. Scudder has shown, Melville used Captain Delano's narrative freely for his own imaginative purposes. In Melville's version of the story, Captain Delano's sealing ship, the *Bachelor's Delight*, has put into the harbor of an uninhabited island off the southern tip of Chili for the purpose of filling her water casks. In the gray dawn, Captain Delano spies a strange ship moving toward shore and in danger of running onto a hidden shoal. He sees that the ship is in an advanced state of disrepair, and surmising that she may be decimated with sickness or lack of food and water, he sets out in his boat to aid her. When he boards the ship, which is called the *San Dominick*, he finds that the decks and the rigging are a shambles and that there is only an uncertain discipline among the men, largely negro slaves over whom the Spanish captain and his handful of Spanish sailors do not seem to have perfect control. Captain Delano attributes all this to the probability that the *San Dominick* has met with some misfortune, such as a storm, an epidemic, or a long calm. Benito Cereno, the Spanish captain, confirms this idea, though he does so with a mysterious evasiveness. He is reluctant to give the facts and puts off Captain Delano's friendly inquiries with a vague indirection which alternately exasperates the stolidly benevolent Yankee captain and rouses his suspicion. Perhaps, he reflects, Benito Cereno may be a pirate; the questions which the Spanish captain asks him concerning the *Bachelor's Delight*—what cargo she has, how large a crew, how many guns aboard—can scarcely be innocent. Yet Benito Cereno looks too much the young aristocrat to be a common cutthroat. Nor is his appearance calculated to arouse suspicion; for though he is a young man—twenty-nine or thirty—he is so attenuated by suffering or disease that he can hardly stand without leaning on the arm of his negro body servant, Babo, who never leaves his master for more than a minute or two. The apparent devotion between the two arouses Captain Delano's pity rather than his suspicion.

Yet there is a mystery aboard the *San Dominick* of which Captain Delano is constantly made aware. Benito Cereno never gives orders directly to the crew but only through Babo; Babo and his master impolitely whisper to each other in Captain Delano's presence; Captain Delano meets what seem to be almost desperately meaningful glances from some of the Spanish sailors; a slave boy slashes the head of a Spanish boy and two negroes trample on an unoffending Spanish sailor without being reprimanded; Benito Cereno falls into a fit of coughing and faintness whenever Captain Delano's questions grow too particular; the whole ship seems to be oppressed with a silent threat of incipient violence, as if everyone aboard were playing a part which he would suddenly put off and appear in his own person.

The sense of mystery and suspense are won in this most Conradian of Melville's stories much as they are in *The End of the Tether*. In Conrad's story the revelation is that the white captain is going blind and that this has been the reason for his remarkable dependence on his colored servant. In Melville's story, this dependence is suddenly explained when Benito Cereno in a final desperate effort jumps over the bulwarks into Captain Delano's departing boat and Captain Delano realizes that the negroes had revolted under the leadership of Babo, had killed all the Spanish officers except Benito Cereno, and had made a slave of their captain.

On the aesthetic principles of unity, coherence, and style, *Benito Cereno* is one of the best single pieces Melville wrote. The mood of the story is fully achieved and maintained to perfection. Melville's characteristic contrasts of light and dark are resolved into a gray monotone occasionally illumined by flashes of fire. As in *Pierre*, the main action begins and ends with the rising and setting of the sun. But we scarcely see the sun in *Benito Cereno*; rather we see its light indirectly through the continuous grayness of an overcast day.

The morning was one peculiar to that coast. Everything was mute and calm; everything grey. The sea, though undulated into long roods of swells, seemed fixed, and was sleeked at the surface like waved lead that has cooled and set in the smelter's mould. The sky seemed a grey mantle. Flights of troubled grey fowl . . . skimmed low and fitfully over the waters, as swallows over meadows before storms. . . . To Captain Delano's surprise, the stranger viewed through the glass, showed no colors.

Heroic actions, such as those in *Moby-Dick*, are absent; in *Benito Cereno* all is muted and somnambulant:

Upon gaining a less remote view, the ship, when made signally visible on the verge of the leaden-hued swells, with the shreds of fog here and there raggedly furring her, appeared like a white-washed monastery after a thunder-storm, seen perched on some dun cliff among the Pyrenees. . . . Peering over the bulwarks were what really seemed, in the hazy distance, throngs of dark cowls; while, fitfully revealed through the open port-holes, other dark moving figures were dimly descried, as of Black Friars pacing the cloisters.

The whole action of the story takes place almost silently. Collisions of objects do not produce the normal volume of noise. The hatchets which certain old negroes are polishing and which they clash together in an occasional ritualistic rhythm sound dull and leaden; the forecastle bell rings "with a dreary grave-yard toll, betokening a flaw." The central figure remains in a twilit stage of consciousness. Benito Cereno is "withdrawn." His spiritless passivity is stirred into action only in the form of sudden vague attempts at communicating with Captain Delano, attempts which are not always distinguishable from nervous starts and twitches.

Repeatedly Captain Delano has the impression that the *San Dominick* and her crew are not objectively real, that instead of boarding a ship and talking with her captain, he is watching a charade or a masque. True, as Captain Delano says, that is the impression one always gets in boarding a strange ship—"the living spectacle it contains, upon its sudden and complete disclosure, has, in contrast with the blank ocean which zones it, something of the effect of enchantment. The ship seems unreal; these strange costumes, gestures, and races, but a shadowy tableau just emerged from the deep, which directly must receive back what it gave." Yet the illusion is not dispelled aboard the *San Dominick* as in Delano's experience it always has been before. Again and again he is made to feel that he is watching "some juggling play" staged for inscrutable reasons by a company of mummers in mask and costume. But there is nothing bland or pleasingly mysterious about the enchanted performance, since every piece of stage business seems to be the symptom of an only imperfectly repressed violence. Actions aboard the *San Dominick* have the overburdened, muted futility which is best represented in dreams or in a surrealist movie sequence. Don Benito seems to "glide" about the deck rather than walk. In a burst of rage, a black boy cuts a Spanish boy on the head with his knife; but the whole action is only a ghostly parody of reality, an almost undiscernible ripple on the quiet surface. The masterly scene in which Babo nicks Don Benito's throat while shaving him and in some unexplained way Don Benito retaliates by gently slashing Babo's cheek is a somnolent, charmed representation of a deathly duel.

The mood of withdrawal, as we have called it, is a literary style in which Melville wrote some of his best prose. It is perhaps a peculiarly American style. In Melville, it is a twofold mood, varying from the infinitely moving lyricism of certain passages in *Moby-Dick* and *Benito Cereno* to a kind of closely knit textural style reproducing the complexity of subdued psychic experience. The lyrical mood carries us away from living experience toward the condition of sleep or death; the textural mood carries us back toward the sense of life. We often use the word "poignant" to describe the sensation of dying away from living experience. In *Moby-Dick* the "seductive god" and master of the Pacific elicits from Melville the poignant lyricism of these words:

When gliding by the Bashee Isles we emerged at last upon the great South Sea; were it not for other things, I could have greeted my dear Pacific with uncounted thanks, for now the long supplication of my youth was answered; that serene ocean rolls eastward from me a thousand leagues of blue.

There is, one knows not what sweet mystery about this sea, whose gently awful stirrings seem to speak of some hidden soul beneath; like those fabled undulations of the Ephesian sod over the buried Evangelist St. John. And meet it is, that over these sea-pastures, wide-rolling watery prairies and Potters' Fields of all four continents, the waves should rise and fall, and ebb and flow unceasingly; for here, millions of mixed shades and shadows, drowned dreams, somnambulisms, reveries; all that we call lives and souls, lie dreaming, dreaming still; tossing like slumberers in their beds; the ever-rolling waves but made so by their restlessness.

Or take the following beautiful sentences from the chapter of *Moby-Dick* called "The Dying Whale":

It was far down the afternoon; and when all the spearings of the crimson fight were done: and floating in the lovely sunset sea and sky, sun and whale both stilly died together; then, such a sweetness and such plaintiveness, such inwreathing orisons curled up in that rosy air, that it almost seemed as if far over the deep green convent valleys of the Manilla isles, the Spanish land-breeze, wantonly turned sailor, had gone to sea, freighted with these vesper hymns.

And then Ahab speaks:

"He turns and turns him to it,—how slowly, but how steadfastly, his homage-rendering and invoking brow, with his last dying motions. He too worships fire; most faithful, broad, baronial vassal of the sun! . . . Look! here, far water-locked; beyond all hum of human weal or woe; in these most candid and impartial seas; where to traditions no rocks furnish tablets; where for long Chinese ages, the billows have still rolled on speechless and unspoken to, as stars that shine upon the Niger's unknown source: here, too, life dies sunwards full of faith."

Life dying sunwards full of faith is almost a definition of Melville's lyrical style—as life dying to be reborn may be taken as a general definition of art. In *Benito Cereno* the lyrical mood occurs in passages like the following:

he saw the benign aspect of nature, taking her innocent repose in the evening, the screened sun in the quiet camp of the west shining out like the mild light from Abraham's tent, a passage which implies that the secret of Ishmael's paternity lies in the West. This mirage of the western light is one of the most poignant of Melville's images.

I include the "textural" style under the general heading of the mood of withdrawal, because though this style re-creates the complexity of living experience, it does so with a twilit consciousness, so that it still retains the muted quality of a dream or silent masque. Consider the following passage from *Benito Cereno*, surely of a very superior order of prose:

To change the scene, as well as to please himself with a leisurely observation of the coming boat, stepping over into the mizzen-chains, [Captain Delano] clambered his way into the starboard quarter-gallery—one of those abandoned Venetian-looking water-balconies previously mentioned—retreats cut off from the deck. As his foot pressed the half-damp, half-dry sea mosses matting the place, and a chance phantom cats-paw—an islet of breeze, unheralded, unfollowed—as this ghostly cats-paw came fanning his cheek; as his glance fell upon the row of small, round dead-lights—all closed like coppered eyes of the coffined—and the state-cabin door, once connecting with the gallery, even as the dead-lights had once looked out upon it, but now caulked fast like a sarcophagus lid; and to the purple-black, tarred-over panel, threshold, and post; and he bethought him of the time when that state-cabin and this state-balcony had heard the voices of the Spanish king's officers, and the forms of the Lima viceroy's daughters had perhaps leaned where he stood—as these and other images flitted through his mind, as the cats-paw through the calm, gradually he felt rising a dreamy inquietude, like that of one who alone on the prairie feels unrest from the repose of the noon.

He leaned against the carved balustrade, again looking off toward his boat; but found his eye falling upon the ribbon grass, trailing along the ship's waterline, straight as a border of green box; and parterres of sea-weed, broad ovals and crescents, floating nigh and far, with what seemed long formal alleys between, crossing the terraces of swells, and sweeping round as if leading to the grottoes below. And overhanging all was the balustrade by his arm, which, partly stained with pitch and partly embossed with moss, seemed the charred ruin of some summer-house in a grand garden long running to waste.

Trying to break one charm, he was becharmed anew. Though upon the wide sea, he seemed in some far inland country; prisoner in some deserted chateau, left to stare at empty grounds, and peer out at vague roads, where never wagon or wayfarer passed.

But these enchantments were a little disenchanted as his eye fell on the corroded main-chains. Of an ancient style, massy and rusty in link, shackle and bolt, they seemed even more fit for the ship's present business than the one for which she had been built.

Presently he thought something moved nigh the chains. He rubbed his eyes, and looked hard. Groves of rigging were about the chains; and there, peering from behind a great stay, like an Indian from behind a hemlock, a Spanish sailor, a marlinspike in his hand, was seen, who made what seemed an imperfect gesture toward the balcony, but immediately, as if alarmed by some advancing step along the deck within, vanished into the recesses of the hempen forest like a poacher.

What meant this? Something the man had sought to communicate, unbeknown to anyone, even to his captain. Did the secret involve aught unfavorable to his captain? Were those previous misgivings of Captain Delano's about to be verified? Or, in his haunted mood at the moment, had some random unintentional motion of the man, while busy with the stay, as if repairing it, been mistaken for a significant beckoning?

Not unbewildered, again he gazed off for his boat. But it was temporarily hidden by a rocky spur of the isle. As with some eagerness he bent forward, watching for the first shooting view of its beak, the balustrade gave way before him like charcoal. Had he not clutched an outreaching rope, he would have fallen into the sea. The crash, though feeble, and the fall, though hollow, of the rotten fragments must have been overheard. He glanced up. With sober curiosity peering down upon him was one of the oakum-pickers, slipped from his perch to an outside boom; while below the old negro, and invisible to him, reconnoitering from a porthole like a fox from the mouth of its den, crouched the Spanish sailor again.

An extraordinary number of concrete images passes through the mind of Captain Delano: mizzen-chains, quarter-gallery, water-balconies, deck, foot, sea-moss, cats-paw, dead-lights, coppered eyes, sarcophagus, panel, threshold, post, and so on. But though it is heavily weighted with allusions and similes, the passage is not oppressive or awkward in the sense of having unassimilated elements. The whole scene is lucid and graceful, and the disparate similes come together in perfect felicity. And despite the factualness of the passage, the scene is still enchanted, a magic texture of psychic experience. The muted, dreamlike quality is still retained, as we perceive from the kinaesthetic effect of the "feeble crash" and "hollow fall" of the rotting balustrade.

Those who think Melville's sensibility is merely imprecise and his language mere vague rhetoric will do well to ponder how wonderfully poised is the universe evoked by the above passage. It is a universe poised upon a present that continually merges with the opulent debris of a dying past and reaches into a vacant and terrifying future. It is a universe in which consciousness is poised between the rich texture of concrete fact existing in time (evoked by the images of decay and the historical references) and a void (evoked by the symbols of space: the dead-lights, the prairie at noon, the deserted chateau, the vague roads). It is a phantasmal world wonderfully conditioned by circumstance and yet trembling with the possibility of entirely unmotivated and irresponsible events, which may happen, as the cats-paw comes, "unheralded, unfollowed"—a world poised between necessity and chance, between reason and madness. Consciousness, furthermore, is poised between the essential experience of different cultures, between the labyrinthine history of Europe and the timeless emptiness of America, between Man in "the recesses of the hempen forest" and Man alone at noon on the prairie. And it is a universe poised between speech and silence, communication and isolation, a universe almost intolerably rich in associable human experience but a universe, nevertheless, in which men must try to communicate with each other with half-formed, half-intended gestures—a universe in which consciousness is completely involved and yet completely alienated. To present a universe thus delicately at rest within the tensions of its own disequilibrium is an *intellectual* feat which disarms all talk of Melville's being merely a "natural" genius.

The great themes *of Moby-Dick* and *Pierre* reverberate, if but distantly, in *Benito Cereno*. As on board the *Pequod,* that static tyranny to which we have applied the mythical name of "Zeus" is the ascendant spirit. The signs are unmistakable. On the stern of the ship is a carving of "a dark satyr in a mask, holding his foot on the prostrate neck of a writhing figure"—the relationship of Zeus and the Promethean hero. On the bow of the *San Dominick* there appears, not the usual figurehead, but the skeleton of the man who had owned the slaves and had been killed by them and fastened crudely under the bowsprit. Death pilots the ship; and on the ship's side have been painted the words, "Follow your leader."

Captain Delano is no Promethean hero. Unsuspicious, "undistrustful," he is a benevolent and courageous man. He is able to save Benito Cereno from the negroes precisely *because* of his spiritual superficiality—his somewhat mindless faith that everything will be all right, his optimistic belief in vitality and goodness. If Delano had lacked this kind of "confidence," he would have failed. As he says to Don Benito:

"the temper of my mind that morning was more than commonly pleasant, while the sight of so much suffering—more apparent than real—added to my good nature, compassion, and charity, happily interweaving the three. Had it been otherwise, doubtless, as you hint, some of my interferences might have ended unhappily enough. Besides, those feelings I spoke of enabled me to get the better of momentary distrust, at times when acuteness might have cost me my life, without saving another's."

(When we read in *The Confidence Man* Melville's attacks on good-natured, optimistic faith, we will do well to recall that in *Benito Cereno* he recognizes its practical utility.) Of course, Captain Delano had been very keenly if inconclusively sensitive to the mysterious terrors of the *San Dominick*. He had even had a moment of profound spiritual illumination:

He was hardly midway in the narrow corridor, dim as a tunnel, leading from the cabin to the stairs, when a sound, as of a tolling for execution in some jailyard, fell on his ears. It was the echo of the ship's flawed bell, striking the hour, drearily reverberated in this subterranean vault. Instantly, by a fatality not to be withstood, his mind, responsive to the portent, swarmed with superstitious suspicions. He paused. In images far swifter than these sentences, the minutest details of all his former distrusts swept through him.

In this sudden influx of confusion and doom, the central values of life and death become enigmatically contradictory. He knows that at the outer door of the corridor there is stationed a gigantic negro in chains, Atufal, who during Captain Delano's visit has been appearing before Don Benito periodically to ask pardon for some obscure offense. Captain Delano suspects that he will be waylaid by Atufal as he tries to pass through the door. The inverted and ambiguous values in this moment of terror are symbolized in the following sentence (which Melville writes as a single paragraph):

The Spaniard behind—his creature before: to rush from darkness to light was the involuntary choice.

Benito Cereno, the white man, is behind him in the dark. Atufal, the black man, is before him in the light. But Captain Delano shakes off the spell, as a spiritually untenacious man does. He passes unmolested into "the light" and sees "his trim ship lying peacefully at her anchor . . . his household boat, with familiar faces in it." The Yankee captain is a good man, committed pragmatically to familiar realities and the domestic virtues.

Captain Delano can therefore rescue Don Benito bodily from the mutinous slaves; but he does not understand that a spiritual rescue is also necessary. He is "astonished and pained" when Don Benito fails to rally from his experience and prophesies his own early death. "You are saved," Delano cries, "what has cast such a shadow upon you?" "The negro," Don Benito answers; and that is the abrupt end of communication between the two men.

Like *Bartleby*, which presents the parallel relationship of Bartleby and his employer, *Benito Cereno* shows the limited grasp on life of the successful American gentleman. It shows that he may do immense good in the world, but that he has a fatal limitation of personality which separates him from other men and renders his dealings with them imperfect and his future dark. "So far may even the best man err," says Don Benito of Captain Delano, "in judging the conduct of one with the recesses of whose condition he is not acquainted." Captain Delano is that familiar fictional American— the man of energy and good will bewildered by the European scene. For though Captain Delano eventually comes through to an equivocal happy ending, he is nearly lost in the miasma of ancient sin, chaos, and decay, an enigmatic world of ruined summer-houses in desolate gardens, of deserted chateaux and rotting balustrades— a savage forest of equivocations, treacheries, and uncommunicated talk among doomed men. The suffering of Don Benito, a son of the old culture, has given him spiritual light, but the ordeal has been fatal. Captain Delano, unacquainted with the further ranges of human experience, lives on. But plainly Melville is guessing that the accomplishment of the New World will be abortive if the American remains ignorant of the Old World's spiritual depths. The European, we see, has "withdrawn" into the Old Night ("the negro," in the abstract sense in which Don Benito uses the word, is to be equated with "Isabel" in *Pierre*), but he has failed to "return." The American, in so far as he is like Captain Delano, remains spiritually unfulfilled because he cannot decisively "withdraw." In Captain Delano we have another false Prometheus, though his failure is spiritual obtuseness rather than a neurotic compulsion to violent "escalade."

2

The Paradise of Bachelors and the Tartarus of Maids is remarkable for its sexual symbolism. The first part of the story is an account, half in reminiscence, of an experience during Melville's visit to England in 1849—of a jolly dinner in London with nine bachelors. Melville finds the bachelors cultivated and amusing. They drink heartily and take snuff liberally but there is no breach of decorum. Their celibacy frees them from the trammels of domestic life. But it also, as Melville observes, makes them superficial. Their grasp upon life is maintained only by their first locking the door against "the thing called pain, the bugbear styled trouble— those two legends seemed preposterous to their bachelor imaginations." Except for this tame observation about the effect of celibacy on the human emotions (a subject which Melville was to consider to better purpose in his poem called "After the Pleasure Party"), the sketch is undistinguished, remaining a piece of that hearty, jocose, rather clumsy wallowing in luxurious foods, drinks, and literary allusions which Melville liked to write from time to time.

But the second section of the story is one of the most uncompromising allegorizations of biological processes on record. Occasionally, it is *too* uncompromising, for Melville does not always find symbols which adequately transmute the brute facts into viable material, so that some of the symbols are monstrous, that is, half symbol, half fact. This is, of course, reprehensible in any work of art, though the half-symbols in this story have at least the psychological validity that they are like the half-symbols of dreams. The teller of the story, who uses the first person, is described as a "seedsman," with a seed-distributing business which extends over the Eastern states. On a bitter cold, gray day in January, he decides to drive to a paper mill some miles distant to order a certain kind of paper which he uses in great quantity as envelopes for his seeds. Wrapped comfortably in buffalo and wolf-skin robes, he rides behind his horse, Black, in the general direction of "Woedolor Mountain," a sort of Berkshire Venusberg. The approach to the mountain is expressed in kinaesthetic and visual imagery appropriate to the mythical identification of the body with the landscape (compare the forests which Milton describes as cloaking the sides of the mountain of Paradise and Melville's own descriptions of landscape in *Typee*): "The forests here and there skirting the route, feeling the same all-stiffening influence, their inmost fibres penetrated with the cold, strangely groaned—not in the swaying branches merely, but likewise in the vertical trunk—as the fitful gusts remorselessly swept through them." The paper mill is in a deep and desolate valley. To get there the traveler must go through a pass in the mountains with "cloven walls of haggard rock" and named the Mad Maid's Bellow's-pipe after a certain "crazy spinster" who once lived in the neighborhood. As the seedsman descends through the pass into the valley, he sees various streams of water which "unite at last in one turbid brick-colored stream, boiling through a flume among enormous boulders. They called this strange-colored torrent Blood River. Gaining a dark precipice it wheels suddenly to the West, and makes one maniac spring of sixty feet into the arms of a stunted wood of gray-haired pines." After passing through a "great, purple, hopper-shaped hollow, far sunk among many Plutonian, shaggy-wooded mountains," the traveler reaches the bottom of the valley. At first he sees nothing but blank, frigid whiteness. But he hears the "whirling, humming sound" of machinery; he looks around and sees a large whitewashed factory standing before him like a "whited sepulchre." In fact there is a whole white hamlet, including the snowy huts of the operatives. It is a submerged, Arctic city; a frozen vision, strangely broken by the violent red river.

The seedsman looks for a place to shelter his horse. A thin, pale girl passes hurriedly from one building to another, but only looks at the visitor, her "eye supernatural with unrelated misery." Finally, he is directed to a shed where he can tie his horse. He then enters the factory and sees "rows of blank-looking counters" at which are sitting "rows of blank-looking girls, with blank, white folders in their blank hands, all blankly folding blank paper." Strange phantasmal machines are to be seen in various parts of the building: "a huge frame of ponderous iron, with a vertical thing like a piston periodically rising and falling upon a heavy wooden block . . . a long apparatus, strung with long, slender strings like any harp." Tending each one of these machines, like a slave, is a pale girl. No human voice is heard, only the relentless hum of the machines.

The owner of the paper mill, who is described as "a bachelor," then appears and orders the only other male in sight to show the seedsman around the plant. The guide is a "dimpled, red-cheeked, spirited-looking little fellow," named Cupid. As the seedsman penetrates into the interior of the factory, he is shown the colossal waterwheel which drives the machinery with power furnished by the blood-red stream. After pausing to wonder at the fact that the red water produces only white pieces of paper, the seedsman is conducted into the "rag-room" where several consumptive, deathly white girls are shredding old rags upon long scythelike blades which stand one before each girl. Cupid jests callously about the blades and the consumptive girls, and the seedsman reflects that "the strange innocence of cruel-heartedness in this usage-hardened boy" is even more tragic and mysterious than the other "mystic sights" he has beheld.

Following Cupid, the seedsman

crossed a large, bespattered place, with two great round vats in it, full of a white, wet, wooly-looking stuff, not unlike the albuminous part of an egg, soft-boiled . . .

"There," said Cupid, tapping the vats carelessly, "these are the first beginnings of the paper; this white pulp you see. Look how it swims bubbling round and round, moved by the paddle here. From hence it

pours from both vats into that one common channel yonder; and then
goes, mixed up and leisurely, to the great machine. And now for that."

He led me into a room, stifling with strange, blood-like, abdominal
heat, as if here true enough, were being finally developed the germinous
particles lately seen.

Before me . . . lay stretched one continuous length of iron framework—multitudinous and mystical, with all sorts of rollers, wheels, and
cylinders, in slowly measured and unceasing motion.

Suddenly the seedsman spies "a sort of paper-fall, not wholly
unlike a water-fall; a scissory sound smote my ear, as of some
cord being snapped; and down dropped an unfolded sheet of perfect foolscap." The sheets of foolscap remind the seedsman of
Locke and his *tabula rasa*: the "human mind at birth," says Melville, is "a sheet of blank paper." The seedsman is overcome with
awe at the relentless precision of the machine. The "inflexible iron
animal" fills him with dread, as if he were about to be devoured
by "some living, panting Behemoth," just as the souls of the pale
virgin girls have been devoured by the mechanical monster. He
falls into a swoon, but is soon ushered out of the factory. In the
cold air, he recovers enough to find his horse and to ascend the
valley on the road by which he had come—an Orpheus turning
his back upon this Tartarus of Maids.

The sexual meaning of the story is adequately projected into
the symbols of the landscape so that we have the clear and completed sense of art. The apparatus of the paper mill provided Melville with a less satisfactory "objective correlative," and, as I have
said, the paper mill symbols do not rise freely or with integrity
from that which they are supposed to symbolize. Like the Titan
Enceladus whom Melville describes in *Pierre*, they fail to struggle
completely out of the earth, remaining only half realized, half
distinguished from the formlessness of the primitive material. In
short, they are the symbols of dreams rather than of art; they remain brutal, repulsive, hopelessly and hugely awkward. Yet the
story partly achieves the level of art, and so we can discuss its
moral and aesthetic sense more confidently than as if it were pure
dream.

The Behemoth which is at once beast and machine we have met
before in Melville—for example, Moby-Dick and the automaton

of Bannadonna. That there was a sexual significance in Melville's idea of the beast-machine has surely occurred to the reader. Yet if Melville had not written the story of the Tartarus of Maids, it might have remained obscure just how much sexual significance he was purposely trying to include in his allegories; this story indicates that the sexual theme in Melville's writing is deeply intended.

We can now be sure that what we have called the Promethean *élan* Melville closely associates with creative sexual power. Prometheus is a phallic divinity. Zeus is everything that inhibits and corrupts the moral, aesthetic, civilizing creativity of sex. He is the machine which unmans heroes—which castrates Ahab, which makes a narcissist out of Pierre, which makes a self-destructive "mechanician" out of the artist Bannadonna, and which sets up the metal phallus-icon in *The Lightning-Rod Man* and tries to make the Promethean hero its idolater. It is obvious, furthermore, that Melville is making a conscious connection between sex and literary activity. The "seedsman" who performs this allegorical intercourse upon a frozen world body is also the disseminator of messages on pieces of paper. Cupid is the guide not only of the sexual man, but of the artist. When the seedsman faints in the oppressive mill, it appears that Cupid may have been Death in disguise—that is, the writer of this story faces the possibility that his sexuality and his artistry may be forms of death from which there is no ostensible return. But that is not necessarily his fate; the hero escapes this frozen and desolate Typee Valley. Unlike Orpheus, the seedsman fails to find Eurydice, his "widely-judging queen," in Tartarus; he finds something more like the Gorgon. But also unlike Orpheus, he looks straight ahead as he escapes.

The remarkable story called *Cock-a-Doodle-Doo* deals with the artist's need for the sense of power and the guilt-feelings which accompany it. This story was quite possibly suggested by Wordsworth's "Resolution and Independence"; Melville quotes Wordsworth's lines about the passing of poets from "gladness" to "madness" and the whole meaning is similar to that of the poem. "Resolution and Independence" is a poem about the emotional crisis of an artist and is hence precisely the kind of poem in which

Melville could have found solace and instruction during the difficult years between 1853 and 1856.

The story recounts how the narrator rises early one spring morning, "being too full of hypoes to sleep," and walks out over the fields and hills. He feels ill and despondent, complaining of dyspepsia and rheumatism. The landscape looks like raw flesh and the cool, misty air and a far-off river seem "fever-and-agueish." He is irrationally interested in disaster, reflecting on certain recent train wrecks and fearing the idea of the steam locomotive, a monster which gets out of control and climbs the backs of other trains. He thinks of brides and infants who disembark from the wrecked trains into Charon's barge and set out baggageless for some "clinkered iron-foundry world." (The style of this story is informal and flexible, keeping the language close to the agitated thoughts of the writer. We get the impression that we are overhearing a man musing to himself.) He thinks rather too violently that if he were made Dictator of North America, he would string up all railway managers, that he would "hang, draw, and quarter; fry, roast, and boil; stew, grill, and devil them, like so many turkey legs." He remembers the bothersome dun who has of late been continually sticking bills under his nose—bills which he cannot pay.

Suddenly he hears the crowing of a cock, miraculous in its clear, joyful, triumphant tone. "Glory be to God in the highest," the fiery voice seems to be saying. And the narrator suddenly finds himself talking to a herd of calves. Listening again to the cock's crow—as exulting as "the great bell of St. Paul's" ringing at a coronation— he perceives a change in the landscape. The sky is now blue; fresh green grass begins to appear; the river flows joyously; and the cheerful whistle of a train can be heard in the distance.

He decides that he must seek out the miraculous rooster. But after walking about the countryside for a day, he gives up the search; apparently no one but himself has heard the cock and he cannot tell precisely from what direction the voice comes. But he continues to hear the song, which each time gives him a sense of strength and freedom so that instead of worrying over his debts, he throws the bill collector out of the house, confidently mortgages the property anew, reads *Tristram Shandy*, and takes a bottle of stout whenever he feels like it.

Then Merrymusk, a mythicized version of Melville himself, enters the story. A hard life—he had once been a sailor and a spendthrift—has given Merrymusk the outward appearance of a wise and sober Solomon. He is now a poor man with an invalid wife and four sickly children. They live in a shack at the edge of a swamp. Merrymusk earns a scant living by sawing wood, and once when the narrator had hired him, he had conceived a great respect for the woodsawyer by observing the wonderful calm intensity with which he performed a task to most people wearisome and disgusting. One day the narrator walks to Merrymusk's shack to pay him some back wages and discovers that Merrymusk owns the miraculous cock. Entranced by the radiant red, gold, and white coloring of the cock, which, as he says, must be Brother to the Sun and Cousin to Jove, he offers to buy it, but he is steadfastly refused.

Inside the shack the narrator finds Merrymusk's wife and children bedridden behind a curtain. But when, at the command of Merrymusk, the cock enters the shack and crows, the whole apartment is irradiated with the glorious sound and the wan faces of the invalids light up with new hope, though, as they realize, there is not the slightest expectation that any of them will recover his health. At this point the narrator first feels terror at the sound of the cock's crow, which reminds him of the voice of some "overpowering angel in the Apocalypse . . . crowing over the fall of wicked Babylon."

On a later visit, the narrator watches in terror while, as the cock gives one world-shattering cry after another, the Merrymusks die one by one before his eyes. And then, mounting to the rooftop, the cock sounds a terrible supernatural scream and falls dead. The narrator digs a grave, buries the Merrymusks and the cock, and has a headstone made with a stone cock perched upon it. From then on, whenever he is depressed, he sings "COCK-A-DOODLE-DOO!"

This story presents us with two pictures of Melville: the dejected and sickly man with certain neurasthenic symptoms who becomes joyful and strong after listening to the cock; and, on the other hand, Merrymusk, who is also buoyed up by the spiritual joy of the cock's song but over whom the cock gains a frightening ascendancy which somehow brings about his death. Wordsworth's formula—the poet's gladness becomes the poet's madness unless he finds a continual regeneration and displacement of vision—is repeated in Melville's story. The idea of madness is indicated by certain obsessive ideas (train wrecks, trains crawling over each other, the earth looking like raw flesh), but more importantly by the single obsessive, slowly intensifying cry of the cock, which (the narrator discovers by inquiry) no one can hear except the central figures of the story. The effect of the song of the cock, as it rises to its finally intolerable intensity, is ambivalent. The golden-voiced cock, a hieratic symbol of sheer power subdued to a majestic form, sings with the very rhythm of universal life. Since power subdued to form is a rudimentary definition of art, it is perfectly natural that the cock should fill the narrator of the story with joy—a joy which is not simply "happiness," but a displacement of vision which changes the narrator's whole perception of life. That is the ambivalent voice at its lower intensity. At its higher intensity the voice is a pure unconditioned affirmation of force, changing as the pitch rises into a hymn of destruction which the Merrymusks listen to with rapt acquiescence while it slowly kills them. And this I take to symbolize what happens when the artist's "gladness" changes to "madness"—though, of course, the artist's gladness is itself a strange amalgam of gladness and madness. The gradually rising cry of the cock is a symbolic statement of the translation of the artist's creative "joy" into a neurotic, libidinal quest for the ecstasy of pure destructive power. Merrymusk, who saws wood with as uncanny an intensity as that with which Melville writes fiction, has fallen victim to this Orphean song-turned-into-a-song-of-destruction, and its ascendancy over him not only keeps him from sawing wood, but brings about his own death and that of his family. Melville, whose artistic appropriation of power was so enormous (think of the ponderous movement and collision of great forces in *Moby-Dick*), must have felt very deeply the injury to human life which his neurosis might involve. The feelings of guilt are plain enough in the pathetic picture of Merrymusk's dying wife and children.

But the upshot of the story is an acceptance of "gladness" at the lower level of ecstasy: the narrator will sing "COCK-A-DOODLE-DOO!" This new resolution and new independence we cannot sup-

pose a poor compromise or a superficiality in a writer who has faced
so terrible a collaboration as that between the cock and Merrymusk. The artist who has had this vision is justified in indicating,
through the death of Merrymusk, that the Merrymusk aspect of
his personality does not point the direction which that personality
will take; that, in fact, the creative artist's personality will be continually reborn out of the continual dying away of Merrymusk.

3

In the thunderstorm at sea, Ahab orders that the ship's lightning rods not be used. Crying that he wants fair play, he challenges
the heavens to do their worst and promises that he will be defiant
to the death. The same situation is re-created in *The Lightning-Rod
Man*. But in this story there is an important difference. Here Melville expresses his faith that the Thunderer will not harm him as
long as he is faithful to his human instincts. The author of *The
Lightning-Rod Man* has exchanged Ahab's mad defiance for a calm
acceptance.

The scene is a cottage in the Massachusetts mountains. The
narrator of the story hears the hollow clatter of someone beating
on the door, instead of using the knocker "man-fashion." It is a
lightning-rod salesman with a specimen of his wares—a Zeus in
disguise. The narrator addresses him as Jupiter Tonans, and wonders if his throne is not on "old Greylock." "The stranger . . .
stood in the exact middle of the cottage, where he had first planted
himself. His singularity impelled a closer scrutiny. A lean, gloomy
figure. Hair dark and lank, mattedly streaked over his brow. His
sunken pitfalls of eyes were ringed by indigo halos, and played with
an innocuous sort of lightning: the gleam without the bolt." The
salesman tries to warn the narrator away from the glowing hearth,
which his Promethean instincts have impelled him to draw near
during the storm. The hearth is a dangerous place in an electrical
storm, says the lightning-rod man; but the narrator will not move.
" 'Mr. Jupiter Tonans,' said I, 'I stand very well here.' " Involuntarily, he steps from the hearth when the lightning-rod man repeats
that the hearth "is by far the most dangerous part of the house."
But he steps back again, assuming "the erectest, proudest posture I

could command." The salesman insists that his lightning rod is the only true one and that it is "of life-and-death use." He then discourses on the nature of lightning, observing that there is a "returning stroke" that flashes from the earth upwards, when the earth is overcharged with electricity. This "strangely inspires confidence" in the author, instead of alarming him as the salesman has thought it would. The lightning-rod man says that during a storm it is best to avoid crowds and especially tall men, at which the narrator exclaims, " 'Do I dream? Man avoid man? And in danger-time too?' " The salesman becomes more aggressive, warning the narrator that he may be reduced to "a heap of charred offal, like a haltered horse burnt in his stall." Still faithful to the hearth, the narrator now sees the lightning-rod man as a kind of celestial confidence man. The salesman's ridiculous "pipestem" is no fit negotiator between "clay and sky. . . . In thunder as in sunshine, I stand at ease in the hands of my God. . . . See, the scroll of the storm is rolled back; the house is unharmed; and in the blue heavens I read in the rainbow, that the Deity will not, of purpose, make war on man's earth." Then the salesman's scowl grows blacker; the indigo circles around his eyes enlarge "as the storm rings round the midnight moon." He flourishes his rod and leaping upon the narrator, tries to drive it through his heart. But the narrator frustrates the attack, dashes the rod under his feet, and throws "the dark lightning-king" out the door—knowing that the impostor will still "drive a brave trade with the fears of man."

The salesman's sample lightning rod is "a polished copper rod, four feet long, lengthwise attached to a neat wooden staff, by insertion into two balls of greenish glass, ringed with copper bands. The metal rod terminated at the top tripodwise, in three keen tines, brightly gilt." Reposing upon his Promethean hearth and refusing this monstrous idol of paternity, the narrator of the story is again the young man of the early novels, concerned with escaping his thralldom to his father. But the reaffirmation is expressed with a positive explicitness hardly attempted in *Redburn* or *White-Jacket*.

Melville again uses the chimney as a symbol in *I and My Chimney*. This piece begins in a leisurely familiar-essay style, describing the great central chimney of the author's Pittsfield home. The chimney is a comfort to an old man—for so Melville imagines himself; it is cozy in winter, it has a mellow air of tradition about it, the old man and the chimney meditate and smoke together during the pleasant hours of old age, and so on. But soon the close involvement of the old man with his chimney begins to be stated in deeper symbolic language. The heavy chimney, uncommonly large, has the ponderous, earth-delving weight and mystery of an Egyptian pyramid, and one day the old man succumbs to an irrational impulse to descend into the "far glens of gloom" in the cellar and dig around the base of the chimney for some lost "memorial." The chimney assumes a relationship with Melville's recurring symbol of the Tower. Usually the Tower is associated with the idea of Light, Space, and the Father; but it also symbolizes the whole range of withdrawal and return, extending as it does down into the earth and up toward the sky. The old man's wife has taken a dislike to the chimney, since it occupies so much space in the center of the house that it interferes with certain renovations she wants to make. First she pleads that a passageway be cut through the chimney and then that the chimney be removed entirely. She calls in an architect named Scribe, who comes to the conclusion that the chimney contains a hidden crypt. The wife assumes that the crypt must be the hiding place of the lost fortune which is said to have belonged to a previous tenant, Captain Julian Dacres, a sea captain and kin of her husband. She is now even more anxious to have the chimney torn down. But the old man is adamant and says that if there is a secret crypt, it ought to remain a secret and ought not to be profanely burst open. That, he feels, would be like bursting into the breast of his dead kinsman. He bribes the architect to sign a document saying that there is no hidden recess in the chimney. With this conclusion the wife must, overtly at least, be content. But she and her daughters keep up their policy of attrition against the chimney, forever tapping it with hammers, measuring it with tape measures, and listening for mysterious noises. Letters appear in the local newspaper, attacking the chimney as an eyesore. The wife draws up plans and estimates for renovating the house, another architect is called in, and once the old man discovers three workmen actually engaged in razing the chimney. But he manages to deflect every attack and to preserve his solitary attachment to the chimney. The chimney is slowly sinking into the earth, and the old man wants nothing but to sink meditatively with it.

Though in *The Lightning-Rod Man* Melville presents himself

as a Prometheus, in *I and My Chimney* he is Zeus. In this story the
intruder is a false Prometheus, a part played by his wife. The old
man is content with everything old: his old cheese, his old Montaigne, his old grapevine, his old chimney. But his wife is a nervous,
probing changer. Though old herself, she has an "infatuate juvenility"; she does not yet conceive of death as a possible reality and
cannot at all understand the old man's acceptance (as he gazes at
the ashes in the fireplace) of the "ultimate exhaustion even of the
most fiery life." She is a progressive spirit, and for her everything
must be new and contain a promise for the future: she is interested
in Swedenborgianism and spirit rapping; she devotes herself to self-
improvement by studying history, French, and music; she rises at
dawn and hates sunsets; she plants her flower garden on the north
side of the house where, it is obvious to the old man, flowers cannot bloom because of the cold north wind. She is, in short, a rather
foolish, mindlessly optimistic woman, and so when she declares
that her purpose is the divine Promethean purpose—to keep the
old man from "stagnating"—he is not much impressed. He is only
confirmed in his godlike posture as "a dozy old dreamer" who
dotes on "seventh days as days of rest."

The chimney containing the encrypted treasure reminds us of
a whole series of similar images in Melville's books, beginning with
the glass ship in *Redburn* and finding expression in such images as
the sarcophagus in the pyramid, described in *Pierre* and symbolizing the young hero's soul. Always before, the impulse has been
to break into the crypt and discover the inner mystery. But here
we find the old man no longer wanting to break in, and indeed
protecting the crypt from those who do. As usual the hidden mystery is to be connected with the father and man's search into the
past for the decisive moral basis of his being. Captain Julian Dacres
represents Melville's father. As Mr. Merton Sealts has pointed out,
"Dacres" is an anagram of "Sacred." The old man (as Melville
imagines himself) is content to accept the mystery as such and to
subside slowly in a kind of wise reverie toward his quiet extinction.

Mr. Sealts has suggested that the secret of Captain Dacres and
his relationship to the old man is their common insanity, real or
imagined, and that Scribe, the architect who comes to examine the
chimney, represents Dr. Oliver Wendell Holmes, who came at the

request of Melville's family to examine Melville for a state of ill
health that was obvious and a state of insanity that was problem-
atical. This interpretation seems very persuasive and it is surely
amusing to watch Melville dealing in his bantering way with the
suspicions of his family. One may assume that to Melville himself it was clear that he was not ready for the madhouse but did
have (in a sometimes morbid form during these years) the artist's
special kind of insanity. He may have speculated that though he
could see his way through his neurosis, in the manner described in
Cock-a-Doodle-Doo, he might yet be destined to cling to it lovingly,
jealously guarding its inviolability, and gradually destroying himself as an artist. But that was a portrait of the artist as *old* man.
And the old man's fate in *I and My Chimney* is not that of the old
man who died after writing *Billy Budd.*

I and My Chimney was written with Ecclesiastes very much in
the author's mind. "I correspond with no one but Solomon," says
the author. The impenetrable secret of the chimney is the God
whom it is vanity to try to understand. And the old man looks for
"no new thing" in the world. The ultimate fate which he envisions
for himself is like the appalling, silent apocalypse envisioned in
Ecclesiastes. Like a great tower, the chimney gradually sinks down,
falling away like a spine surrounded by interior organs, as the
rooms of the house surround the chimney. The old man desires
only to meditate and gain what wisdom he can before the subtle,
muted demolition of body and mind is completed, before, as he
says, the golden bowl is finally broken. This vision of destruction
he is determined to keep, as against that implied by his wife. For,
indeed, the "improvement" which she urges on him with "her terrible alacrity" is only "a softer name for destruction." The total
effect of the story is not a feeling of pessimism or morbidity. The
truly "morbid" person in the story is the wife who every spring
blithesomely plants her flowers precisely where the north wind will
kill them.

In considering the two short sketches called *Jimmy Rose* and
The Fiddler, we have to remember a similarity between the career
of Melville and that of his father. Both of them moved, or "withdrew," from the city after a period of success, his father as a mer-

chant and Melville as a writer of travel stories. *Jimmy Rose* and *The Fiddler* are stories of men who withdraw into obscurity and then in a modest way and with quiet wisdom "return."

The narrator in *Jimmy Rose* presents himself to the reader as a man who had lived in the city in early life, had moved to the country, and now, leaving his "white-blossoming" orchard, returns to the city, an old man with a "white-headed cane" and "white hairs." Unexpectedly he has inherited a magnificent old house near the Battery on a street once inhabited by wealthy merchants but now mostly lined by warehouses. He associates the old house with the memory of Jimmy Rose, who had once lived there and whose story is thus brought to the old man's mind.

Jimmy Rose had been a wealthy merchant, a sort of Cosimo the Magnificent, and had lived well in an expansive but genteel manner. He entertained frequently and well and became a social arbiter, admired for his taste, his dress, his wit, his French furniture, his bounteous board, and his delicate wine. But suddenly he failed in business and disappeared from view, accompanied by the jibes and imprecations of his fair-weather friends. The narrator recalls how he had tried to find out where the ruined man was living, in order to help him if his plight were, as he feared, desperate. He learned that Rose had shut himself up like a prisoner in the old house, the only piece of property he still owned. On a bleak, snow-swept day, the narrator found the house shuttered, locked, and desolate. After vainly knocking on the door several times, he succeeded in getting Jimmy Rose to speak through the keyhole. Rose refused to believe that the visitor was a friend or that, if he were, his intentions could be anything but treacherous. The narrator left sadly when Jimmy Rose pointed a pistol through the keyhole.

The narrator did not see Jimmy Rose for twenty-five years, during which time he imagined him to have died or to have become a pale wraith sitting alone in the front room of the great house, which was papered with a magnificent floral design—roses whose crimson must have faded and withered with time as inevitably as Jimmy's once remarkable ruddiness. Jimmy, however, gradually emerged from the semimadness which had impelled him to shut himself up in the house. He was "too good and kind" to be a misanthrope forever; he came to think it "irreligious" to shun mankind.

When the narrator next saw him, Jimmy Rose had become a

sort of jester in the homes of the wealthy people he had once so lavishly entertained. He had enough money to dine once a day on meal and milk, and he usually got a little bread and tea by dropping in on one of his acquaintances at teatime. His clothes were threadbare but his cheeks were alight with a miraculously eternal ruddiness. He was as courtly as ever and paid for his bread and tea by making graceful compliments to his hostesses or by discoursing on current political and literary affairs which he studied in the public reading rooms. Although he was well aware of the abjectness of his position and the hidden contempt which his hosts and hostesses felt for him, he appeared to have attained a state of inner calm and quiet, an uncrushable joy which put him beyond the kind of humiliation his acquaintances were able to enforce. The "undying roses" still bloomed in "ruined Jimmy's cheek."

As the story ends, the narrator sits in the house he has inherited, contemplating the rose-paper room where Jimmy, now dead, had cowered in his madness, and pondering the mystery of Jimmy's return to the world. How is it possible, he wonders, that "after that gay, dashing, nobleman's career, he could be content to crawl through life and peep about among the marbles and mahoganies" of the world whose acclaim he once commanded?

At the beginning of *The Fiddler,* a poet named Helmstone has just read a damning review of his cherished tragic poem. In a fit of despondency over his failure to achieve fame, he rushes out into Broadway, where he sees crowds of eager people moving into a side street where there is a circus with a much admired clown. Bitterly pondering this piece of irony, the poet is accosted by his old friend Standard, and in another moment they are joined by Hautboy, to whom Standard introduces Helmstone. The appearance of Hautboy is enough to soothe the poet's stormy passions. His face is ruddy, animated, and sincere. There is a strange juvenile look about him. At first sight his hair seems prematurely gray, but in reality, Helmstone decides, it indicates that he is forty or over. With good humor and vivacity, which act upon Helmstone like "magic," Hautboy hurries them off to the circus to see the clown. At the circus, Helmstone is more interested in observing the genuine joy which the clown arouses in Hautboy than in watching the clown himself. The marvelous, graceful juvenility of Hautboy makes

Helmstone compare him with "some forever youthful god of Greece." But looking away from Hautboy, Helmstone becomes gloomy again over the thought that if he were to take the clown's place and give a reading of his tragic poem, he would be hooted instead of applauded. But again he looks at Hautboy's face and finds its "radiance" a reproof to his intolerant pride. "At the very instant I felt the dart of the censure, his eye twinkled, his hand waved, his voice was lifted in jubilant delight at another joke of the . . . clown."

The performance over, they repair to a tavern for stew and punch. Here Helmstone perceives that besides vivacity and humor Hautboy has deep, serene good sense, excellent judgment, and the ability "to hit the exact line between enthusiasm and apathy." Espousing neither the dark side of life nor its bright side, he understands both sadness and gaiety. Rejecting all solutions, he acknowledges every fact. To Helmstone it is a revelation that such wisdom and such cheerfulness can exist in a man and yet not "arise either from deficiency of thought or feeling." Helmstone realizes that in making this "new acquaintance" he has in fact made a new acquaintance with the possibilities of life.

When Hautboy leaves the table for a short time, gloom again overtakes the disappointed poet. An artist who cherishes his sickness too dearly, he sneers at Hautboy, intimating that his cheerful good sense is made possible only by his lack of genius. "Genius, like Cassius, is lank," he says; and Hautboy is anything but lank. Standard, the friendly Philistine, suggests that Hautboy had once had genius, "but luckily getting rid of it, at last fatted up." To which Helmstone answers: "For a genius to get rid of his genius is as impossible as for a man in the galloping consumption to get rid of that." Then he sums up his case against Hautboy: his opinions are clear only because circumscribed; his passions are docile only because they are feeble.

Nothing tempts him beyond common limit; in himself he has nothing to restrain. By constitution he is exempted from all moral harm. Could ambition but prick him; had he but once heard applause, or endured contempt, a very different man would your Hautboy be. Acquiescent and calm from the cradle to the grave, he obviously slides through the crowd.

Later they go to Hautboy's modestly furnished rooms on the fifth floor of a warehouse to hear Hautboy play the fiddle. Though he plays only "Yankee-Doodle" and other "carefree airs," his miraculous style enchants Helmstone anew. His "whole splenetic soul capitulates to the magical fiddle," and he stands before Hautboy as the charmed bear stood before Orpheus.

When they have left Hautboy's rooms, Standard finally tells Helmstone the fiddler's real name, which the poet recognizes as that of a young prodigy who had once been an actor and for a short time had been everywhere acclaimed a great genius.* That he was a genius Helmstone could testify, for he himself could remember seeing the young actor perform. Now Hautboy makes a living by going from house to house and giving violin lessons. He is still a genius, and though no one recognizes him as he walks along Broadway, he is still happy.

"I have heard your poem was not very handsomely received," Standard says suddenly. "Not a word of that," cries Helmstone. "Shall not my petty affair be as nothing, when I behold in Hautboy the vine and the rose climbing the shattered shafts of his . . . temple of Fame?" And next day Helmstone tears up his manuscripts, buys a fiddle, and goes to take regular lessons with Hautboy.

The temple of Melville's own early fame had been similarly shattered, but, he decides, that is no reason to suppose that his genius has been irredeemably shattered too or that there is anything contemptible about redirecting his genius to less momentous undertakings. It is part of nature's process, as he had observed in *Moby-Dick,* to weave green foliage on the trellis of the dead white bones of the whale after the tempests have cast him on shore. Taking different forms and fulfilling different purposes, life slowly renews itself after death. Melville's short stories of the 1853–1856 period were vines and roses growing around a ruined tower.

* "Hautboy" Melville probably intends to mean "the boy who has flown high." "Helmstone" equals "the human clay capped by intelligence"—cf. the name "Pierre" and Pierre's determination to strike through the visor of the "Black Knight" (himself) who confronts him. Both "Hautboy" and "Helmstone" symbolize the polar extremes of height and lowness which Melville connects with the idea of the Fall of Man.

V

Israel in the Wilderness

Melville wrote the short novel called *Israel Potter* in 1854, taking the outline of the story from an account of the adventures of an obscure American hero which he found in a little volume made of "sleazy gray paper" and which he "rescued by the merest chance from the ragpickers." It is a lighthearted and unpretentious book, falling partly within the picaresque tradition. There are a number of incidents which remind one of Smollett: pants-tearings, rough doings in the English countryside and in English inns, humorous and adventurous meetings between rustics and noblemen, the triumph of gaiety and animal spirits over artificiality and cruelty on the one hand and sadness and violence on the other. But the debt to Smollett is slight. *Israel Potter* is a distinctly American book. The rapidly shifting scenes and the often inconsequential adventurousness, commented upon by a humorous or oracular muse, remind one of Melville's earliest novels. But *Israel Potter* is, perhaps, more beguiling than most of these. There are somber depths in the book, but they are less oppressive than in *Typee*. The self-conscious erudition, the rather heavy heartiness, the sometimes awkward language, the slightly oafish philosophizing of *Omoo* and *Mardi* Melville has pretty much purged by the time he arrives at *Israel Potter*. His style has become more mature, lighter, more sunny and open. It has achieved the nimbleness and efficiency which will animate *The Confidence Man,* though in that book it will gain a toughness and satirical edge unknown to *Israel Potter*.

As in *Billy Budd,* the action takes place at the time of the Revolution, a spectacle which always inspired Melville with thoughts of heroic accomplishment, bright hopes for the future, the nobility of the republican purpose, and the rights of man. As we have noticed and will again, Melville tended to imagine the most admirable of human undertakings as happening in a primordial world, opening out into lyrical or epical spaciousness and light. For Melville, the Revolution was the primordial age of the Americans. Israel Potter has many affinities with the other folk heroes who emerged so suddenly—as if from an unhistoried void—in the period of the Revolution. He was born among the hills of western Massachusetts, but soon, rebelling against his father's tyranny, took to the road. Like the typical Yankee folk hero, he became a jack-of-all-trades: a farm hand, a surveyor of wild forest lands, a hunter and trapper, a peddler among the frontier villages and Indian settlements. Fearlessly self-reliant, independent, and shrewd, he bargained and swapped his way through periods of prosperity and poverty. Later, this wandering Ishmael went to sea as a harpooner out of Nantucket. Through all his ups and downs Potter kept his ceaseless energy and easy-going humor. In appearance he was well made and agile; he had freckles and "lank and flaxen hair." His character combined the "gentleness of the dove" with the "wisdom of the serpent." He was rustic without being loutish, refusing through sheer inability rather than ill will to address an English gentleman as "Sir John," but managing to ingratiate himself with the gentleman even as he continued to call him Mr. Millet. Meeting certain English fops and exquisites, Potter is obviously their superior, and they perceive neither his manly strength nor his shrewd wit. In an encounter with King George himself, Potter has the better of it, treating the king with a noble civility while extolling the stubborn courage and high spirits of the colonists with whom Israel himself had fought at Bunker Hill. Faced with Potter, the king can summon no other mode of conduct than a kind of stammering urbanity and forced broadmindedness about the propriety of his talking with an obscure and intransigent rebel. Later, on a British ship which he has boarded by mistake, Potter, assuming the mask of the smooth-talking Yankee peddler, is able by a series of incredible falsehoods to convince the none too gullible British officers that he is a true Englishman properly signed aboard the ship. As Constance Rourke has shown, the agile, jig-dancing, shrewd, talkative, humorous, flaxen-haired hero was well known in the folklore of the first decades of the last century as Brother Jonathan, the figure who was gradually to change into Uncle Sam himself. Again, Israel Potter has strong affinities with Major Jack Downing and

Sam Slick, two humorous characters of the popular literature of the 1830's and 1840's who combined the character of the peddler with those of the hero and the politician and the foreign diplomatist.

Potter had fought with the "terrible farmers" of Bunker Hill, but, having been assigned to sea duty because of his whaling experience, he was later captured by the British and sent to England as a prisoner. In England he escaped his captors, on the Smollettian pretext of having to step outside of an alehouse to relieve himself, and after several incidental adventures found his way into the hands of some Englishmen friendly to the American cause: Horne Tooke, John Woodcock, and James Bridges. These republican-minded dissidents took Potter in, fed and clothed him, and finally sent him on a secret mission to Benjamin Franklin in Paris, with certain vital documents hidden in the false heel of a specially made boot.

The interest of *Israel Potter* is threefold: for the lively story itself, for its embodiment of certain of Melville's lifelong themes, and for the portraits of three American figures who are half historical and half legendary: Franklin, John Paul Jones, and Ethan Allen. As Melville re-creates him during the time of his embassy to the French, Franklin is a strange combination of the Magian and the practical man, with rather more of the Magian, in the sense of wizard or medicine man, in him than one might expect. Melville's attitude is humorously hostile. He makes his Franklin stand halfway between such fabulous zanies as Babbalanja in *Mardi* and that marvelous figure he was yet to create, the confidence man. Franklin is at once a likable, fairy-tale philosophizer and a charlatan. But he is rather more the confidence man than Babbalanja, so that he becomes in fact a sort of preliminary sketch for that deft and nimble fake who peddles his way through Melville's great satire. When we first see Melville's Franklin, he reminds us of an alchemist or a Paracelsus. Wrapped in a rich gown, the present of an admiring *marchesa,* and looking like a conjuror with his black skullcap, "the man of gravity" sits at a round table which is covered with manuscripts, models of inventions, pamphlets and books of all kinds. On the "necromantic" walls are charts, barometers, and maps of the New World. After he has greeted Potter, delivered a speech against the iniquity of tight boots and high heels such as he spies upon his countryman's feet, and made a note to get out a pamphlet on the subject, he learns that Potter bears secret messages for him in these very boots. Potter tells the grave man of utility how a suspicious-looking French bootblack has attempted to tamper with the secret heel, and Franklin replies, in a mood any reader of *The Confidence Man* will recognize, that Potter needs more confidence: "Sad usage has made you sadly suspicious, my honest friend. An indiscriminate distrust of human nature is the worst consequence of a miserable condition, whether brought about by innocence or guilt. And though want of suspicion more than want of sense sometimes leads a man into harm, yet too much suspicion is as bad as too little sense." During their relationship, Potter receives these sanctimonious speeches with a sort of amused, rustic impenetrability, repeatedly playing the innocent dupe to Franklin's righteous wiles yet always emerging the superior figure. When, for example, "the mild sage" gives Potter the following advice: "At the prospect of pleasure never be elated; but, without depression, respect the omens of ill," Potter feels as if "a plum-pudding had been thrust under his nostrils, and then as rapidly withdrawn." Franklin is always robbing Potter of something, and we always sympathize with the victim. Thus when Franklin invites Potter to stay to dinner, "free of cost," dinner consists of bread (not pastry, for pastry is "poisoned bread") and "white wine of the very oldest brand," which Potter soon discovers is plain water. Later, when Potter is installed in a room adjoining Franklin's (they are in a lodging house in the Latin Quarter), Franklin removes certain pleasant furnishings which Potter has got only to the point of inquisitively admiring: a bottle of Otard which Franklin calls "poison"; some Eau de Cologne ("a senseless luxury"); and some sugar ("bad for the teeth"). Then, warning Potter against a tempting chambermaid on whom our young hero has his eye, Franklin withdraws, leaving Potter to reflect, "Every time he comes in he robs me . . . with an air all the time, too, as if he were making me presents."

Melville observes that Franklin is like Jacob: a dedicated patriarch and protector of his people who has both the rusticity of the shepherd and the worldly wisdom and tact of the diplomat. If Jacob was a "tanned Machiavelli in tents," Franklin is a canny rustic in knee breeches. Again, Franklin is like Hobbes: "Indeed, making due allowance for soil and era, history presents few trios more akin, upon the whole, than Jacob, Hobbes, and Franklin; three labyrinth-minded but plain-spoken Broadbrims, at once politicians and philosophers; keen observers of the main chance; prudent courtiers; practical magians in linsey-woolsey." Under Melville's gently acerb portrait there lies a severe satire which emerges in full force only when he comes to assess the American character in *The Confidence Man*. For, admittedly, it would be difficult to be more American than Franklin. Humorous, gifted, agile-minded, grave without being truly serious, Franklin is "the type and genius of his land." "Printer, postmaster, almanac maker, essayist, chemist, orator, tinker, statesman, humorist, philosopher, parlor-man, political economist, professor of house-wifery, ambassador, projector, maxim-monger, herb doctor, wit: Jack of all trades, master of each and mastered by none," he is "a sort of handy index and pocket congress of all humanity." Only when we have understood *The Confidence Man* will we fully detect the acid ambiguity of epithets such as orator, philosopher, parlor-man, professor of house-wifery, ambassador, and herb doctor. Still, Franklin was only *one* type of American. He was, says Melville, everything but a poet, and in other American types there was poetry. Poor Potter himself was, by comparison, a poet. Here, he says as Franklin makes off with his Otard, his Eau de Cologne, and his sugar, "you better take the whole furniture, Doctor Franklin. Here, I'll help you drag out the bedstead." "My honest friend," says Franklin solemnly, holding the two bottles under his arms, "my honest friend, the bedstead you will want; what I propose to remove you will not want." "Oh, I was only joking," says Potter. The joke is low-keyed and mild, but what have Ahab and Franklin in common if not a fatal incapacity to cherish "the humanities" and to cultivate "the low enjoying powers"?

There is another American type who has a sterner and more heroic poetry than Potter. John Paul Jones, "a rather small, elastic, swarthy man," flashes upon the scene with the barbarous civility of "a disinherited Indian Chief in European clothes." An American by temperament and conviction if not by birth, he has "an unvanquishable enthusiasm, intensified to perfect sobriety, couched in his savage, self-possessed eye. He was elegantly and somewhat extrava-

gantly dressed as a civilian; he carried himself with a rustic, barbaric jauntiness, strangely dashed with a superinduced touch of
the Parisian *salon*. . . . A wonderful atmosphere of proud friend-
liness and scornful isolation invested him . . . there was a bit of
a poet as well as the outlaw in him, too." Demanding that Franklin
furnish him with a ship, he orates in the manner of the frontier
folk hero. He declares himself "an untrammelled citizen and sailor
of the universe"; and sitting erect as "an Iroquois," he rhapsodizes
upon the feats he will accomplish: "Give me the *Indien,* and I will
rain down on wicked England like fire on Sodom." The sultanism
of the fated killer is as much a part of Melville's Jones as it is of
Ahab: "to be effectual, war must be carried on like a monsoon,
one changeless determination of every particle towards the one
unalterable aim. But in vacillating councils, statesmen idle about
like the cats'-paws in calms . . . why was I not born a Czar?"
Having been introduced to Potter and having learned that Potter
was once in the brigantine *Washington,* Jones asks, parading and
posing like a "Sioux demanding homage to his gewgaws": "Did
your shipmates talk much of me? What did they say of Paul Jones?"
"I never heard the name before this evening," says Potter, and the
blunt answer immediately endears him to Jones.

But though a violent man of action, Jones is given to long periods of "reverie." Put up for the night in Potter's room, he insists
that Israel shall have the bed. Jones spends the night walking up
and down, looking sardonically into the mirror, studying the caba-
listic tattooing on his arm, and musing upon his past and future
enterprises. All night, like a prophetical ghost of tragedies to come,
"this jaunty barbarian in broadcloth" walks up and down in "the
heart of the metropolis of modern civilization." In the morning,
"care-free and fresh as a day-break hawk," he leaves "with his light
and dandified air," having kissed the chambermaid as if he had been
saluting a frigate. Later, Israel Potter sails on the *Ranger* and the
Bonhomme Richard as Jones's quartermaster, and we catch many
stirring glimpses of this "democratic sort of sea-king" with his
Scotch bonnet as he raids Whitehaven and fights the *Serapis.*

The terrific battle between the *Richard* and the *Serapis* is masterfully described in two long chapters. And Melville takes the occasion to symbolize once again the two modes of behavior which we

have called, speaking generally, Prometheus and Zeus. The *Serapis* and her Old World crew fight like a machine. Behind the guns of the *Serapis,* "tall and erect, the Egyptian symbol of death, stood the matchman, immovable for the moment, his long-handled match reversed. Up to their two long death-dealing batteries, the trained men of the *Serapis* stood and toiled in mechanical magic of discipline. They tended these rows of guns, as Lowell girls the rows of looms in a cotton factory. The Parcae were not more methodical; Atropos not more fatal; the automaton chess-player not more irresponsible." On board the *Richard* too there was the mechanics of discipline; yet it was quickened by the Promethean spirit of flexibility and sudden inspiration. Jones "flew hither and thither like the meteoric corposant-ball, which shiftingly dances on the tips and verges of ship's rigging in storms. . . . Yet his frenzied manner was less a testimony of his internal commotion than intended to inspirit and madden his men."

As Melville pictures him, there is much of the Promethean spirit in John Paul Jones. But Jones is, in Melville's final estimation, more an Ahab than a Bulkington.

The career of this stubborn adventurer signally illustrates the idea that since all human affairs are subject to organic disorder, since they are created in and sustained by a sort of half-disciplined chaos, hence he who in great things seeks success must never wait for smooth water, which never was and never will be, but, with what straggling method he can, dash with all his derangements at his object, leaving the rest to Fortune.

This was precisely Melville's deepest fear about the American character: that it would turn out to be inorganic, unstable, possessed by an enormous impatience which would lead it to plunge violently into undertakings for which it was unprepared. The penalty, as Melville tried to demonstrate in diverse ways, was that the American would be "unmanned." And though he cannot say it without pride, still there is a vast reservation in his prediction that "intrepid, unprincipled, reckless, predatory, with boundless ambition, civilized in externals but a savage at heart, America is, or may yet be, the Paul Jones of nations."

In Melville's portrait of Ethan Allen we have the American character stabilized, principled, and organic. Yet, as with Bulkington and Melville's other Handsome Sailor, we are not sure what, beyond a wonderful promise, the character of Ethan Allen is—whether it is a miracle out of time and context or whether, after all, it implies a stabilized, principled, and organic American society which we think cannot exist only because we do not yet understand our own culture well enough. This is the tantalizing question the character of Melville's Ethan Allen leaves us with. It is, at any rate, a wonderful enough character so far as we see it. As Israel Potter sees Allen, he is Samson among the Philistines, a reviled prisoner of war chained in the courtyard of Pendennis Castle. A truly Patagonian figure, he towers bravely and defiantly above the heads of the contemptible soldiers and townspeople around him. Eloquently he defies his enemies and praises the spirit of freedom in resounding periods which belie the rudeness of his ragged beard and his torn, half-Indian dress. Proclaiming himself the champion of the rights of man, he discourses upon the duties of the Christian gentleman as readily as upon the nature of reason and the problems of theology. Courteous, haughty, his whole mien bespeaking his experience and mastery of every dark and every exalted emotion, alternately pacific and ferocious, the flower of man's spiritual agony in the New World, Allen is the "true American." He is "a curious combination" of Hercules, the culture hero and civilizer; of Joe Miller, the quickening spirit of folk humor; of Bayard, the Christian chevalier; of Tom Hyer, the popular American champion. He exhibits no trace of the New England character. Though born in Connecticut, he is "essentially Western." It is as much as we get explicitly from Melville on the character of the "true American," the true Prometheus. The rest we must discover by indirection.

Like the nation for which he was named, Israel Potter wanders for forty—indeed fifty—years in the wilderness. We lose sight of him after he has been captured again, released after the wars are over, and has finally lost himself in London, where for long years he lives in poverty and obscurity. At the end we catch a brief glimpse of our "plebeian Lear or Oedipus," returned as an old man to the place of his birth and murmuring "Father" as he prods at the ruined stones of the house he was born in.

The London, or City of Dis, into which Potter disappears Melville describes with Blakeian overtones:

The Thames, which far away, among the green fields of Berks, ran clear as a brook, here, polluted by continual vicinity to man, curdled on between rotten wharves, one murky sheet of sewerage. Fretted by the ill-built piers, awhile it crested and hissed, then shot balefully through the Erebus arches, desperate as the lost souls of the harlots, who every night took the same plunge. Meantime, here and there, like awaiting hearses, the coal scows drifted along, poled broadside, pell-mell to the current.

And as that tide in the water swept all craft on, so a like tide seemed hurrying all men, all horses, all vehicles on the land. As ant-hills, the bridge arches crawled with processions of carts, coaches, drays, every sort of wheeled, rumbling thing, the noses of the horses behind touching the backs of the vehicles in advance, all bespattered with ebon mud—ebon mud that stuck like Jews' pitch. At times the mass, receiving some mysterious impulse far in the rear, away among the coiled thoroughfares out of sight, would start forward with a spasmodic surge. It seemed as if some squadron of centaurs, on the thither side of Phlegethon, with charge on charge, was driving tormented humanity, with all its chattels, across.

A man born "in a virgin clime where the only antiquities are the forever youthful heavens and the earth," a son of Space, has been swallowed up by Time, by the black, lightless stones of London and the age-old rhythms of its misery.

VI

The Sweet Voice

One reason for the general underestimation of *The Confidence Man* is the failure to see that, like *Israel Potter,* it is a book of folklore, that it examines the American character as it manifests itself in folk ideals. The confidence man is one of the most extraordinary figures in American literature. Melville was aiming very high when he created this character, and it has not yet been seen, I believe, how well he succeeded. If he succeeded, he did so because by the time of *The Confidence Man* (1857) his satiric vision of American life had attained its full clarity and he was ready to make his one definite adverse statement. Earlier, in *Moby-Dick,* he had achieved the fullness of his lyric-epic comprehension of the American spirit. But his work would have been less complete without what one is tempted to call his second-best book, in which he was able to display a ripe satirical intelligence in a style unique among his writings for its leanness, nimbleness, and jaunty vigor.

The action of *The Confidence Man* takes place on April Fool's Day, the day of the American Saturnalia, the Festival of the Practical Joke. The scene is a Mississippi river boat, the *Fidèle,* bound from St. Louis to New Orleans. The boat is the American world in miniature. The passengers are

parlor-men and backwoodsmen; farm-hunters and fame-hunters; heiress-hunters, gold-hunters, Buffalo-hunters, bee-hunters, happiness-hunters, truth-hunters, and still keener hunters after all these hunters. Fine ladies in slippers, and moccasined squaws; northern speculators and Eastern philosophers; English, Irish, Germans, Scotch, Danes; Santa Fe traders in striped blankets, and Broadway bucks in cravats of cloth of gold; fine-looking Kentucky boatmen, and Japanese-looking Mississippi cotton-planters; Quakers in full drab, and United States soldiers in full regimentals; slaves, black, mulatto, and quadroon; modish young Spanish Creoles, and old-fashioned French Jews; Mormons and Papists; Dives and Lazarus; jesters and mourners; teetotalers and convivialists; deacons and blacklegs; hard-shell Baptists and Clay-eaters; grinning negroes and Sioux chiefs solemn as high priests.

The book is a "masquerade" and the passengers a company of masks—a visionary, shifting, variegated tableau of American life, agitated by "the dashing and all-fusing spirit of the West."

At St. Louis the confidence man boards the *Fidèle*. He is an elusive figure, a portmanteau character who wears a variety of masks, shifting from one to another with his light-fingered dexterity almost before the very eyes of the passengers. At the center of this complex figure is the Yankee peddler. In the New York sporting journal *Spirit of the Times*, one could read (in 1850) a humorous sketch about "the Erasive Soap Man." He was "a sharp-eyed fellow, with a sanctified look," whose sanctification could be explained by the fact that his soap-selling spiel was always embellished with moral and philosophical uplift. "Gentlemen," he would say, "gentlemen, I offer you a splendid article, a superb article, an incomparable article. . . . Magical, radical, tragical, erasive soap!" His soap would clean man's body and his clothes. But more than that, if taken internally it would make the tongue-tied eloquent. Finally, the virtues of erasive soap were so expansive that they would ensure "the peace and welfare of society and the world." Melville's confidence man is based upon this folk figure, this smooth-talking, long-legged wizard, as Constance Rourke describes him, whose "driving pantomime and slow, high talk" beguiled the credulous, this magnetic medicine man into whose pockets the coin and silverware of householders were mystically impelled as he walked and talked in his jig-time quickstep. In public he always assumed his mask, so that, as Melville says of his confidence man, he left one "at a loss to determine where exactly the fictitious character had been dropped, and the real one, if any, resumed."

Melville's confidence man is a composite figure. The figure which Melville had appropriated from folklore was, in fact, already composite. He embodied the Yankee and the Westerner. On the popular stage in the decades immediately preceding Melville's book, the peddler had merged into the figure of Brother Jonathan, who came gradually to be presented in a striking costume: flaxen wig, white bell-crowned hat, blue coat with long tails, red-and-white trousers.

Finally, the Yankee peddler had become Uncle Sam. In the richly caparisoned figure who stepped jauntily aboard the *Fidèle,* the perceptive passenger might have caught a glimpse of Brother Jonathan, for though the confidence man wore cream colors instead of red, white, and blue, he had Brother Jonathan's fair cheek, his flaxen hair, and his high white fur hat.

The strange figure appears to be from some other world; he is a mythical being. Later in the book, as the confidence man descends into the hold of the *Fidèle,* he will be compared with Orpheus humming his magic song on "his gay descent to Tartarus." The confidence man is another of Melville's false heroes, the Promethean-Orphean figure who seems to be the bringer of life and civilization to his people but who is not what he seems.

As the stranger steps aboard, an act described as an "advent," he sees a posted circular offering a reward for "a mysterious impostor, supposed to have recently arrived from the East." As the man in cream colors stands with the crowd reading the circular, a peddler hawks a book containing "the lives of Measan, the bandit of Ohio, Murrel, the pirate of the Mississippi, and the brothers Harpe, the thugs of the Green River country in Kentucky"; and Melville interposes a warning that America must not be complacent because it has eliminated these famous renegados and murderers, for this is a nation in which, though wolves grow extinct, the foxes flourish. The man in cream colors then walks about the crowded decks. In his hand he holds a slate on which he writes slogans for the passengers to read: Charity thinketh no evil; Charity endureth all things; Charity never faileth. The passengers are annoyed by what they suspect is some kind of hoax; they feel vaguely sullen and resentful. They jeer at the strange figure; somebody hits him. Finally he conveys to the crowd the idea that he is a deaf-mute; then, mysteriously, he disappears.

Later he is spied sleeping in a corner; in his sleep he appears oddly mild and lamb-like.* He is, in short, a cruel, chimerical mask

* It is possible by a complicated process of circumnavigation to read *The Confidence Man* in a manner quite opposite from my own reading. The argument can be made that the confidence man is not a false hero but a true one, and specifically the true Christ. Melville (so the argument goes) was concerned to show how in a corrupted and commercial America the true Christ must operate, to show, in other words, that Christ can convert people to charity and faith only by means of confidence tricks. Thus Melville's book becomes a sort of latter-day of Christ, the very impostor advertised by the circular as "supposed to have recently arrived from the East." The Yankee peddler, Brother Jonathan, Uncle Sam, Orpheus, Christ—these are the main components of the character of the confidence man. Taken together, they embody virtues which would assure the success of the American venture: the acute humor of the peddler; the simple manliness of Brother Jonathan; the strength and patriarchal authority of Uncle Sam; the leavening ease and creativeness of Orpheus, the Civilizer; the charity of Christ, and his spiritual agony and vision of another world. All this Melville implies by attributing to the confidence man the opposite characteristics of these figures: the dishonesty of the peddler; the narrow-minded guile and provincialism of Brother Jonathan; the power worship and obscene senility of Uncle Sam; the spiritual sleight of hand of Orpheus; the effeminacy and sick humility of Christ. Above all, the frightening thing about the confidence man is that he is not a man; the perpetually shifty mask never quickens into the features of a human being.

Soon we see a crippled negro named Black Guinea, painfully moving about the deck on the stumps which were once his legs. Black, deformed, standing no higher than a large dog, he mumbles a curious tune and begs from the passengers. Opening his mouth widely and grotesquely, he catches the pennies and buttons which the gamesome passengers toss into it. A cynical man with a wooden leg emerges from the crowd and accuses the negro of being an impostor, insinuating that the negro's legs are not crippled but merely cunningly bound up to look crippled. He is a contemptible,

---

gospel. Now although I believe there is some ground for this argument, it seems to me finally only a minor ambiguous theme of the book and by no means a full account. The confidence man is a consummate and all-out pharisee; that is the great fact no argument about the book can get around. If he sometimes seems to be like Christ as the story goes on, that is in accordance with the essential paradoxical nature of pharisaism and cannot be accounted for by saying that the confidence man really is Christ and is only acting like a pharisee in order to make converts.

The fact that the confidence man displays certain Christlike traits in the later parts of the story seems to me less important than the striking fact that when he appears actually to be Christ, he has been *put to sleep* by the author. This I take to be an overt gesture of dismissal of the confidence-man-as-Christ from the conscious, meaningful, and discussable levels of the book. The Christ in Melville's unconscious mind, the "sleeping Christ," as we have called him, had great influence on Melville's works. But it is a mistake to make Melville more explicitly Christian than he actually was.

scaled-down version of Ahab—the earth-shaking willfulness with
which the whale hunter hurled his harpoon at the White Whale's
mask reduced to a commercial man's small cynicism. His suspicion
is contagious, and the crowd begins to question the negro. The
negro, who, we begin to realize, is the confidence man in disguise,
defends himself and gives a list of respectable people aboard the
ship who know him and will vouch for his honesty. Someone sets
off to find one of these alleged friends of the negro, but they all
seem to have disappeared or not to have been on board at all. As
the masquerade proceeds, the confidence man himself will turn up
in the guise of some of these friends. But meanwhile a handsome
young Tennessee preacher of heroic mien and noble purpose steps
forward to defend Black Guinea and challenge the man with the
wooden leg. It is reminiscent of Bulkington, the true hero, facing
his enemy, Ahab.

Assuming the role of a businessman and calling himself John
Ringman, the confidence man approaches a merchant, addresses
him by name, and affects to be an old acquaintance. The merchant
honestly declares that he never met a John Ringman or if he did,
he has forgotten him. But the confidence man soon convinces the
merchant that they are old friends, that he had once visited the merchant's home and met his family. It is easy work for the confidence
man: "A not unsilvery tongue . . . was his, with gestures that
were a Pentecost of added ones, and persuasiveness before which
granite hearts might crumble into gravel." Soon he has borrowed
some money from the merchant and disappeared.

As the scene shifts, the confidence man becomes "the man with
the weed in his hat"; he pretends to be mourning a lost wife. He
strikes up a conversation with a studious sophomore from college
whom he spies leaning on the rail and reading Tacitus. After many
pleasantries, which the bashful sophomore resents, the confidence
man succeeds in drawing him into a discussion of Tacitus. Taking
the book, he reads: "In general a black and shameful period lies
before me." This appears an unhealthy point of view to the confidence man. What this country needs at the present hour, he says, is,
not Tacitus, but confidence—a belief in progress and hope that
all is for the best. And he tries to argue the sophomore into throwing the book overboard.

Moving about the deck with his jaunty air and his Pentecost of
tongues, the confidence man now poses as an agent for the Seminole
Widow and Orphan Asylum. He is, we hear, the type of the "righteous man." Soon he meets a "good man." The good man is "perhaps
sixty, but tall, rosy, between plump and portly, with a primy, palmy
air." He wears one white kid glove; his other hand, though un-
gloved, is equally white. He seems supernaturally immune from dirt;
the soot which falls on the other passengers does not besmirch
him. He has a negro body servant who does all his touching and
handling. We suddenly realize that he is God, but he is God without the knowledge of evil: "scarcely could he have known ill, physical or moral"; his nature exempts him from knowing evil either by
observation or philosophy. Easygoing, benevolent, innocent, the
God of the good man, of free and easy progressivism, of improvement, service, uplift, and confidence, he is a soft touch for the
confidence man; for in the whiteness of this God there is no terror
or mystery, no reason for any enmity between him and man. He
listens attentively as the confidence man describes his charitable
schemes—which are more extensive than one might suppose. The
confidence man is recently back from the World's Fair in London,
where he went to exhibit a marvelous new easy chair for invalids
which he has invented. Also, while he was attending the fair, he had
issued a prospectus of his proposed World's Charity. This is to be
an organization designed to handle the world-charity problem by
the methods of big business. The whole situation, he believes, can
be cleared up all over the world once charity is properly organized. "Missions," he says, "I would quicken with the Wall Street
spirit." Why should mankind go on suffering from hunger, disease,
and neglect, not only in America but in China and elsewhere, when
the Wall Street spirit could soon solve the whole problem? People
need only place their confidence in him and he will organize the
World's Charity, a kind of universal easy chair for the whole of
mankind. The "good man," though politely skeptical about the
World's Charity, gives the confidence man several virginal bills for
the Seminole widows and orphans.

The scene dissolves and the confidence man emerges in the mask
of "the man in the travelling cap," representing the Black Rapids
Coal Company, a dubious or nonexistent corporation. He ap-

proaches the merchant of whom, in another guise, he had borrowed the money. Again the merchant succumbs to the impersonal silvery tongue and buys some bogus stock. They get into a discussion of the crippled negro. Possibly a worthy fellow, thinks the confidence man, but we must be careful not to misplace our sympathy. Perhaps he doesn't suffer so much as one might think. Perhaps the suffering may "exist more in the pity of the observer than in the experience of the observed." The confidence man, we see, is an emotional cutpurse as well as a monetary one.

The merchant tells a story about the man with the weed in his hat (the confidence man) to the man in the traveling cap (also the confidence man). The man wears the weed, it appears, not for a dead wife, but for a wife from whom he has parted. The wife's name was Goneril.* She was young, lithe, straight, and attractive, but she had something "stony" in her character. She takes to eating "dried sticks of blue clay" and to brushing against handsome young men, as if by mistake. When Goneril begins to persecute their seven-year-old daughter, the husband takes the child away. A women's-rights organization becomes interested in the case and urges the wife to bring legal action. Through the courts she succeeds in winning back the child and bankrupting the husband. Outraged and desperate, the husband pleads his wife's mental and emotional aberrations, whereupon he is himself judged insane. He flees before he can be shut up in an asylum, wearing a weed in his hat in memory of the young Goneril he once knew.

In accordance with his way of pooh-poohing everything tragic, pathetic, or morally complex, the confidence man proceeds to dissolve the moral values of the merchant's story in a solution of philanthropic sentiment. He sets about systematically obscuring the just behavior of the husband and the active evil of the women's-rights organization. The husband, he thinks, should have used "reason," he should have had more "confidence"; perhaps he was too hasty. If, says the confidence man, we admit any mystery or ambiguity in moral questions, people will take this to be a weakness. We must have confidence that the whole thing worked out for

---

* Egbert S. Oliver has pointed out that Goneril is based on the personality of Fanny Kemble, who summered near Melville at Lenox and whose divorce suit made a great noise in the 1850's.

the best in the end, despite the hardships imposed upon the husband. Yet it is, of course, the confidence man himself who obscures moral issues in mystery and ambiguity—either by hedging when the issue is clear-cut or by making a complex and difficult moral situation deceptively simple.

"Speeds on the daedal boat as in a dream." Briefly, the Promethean fire of the sun appears from behind the clouds which have darkened the scene, lighting and warming the passengers. The confidence man now appears as an herb doctor and delivers a long spiel in which he attacks "chemical practitioners" as dealers in artificial and deadly medicine. Herbs are the only specific that can cure the sick and rejuvenate the aged, for herbs contain the life principle. "Health is good," he says, "and nature cannot work ill." He quotes Virgil:

> "This is no mortal work, no cure of mine,
> No art's effect, but done by power divine."

The confidence man is a bogus peddler of the divine creative *élan,* a smooth-talking American Prometheus. Later our attention is directed to a sick old miser who has staggered on deck from his cabin in the hold. Raging decrepitly, he complains that a mysterious stranger has descended "like Orpheus" into the hold and relieved him of $100. The confidence man, not content with having robbed the miser, accosts him disguised as a purveyor of patent medicines and soon sells him a panacea called the Omni-Balsamic Reinvigorator.

But meanwhile a quick change of scene takes us into the lounge of the *Fidèle,* where the confidence man is trying to sell the passengers an ointment called the Samaritan Pain Dissuader. Into the lounge there ponderously strides a heroic figure "slanting his tall stature like a mainmast yielding to the gale, or Adam to the thunder." He is, says Melville, "a kind of invalid Titan in homespun"—a great stooped shaggy man with a beard "like the Carolina moss." He carries a heavy walking stick of swamp oak and has only just boarded the *Fidèle* at a little frequented landing, where he had been seen to emerge at the riverside from a clearing in the forest which was like a "cavernous old gorge." With him is a little girl in moccasins. She seems to be of "alien maternity"; perhaps she is a

Creole or part Comanche. She wears an Indian blanket, and her
eyes are extraordinarily large and "inky as the pools of falls among
mountain pines." In this invalid Titan the reader will recognize
another one of those we have called Melville's Maimed Men in the
Glen—Pierre, Ahab, Donjalolo, and the hero of *Typee*.

Parading a story of how the Samaritan Pain Dissuader had cured
"a Louisiana widow (for three weeks sleepless in a darkened chamber) of neuralgic sorrow for the loss of husband and child, swept
off in one night by the last epidemic," the confidence man claims
that his balm is "a certain cure for any pain in the world." In
answer to which the invalid Titan asks in a voice ringing with intimations of unknown spiritual agonies, "What was that last you
said?" The question "was put distinctly, yet resonantly, as when a
great clock-bell—stunning admonisher—strikes one; and the stroke,
though single, comes bedded in the belfry clamor." The bell sounds
the doom of the false Prometheus, as it had done in *The Bell Tower*.
The confidence man repeats his allegation, adding that the ointment is not an opiate, that it kills pain without killing feeling. "You
lie!" says the Titan. "Some pains cannot be eased but by producing
insensibility, and cannot be cured but by producing death." And he
all but fells the confidence man with a terrible blow. But again the
scene changes quickly; the invalid Titan and the little girl disappear;
the confidence man miraculously recovers from the blow and with
characteristic good cheer makes it known that he would be the last
man to bear his attacker any malice, as well as the first to turn the
other cheek.

The confidence man soon becomes the Happy Bone-Setter. On
deck he finds a man on crutches who is posing as a war veteran and
begging from the passengers. The confidence man, assuring him
that his legs can be easily mended, learns that the cripple is not
really a wounded veteran but that his legs are rotting away with a
disease he caught while languishing for several years in jail. It seems
that the man had unfortunately been a witness to a murder and
that in the legal entanglements of the case the murderer had been
proved innocent and the witness guilty, if not of murder then of
certain obscure crimes which merited a long imprisonment. "What
about this free Ameriky?" asks the bitter cripple. It is most certainly forever free, or will be, answers the confidence man (who

now refers to himself as "Mr. Truman"), if we only have confidence enough to believe that everything is in general improving.

As he first "unmasked" and then felled the ointment peddler, the invalid Titan was playing a part well known in American folklore: the part of the frontiersman taking revenge on the Yankee peddler for his easy talk, his sly dishonesties, and his false doctrines. The next scenes of Melville's book center upon this situation. Out of the weltering masque the figure of the "Missouri bachelor" sharpens into focus and confronts the confidence man. He is a civilized version of the wild frontiersman, but he retains many of the original characteristics. He is

somewhat ursine in aspect; sporting a shaggy spencer of the cloth called bear's-skin; a high-peaked cap of raccoon skin, the long bushy tail switching over behind; raw-hide leggings; grim stubble chin; and to end, a double-barreled gun in hand—a Missouri bachelor, a Hoosier gentleman, of Spartan leisure and fortune and equally Spartan manners and sentiments . . . not less acquainted . . . with philosophy and books, than with woodcraft and rifles.

No Omni-Balsamic Reinvigorator for him, he says, talking about the peddler of medicinal herbs. There is no special virtue in natural remedies as against artificial ones. Quite the contrary. Nature, as he has learned, is evil. Herbal remedies are likely to be poisonous: "What's deadly nightshade?" he sneers. "Yarb, ain't it?" Nature may be as fine as the poets say it is. But, he asks, who froze my teamster on the prairie and who caused the river to sweep away my $10,000 plantation?

Spying a victim worthy of his talents, the confidence man appears and objects to what the Missourian has been saying. There ensues an encounter well known in the humorous literature of Melville's time. "And who of my sublime species may you be?" the frontiersman growls at the confidence man, "turning short round upon him, clicking his rifle-lock with an air which would have seemed half cynic, half wild-cat were it not for the grotesque excess of the expression, which made its sincerity appear more or less dubious." The confidence man suspects that the Missourian's remarks cast imputations upon his character.

"Suppose they did?" with a menacing air.

"Why, then—then, indeed," respectfully retreating, "I fall back on my previous theory of your general facetiousness. I have the fortune to be in the company with a humorist—a wag."

"Fall back you had better, and wag it is," cried the Missourian, following him up, and wagging his raccoon tail almost in the herb-doctor's face. "Look you!"

"At what?"

"At this coon. Can you, the fox, catch him?"

And the Missourian leans on his rifle, looking at the confidence man's face "with no more reverence than if it were a target."

Still, the confidence man is able to engage him in conversation. It appears that the Missouri bachelor is seeking a hired boy but that he despairs of finding one that is neither dishonest nor lazy. Repeatedly he has placed his confidence in hired boys and repeatedly he has been disillusioned with human nature. "Yes, sir, yes," he says, "my name is Pitch and I stick to what I say. I speak from fifteen years' experience; five and thirty boys; American, Irish, English, German, African, Mulatto. . . . All rascals, sir, every soul of them." The confidence man then briskly sets to work to convince the Missourian that what he really wants is a machine, not a boy. A machine is the only good and faithful servant to be found in this corrupt world. Having planted this idea in the mind of the man from Missouri, the confidence man disappears. But he quickly reappears, this time as the traveling representative of an employment bureau known as the Philosophical Intelligence Office. Ducking and groveling with the obsequiousness of an insignificant man who represents an organization, he tells the Missouri bachelor who he is and asks if he can be of service. The Missourian says that he is in search of a machine to do the work of a hired boy. The representative of the Philosophical Intelligence Office is shocked by this evidence of lack of faith in mankind and he intimates that we find ourselves in a most degraded state of affairs when we begin to favor machinery over men. Summoning the full myriad of his silver tongues, he launches into a speech about the inevitable progressive improvement of mankind. As usual he works both sides of the street, maintaining on the one hand that there is no organic necessity which makes it inevitable that a certain kind of boy should become a certain kind of man and, on the other hand, that there is a natural principle according to which every change in human morality is progressive. "The child," he asserts, "is not father to the man." The principle of organic development which such an idea implies is repugnant to every right-thinking man. How horrible that a man should develop from a boy! But surely we need not entertain such a thought. The man is simply a *successor* to the boy, and though the boy be bad, the man is good. The flower merely succeeds the bud; the one is present, the other is past; there is no organic connection between them. From our privileged vantage point in this great progressive land, says the confidence man in effect, standing as we do upon the pinnacle of earthly success, prepared for us by the old unenlightened and undemocratic generations, we have the happiness to behold the principle of the universe —the wondrous successions, according to which light succeeds darkness, day succeeds night, reason succeeds superstition, goodness succeeds evil, innocence succeeds guilt, democracy succeeds tyranny, and confidence succeeds all manner of doubting, introspection, and perplexity. "In the natural advance of all creatures," asks the confidence man, "do they not bury themselves over and over again in the endless resurrection of better and better?" If the confidence man peddles a phony Promethean *élan,* he also peddles a cant version of Melville's own belief about progress: that it proceeds in a developmental rhythm, that progress is wrung from an unamenable universe by the suffering and death and, as we shall see, the Fall of enlightened men.*

But the confidence man's sales talk is persuasive. As Melville

* Later in *The Confidence Man,* Melville thrusts satirically at those who discount development, history, and the past. A disciple of Mark Winsome—a kind of Emersonian figure, a pinchpenny and sublime somnambulist—cries, "I will hear nothing of that fine babble about development and its laws." Certainly Melville would have detected the silver tones of confidence in Emerson's "Self-Reliance":

"Is the acorn better than the oak which is its fulness and completion? Is the parent better than the child into whom he has cast his ripened being? Whence, then, this worship of the past? The centuries are conspirators against the sanity and authority of the soul. Time and space are but physiological colors which the eye makes, but the soul is light . . . and history is an impertinence and an injury, if it be anything more than a cheerful apologue or parable of being and becoming."

Later, Melville was to underline the following sentence in his copy of Emerson's *Conduct of Life:* "In front of these sinister facts, the first lesson of history is the good of evil. Good is a good doctor, but Bad is sometimes a better." Melville noted in the margin, "He still bethinks himself of his optomism [*sic*]—he must make that good somehow against the eternal hell itself."

suspected, it was persuading nearly all of his countrymen and would continue to do so. Even the Missouri bachelor, on whose steadfastness the reader had so much wanted to depend, begins to lose his skepticism. Perhaps he was wrong to lack confidence; he will reconsider. Significantly, the line that finally softens the Missourian is a flattering appeal to snobbery, propriety, and easy optimism. Momentarily, at least, the Missourian is in such a spell that he cannot tell April Fool's Day from a summer evening. "Ah, sir," says the confidence man, "permit me—when I behold you on this mild summer's eve, thus eccentrically clothed in the skins of wild beasts, I cannot conclude but that the equally grim and unsuitable habit of your mind is likewise but an eccentric assumption, having no basis in your genuine soul, no more than in nature herself." To get back to business, the traveling representative will find a hired boy through the Philosophical Intelligence Office. The man from Missouri pays in advance. And though, almost as he hands over the fee, he realizes that he has been taken, the traveling representative has silently disappeared in the crowd. Left to ponder what has happened, the Missourian tries to fathom the character of the man who has taken him, "that threadbare Talleyrand, that impoverished Machiavelli, that seedy Rosicrucian." His conclusion, sinister enough, is that since all the "sleek speech" and insinuating flunkeyisms and philosophizings of the confidence man have netted him only two or three dollars, he drives his trade "more for the love than the lucre."

The Missourian resolves to become a confirmed misanthrope. His previous realism has proved an inadequate view of things. He will cut himself off entirely from mankind, content to play the outcast and to call himself Ishmael. But the confidence man is not through with him yet; he must try to make the final touch. A jaunty "cosmopolitan," gaily dressed in what is brightest from all the national costumes of the world, approaches the Missourian. He comes, he says, as "an ambassador from the human race"; he has "a fraternal and fused feeling for all mankind." He hopes that the misanthrope in coonskin and rawhide will soon regain his confidence in his fellow man. But the Missourian successfully resists these jovial advances by sullenly clicking his rifle.

The man from Missouri now recedes into the background, still

clicking his rifle, and the masquerade goes on, centering again during the next episode on the relation between Easterner and Westerner. The smiling, gaily clad, nimble cosmopolitan meets a man
"with the bluff *abord* of the West." They strike up an acquaintance;
the man is disposed to talk about Indians and Indian fighters. Oh,
Indians, says the cosmopolitan, they are the noblest of men, "I
admire Indians." The confidence man's new friend then proceeds
to tell the story of Colonel John Moredock, "an Indian-hater *par
excellence*." * Moredock was a frontier hero, a sort of Crockett,
but without the flashy egotism. He was a lonely man; he was
thoughtful, strong, unsophisticated, impulsive, on the whole unprincipled. Living almost exclusively among the works of God, still
there was little in him of a godly mind. As an athlete, Moredock
"had few equals; as a shot, none; in single combat, not to be
beaten." He had an "eye like Lochiel's; finger like a trigger; nerve
like a catamount's." He was grave, courteous, gentlemanly, could
on occasion be convivial and tell "a good story," though not about
himself. He was "silky bearded and curly headed, and to all but
Indians juicy as a peach." Like Ahab, Moredock had his humanities. But also like Ahab, he had suffered terrible wrongs from an
adversary with whom he must fight to the death, though the battle
transform his whole being. As an Indian-hater Moredock is an
ascetic, a dedicated and fated hunter, his blind but cunning rage
expending itself against the enemy who slew and burned his mother
and eight brothers and sisters. The confidence man's new friend
recounts the main episodes of Moredock's campaign against the
Indians, sometimes carried out in heroic, solitary forest vigils and
ambushes, sometimes at the head of small bands of frontiersmen.
The confidence man is horrified at this account of a man absolutely
dedicated to hatred and murder and can only cry, "Charity, char-

* Melville took his account of Moredock's life from "Indian-hating—Some
Sources of This Animosity—Brief Account of Col. Moredock," Chap. VI, Vol. II,
Sketches of the West, 1834, by James Hall. Melville writes as if quoting Hall, but
though he retains the main facts of Moredock's life, he freely rephrases Hall's
account. In Hall's *Wilderness and the War Path*, 1846, there is a chapter called
"The Indian-hater," in which a self-righteous traveler confronts a certain Samuel
Monson, who, like Moredock, is a dedicated Indian killer. The pious traveler
throws up his hands in horror and cries, "Wretch—miscreant—murderer! Begone!"
Monson then explains his grievances against the Indians, just as the storyteller in
Melville's book tries to explain the motivations of Moredock's Indian killing to the
pious cosmopolitan.

ity!"—there being no resources in his character which would allow him to accept such willed intransigence as a possible human reality.

The man who has spun the tale does not take kindly to the pious figure before him, but he assents to the confidence man's invitation to a friendly drink. They now introduce themselves: the teller of the tale is called Charles Arnold Noble and the confidence man presents himself as Francis Goodman. The theme of the Westerner versus Easterner is dropped at this point, or at least broadened out and abstracted so that Noble, in the ensuing conversation, stands for the free spirit, generosity, and good humor, and Goodman stands for righteousness, timidity, and puritanical conservatism. As they sit together over their drinks, the confidence man delivers himself of a two-faced paean to the glorious free press of America, which has brought American culture to such unprecedented heights and played such a commendable part in furthering the progress of democracy by its courageous plumping for "true reform." During this discourse, Noble becomes more and more irritated with Goodman, for whereas Goodman repeatedly interrupts himself to extol conviviality and the humanizing virtues of a pleasant drink and a good cigar, he does not himself touch either one, leaving Noble to drink and smoke alone. After a spirited defense of puritanism by Goodman, Noble, by now thoroughly nettled, exclaims, "Hey-day and high times indeed . . . sons of the Puritans forsooth!" But they soon get into an argument about Polonius and Laertes, the central issue being: Was Polonius fit to advise his son? Goodman says that he was eminently fitted to do so, and he makes of Polonius a sort of Father image, a symbol of justice and perfection. Do not "the snowy locks" of Polonius bespeak his purity, his righteousness, and his charity? We must have confidence in our patriarchs, he says; surely, ripeness *is* all and "old age is ripeness." These admirable qualities are precisely what Noble does not see in the character of Polonius. To Noble, Polonius's snowy locks are emblems of his senile tyranny, his complacent denial of all open and hopeful values. For him Polonius is an evil old man, kept on his legs by no more human force than "nature's automatonism."

Having defended old age as against youth, the confidence man proceeds to a story about a young man whom he calls "Charlemont, the gentleman-madman." Cryptically, irresponsibly, and with a sneer, he tells the story to Noble. Charlemont was a successful young merchant in St. Louis. He was graceful, witty, gay; he was loved and toasted by the best society. At the age of twenty-nine he became strangely morose and began to cut his friends with a fierce rudeness. He went bankrupt and disappeared suddenly and completely. After several years he just as suddenly reappeared. Where he had been and what he had been doing no one ever discovered. He just turned up one bright spring morning, "a restored wanderer." He quickly became once again the gay and witty toast of St. Louis society, "grew up like golden maize in the encouraging sun of good opinions." The young merchant offers the following explanation for his behavior, without going into any further detail:

If ever, in days to come, you shall see ruin at hand, and, thinking you understand mankind, shall tremble for your friendships, and tremble for your pride; and, partly through love for the one and fear for the other, shall resolve to be beforehand with the world, and save it from a sin by prospectively taking that sin to yourself, then will you do as one I now dream of once did, and like him you will suffer.

Except in relation to the whole of Melville's work, this cryptic story of Charlemont remains obscure. But if we recall again the theme of withdrawal as it appears in the other works, the story begins to make sense. As we have noted, both Melville and his father, the one as an artist and the other as a merchant, withdrew from the world after a period of success. In the story of Charlemont (as in *Jimmy Rose* and *The Fiddler*) Melville is pondering what Toynbee calls "schism in the body social"—that is, the schism which appears in a declining or unhealthy culture between the dominant classes and creative individuals. It is a "sin," Melville seems to be saying, for the dominant classes to cut off its Charlemonts. But in an unhealthy society—that is, American commercial society—the inevitable schism will appear. The genuinely creative individual will take up the challenge by voluntarily withdrawing. He will suffer the ordeal of spiritual isolation and will finally return, "a restored wanderer," to the body social. The confidence man would be the last to admit that the story of Charlemont had any significance or any relation to reality. Is your story true? asks Charles Arnold Noble. "Of course not," replies the confidence man.

A quick transition to a new episode brings a new character to the unconvivial table of Goodman and Noble. This character, Mark Winsome, is new in the sense that we have not yet met him in person, but we have met him in spirit: he is an embodiment of many of the confidence man's attitudes. He plays the part so well, indeed, that in this particular scene the confidence man seems positively admirable by comparison. It has not been clear in the scenes with Noble how much the confidence man (Goodman) has remained also the "cosmopolitan." But as Winsome appears, the confidence man again emerges clearly in his cosmopolitan's mask. Some writers have conjectured that Mark Winsome is intended to be a portrayal of Emerson; also it has been flatly denied on the ground that there is no positive proof of Melville's intention. My own feeling is that Winsome, though not intended to be an actual portrait of Emerson, is quite consciously intended to be the Emersonian man, a sort of vessel of Emersonism, and that some of his traits are derived directly from Emerson. Certainly Melville makes covert references to Emerson's essays on friendship and self-reliance. And Winsome, described as "a mystic," surely looks not unlike the Emerson Melville had once heard delivering a lecture: "a blue-eyed man, sandy haired, and Saxon-looking; perhaps five and forty [Emerson was fifty-one or fifty-two as Melville wrote]; tall, and but for a certain angularity, well made; a touch of the drawing-room about him, but a look of plain propriety of a Puritan sort, with a kind of farmer dignity." Thoughtful, rosy, youthful, the whole man was toned by "one-knows-not-what of shrewdness and mythiness, strangely jumbled; in that way he seemed a kind of cross between a Yankee peddler and a Tartar priest, though it seemed as if, at a pinch, the first would not in all probability play second fiddle to the last." Mark Winsome is immensely pleased with the natty cosmopolitan. Surveying his jaunty carriage and his colorful clothes, he says, "Yours, sir, if I mistake not, must be a beautiful soul—one full of all love and truth; for where there is beauty, there those must be." Then, with "infantile intellectuality," as Melville steps in to say, Mark Winsome descants upon the sublime inseparableness of goodness and beauty, extending his generalization to include the rattlesnake, which God in his bounteousness has made at once so good and so beautiful. Even the cosmopolitan cannot stomach this, and he shrinks from Winsome's cold, blue eye, which makes him seem "more a metaphysical merman than a feeling man."

The cosmopolitan invites Winsome to take some wine, but Winsome replies that his regard for wine is so extreme that he never partakes, fearing that to do so would be to destroy the beautiful abstraction. Having listened further to Winsome, the cosmopolitan asks if his opinions do not seem somewhat inconsistent. To which Winsome readily assents. Oh, yes, he says, "I seldom care to be consistent." Drinking bracing draughts of ice water, and looking at once the type of the mystic and "keen Yankee cuteness," Winsome descants upon metempsychosis, bewildering the cosmopolitan with occult references to the Egyptians and to certain obscure Greeks. As the cosmopolitan tries to change the subject, a demented wandering poet stops at the table to beg a coin in return for a sample of his wares. The cosmopolitan genially gives the fellow some money, but Winsome merely fixes him with a cold, reproachful stare.

A man named Egbert approaches the table and is introduced as Mark Winsome's disciple. Egbert is "a commercial-looking gentleman of about thirty" and "the first among mankind to reduce to practice the principles of Mark Winsome." So Winsome himself says, dropping some edifying thoughts on the relation of philosophy and trade as he turns to leave: "If still in golden accents old Memnon murmurs his riddle, none the less does the balance sheet of every man's ledger unriddle the profit or loss of life," and "Swedenborg, though with one eye on the invisible, did he not keep the other on the main chance?" After a long discussion of the meaning of friendship, during which the cosmopolitan and Egbert pledge themselves eternal friends, the cosmopolitan tries to borrow some money. But, says Egbert, "I give away money, but never loan it; and of course the man who calls himself my friend is above receiving alms"—with which the scene is ended. These passages on Emersonism, sharp and incisive as they are, speak undeniable truths about Emerson. But they should not be taken as representing in any complete form Melville's opinion of Emerson. The two men were deeply divergent in temperament. Melville with his sense of evil, his heroic intimations of space, history, destiny, and person-

ality, and his sympathy for the Western spirit would find much in
Emerson which he could not share or approve. Yet his attitude
toward Emerson was by no means uniformly adverse.*

An interpolated story between the Mark Winsome episode and
the concluding scenes of *The Confidence Man* seems to me a blemish in an otherwise fairly well planned book. It is a story of a
candlemaker named China Aster and his vicissitudes in business—
his borrowing money, his going in debt, his failure in business, his
death. The money-borrowing and friendship themes give the story
a rather specious connection with the Egbert episode. But the story
is unnecessary, and by failing to advance the movement of the book
or to sharpen the moral point it strikes the reader as a piece of
padding which the author ought to have left out. It has a mild
autobiographical interest. As he wrote *The Confidence Man,* Herman Melville, the Promethean light-maker, was in debt and full of
apprehensions about the future, as was China Aster, the candlemaker. The name is entertaining: an aesthete's name reminding
one of stars, and flowers, and exotic utopias, or perhaps teacups.
The rough and hearty man of whom Hawthorne could complain
that he didn't change his shirt often enough could, on occasion,
think of himself as an exquisite among the philistines.

After stopping in at the shop of the *Fidèle's* barber, where he
gets a free shave and argues the barber into taking down his "No
Trust" sign, the confidence man descends into the cabin of the old
gentleman who is to be his last victim. This old gentleman is, I
take it, Melville's version of Uncle Sam, of whom there is something in the character of the confidence man himself. It is a large
cabin, with several curtained bunks placed around the walls. The
old man, neat and comely, keeps a lone vigil at a perfectly round
table in the center of the room. He is reading a book. The whiteness of the marble table-top and of the old man's hair is lighted by
a solar lamp hanging above the table. The light grows alternately
bright and dim at the center of the room and fades into obscurity
at the periphery. There is an unlit lamp—like a "barren planet"—
by each of the berths, and in each berth is a sleeper. As the confidence man approaches and sits down at the table, he notices that

* This question has been studied by William Braswell in *American Literature,*
November, 1937.

the old man seems to have the "hale look of greenness in winter"; his hands, tanned from bygone summers, might be those of a well-to-do farmer, happily dismissed, after a thrifty life of activity, from the fields to the fireside—"one of those who at three-score-and-ten are fresh-hearted as at fifteen." Yet is there not something too complacent in the old man's mien? Does he not seem, Melville asks, a little too much like Simeon, convinced at last that he has beheld the "Master of Faith"? Is he not, even, one of those "to whom seclusion gives a boon more blessed than knowledge, and at last sends them to heaven untainted by the world because ignorant of it"? There is something soft and easygoing in the old man's character, and of this the confidence man knows how to make use. The old man has been reading the Bible. Borrowing it for a moment, the confidence man turns to the Apocrypha and reads:

"Believe not his many words—an enemy speaketh sweetly with his lips. . . . With much communication he will tempt thee . . . and speak thee fair, and say What wantest thou? And if thou be for his profit, he will use thee; he will make thee bear, and will not be sorry for it. Observe and take good heed. When thou hearest these things, awake in thy sleep."

But as the confidence man soon convinces the old man, this is indeed apocryphal and so need not be taken seriously or allowed to destroy confidence.

A bedraggled boy, a "juvenile peddler, or *marchand* . . . of travellers' conveniences," enters the cabin and approaches the table. "All pointed and fluttering, the rags of the little fellow's red-flannel shirt, mixed with those of his yellow coat, flamed about him like the painted flames in the robes of a victim in *auto-da-fé* . . . his sloe-eyes sparkled . . . like lustrous sparks in fresh coals." The strange boy comes with warnings about the uncertainty of life in these modern lawless days. He is peddling door locks and a device for detecting counterfeit money. The old gentleman suddenly grows weak and senile; he complains that he is losing his memory. He thinks that on the whole he had better buy a lock for his cabin door and a counterfeit-detector. The youth then tries to sell the confidence man a lock, but the confidence man refuses, saying, "Excuse me, my fine fellow, but I never use such blacksmith's things." The confidence man then lulls the old gentleman into a false sense of security, telling him that what he needs is confidence, not locks and counterfeit-detectors. Like a long-desired opiate the sweet voice dims the brain of the old man. Have confidence, it says. Rest assured. There is a very active "Committee of Safety" in Heaven. "Jehovah shall be thy confidence." The fluctuating light of the solar lamp slowly dies down. "Let me extinguish this lamp," says the sweet voice. And the book ends, as the confidence man turns out the light and gently leads the old man away. It is like the end of *Pierre,* where a celestial confidence man extinguishes the sun.

Seen in relation to Melville's other books, the symbolism of this final episode of *The Confidence Man* is understandable. At the immediate cultural level the old man has clear affinities with Uncle Sam; yet in the larger symbolism of Melville's universe, he is the Old God and Father of all the planets sitting at his death-white table at the center of the universe. The inhabitants of the planets sleep in the dark and suspect nothing of the cosmic crisis at hand. The youthful, fiery Prometheus tries to warn the Old God that all is not well, that he must meet life's dangerous challenges, that he must break the comfortable stasis into which he has settled. Prometheus is the eternal heretic who suffers from the persecution of the complacent, corrupt, and retrogressive God. It is his purpose to defeat the universal inquisition by which the Old God tries to rule the world; it is his purpose to awaken the sleepers, to enflame the death-white stone with his fiery *élan,* to force the Old God into motion. The purpose of the confidence man is to persuade the Old God that all is well in His universe. It is the confidence man's finest moment, his most cherished opportunity, his ultimate sales talk.

The Confidence Man is often said to be a disorganized fragment which Melville intended to finish but never did. The final sentence —"Something further may follow of this Masquerade"—does seem to indicate that Melville thought of adding more to it or of writing a sequel. However that may be, the book stands well enough in its present form. There is nothing to make one suppose that Melville suddenly dropped *The Confidence Man* in mid-career because he had reached a nadir of disgust and disillusion which made the subject unbearable to him. True, *The Confidence Man* is a disillusioned and savage book. But the author who wrote it was a buoyant, vigorous, incisive man who was achieving a new style and who found as much pleasure as he did disgust in the folkways he was portraying. "Hey-day and high times indeed!" A man cannot write a book like *The Confidence Man,* strong and compassionate to the last page, and then suddenly throw it aside in a rage of impotent despair, and even if he could, it would not affect what he had written. The book is carefully planned. It has the unity of any episodic work, the unity of the pervading themes. It has the dramatic unity of a dialectical movement of ideas. It is unified by the character of the confidence man, which, though it is a portmanteau character and tends to merge and then separate itself from other characters in the book, can be meaningfully summed up. The final episode, furthermore, makes a general symbolic and thematic statement.

The Confidence Man is a supreme achievement. More than any of his other writings it establishes Melville's claim to moral intelligence; it is an intellectual act of the greatest force and authority. The usual liberal-progressive line on this book is that the author's vision was warped and obscured by his "pessimism" and sense of personal failure. The reluctance of the liberal-progressive mentality to see *The Confidence Man* for what it is, is easy to understand: *The Confidence Man,* with its wonderful lilting poetry of motion and mask and its brilliant satirical thrusts shining against a dark but unoppressive backdrop, is an attack on liberalism; worse yet, it is an attack by a liberal.

The confidence man, that beautifully conceived and executed phantasm, represents all that was wrong with the liberalism of Melville's day: its commercialism, its superficiality, its philistinism, its spurious optimism, its glad-handed self-congratulation, its wish-fulfilling vagueness, its fondness for uplifting rhetoric, its betrayal of all tragic or exalted human and natural values, its easy belief in automatic progress. Yes, sir, smiles the confidence man, it is "the age of joint-stock companies and free-and-easies. . . . Yes, we golden boys, the moderns, have geniality everywhere" and some day we must have the "whole world genialized."

The liberal—let us not make a mistake Melville himself never made—is morally right in his objectives. Reaction is no answer. But just as Zeus must perpetually be saved from himself, so, Melville saw, liberalism must be perpetually saved from *it*self. The confi-

dence man is an abolitionist: when the Missouri bachelor asks him
point-blank whether he is or not, he delivers a long, obscure spiel
meaning "Yes." But this does not mean that Melville was in favor
of slavery. It means that abolitionism had to purge itself of the
spirit of Confidence. The confidence man can ruin every hopeful
liberal movement, and the Missouri bachelor understands why.
"You are the moderate man," he says, "the inveterate understrapper of the wicked man. You may be used for wrong, but you
are useless for right." Surely these words strike home to anyone
who has watched the modern American liberal movement break
down and surrender its responsibility because so many of its pro-
ponents have become "understrappers" to Soviet foreign policy
and the American Communist party. To become a party member
or a fellow traveler has been in our time the ultimate suicide of
the errant liberal mind—that mind which, as Melville knew, is outwardly bland and mild but inwardly the self-devouring prey of
exaggerated guilt, hostility, and the dark desire for surrender and
death. And what an ingenious array of ways and means to this end
have been invented! This softening-up process, this elaborate and
evasive rationalization is the chosen province of the confidence
man. Today the peddler of spiritualism, hybrid corn, persecuted
Christliness, little people-ism, and short cuts to international felicity
is fully as busy as was the peddler of bogus transcendentalism, the
Omni-Balsamic Reinvigorator, hermaphrodite saintliness, and universal easy chairs.

The work of the confidence man is to destroy moral distinctions,
to keep our fallible minds from making choices. When he was in
favor of capitalism, he told us that Wall Street and charity were
synonymous. Now that he wishes to reform capitalism (it is a
question whether he really does, since so many of his liberal views
have precisely the same superficial moral quality as capitalist apol-
ogetics), he tells us that, like Russia, America is a police state or
that, like the Russian press, the American press is in the hands of
the ruling class. The confidence man always wants us to present
ourselves to the world as neutrals; the sullen and defensive sellout
to a center of power or authority, if it is made at all, must be made
behind the façade of neutrality. And yet is it not exactly the condition of neutrality itself for which the liberal mind longs in times of

stress and difficulty? I take it that the white suit worn by Melville's confidence man, when he boards the river boat and when he appears as the liberal-progressive god, symbolizes neutrality—a universe where everything cancels out, where moral distinctions disappear, where all the light and dark colors are expunged, where consciousness, vitality, and action are purged of all natural grossness and efficacy, where man is "unmanned."

The American liberal mind has no idea of its own momentousness or of its own tragic career. The liberal habitually shields himself from this self-knowledge by convincing himself that he is a "harmless" man, that he is persecuted and powerless, that he is "just a confused liberal." Intellectually, he preserves himself from self-knowledge by refusing to admit that moral choices have far-reaching consequences and that thought, no matter how ordinary or workaday, has its complex resonances of moral, mythical, religious, and cultural meaning. The liberal man—any man who thinks and feels—lives momentously every day, in heaven, on earth, and in hell. The liberal, since he generally has unusual intelligence, ought more than other people to be aware of these resonances; and, since they are his and mankind's, he ought to be responsible to them. When Melville calls the confidence man "moderate," he means to denounce him for this failure of consciousness and responsibility. The myth which was central in Melville's mind during his whole lifetime—the Fall of Man and the symbolic polarities of Light and Dark, Space and Time, Father and Son, and so on, which derive from it—has precisely the quality of rich extension the liberal mind lacks. And of course this is the very myth the confidence man devotes himself to destroying.

The confidence man denies, in effect, that Ahab and Pierre are parts of the liberal personality, that their fates are tragic resonances of the liberal fate. The symbol of whiteness shows us that Melville makes this connection. Ahab abdicates from humanity and merges himself, in his violent and flamboyant rectitude, with the whiteness of the whale. Pierre "unmans" himself and, in his adolescent slavery to the absolute, merges himself with the whiteness of his pure father. And the confidence man escapes from the tensions and antinomies of life into the whiteness of his neutrality. This he does sullenly, passively, and without heroism. His form of death endures in life. He is more thorough even than Ahab and Pierre. For his final act of confidence is to deny the distinction between life and death.

In *The Blithedale Romance* Hawthorne undertook to show, among other things, how a group of generous and well meaning reformers can contrive with a fatal ingenuity exactly the kind of culture designed to destroy its most beautiful and touching member—the fair Zenobia. In *The Princess Casamassima* Henry James showed how another sort of liberal-revolutionary culture could defeat a woman, the Princess, somewhat like Hawthorne's Zenobia, and destroy a fair and brave young man. But to look into the volumes of American criticism dealing with these authors is to discover that, like *The Confidence Man,* these books are strangely neglected.

If our new liberalism of the 1940's—of which in political theory Mr. Arthur Schlesinger, Jr., is the most brilliant spokesman—is to merit its assertion of superiority over the bankrupt liberalism of the thirties, it must establish itself in the best tradition of the American past. The search of the older liberalism for "social realism" led it to a most culpable underestimation of Hawthorne, Melville, and James. We perceive now that realism can be moral, spiritual, and cultural, as well as "social." And we realize that liberalism tends to commit suicide by reducing itself to a stance of rectitude, a bondage to the absolute, or a mechanism for denying the necessity to think and feel. Liberalism has fantastically underestimated the conditions of survival in the modern world. The first condition of survival for any body of thought is the lively faculty of self-criticism. (This is especially true of liberalism, since in our time the attacks on liberalism by the religious and the conservative have been uniformly superficial or anachronistic.) On this score, *The Confidence Man* ought to be scripture.

VII

From Tartarus to Tivoli

The idea that he was living in Tartarus during the years from 1853 to 1856 often occurred to Melville. During these years he had found his way to certain kinds of reconciliation with life at less extreme levels of intensity than those to which his two most ambitious novels had been devoted. He had had periods of what Wordsworth called the poet's "joy," and out of this positive exhilaration had written such superior works as *Benito Cereno, Israel Potter, The Confidence Man,* and *The Encantadas* (to which we turn in a moment). Still, he had gone through long periods of suffering, depression, and debility. In Homer's picture of the inmates of Tartarus, Melville would have found a symbolization of some of his own states of mind. There was Tityus, the bound Promethean giant, whose liver was being eaten by two vultures. There was Tantalus, thirsting and hungry, whose mouth the abundant waters and the fruit perpetually eluded. And there was Sisyphus, grinding out his life into the dead weight of the stone which he was condemned to roll eternally up the hill. Melville as Tityus: the man who had withdrawn to suffer his ordeal. Melville as Tantalus: the man in a dry season searching for new sources of sensuous experience, the exhausted man searching for fact. Melville as Sisyphus: the dogged, laborious writer of fiction.

The Encantadas, Melville's fancied version of the Galápagos Islands, are a veritable Tartarus. From atop a high stone tower, the Rock Rodondo, which rises into the upper spaces above the Pacific, one can survey the Enchanted Islands, as one surveys an ancient city from the Campanile or the Bell Tower of St. Mark. From the top of this solitary white tower one has a "Pisgah view," a "view of space." The islands themselves are like twenty-five heaps of cinders dumped in a vacant lot. They are extinct volcanoes and look like a world burnt out by a "penal conflagration."

The islands are apples of Sodom, "once living things malignly crumbled from ruddiness into ashes." The special curse which "exalts" the islands "in desolation" is that they never change; they know neither autumn nor spring; they are transfixed in a seasonless waste. Yet there is the continual illusion of change, of pantomimic, protean movement. The Encantadas appear to shift position; they are surrounded with treacherous currents, so that a mariner may be caught in an irresistible offshore tide or a merciless indrift; they are wandering islands, notorious among navigators. And the islands themselves seem to change, taking on the appearance of a distant sail, a great city, or a ruined fortification.

Next to no animal life stirs here except the great tortoise, making his charmed, archaic, stonelike motions among stones: "the long languid necks protruding from the leafless thickets . . . the vitreous inland rocks worn down and grooved into deep ruts by ages and ages of the slow draggings of tortoises in quest of pools of scanty water."

The islands will drive any man who lives there to the greatest feats of human endurance or to the lowest depths of human depravity. Hunilla, an Indian woman who had come from Peru with her brother and husband, had lived there, no one could tell how long. Seated on a cliff, peering through a thicket, she had watched, as if sitting in a "high balcony" or looking out of a cave, the "sham tragedy" in which her husband and brother had died. It was as if "an invisible painter" were painting the scene as she watched the raft slowly break up on the distant reef and saw the two men sink down. "A dumb show" seen from a "blasted tower." That is the way many things looked to Melville during these years.

But Hunilla lived on, though the ship which had contracted to pick her up never returned. Putting her "trust" in the single fact of existence itself, she endured. It was possible to undercut all questions of reality and appearance, desire and knowledge; it was possible to live below them.

On one of the islands, fatherless Oberlus lives, or did once. Somehow, he urges his crops of desiccated potatoes and pumpkins out of the stones and sells them to the occasional ships which put in at his island. He is another of Melville's Maimed Men in the Glen. A "wild white creature," he lives in a desolate vale in a den of lava and clinkers. He is a dried-up shell of a man, whose only "potency" is an old musket which he uses to kill or enslave the occasional sailors who find themselves abandoned on the island. There is no central core in this man; no sex, no morality, no mind. He is distinguishable from the tortoises only by his "larger capacity for degradation." The islands have sterilized "the whole moral man" out of him. He is less human than Jackson in *Redburn* or Claggart in *Billy Budd*. The last we see of Oberlus, he cowers in a brick jail in the dusty plaza of a South American town. He is "a creature whom it is religion to detest, since it is philanthropy to hate a misanthrope."

In the last three chapters we have noticed some of the ways in which Melville treated the theme of withdrawal and return during the early 1850's. The protean, illusory, archaic world of the Encantadas represents the more withdrawn reaches of life. But the tortoise, a creature in whom life has withdrawn almost to the condition of stone, nevertheless also symbolizes certain modes of the return, the ascent back up the scale of life. We notice that "the spectre tortoise when emerging from its shadowy recess" displays not only its "dark and melancholy" back but also its breastplate, which is comparatively bright with "a yellowish or golden tinge." Melville remembers how strangely affected he was when some of "these mystic creatures" were brought from their "unutterable solitudes" to the "peopled deck" of his ship. "They seemed newly crawled forth beneath the foundations of the world." He thought of their "dateless endurance," their enormous capacity for sustaining life in an inert world, their quality of making themselves citadels against "the assaults of Time." Sleeping under the deck, he could hear the tortoises moving about above him, the "slow, weary draggings" of these ponderous Sisyphean beings whose resolution or stupidity was so great that they would never go aside for any impediment. At sunrise Melville found one of them "butted like a battering-ram against the immovable foot of the foremast, and still striving, tooth and nail, to force the impossible passage." And he reflected that "these tortoises are the victims of a penal, or malignant, or perhaps a downright diabolical enchanter. . . . I have known them in their journeyings to ram themselves heroically against rocks and long abide there, nudging, wriggling, wedging, in order to displace them, and so hold on their inflexible path. Their crowning curse is their drudging impulse to straightforwardness in a belittered world." Yet though these creatures might be accursed, they survived. At times one must be like a tortoise, pushing one's way out from under the dark recess at the foundation of the world, wedging one's way among rocks, wriggling, nudging, and enduring. In a dream Melville saw himself and two Brahmins riding with crossed legs on the backs of three tortoises. Melville rode before the two Brahmins, one of whom was on either side. Their foreheads formed a tripod "which upheld the universal cope."

2

A man looking out under the cope from the Tartarean Enchanted Isles will easily be convinced that Paradise is not in heaven but in the living commotion of society and nature. And it was this sense of life which Melville was recapturing in 1856–1857 when he traveled to Europe and the Near East (on the recommendation and at the expense of his in-laws). He was emotionally exhausted when he set out on his travels, and he had an enormous appetite for sensuous experience, for watching people do things, for examining every object that he could see. He wanted to recover his sense of fact and of living reality and to find his way again to the sources of energy. He wanted, as he said, "to saturate his mind."

The *Journal Up the Straits* records the trip, from Glasgow to the Mediterranean, Constantinople, Egypt, Palestine, Athens, Naples, Rome, Florence, Venice, Milan, and back to England. The style is telegraphic, spontaneous, and fragmentary. It is, indeed, a breaking up of style—a sort of hungry setting down of nouns, adjectives, verbs, and adverbs in order to bring the sense of life as immediately as possible into consciousness. For Melville the voyage was always, as he said at the beginning of *Moby-Dick*, a "breaking up of the ice-bound stream." I shall not try to schematize my account of Melville's *Journal*. (Quotations from the *Journal*—I use Raymond Weaver's edition—are always subject to correction; Melville's handwriting was sometimes illegible.)

On November 24, Melville sailed through the Pillars of Hercules and recorded his impression of great size and power, subdued in majestic calm: "Insular Rock. Sunset. Rock strongly lit, all the rest in shade. Vast heigth. Red sky. Sunset in the Straights. Gate of the East. Many ships . . . Calm within Straits. Long swell took us. The Mediterranean." Here was "such weather as one might have in Paradise."

On December 2 he disembarked at Syra and was struck by the "animated appearance of the quay: colorfully dressed men weighing bales, counting codfish, sitting at tables on the dock, smoking, talking, sauntering. . . . Picturesqueness of the whole. Variety of it. Greek trousers . . . white petticoats . . . Fine forms." It looked like a wonderfully animated masque, as if someone had taken "all the actors of opera in a night from the theaters of London" and set them down at Syra.

At Salonica one observed the contiguity of dead and live cultures: Greek churches turned into mosques; the remains of a triumphal arch bearing the Roman eagle. The weather was mild and gloriously clear. The "uproar" of the mixed European-Asiatic crowds. "Two negresses, faces covered to conceal their beauty," came aboard the ship as passengers. "Cold and snowy" in the sun, Mount Olympus looked down on the scene. The gods seemed to take no interest. At night Olympus "glittered at top with ice" and looked unreal, as compared with some "very pretty women" belonging to a "fine old effendi" who had come aboard.

The first sight of Constantinople was erotic, a woman lifting her skirts. The fog lifted slowly, allowing only part of the city to be seen. "Could see the base & wall of St. Sophia but not the dome. It was a coy disclosure, a kind of coquetting, leaving room for imagination & heightening the scene."

The first day in Constantinople (December 13) Melville took "a terrible long walk." He felt oppressed and longed for space. "Perfect labyrinth. Narrow. Close, shut in. If one could get *up*. Aloft, it would be easy to see one's way out. . . . Soar out of the maze. But no."

The "Burnt Column" interested him; he visited it twice. He found it "black & grimy enough & hooped about with iron. . . . It leans, is split & chipped & cracked." It was like a statue of Ahab, the son and king-father, blasted by fire.

Nature and man conspired to lead Melville through the rhythm of withdrawal and return. In Constantinople he descended into the Cistern of 1001 Columns. You look "down into a grove of marble pillars, fading away into utter darkness. A palatial sort of Tartarus . . . Used to be a reservoir. Now full of boys twisting silk. Great hubbub. Flit about like imps. Whir of the spinning jennies . . . Terrible place to be robbed or murdered in." A Tartarus of Boys to match the Tartarus of Maids. He does not describe getting back out: he just says, "Came out." A return to the world at its busiest point: "To the Bazarr. A wilderness of traffic. Furniture, arms, silks, confectionery, shoes, saddles—everything. . . . Immense crowds. Georgians, Armenians, Greeks, Jews & Turks." Then he visited a "Tower of vast girth & heigth in the Sarecenic style—a column. From the top, my God, what a view!"

In Stamboul on December 14 he again thought of the "ghost of Rome," which, as he contemplated the aqueduct of Valens, "seemed to stride with disdain."

The Jewish, Greek, and Armenian women he saw in the streets of Constantinople struck him as being singularly beautiful as compared with English and American women. He saw "lovely girls" peeping coyly out of paupers' hovels like lilies and roses in cracked flowerpots.

On December 15: "mounted the Genoese Tower. A prodigious structure. 60 feet in diameter. 200 or more high. Walls 12 thick."
The Tower is the symbol of man's ego and his command over space. *Moby-Dick,* Melville thought, was a tower. He found the dome of St. Sophia a marvelous "appropriation of space." The problem of the artist was how to appropriate space. Unappropriated it was sheer sterilized emptiness, the greatest horror man could know, or fail to know. To unmask Space and to mask it again in

man's measurement was the problem. Melville traveled about Europe and the Near East to see how man had measured space.

After he had visited the Genoese Tower, he was followed for two or three hours through the streets by "an infernal Greek, & confederates. . . . The mere mysterious, persistent, silent following." It was like the mindless hunt of the backwoodsman after the Indian or the ship after the White Whale.

The tree and the tower. These are often linked in Melville's mind. "The Cypress a green minaret, & blends with the stone ones. Minaret perhaps derived from cypress shape. The intermingling of the dark tree with the bright spire expressive of the intermingling of life & death." The tree is nature's appropriation of space, mindless but living. The tower performs the conscious appropriation in the form of art, which is a kind of death.

At Smyrna on December 21, Melville dined with a Captain Orpheus.

On December 31, Melville visited the Pyramids. They terrified him. They were Space itself, giving the idea of vastness more than any natural object, dwarfing man and swallowing him, casting no shadow for the better part of the day. Climbing the pyramid, Melville found himself "oppressed by the massiveness & mystery." He felt awe and terror and dreaded the Arab guides, who seemed so much at home here and one of whom "offered to lead me into a side-hole." In the interior of the pyramid he thought that here the idea of Jehovah had been conceived. The avenging God and maimer of men was a "terrible mixture of the cunning and awful. Moses learned in all the lore of the Egyptians."

The pyramid endures against all the laws of nature, a tower that refuses to collapse, despite the ruin of the outer shell. It refuses both death and rebirth. *"No vestige of moss upon them. Not the least. Other ruins ivied. Dry as tinder. No speck of green."*

The pyramid terrified Melville because it is a tower that does not measure space. "The vast plane. No wall, no roof. In other buildings, however vast, the eye is gradually innured to the sense of magnitude, by passing from part to part. But here there is no stay or stage. It is all or nothing. It is not the sense of height (or breadth or length or depth that is stirred) but the sense of immensity. . . . Its simplicity confounds you. . . . It refuses to be studied or adequately comprehended. . . . A dead calm of masonry." The thought of the labor and damage to human life that had produced the pyramid was overwhelmingly ironic, for "Man seems to have had very little to do" with building it. It represented man's absorption into the faceless void, the sterilization of personality. Like the idea of God, the pyramid was conceived by a supernatural being, the priest.

The whole landscape of Egypt from Pompey's Pillar to Cheops seemed painted by an invisible painter: "unreal & a panorama."

After the Pyramids it was a relief to be in the great square of Cairo, which was space peopled and principled. "Large extent of square . . . Leapers, tumblers, jugglers, smokers, dancers, horses, swings (with bells), sherbert, &c. Lovely at evening. In morning, golden sun through foliage . . . Paradise melted and poured into the air."

During January of 1857 Melville was in Palestine. Palestine was stone. "Whitish mildew pervading whole tracts of landscape— bleached—leprosy—encrustation of curses—old cheese—bones of rocks—crunched, gnawed & mumbled. . . . No moss as in other ruins—no grace of decay—no ivy—the unleavened nakedness of desolation—whitish ashes—lime-kilns—You see the anatomy— compares with ordinary regions as skeleton with living & rosy man." The whole land was "a sickening cheat" in general as the Holy Sepulcher was in particular. The landscape accounts for "the ghastly theology" of the prophets. Nothing relieves it except caves and glens as sterile as the rest of the country. In "the emptiness" of this "lifeless antiquity" the Jews live "like flies that have taken up their abode in a skull." Could Christ have lived here? He must have been of stone. "The Stone Christ . . . The arch—the stone he leaned against—the stone of Lazarus &c." There was nothing in Palestine to inspire one to resurrect the young hero to whom one had given the name "Pierre."

Naples, where he landed on February 18, was full of life and

commotion. "Strada de Toledo. Noble street. Broadway. Vast
crowds. Splendor of city. Palace—soldiers—music." Outside of
Naples he visited Lake Avernus. "In a crater Lonely look. Flags
on water side. Melancholy old temple. Curious they should have
fabled hell here. Cave of Sybil. Gate. (Narrow one to hell, here)
Torches. Long grotto, many hundred feet, fast walk . . . Many
other caves to right & left. Infernal enough—What in God's name
were such places made for, & why? Surely man is a strange animal.
Diving into the bowels of the earth rather than building up towards
the sky. How clear an indication that he sought darkness rather
than light."

He found Rome "hypochondriac" and he was sick while he was
there. But it was wonderfully impressive too, and he visited pal-
aces, museums, and ruins assiduously. As he went farther north,
his mood became gay and contented, and he took things lightly.
At Florence he saw "the 3 Fates of M. Angelo," and wrote, "Admirable expression. The way the one Fate looks at another—Shall
I?—The expectancy of the 3d." In Venice he climbed the Bell
Tower, and it did not disturb him. On April 5: "Breakfast on
St. Marks. Austrian flags flying from their masts. Glorious aspect
of the basilica in the sunshine. The charm of the square: The snug
little breakfast there. Ladies. Flower girls—musicians. Pedlers of
Adriatic shells. Cigar stores &c &c.—Sat in a chair by the arcade
at Mindel's sometime in the sun looking at the flags, the sun, & the
church. (The shadow of the bell-tower . . .)"

Back in England by the end of April, it was Oxford which
charmed him most. He felt a great affection for "the mother country" and thought that Oxford and its way of life were a clear rebuke
to the sophomoric chauvinism of Americans.

At the end of the *Journal,* Melville jotted down some thoughts
for further consideration. Among these is:

From *Tartarus to Tivoli*
is but a step or two.

This refers to his entry of March 20, on which day he had taken a side trip from Rome to Tivoli. "At 6 A.M. started for Tivoli. Chill, grey ride across Campagna. Lake Tartarus. Travertine.—Villa of Hadrian—Solemn scene & solemn guide—Extent of ruins—fine site . . . Tivoli on heigth. Temple of the Nymph overhanging—paths—gallery in rock—Claude—not to Paradise, but Tivoli—shading—middle tint." There was no Paradise, no celestial Paradise, beyond the borders of Tartarus. But there was Tivoli, the City of Man, high up and seeking light. There was Hadrian's Villa, whose broken columns would remind man of the king-father, and the temple of the Tiburtine Sibyl, the dark woman who once spoke magic words which were now a somber memory. Behind Tivoli was a deep glen, the gorge of Anio. In the opposite direction one looked across the wide Campagna to Rome. Immediately beneath the notation at the end of the *Journal* about Tartarus and Tivoli, Melville wrote, "The Cenci Portrait." In Rome, Melville had stood before Guido Reni's portrait of Beatrice Cenci as, in *Pierre,* he had made Lucy do. Rome was Babylon, and it had made him sick with its hypochondriac air of ancient corruption. Tivoli was the New Jerusalem but not the New Jerusalem of the Apocalypse. Tivoli lifted itself above the plain, but was earthbound. It sought space, but peopled and principled it. It sought light, but of a middle tint.

At the end of the *Journal Up the Straits,* Melville had been further confirmed in his humanism, his "bias for a life with men." Like exile itself, travel brought one wisdom. One must accept the conditions of manhood, perceiving that consciousness is awareness of one's own attempt to comprehend these conditions, and that sensibility is the awareness of the tensions and reconciliations of life's rhythms. Melville's humanism could not be described as gladsome or optimistic. But he had not surrendered all hope and become "morbid" and "pessimistic"—far from it. Traveling north, he was happy; he was prepared to be puckish about Michelangelo's Fates and sit contentedly in the shadow of the Bell Tower. There was still the long afternoon of life, a time for reflection, reverie, myth, and, if one could manage it, poetry. But this did not gainsay the fact that the afternoon would be followed by the evening and that the evening might be austere. There might be (as Melville wrote at the end of his description of the Tivoli trip) a "chill ride home in the evening."

VIII

Amor Incensed

In the middle of Melville's poem called "After the Pleasure Party" *
there is a denunciation of whatever meddling god it was who separated the original hermaphrodite human being—that Old Adam
of the occult myths—into two beings of opposite sex. The poem
speaks of the dangers of slighting Cupid. "Fear me, virgin . . ."
Cupid warns in the epigraph,

> never
> Brave me, nor my fury tempt:
> Downy wings, but wroth they **beat**
> Tempest even in reason's seat.

The pleasure party had been held, apparently, in Italy. (Melville
seems to be recalling an incident of his 1856–1857 travels.) The
marble pillars of a splendid house had gleamed down a long slope,
through "green halls" of foliage, terrace by terrace down to the
"starlit Mediterranean Sea." It had been a paradise, a place and a
time for the release of "rending pangs" and for the expression of
passionate words long grown vague and impotent in the hot
atmosphere of fantasy—the discontent of "long revery," which
was quite the opposite of the outward expression which the scene
of the pleasure party seemed to demand. The starlit waves of the
Mediterranean flowed endlessly upon the shore; and Urania, the
poet's muse, reflected that they were like the rhythms of sexual
desire. In the procession of the waves, the warning of Amor was
to be discerned:

* This poem was not published until the *Timoleon* volume of 1891. The date
of composition is uncertain. I would suggest, however, that Melville's poem is an
elaboration upon Matthew Arnold's sonnet called "Austerity in Poetry," and that
Melville read this sonnet (he underscored some of the lines) in 1871, since that is
the date penciled under his autograph in his volume of Arnold's poems. Both
Melville's poem and Arnold's are concerned with the poet's muse, who is at once
radiant and celibate, and both describe a "festal" occasion.

> Tired of the homeless deep,
> Look how their flight yon hurrying billows urge,
> Hitherward but to reap
> Passive repulse from the iron-bound verge!
> Insensate, can they never know
> 'Tis mad to wreck the impulsion so?

Urania then recalls the sudden upwelling of sexual desire she had
experienced at the pleasure party; it had been such an overwhelming
demand, such an overturning of all the verities of her celibate life,
such a Sapphic storm in a vestal soul, that she had wanted to escape
by sleeping or dying.

> An art of memory is, they tell:
> But to forget! Forget the glade
> Wherein Fate sprung Love's ambuscade,
> To flout pale years of cloistral life
> And flush me in this sensuous strife.
> 'Tis Vesta struck with Sappho's smart.
> No fable her delirious leap:
> With more of cause in desperate heart,
> Myself could take it—but to sleep!

The impassioned Urania realizes with a shock that "one's sex,"
however long "faded," has a "dear desire" to "assert itself" and to
achieve the sense of power through the assertion: "the dear
desire through love to sway." The sexual impulse is like geysers
that aspire to win their fervid way "through cold obstruction." But
in the muse who is speaking, the geysers have been "baffled," and
so an arid, destructive fire sweeps through her soul, like uncon-
trollable prairie fires feeding on withering weeds. With the energy
of this raging fire, Urania, goddess of astronomy, has spun her
fantasies:

> O reaching ranging tube I placed
> Against yon skies, and fable chased
> Till, fool, I hailed for sister there
> Starred Cassiopeia in Golden Chair.

But the fantasies of myth and art produced at the expense of
celibacy may drive the artist mad:

> In dream I throned me, nor I saw
> In cell the idiot crowned with straw.

The invasion of sexual desire has destroyed Urania's pleasurable dream world and has left her "enlightened, undeceived." The poem goes on to ask whether she will find anything in the cold future beyond "envy and spleen."

There follow three stanzas in which we discover the main theme of the poem. In the first stanza Urania recalls an enticing girl whom the poet had seen on his travels. The girl had walked beside the carriage in which the poet rode, and she carried a "blossoming rod," apparently a "sceptre of May-day." Amor's "glance" fell "moistly" on the peasant girl, and the "petty hell" of the poet's passions was fired. But the envious muse tries to convince herself that the girl was a "cheat," saying that her buds concealed her briars even as her innocence concealed her wiles—and in short, that there was more pain than pleasure to be found in the girl, and any relation the poet might have with her would be a disappointment and a betrayal of all noble passions. In the second stanza Urania recalls that at the pleasure party the guests had reclined in sylvan groups "like the Decameron folk." The muse demands of Amor whether he supposes that because she is not "roseate" but only plain and lone, she had felt "no sun" nor thrilled "with Spring." She taxes Amor with his neglect, complaining that his arm is always about "some radiant ninny flung," and finally admits that if she could she would gladly exchange her "starry lore" for the "veriest wanton's rose." In the third stanza Urania bursts out petulantly against whatever "Cosmic jest or Anarch blunder" it was that

> The human integral clove asunder
> And shied the fractions through life's gate,

and declares that she longs to plunge "deeper than Sappho," since only such a "surge" of passion can overcome the separation of the sexes and achieve the cruelly elusive paradisaical state in which "halves" are perfectly "matched."

Melville writes of sex in this poem as a part of the world whose dominion is contested by Prometheus and Zeus. The division of the sexes is an obstacle in the path of man, placed there by an anarch. It is another lure of God. If the challenge is taken up, if sex urges against nature (that is, against the division of the sexes) profoundly and powerfully, the obstacle is overcome and the work

of the Promethean *élan* is accomplished. But if the challenge is met
with a "shallow surge," the Promethean purpose is defeated.

The poem goes on to repeat the statement that Urania's fantasies
have been dispelled: "light" has broken, and "disillusion opens all
the shore." The poet then says that he does not know the final
fate of Urania, but he confronts her with three different visions of
life as possible sources of renewed art and fantasy. He tells us that

> late in Rome
> (For queens discrowned a congruous home)
> Entering Albani's porch she stood
> Fixed by an antique pagan stone
> Colossal carved.

The pagan statue aroused in Urania the most profound and turbu-
lent passions; she was all but overcome and could rally her senses
only after her "surged emotion" had subsided. For a moment she
seemed ready to take the deep "plunge" which would have set free
her "sex" and her "selfhood."

But Urania cannot face these Sapphic extremities; they only
make her want to flee to a nunnery:

> by Mary's convent shrine,
> Touched by her picture's moving plea
> In that poor nerveless hour of mine,
> I mused—A wanderer still must grieve.
> Half I resolved to kneel and believe.

At this point we begin to see that the alternative visions Melville
poses in this poem are alternatives we have met before. Failing to
be the creative spirit (symbolized by Sappho), she can take the veil
—that is, become one of the Divine Inert which Christianity exalts.
But her urge toward self-assertion and power are too great to allow
this. Finally, she can court spiritual disaster, like a literary Ahab.
This, we gather, will probably be her fate. For suddenly she invokes
another virgin, but an armed and helmeted one: Athena. She will
follow the severe, gray-eyed goddess who sprang from the head of
Zeus and who bore on her shield the image of the Gorgon's head.
Surely, cries Urania, Athena is "self-reliant, strong and free" and
is far from all "that which makes the sexual feud And clogs the
aspirant life." In Athena

> power and peace unite,
> Transcender! raise me up to thee,
> Raise me and arm me!

But the poem ends with the abrupt statement that this is a "fond appeal." The celibate muse will never transcend the demands of sex; and "Art inanimate" will never be recalled to life by such passions as Athena may bring to it.

Melville's poem, then, makes the statement that art depends on sex and that prolonged failure to find one's other "half," though for a while it may produce wondrous and far-ranging fantasies, finally leaves one's art "inanimate." Can we very well avoid seeing in *Moby-Dick* the spacious fantasies of an obscurely celibate writer, or hearing in *Pierre* the mutterings of the "idiot crowned with straw" at the expense of whose sufferings those fantasies were created?

2

Why should Melville have made Urania visit the Villa Albani rather than some other museum? During his Mediterranean trip Melville had visited this Roman villa on two occasions: Saturday, February 28, and Saturday, March 14, 1857. On the first of these days he wrote in his *Journal*:

At 12 M. was at Borghese Villa. Extent of grounds—peculiar odor of Italian gardens—deep groves—cold splendor of Villa—Venus and Cupid—mischievous look of C.—Thence to Villa Albani—along the walls—Antinous—head like a moss-ross with curls & buds—rest all simplicity—end of fillet on shoulder—drapery, shoulder in the mantle—hand full of flowers & eyeing them—the profile &c.

One gathers that Antinoüs had a special appeal for Melville. Several days before he saw the Albani Antinoüs, he had seen a statue of him in the Capitoline Museum and he had written:

Antinous, beautiful.—Walked over to the Pincian Hill—Gardens and statuary.—overlooking Piazza del Popolo.—Fashion & Rank—Preposterous touring within a stone's throw of Antinous. How little influence has truth in the world!—Fashion everywhere ridiculous, but most so in Rome. (Music on Pincian). No place where lonely man will feel more lonely than in Rome.

The statue of Antinoüs had made Melville suddenly self-conscious and lonely and had filled him with momentary despondency over "fashion" and the aimless occupation of "touring."

The bas-relief of Antinoüs at the Villa Albani had seemed to Winckelmann "after Apollo and the Laocoön, perhaps the most beautiful monument of antiquity." It depicts a sad, beautiful youth with a thoughtful forehead and deep, dreamy eyes. "The nose is straight," says Symonds, "but blunter than is consistent with the Greek ideal. Both cheeks and chin are delicately formed, but fuller than a severe taste approves; one might trace in their rounded contours either a survival of infantine innocence and immaturity, or else the sign of rapidly approaching over-bloom." Antinoüs, born in Bithynia, had been the favorite of the Emperor Hadrian, to whom he had seemed to symbolize the lost Greek spirit. He had been drowned during a boating party on the Nile, and the flowers he is represented as holding in his left hand are water lilies from the river. His death is said to have been self-inflicted, for an oracle had told him that he might save the life Hadrian by killing himself. After his suicide he was worshiped as a demigod, and his beauty became the touchstone of the artists. "His features were utilized to represent all the young male gods on Olympus," says Stobart. "In their tragic beauty we see a mirror of Greece tinged by the Orient, as if Dionysos had wedded Isis and this were the offspring." If the differing sexes meet in Antinoüs, so do differing cultures.

At the Villa Albani, Melville would have seen other art works which might have had a special meaning for him: an Athena, with her helmet, her spear, and her Medusa shield; a Zeus; an Aphrodite with Eros; a head of Sappho, "the energetic forms of her face showing extraordinary strength of feeling, will, and ability," says W. Helbig, "her massive chin and full lower lip showing a strongly developed sensuality . . . her grave expression made mild by the longing look of her almond-shaped eyes." The Villa Albani was an ideal place to test the emotions of the virginal Urania.

Concerning his second visit to this villa, Melville wrote the following obscure but tantalizing lines:

Second went to Villa Albani. Father Murphy. Mrs. S. Caryatide. The long lines of foliage—architecture of villa, richness of landscape. Fine site.—to B. of Diocletian Church.

Father Murphy. Did Melville see an acquaintance of this name at the villa? Perhaps this is the priest he refers to in the entry for Tuesday, March 3: "A cold rain, windy, dirty & horribly disagreeable day. Dinner & to bed.—The Peruvian & Pole.—The Irish Priest." But for Melville the words "Father Murphy" bore an older memory, a memory of Tahiti and the South Seas. In *Omoo* Melville relates how an Irish priest named Father Murphy befriended him and his companions while they were languishing in a British jail. Father Murphy was a handsome, ruddy, middle-aged man with such a liking for French brandy that he usually "glowed" and walked a bit unsteadily. And, like the other priests on the island, he was accustomed to convert the most delectable maidens to Christianity before turning his attention to the rest of the natives. "I never drink French brandy but I pledge Father Murphy," wrote Melville in *Omoo*. "His health again! And many jolly proselytes may he make in Polynesia!" The Christian priest served to associate in Melville's mind the sensual qualities of two pagan cultures, the Mediterranean and the Polynesian. But on the day of his second visit to the villa, Melville made other associations.

Mrs. S. Caryatide. A caryatid stands immediately at the rear of the porch of the villa. Quite possibly the "antique pagan stone" which so moved Urania in Melville's poem, it is a headless bacchante upon which the head of a caryatid has been superimposed. But who is the Mrs. S. whom Melville associates with the bacchante? Presumably Mrs. Saunders, the wife of an American missionary to Palestine whom Melville met on his travels. On January 23 he wrote in his *Journal*: "Mrs. S, an interesting woman, not without beauty, and of the heroine stamp, or desires to be. A book lying on her table, entitled 'Book of Female Heroines,' I took to be exponent of her aspirations. She talked to me, alone, for two hours; I doing nothing but listen." Did this female heroine resemble the bacchante and was Melville taking a perverse pleasure in thus linking this self-mortifying Christian missionary lady with a wild nymph who had assisted, no doubt, at the dismemberment of Dionysus? If so, it is the same kind of spleen he exhibits by suddenly making the celibate Urania the victim of her own sexual desire.

Lines, architecture, landscape, site: these are images of space.

Foliage: an image of richness. Consider for a moment certain hints thrown out by Charles Olson in his *Call Me Ishmael*. Olson writes that the aesthetic mode of Melville's great image, Space, is Magic; and that the setting of the image is pre-Christian—pagan and Old Testament. From the Villa Albani, Melville went to the church of Maria degli Angeli, built upon the ruins of the Baths of Diocletian. On the day of his first visit to the villa, he had taken the same tour:

Thence to the Baths of Diocletian—Church—monument of 8 columns. —S. Rosa's tomb. The four fountains—Monte Cavallo—colossal horses from ruins of baths—like finding the bones of the mastadon— gigantic figures emblematic of gigantic Rome.

Of the following day's trip he wrote:

To Monte Cavallo—colossal equestrian group, found in Baths, basin also, obelisk—most imposing group of antiques in Rome.—People these Caracalla baths anew with these colossal figures—Gigantic Rome. —St. Peter's in its magnitude & colossal statuary seems an imitation of these fragments. The grass growing in the Square.

On a later day he visited the Rospigliosi Gallery and wrote:

Aurora—Floats overhead like sun-dyed clouds—The Mirror—The lovers seated there. Samson pulling down the temple—gigantic—unfortunate hint at fall of Aurora.

Like Vico, Melville thought of the earliest age as the age of giants, of great spaces, and of the first light. The early ages of Rome he imagines to be revived in the colossal stone horses, which are like the fossil bones of mastodons. In a chapter of *Moby-Dick* called "The Fossil Whale," Melville had written: "I am, by a flood, borne back to that wondrous period where time itself can be said to have begun; for time began with man. . . . I look around to shake hands with Shem. I am horror-struck at this ante-mosaic, unsourced existence of the unspeakable terrors of the whale, which having been before all time, must needs exist after all humane ages are over." The erotic, soaring fantasy of the first dawn had disappeared with the beginning of time. Aurora, like Lucy and Urania the goddess of light and space, had fallen. Samson, the wounded titan, had pulled down the temple, destroying the antique representation of space.

In the church of Maria degli Angeli, at the Diocletian Baths, are two wall paintings of the Fall of Simon Magus. "The Fall of Simon Magus," wrote Melville in his *Journal*. "Meridian line." Simon the Samaritan sorcerer had made a supreme flamboyant attempt to discredit Christianity and reassert the dominion of the pagan Powers and their primitive magic. While the Emperor Nero watched in amazement, the inspired magician, wrapped in his supernatural cloak, stepped into the blue abyss of the Roman sky and soared slowly over the city. With the purest exhilaration, Simon Magus felt himself enthroned in space, at one with the ecstatic forces of the universe, and in control of the city which extended its streets and its squares far below him. In "The Fossil Whale" Melville had written (a passage I have already quoted in part):

Give me a condor's quill! Give me Vesuvius' crater for an inkstand! Friends, hold my arms! For in the mere act of penning my thoughts about this Leviathan, they weary me, and make me faint with the out-reaching comprehensiveness of sweep, as if to include the circle of the sciences, and all the generations of whales, and men, and masto-dons, past, present, and to come, with all the revolving panoramas of empire on earth, and throughout the whole universe.

But soon Simon's afflatus began to wane; doubts assailed him; a subtle enervation seeped into his veins. The clutch of the demons' aery hands, which bore him up, gradually relaxed. The blitheful cloak began to weigh heavily. The Evil One himself came through the sky to whisper courage in Simon's ear and to upbraid the at-tending demons for their weakness. Far below, Nero watched; and Peter and Paul prayed to the Christian God that He would vindi-cate Himself by causing Simon Magus to fall out of the sky. Simon was overcome with dismay and grew angry, cajoling and threaten-ing the demons. But gradually he descended, and then, the magic *élan* entirely dispersed, he fell bleeding at the feet of the emperor.

Meridian line: the line between the magical ascent in the morn-ing into space and light and the slow, tortured descent of the magician in the afternoon, borne down by Christianity with its weight of suffering and personal agony, its dark mysteries, its time-consciousness. *Moby-Dick* was such a meridian line, and the slow descent of the magician who created it ended in the broken body of Billy Budd.

Melville's muse was Urania, goddess of space, and he sought her in the monuments and ruins of Mediterranean antiquity. But what has the goddess of space to do with sex and pleasure parties? Intuitively, Melville knew that the myth of the sex act is man's appropriation of space, his magic flight, his willed negation of time.

IX

The Meteor of the War

In the years between 1857 and 1860 Melville traveled about the country giving lectures on "Statuary in Rome," "The South Seas," and "Travelling." He was also writing poetry. In 1863, after repeated failures to get a job in the consular service (a trip to Washington gained him a handshake with Lincoln), Melville ended the thirteen-year sojourn at Pittsfield, moving his family (which now included four children) to 104 East 26th Street, New York City. In 1866 he began his twenty-year stint as a district inspector of customs; and also in that year he published a book of poems called *Battle-Pieces and Aspects of the War.*

Melville wrote his Civil War poems gravely and compassionately, with no trace of presumption assuming the role of counselor to the nation. With the humility of one who explicitly disclaimed any program or even any consistent attitude and with the serious candor of one who assumed, however gratuitously, that it was still the poet's duty to counsel generals and legislators, he wrote:

> I muse upon my country's ills—
> The tempest bursting from the waste of Time
> On the world's fairest hope linked with man's foulest crime.

We have seen that in his early books Melville's chief fear for the future of the United States was that its leaders would lose the Promethean *élan,* that having made the Revolution and founded the Republic, the American spirit would somehow petrify and be unable to regenerate itself in preparation for fresh creative acts. He feared a "reversal of roles," in which the victory over tyranny would revert to the vanquished, leaving America no longer the St. John of the wilderness crying prophetic words of political wisdom.

But Melville's ardent, heroic republicanism had always had a conservative streak. His search for the father (which took a politi-

cal character in his reverence for the founders of the Republic),
his admiration for old, landed families like the Glendinnings, his
perception of the necessity of law—these attest to his conservatism.
But in the Civil War poems there appears a new conservatism
which was to tincture all of Melville's later political thinking. In
one of its aspects, at least, he could not help seeing the disastrous
war as the work of Prometheus. "All wars are boyish," he exclaims
in one of the poems. He saw the war as a sudden turning over of
destiny to the young men, and he feared that what these young
men were creating was nothing less than a decisive breach with
history and nature which would leave the country without purpose
or direction. The tragedy of the war seemed to Melville to be its
mindless destruction of the past, which he feared might make it
impossible for America to pursue those courses of further development necessary to fulfill "the Founders' dream." In the Civil War
poems, Prometheus is no longer the tragic suffering hero; he has
become a "collegian" who gaily takes his country's destiny in hand
as if he were going to a picnic—a youth who can be "enlightened"
only by the glare of a volley of rifle fire. The breach in history is the
central idea of the Civil War poems.

2

Melville's forebodings are expressed in one of his best poems,
"The Portent," written in 1859:

> Hanging from the beam,
>   Slowly swaying (such the law),
> Gaunt the shadow on your green,
>   Shenandoah!
> The cut is on the crown
> (Lo, John Brown),
> And the stabs shall heal no more.
>
> Hidden in the cap
>   Is the anguish none can draw;
> So your future veils its face,
>   Shenandoah!
> But the streaming beard is shown
> (Weird John Brown),
> The meteor of the war.

The expert poise and movement of these lines nicely fits the subject matter. Swinging from the beam, the body is like a ship's lantern, like the solar lamp in the last scene of *The Confidence Man*. But it casts not light but darkness. It sways according to the natural law which moves all bodies, animate or inanimate. Yet this fateful sway is neither known to, nor directed by, the man who sways. Perhaps this will be America's fate. (In this sense John Brown is "weird.") The face of the future is veiled, not conscious of what convulsive events are taking place or of what they portend. The image recurs in Melville's later poem "Timoleon," where the hero is present but unmindful of what is going on—his face being "muffled"—while his companions kill his brother. All we see of John Brown's face is the streaming beard, a meteor which suddenly appears in ostensible violation of the order of things.

In *Clarel* (1876) Melville was to make it clear that he extended the idea of withdrawal into a general characterization of modern times. He was to say that the modern world was a kind of universal Encantadas or Palestine, a sterile land from which all heroic vitalities had somehow disappeared. Though perhaps more profoundly conceived, it is the same image as Arnold's ebbing sea in "Dover Beach." The question which Melville poses in various forms is whether in our time or in our society there will ever be a "return." The Civil War poems make a particular application of the idea that certain admirable and necessary qualities of life have been withdrawn. What has been withdrawn is the "faith" or "dream" of the founders, by which Melville means a reasoned, free, heroic form of republicanism. He pictures the estrangement between the founders and their heirs in two ways: first, as the work of History, which in a kind of Indian-giving has taken back the political blessing it once bestowed, and, second, as the work of Man, that perpetually falling creature who has now fallen away from the founders. "The Conflict of Convictions" (1860–1861) opens with a stirring summons to the "Hope" which the founders had aroused in the hearts of men:

> On starry heights
>   A bugle wails the long recall;
> Derision stirs the deep abyss,
>   Heaven's ominous silence over all.
> Return, return, O eager Hope,
>   And face man's latter fall.

Hope does not return from the abyss, for this is a disheartening
moment. As Melville says in a note to the poem, "The gloomy lull
of the early part of the winter of 1860–1, seeming big with final
disaster to our institutions, affected some minds that believed them
to constitute one of the greatest hopes of mankind, much as the
eclipse which came over the promise of the first French Revolution
affected kindred natures, throwing them for a time into doubts and
misgivings universal." Hope, he says in the poem, standing motionless like a stone in a garden run to weeds, seems to contain not
even the promise of comets which, though "gone a thousand years,
Return again."

The conflict in Melville's convictions arose from his mingled
hopes and fears for the young men who were fighting the war. In
"The March into Virginia," where he observes that "all wars are
boyish, and are fought by boys," he speaks gravely of the "ignorant impulse" of young hearts that spurn precedent and the warnings of the wise. Knowledge, he feared, would come to these
soldiers only in death, whether they were young collegians "with
golden mottoes in the mouth" or youths who felt nothing but a
"rapture sharp" as they went off to war—for "what like a bullet
can undeceive?" It was this sense of the mindlessness of the young
soldiers—the feeling that, as he wrote in a later poem, "little boy-
gods" were spinning "the whizzing world"—that led Melville to
fear that however just the cause of the North, the war would be
turned into a purely destructive act, that even if the young soldier
were not killed, he would return, like the student in "The College
Colonel," without "self" because exiled with an "Indian aloofness" from the world of his fellow men. If the young soldiers should
fail to turn the war into a creative act, Melville says in "The Conflict of Convictions," then indeed the fatal breach with history will
have been made. The Civil War will have abolished the American
past and the future that past implied. The "blissful Prime" of the
revolutionary days will prove to have been the end of time. The
penalty for this nihilism will be "Power unanointed" and such
"dominion" as was "unsought by the free." The Iron Dome of the
Capitol will be the symbol of tyranny. The "Founders' dream shall
flee" when the Iron Dome, strengthened by the stress of the war,
"flings her huge shadow" over the land. Then shall "death be busy
with all who strive."

Yet though the "elders" mourn the passing of America's revolutionary "Prime" and fear for what their successors will do, America's destiny is inevitably in the hands of the young. As the Iroquois proverb says,

> Grief to every graybeard
> When young Indians lead the war.

This kind of thought could always stir a Promethean optimism in Melville. And in "The Conflict of Convictions" he is still able to take comfort from the thought that though the God who rules is old and though "Heaven with age is cold," the "light" may yet prove to be on the "youthful brow," giving the Promethean "Forethought" to the young as the miner's light allows him to see through the darkness. The young men can still force the Old God into fresh creative motion:

> The Ancient of Days is forever young,
>   Forever the scheme of Nature thrives;
> I know a wind in purpose strong—
>   It spins *against* the way it drives.

A Promethean wind, surely, driving the world on toward its natural fulfillment by spinning against it, creating new forms of life through suffering and death. If it should be that America is still in possession of the Promethean *élan*, there is no need to fear even the most terrible extremities:

> What if the gulfs their slimed foundations bare?
> So deep must the stones be hurled
> Whereon the throes of ages rear
> The final empire and the happier world.

But in this early period of the war, Melville's convictions remain in conflict, and he ends his poem with the statement that "Wisdom is vain, and prophecy."

3

Along with his fear that America might be cutting itself off from past and future and condemning itself to a directionless present, we find the statement that this present may turn out to be a new barbarism or archaism. If all the creative rhythms of life retreat, as it were, into the swaying corpse of John Brown, man will retreat out of history and civilization into the old night from which Orpheus, the maker of rhythms, had once led him. In "The Armies of the Wilderness" we read:

> The fight for the city is fought
>   In Nature's old domain;
> Man goes out to the wilds,
>   And Orpheus' charm is vain.
>
> In glades they meet skull after skull
>   Where pine-cones lay—the rusted gun,
> Green shoes full of bones, the mouldering coat
>   And cuddled-up skeleton.

It is the pervasive theme of reversion. In "The House-Top: A Night Piece" (1863) Melville speaks of the forces which drag mankind in a spiritual or social crisis back to an archaic level of life. Melville appended the following note to this poem: " 'I dare not write the horrible and inconceivable atrocities committed,' says Froissart, in alluding to the remarkable sedition in France during his time. The like may be hinted of some proceedings of the draft-rioters."

> No sleep. The sultriness pervades the air
> And binds the brain—a dense oppression, such
> As tawny tigers feel in matted shades,
> Vexing their blood and making apt for ravage.
> Beneath the stars the roofy desert spreads
> Vacant as Libya. All is hushed near by.
> Yet fitfully from far breaks a mixed surf
> Of muffled sound, the Atheist roar of riot.
> Yonder, where parching Sirius set in drought,
> Balefully glares red Arson—there—and there.
> The town is taken by its rats—ship-rats
> And rats of the wharves.

In such times of "ravage" and vexing of blood, one can scarcely argue that the social contract or the power of reason preserves the state. No, it is preserved, or at least *has* been preserved, by the magic song of Orpheus, the primitive culture hero who plays upon the mimetic faculties of his people with his dark music. But now the Orphean music is drowned out by cannon and insurrection.

All civil charms
And priestly spells which late held hearts in awe—
Fear-bound, subjected to a better sway
Than sway of self; these like a dream dissolve
. . . man rebounds whole eons back into nature.
Hail to the low dull rumble, dull and dead,
And ponderous drag that shakes the wall.
Wise Draco comes, deep in the midnight roll
Of black artillery; he comes . . .

A Republic-become-Chaos will embrace Draco with all the intense
joy of passivity and submission:

. . . the Town, redeemed,
Gives thanks devout; nor, being thankful, heeds
The grimy slur on the Republic's faith implied,
Which holds that Man is naturally good,
And—more—is Nature's Roman, never to be scourged.

Orpheus "withdraws" into Hell to rescue his lost Eurydice, the
"queen," the "widely-judging one." But having charmed Hades
and the subject shades with his lyre, Orpheus looks back as he is
leading Eurydice out of the darkness; and this act, this reversion,
this submission to the wish-dream of the archaist, causes Eurydice
to disappear. Orpheus thus betrays his role as civilizer and fails to
lead the widely judging queen back into the world and the light.
Melville was anything but an acrimonious partisan during the war.
But the South seemed to him to be guilty of the Orphean betrayal.
The North he conceived to have "Right on its side because, however blindly, it was fighting on the side of History and natural
Law." The North might be a paltry sort of Orpheus. But it looked
ahead.

4

In the poem called "America," written as the war ended, Melville presents the Civil War not as an act of nihilism or archaism,
but as an ordeal prelusive of spiritual renewal. The poem begins
with a placid and gladsome picture of the Capitol building. Over
the "sunny Dome" the flag floats majestically. America is symbolized as a young mother, an unusual image for Melville. "Young
maternity" enfolds her children exultingly to her heart. But then

the storm comes, the children fly at each other's throats, and the
young mother is speechless and pale at "the fury of her brood."
The flag streams wildly in the sky; over the spear point of the flag-
pole "the ambiguous lightning plays"—ambiguous because it may
be either the creative or the destructive fire. When the storm sub-
sides, the young mother lies in a deathlike sleep, her "fair cold
form" wound in the silk of the flag, a "shining shroud," which,
however, cannot warm the sleeper with its "ruddy hue."

> . . in that sleep contortion showed
> The terror of the vision there—
> A silent vision unavowed,
> Revealing earth's foundation bare,
>   And Gorgon in her hidden place.
> It is a thing of fear to see
>   So foul a dream upon so fair a face,
> And the dreamer lying in that starry shroud.

The idea that when the extreme foundations of reality and the last
secrets of human depravity are laid bare man will face the terrible
female monster who turns everything to stone is very common in
Melville. In this poem America dreams of facing the Gorgon, or
passes through the experience of wishing herself transformed into
the Gorgon. Perhaps the Gorgon is the most horrifying possible
image of America: the enchantress, murderess of all who seek out
her sanctuary, the treacherous mirage of the Plains, daughter of the
incestuous coupling of the primeval Land and Sea.

The Gorgon is the ultimate vision of America's withdrawal, and
it makes possible her return. For though John Brown swings in
the mechanical rhythm of death, America, the young mother,
emerges on the returning beat of the life rhythm:

> But from the trance she sudden broke—
>   The trance, or death into promoted life.

Her face is now "purified" by pain and its calm look bespeaks a
hopeful future:

> . . . triumph repressed by knowledge meet,
> Power dedicate and hope grown wise,
>   And youth matured for age's seat—
> Law on her brow and empire in her eyes.

Before the Civil War (in *Pierre*), Melville had written:

The democratic element operates as a subtile acid among us, forever producing new things by corroding the old; as in the South of France verdigris, the primitive material of one kind of green paint, is produced by grape vinegar poured upon copper plates. Now in general nothing can be more significant of decay than the idea of corrosion; yet on the other hand, nothing can more vividly suggest luxuriance of life than the idea of green as a color; for green is the peculiar signet of all-fertile Nature herself. Herein by apt analogy we behold the marked anomalousness of America, whose character abroad, we need not be surprised, is misconceived, when we consider how strangely she contradicts all prior notions of human things; and how wonderfully to her, Death itself becomes transmuted into Life. So that political institutions, which in other lands seem above all things intensely artificial, with America seem to possess the divine virtue of a natural law; for the most mighty of Nature's laws is this, that out of Death she brings Life.

This faith in the durable viability of American institutions survived the war, as we see from the poem "America." But the new note of caution and conservatism is obvious. For Melville's political attitude now included the conservatism of one who (in "The House-Top") could warn the nation against the "Atheist roar" and "red Arson." Melville's growing conservatism was not an unreasoned or despairing reactionism. It came rather from his increasing awareness of the difficulty of achieving a political state capable of really regarding man as "Nature's Roman" and really preserving the rights of man, which Billy Budd salutes in Melville's last book.

5

As Mr. Robert Penn Warren has pointed out, Melville's Civil War poems deal with certain kinds of disruptions, disconnections, and antinomies and symbolically affirm that these can be reconciled or made whole again by the processes of nature and human life. Melville was searching, Mr. Warren says, for "mechanisms of meliorism." In "Shiloh" we read how nature reconciles the enemies through the

natural prayer
Of dying foemen mingled there—
Foemen at morn, but friends at eve—
Fame or country least their care:

(What like a bullet can undeceive!)
But now they lie low,
While over them the swallows skim,
And all is hushed at Shiloh.

In another poem we read how "thousands" lying on the sod of
Malvern Wood are one with the musing and brooding of this forest
which renews itself with each spring. In "Battle of Stone River"
Melville expresses the faith that however destructive of the past
the war may be, it is already creating a new past and new forms
of understanding the past:

In days to come the field shall blend,
The story dim and date obscure;
In legend all shall end.

And in a poem on Stonewall Jackson, Melville, reasserting a historical continuity, a unity of experience through time, writes:

A Modern lived who sleeps in death,
Calm as the marble Ancients are.

Striking this note of reconciliation with the processes of nature,
art, and time, Melville sought to heal the breach with history which
he feared the Civil War was making.

The poem called "A Canticle" is Melville's most positive affirmation that despite the Civil War, America might still grow "toward the fulness of her fate" and that Humanity might still find
(as he says in another poem written at the end of the war)
"Freedom's larger play." "A Canticle" combines certain images
from *Moby-Dick*—whiteness and the rainbow—with the idea of
the Fall of Man. The central trope of the poem is the stream of
humanity, made up of confluent streams which meet at the brink
of a "Titanic" precipice and fall into a gorge. Like the American
nation, the stream moves with an impulse "mysterious as the tide,"
with a deep, devoted power. From the unsounded abyss of the
gorge,

The Giant of the Pool
Heaves his forehead white as wool.

It is Death, the white monster, swallowing up the falling "hosts of
human kind." But spinning like the Promethean wind, against the
way it drives, the plunging stream perpetually leaves behind it a

delicate but inexpungeable rainbow, which, though it may hover fitfully or be paled to "blankness" by "a wind from heaven," is "incessant in renewal," the indestructible emblem of man's triumph over the white giant. Watching the rainbow in the spout of the whale, Melville (Noah in a whaleboat) had taken it as a symbol of the beauty and endurance of aesthetic and moral values. In "A Canticle" the rainbow assumes a political meaning; it signifies that whatever convulsions may interrupt history, the generations

> in their flowing
> Ever form the steadfast state.

It might have been plausibly predicted that so great a catastrophe as the Civil War would make Melville increasingly religious, that he would see in the "boys" who fought the war the figure of the young hermaphrodite Christ who slept unquietly in the recesses of his mind. It might have been predicted that Melville's thought would have taken the direction indicated by these lines of Robert Lowell's:

> When Chancellorsville mowed down the volunteer,
> "All wars are boyish," Herman Melville said;
> But we are old, our fields are running wild:
> Till Christ again turn wanderer and child.

Yet quite the opposite was the case. Christ, the Beatified Boy, entered very little into Melville's conscious thoughts after *Pierre,* though this figure was to achieve a startling recrudescence in *Billy Budd.* The emphasis of the war poems is all on the human and the adult. Looking out over a disrupted nation, Melville found that the war had confirmed him "in his natural bias for a life with men." He found hope in the qualities displayed by some of the Civil War leaders: he wrote of Lee like a versifying Plutarch and took comfort in the thought (at the fall of Richmond) that "God is in Heaven, and Grant in the Town." And as he wrote in "On the Photograph of a Corps Commander":

> Nothing can lift the heart of man
> Like manhood in a fellow man.
> The thought of heaven's great King afar
> But humbles us—too weak to scan;
> But manly greatness men can span,
> And feel the bonds that draw.

The war for Melville was a human tragedy rather than a battle of, or with, Titans and gods. In a prose "Supplement" to *Battle-Pieces,* in which he wrote with a dignified formality, gracefully drawing historical parallels and rounding his periods with fulsome metaphors, Melville warned of the "difficulties great and novel" which the postwar period faced. As one "who never was a blind adherent" and who "counted on the indulgence of his countrymen," he pleaded for common sense and Christian charity, for patriotism free of narrowness and for intellectual fair-mindedness free of political trimming. "Noble was the gesture," he wrote, "into which patriotic passion surprised the people in a utilitarian time and country; yet the glory of the war falls short of its pathos—a pathos which now at last ought to disarm all animosity." And again:

Let us pray that the great historic tragedy of our time may not have been enacted without instructing our whole beloved country through terror and pity; and may the fulfillment verify in the end those expectations which kindle the bards of Progress and Humanity.

The countrymen on whose indulgence the customhouse poet counted bought, alas, only 525 copies of *Battle-Pieces* during the first ten years of its publication. But by 1876 Melville had completed his long poem *Clarel,* "a metrical affair, a pilgrimage or what not, of several thousand lines, eminently adapted for unpopularity." The idea of writing a pilgrimage had its special felicity; for whether he was writing the poem or working at his job, the customs inspector, once a traveler himself, was examining the baggage of travelers.

X

"Just Reason, and Appeal for Grace"

I have said that in Melville's later works we find him seeking for
a revised Promethean humanism, a meaningful vision of life at a
lower level of ecstasy than that which inspirits *Moby-Dick* and
Pierre. This more modest understanding of life demanded a set of
symbols different from, but complementary to, the symbols of the
Promethean-heroic theme. The most pervasive of these symbols
were adumbrated in *Pierre* and the short stories of the 1850's,
such symbols as Stone versus Water and Earth or Vine versus
Rose. Given the lowest state of life at which man can endure—
Melville asks in effect—given the low, enduring life among rocks
and sterility, how do forms of beauty and fertility emerge? In *Clarel*
(1876) he asks: What are the chances, in an age sterilized by
doubt and apathy and haunted by the ostensible failure of the revolutionary movements of the time, that art and intelligence and social
morality can continue to flower?

There is much that is solitary in Melville's thought. And yet his
later works place him squarely in the tradition of Victorian thought.
Clarel is the work of a man well versed in the controversies of his
day and shows Melville to have been a student of the political revolutions of the nineteenth century, of the scientific discoveries of
the time, and of the "higher criticism" of myth and religion. *Clarel*
will very much remind us of the work of Matthew Arnold and
Arthur Hugh Clough. (Arnold's "Empedocles on Etna," which
Melville read in 1871, especially comes to mind.) And the imagery
of the poem, furthermore, will make the reader think that if *Clarel*
were mercilessly compressed, it would sound a great deal like T. S.
Eliot's *Waste Land*.

A passage from *The Journal Up the Straits* indicates Melville's
partial commitment to a kind of liberal-skeptical thought which
now seems unsatisfying. En route to Egypt he found the Greek

islands, as they appeared from the sea, "sterile & dry." They looked worn, meager, "like life after enthusiasm is gone." Surveying the island of Patmos, Melville exclaims that he "could not realize that St. John had ever had a revelation here. . . . When my eye rested on arid height, spirit partook of the barrenness.—Heartily wished Niebuhr & Strauss to the dogs. The deuce take their penetration & acumen. They have robbed us of the bloom. If they have undeceived anyone—no thanks to them." We cannot think very highly, sophisticated in doubt as we are, of the "bloom" theory of art which Melville implies in this passage. We want to reply that the kind of profound poetic consciousness of life as aesthetic fact which produces works of art is perfectly unassailable by "Niebuhr & Strauss" and that we are probably well off without the kind of "bloom" which the "higher criticism" succeeded in blighting. The "bloom" theory is, of course, an underestimation of art—making of art, as it does, a kind of airy dream which is dispelled when confronted by a scientific fact. Melville was enough a man of his time to pay homage to this theory (he allows the most intelligent character in *Clarel* to sigh over the thought that the telescope has made Diana's moon into a "clinkered blot"), yet in *Clarel,* as in his work as a whole, he successfully transcends the limits of this theory. *Clarel* is a search for an intelligent point of view and not a lament over the advent of science.

Melville's poem runs to over six hundred pages. It consists of a long series of somewhat loosely connected and often prolix cantos, mostly in rhymed tetrameters. The scene is the Holy Land (several of the incidents and much of the description are taken from the record of Palestine in *The Journal Up the Straits*); the characters are American and European travelers. The poem is an "education," the central theme being the developing thoughts and emotions of a young American divinity student. Clarel comes to Palestine already an unhappy skeptic. If the Plain of Sharon with its scarlet "Rose" gives him a momentary feeling of elation, he is soon depressed and frightened by the terribly stony landscape and "the blank, blank towers" of Jerusalem. Leaving books and Europe behind, Clarel has come to Palestine to submit himself to "nature's influx of control," to get back in some way (about which he is not clear) to the sources of life and the origins of Western myth and religion. He reflects that the American mind, though "shrewd," is "local" and tends to "avoid the deep" and that avoiding the deep "saves not from the storm." The New World, he thinks, lacks "the Semitic reverent mood." Fine of feature, pale, "all but feminine" in aspect, Clarel travels among the relics of biblical culture, seeking a firmer, deeper understanding of life than he has so far attained in his "collegiate groves."

The other main characters in the poem symbolize modes of life or thought bearing upon the education of Clarel. There is Nehemiah, "a harmless vagrant," an aged and attenuated American pilgrim who goes about Palestine, clutching a copy of the Bible and dispensing tracts to men of all religions, announcing the coming of the New Jerusalem. Clarel is deeply touched by the old man's other-worldliness, and for a time Nehemiah acts as Clarel's guide. Later it is hinted that Nehemiah had once been a mariner who had undergone terrible ordeals at sea. In hinting at Nehemiah's background, Melville seems to have had in mind Captain Pollard, the ill fated Nantucketer described in Obed Macy's *History of Nantucket*. Captain Pollard's ship, the *Essex* (the story is masterfully retold in Olson's *Call Me Ishmael*), had been rammed and sunk by a whale. The ship's company had spent weeks of indescribable hardship in open boats; nearly all the men had died and several of them had been eaten by the survivors. In his old age Captain Pollard had taken to hiding caches of food in the attic of his Nantucket home. The saintly Nehemiah, when not dispensing tracts, occupies himself with removing stones from the mule paths of Palestine in preparation for the second coming, though each stone but reveals another. He dies, leaving Clarel to seek a new friend and to wonder at the fact that so much saintly dedication had produced nothing but a "poor thin life."

Much of Clarel's education comes from observing "extreme" modes of behavior. From the extreme saintliness of Nehemiah, his attention is turned to the extreme bitterness of Celio. Clarel perceives that Celio is somehow a "brother in spirit." He is an Italian youth of good family. A hunched back is the outward sign of his inward torment. Alienated from his Church and his family and the girl he was supposed to marry, he symbolizes an extreme form of exile which Clarel had never before imagined. Vibrant with the zeal of a Savonarola, the grief of a Leopardi, the suffering of a St. Stephen, Celio's temperament is different from either "the Attic calm" or the "Saxon phlegm." Renouncing all thoughts of the future, scorning the New World, Celio seeks only the past. To Clarel, who at the beginning of the poem thinks of Christ as symbolizing liberation, spirit, and freedom, Celio's attitude is shocking. For Celio upbraids Christ with a sadistic ambivalence, charging him with being a cruel mystery and mocking enigma who came to earth in order to establish in men's minds the treacherous illusion of the Other World:

> For this Thou bleedest, Anguished Face;
> Yea, Thou through ages to accrue,
> Shall the Medusa shield replace:
> In beauty and in terror too
> Shalt paralyse the nobler race—
> Smite or suspend, perplex, deter—
> Tortured, shalt prove a torturer.

Unable to find a principled meaning in Christianity, Celio is equally unable to find a meaning in nature. He upbraids the sun itself; the sunrise is simply a pageant contrived to conceal the real order or disorder of Nature. Fainting amid a "contending press of shadowy fiends and cherubim," Celio dies, filling the night air of Jerusalem with his agonized cry. The death of Celio is a further step in Clarel's education. It leads him to contemplate the fact of death; for a while he puts "all else by" to "get at items of the dead." In his contemplations he begins—but only begins—to find "a second self," a stronger self,

> with the heart to brave
> All questions on that primal ground
> Laid bare by faith's receding wave.

Running somewhat scantily through the discursive texture of the poem, there is the love story of Clarel and Ruth. Ruth is the daughter of Nathan, an American of pilgrim stock, and Agar, an American Jewess. Nathan symbolizes the puritan New Englander whose family had moved westward with the frontier, leaving the White Mountains of New Hampshire, with "legacies of farms behind," and seeking the "parks and pastures of the sun." The West had made a potential pagan of Nathan. "The power of vast space" daily beheld from the door of the log cabin, the Indian mounds mysterious as the Pyramids, a bleached skull on the prairie, like a "vase vined round and beautiful with flowers"—these things give him a pre-Christian outlook. Listening to the spirits of air and season which rustle in the corn, watching "the breasts of Ceres swell," Nathan becomes "heathenized" against his will. Reading the works of an unbeliever (presumably Paine), he is confirmed in his un-Christian views. But Paine converts Nathan's paganism into a kind of dry and unsatisfactory pantheism, so that Agar, when he meets her, comes to him with her Jewish faith, as rain comes to a drought. He marries Agar, adopts her religion, and decides to go on a mission to Palestine to reconvert the backsliding Jews. An American turning back into the past, he is resolved to ignore "Rome and Luther" and return to "the crag of Sinai." In Palestine he establishes a farm and tries, without success, to educate the Jews in religion and modern methods of agriculture. He is killed by marauding Arabs.

Ruth remains a symbolic being and is never convincingly described as a real woman. But this has a certain felicity, because, as the poem makes clear, Clarel is still too sexually immature to see Ruth as anything but a symbol. She is usually said to be like "light" or a "dove"; her pure beauty makes Clarel think that "Paradise is possible": she is also symbolized as a "bud" and a "rose." And there are certain dark meanings in her character, for though a creature of light, she is also a "young raven," And when Clarel leaves her, temporarily as he thinks, to travel to Bethlehem, it occurs to him, in some way he does not understand, to think of Ruth as a ruinous fount, which in turn brings a lingering "memory of the Golden Bowl." The prospective marriage of Clarel and Ruth would be a symbolic union of America and the Old World. The separation of the two lovers, while Clarel makes his pilgrimage to Bethlehem, is for Clarel a period of spiritual preparation for this symbolic marriage.

On the journey to Bethlehem, Clarel is accompanied by Vine, a shy, retiring, but intelligent American; Rolfe, an American from the frontier who turns out to be the intellectual hero of the poem; Derwent, an Anglican Broad Churchman; Mortmain, an apocalyptically disillusioned Swedish revolutionary; and Ungar, a Catholic from the American Southwest.

Of these characters, Vine is the most elusive. It is sometimes said that Vine is intended as a partial portrait of Hawthorne, and this seems to me very probable. The name "Vine" is significant of the man's character. He seems to have grown close to earth in secret and shadowed places. Some "aloofness" or "privity" has cooled his blood. Vine reminds Clarel of a dim figure in a sheltered garden in which glowworms occasionally show their lights. Or again, Vine seems to gleam in the shade like the Golden Bough, and his rare comments appear to shine forth from his dark mind. In a canto called "Bell and Cairn," Melville writes that Vine's mouth shows that nameless kind of suffering which one observes in the portrait of Beatrice Cenci. Clarel, desiring to know which of his companions "sees aright," at first is impressed by Vine, not only by his apparently deep, rich temperament but by the acumen of his rare utterances. Later it is made clear that for Clarel this attraction has a strong homosexual element. Clarel feels a "thrill" of "personal longing" for Vine, and (as the company approaches the ancient site of Sodom) he ventures an uncertain declaration of love, making known a "feminine . . . passionate" desire to call Vine "brother." Vine quickly repulses Clarel with an inarticulate, dark frown. This rebuke, part of Clarel's education, makes him feel "sick" and "foolish" and leads him to ask himself how he could have found place in his heart for "such solicitudes Apart from Ruth." The joyous ringing of a monastery bell seems to give voice to Clarel's own happiness, for he no longer feels the need of "winning" Vine or of "coming at his mystery." Later it is symbolically intimated that the Vine is the enemy of the Rose—that the Vine grows most readily on the "death-bed of the rose," and that the never withering amaranths which the Vine boasts of putting forth in place of the dying Rose are a "fond conceit."

Clarel's attachment to Vine had been partly due to his feeling of revulsion at what seemed to him the intemperate language and violent thoughts of Rolfe. Finally, Clarel comes to realize that in the presence of Rolfe he is

in attendance on a mind
Poised at self-center and mature.

Rolfe, a man of rich and complex centrality, with certain overtones of more extreme modes of thought, is in fact the Promethean humanist Melville himself wanted very much to be during the latter half of his life. Rolfe is a peculiarly American kind of hero. He appears to have been a "trapper or pioneer." His "genial heart" and "brain austere" imply a tinge of the soil, and he has been in the past a "messmate of the elements" as well as a student of books. His trip to Palestine is not so much a desperate pilgrimage as another journey during which he entertains some hope of gaining "some lurking thing." His outspoken realism shocks the still tender Clarel and makes Vine retire into his "dumb castle." Rolfe's is the first vigorous voice to speak in the poem. He begins by expressing a realistic view of the power and even the human justification of the Roman Catholic church. The priest, he says, will in the long run never decline in either temporal or spiritual power. Religion will go on to the crack of doom, or at least as long "as children feel afright In darkness." And for Western society the Catholic church will always be "religion's ancient port." As for science, as for comparative religion whether or not it proves the affinity of Christ and Osiris, these disciplines, for all practical political and religious purposes, will simply deepen and enlarge the frightening ignorance of man. (Although Rolfe is himself staunchly anti-Catholic, his argument is much akin to that of a Dominican monk who appears briefly on the scene to prophesy that man will eventually forsake his modern barbarism and his Red Republic, the modern "Scarlet Dame," and return from his "moral dispersion" to the church, admitting finally that " 'Tis Abba Father that we seek.") While admitting that science "has her eagles," Rolfe deplores the general effect of "Niebuhrisation," saying that "doubt's heavy hand Is set against us," and that the result of disillusion through science has been an apotheosis of "King Common-Place." Throughout Rolfe's argument runs the idea that the nineteenth century is an emasculated era; it is a period in which the best of human thought and emotion has been "withdrawn," and Rolfe's idea of a happy future involves a "return" of life to the sterile world the withdrawal has created. He has a deep faith that below the superficial level of scientific knowledge there is an age-old "persistent flow" in "earth's vitals" which science cannot gainsay, however much it may seek to "neutralize" the universe or expunge its "taint" of evil. "The depths of Being moan," he says,

> Though luminous on every hand
> The breadths of shallow knowledge more expand.

In attacking the too optimistic liberalism of Derwent and his easy belief that "the bias" of the day leans away from authority, Rolfe says that a long view of history shows that men "get tired at last of being free" and tend to abase themselves before

> Law scribbled by law-breakers, creeds
> Scrawled by the freethinkers, and deeds
> Shameful and shameless.

And he makes clear his opinion that the beneficiary of the modern political revolutions will not be the liberal, who has given them his mild support, but "Rome" and the "atheist." He sees whole Protestant nations "doing their own undoing" and whole schools of Protestantism and liberalism being used as fronts by the "law-breakers"—bases "of operations sly." Is it irreverent for an American to have such opinions? asks Rolfe. Then let American democracy give Americans just reason for reverence.

Rolfe is able to see life as a mixture of dark and light, of pain and pleasure. His own temperament is a mixture of "earnestness and levity," so brilliant and exhilarating that Clarel is at first frightened by it. Though rigorously realistic about human nature and the practical workings of human affairs, and though openly contemptuous of Laodicean liberalism, Rolfe is himself a liberal and entertains hopes for the future of American civilization. He appears in this light in an argument with Ungar, a kind of extreme version to Rolfe himself. A frontiersman from the Southwest, Ungar is part Cherokee, and Catholic in religion. A southern officer in the Civil War (though he had been against slavery), he has become a refugee from his own country, from

> the immense charred solitudes
> Once farms . . . and chimney stacks that reign
> War-burnt upon the houseless plain.

A spiritual casualty of the war—that "Bridge of Sighs" between "contrasted eras"—he has the implacable bitterness of the dis-

possessed. And because of his Indian blood, Ungar has set his hand
against every Anglo-Saxon:

> The Anglo-Saxons—lacking grace
> To win the love of any race;
> Hated by myriads dispossessed
> Of rights—the Indians East and West.
> These pirates of the sphere! grave looters—
> Grave, canting, Mammonite freebooters,
> Who in the name of Christ and Trade . . .
> Deflower the world's last sylvan glade.

A believer in the divine right of kings and medieval culture, Ungar
berates the modern masses, whose education, he thinks, only serves
to lead them into ever more perilous abysses of ignorance. Democracy, he believes, has turned into the "arch-strumpet of an impious
age"—

> Harlot on horseback, riding down
> The very Ephesians who acclaim
> This great Diana of ill fame!

As for the arts and skills of which the progressive West is so proud,

> Your arts advance in faith's decay:
> You are but drilling the new Hun
> Whose growl even now can some dismay;
> Vindictive in his heart of hearts,
> He schools himself in your mines and marts—
> A skilled destroyer.

Railing against the "impieties of Progress," Ungar predicts that the
American civilization will disintegrate and will meet its doom in a
new Thirty Years' War. No less apocalyptic a future can come to
this New World already debased with "equality," glutted with
material success, barbarized, and disennobled. And the final result
will be a

> Dead level of rank commonplace:
> An Anglo-Saxon China, see,
> May on your vast plains shame the race
> In the Dark Ages of Democracy.

But Rolfe's arguments against Ungar are persuasive. Without over-
rating them, he finds reason for hope in the development of arts
and skills in the Western world. These arts may "ripen" and help

to bring about a "happy sequel." When Ungar argues that we need God and not Progress, Rolfe quickly accuses him of dealing in "void abstractions." Rolfe puts his faith in a reasoned and skeptical naturalism. Admitting, if Ungar wishes, that "God is God, and men are men," he asks, "What then?" and continues by saying:

> There's Circumstance—there's Time; and these
> Are charged with store of latencies
> Still working in to modify.
> For mystic text that you recall,
> Dilate upon, and e'en apply—
> (Although I seek not to decry)
> Theology's scarce practical.

He then goes on to speak of the "vast reserves" and "untried fields" of America which still delay "the class-war" from which alone "serious trouble" might spring. Meanwhile, it is still possible to effect a "firm founding of the state." And again he voices his belief in the rhythmic "persistent flow" of life, pointing out that whatever upheavals America faces, "spasms but tend Ever, at last, to quiet."

The complex humanity of Rolfe, who contradicts Ungar while admitting that "he's wise," continues to baffle and even disgust Clarel. Having decided that Vine does not entirely "see aright," Clarel has placed his faith in Derwent. The Anglican clergyman is another portrait in Melville's gallery of liberals, taking his place beside Plinlimmon, the Reverend Mr. Falsgrave, the Benjamin Franklin of *Israel Potter,* and the confidence man. But while it is made clear that the moral-intellectual weakness of Derwent is "confidence," he is portrayed without bitterness and is, in fact, a likable man. He is brisk, pleasant, handsome, possibly a little vain. Speaking of the "inherent vigor" of man's life, he believes that the decline of civilizations is only the unfortunate by-product of earth's perpetual reformation: "true reform," as he thinks, "goes on By nature." He takes pride in his own rather boyishly athletic-Christian manliness. A German-Jewish geologist who appears now and then pounding comically among the rocks with his hammer and who believes that "all is geology" and has never heard of Moses, Derwent pronounces "sterile." He is inclined to dismiss St. Francis as "effeminate," and for this is remonstrated with by Rolfe, who

admires St. Francis' "Christliness" as against the Charles-Kingsley-
like heartiness of Derwent. With an unshakable faith in modern
times—"maintaining the fine progressive part"—Derwent declares
that the world is at last "too civilized" for "Rome." Playing the
middleman, not with trouble and anguish, but by beguiling himself
with easy compromises, he defends science against the religionists
and religion against the scientists. Rolfe sees that Derwent's easy
belief in both science and religion is, though "generous," an illusion, and he shocks Clarel by remarking of Derwent that "his idol's
an hermaphrodite." Still, Rolfe's good-natured attacks on Derwent
begin to make Clarel wonder if "liberal thought" does not tend to
be caught halfway down a "slippery glacier."

Rolfe sees that Derwent is accustomed to "mask the thrill" of his
own emotions. Because, presumably, he has extreme emotions of
his own but will not admit it to himself, he is secretly disturbed at
the extremes of emotion in others. He is as much worried by
ecstatic joy as by profound grief and is deeply upset by the appearance of a youth on horseback singing a joyous song while he rides
toward the Jordan to dip his mother's shroud in the holy water. He
obscures his own feelings about Mortmain by insisting that Mortmain is mad. Mortmain, once a youth of generous heart and high
aspirations (he seems to have been a sort of Swedish Pierre), had
become a famous figure in certain republican-revolutionary movements on the Continent. Completely disillusioned, he now says:

> Man's vicious: snaffle him with kings;
> Or, if kings cease to curb, devise
> Severer bit.

Apocalyptically, he announces the coming extinction of mankind
and "the funeral" of the gods. If there is still any God, so he thinks,
God is the Red Destroyer, the modern "God of Habakkuk."

> He storms in Paris. . . .
> He's over the Rhine—He's at Berlin—
> At Munich—Dresden—fires Vien . . .
> In Rome; London's alert.

In an ecstasy of suffering and self-castigation, Mortmain retires
into the hills alone, seeking some last vestige of religious light. He
later returns to the company, not transfigured or refreshed, but

with prophetic exhortations to repent while "the armed world" still "holds its own." Sitting on a camel's skull by the Dead Sea near where the travelers suppose Sodom to have been, Mortmain discourses upon evil and innocence, expressing for a moment Melville's own conclusions. The carnal sins of Sodom were the vulgar, excusable sins compared with those which are more deeply evil. The really culpable sin is (as in Dante) fraud, varying in degree from confidence to hypocrisy. The real sinners are those who "serve Mammon" through "holy forms"; those who know the world "yet varnish it"; those "who trade on the coast of crime Though landing not." Sin is deeply and naturally motivated at subconscious levels. But despite the origin of sin, the sinful man is shallow, for sin "shuns" all knowledge of the "deeps": "Sin acts"; it does not reflect. Innocence Mortmain defines as reflection upon evil and the deeps from which evil springs. He is innocent whose thought "sweeps the abyss that sin has wrought" and who with "true heart"

> Moves as along the ocean's bed
> Amid the dragon's staring crew.

Often in Melville the vision of absolute evil is symbolized by a Medusalike woman. As Mortmain descants on sin and innocence, he gazes with rapt fascination into the slimy waters of the Dead Sea. Thinking apparently of his own Medealike mother (elsewhere he calls nature "Circe's sty"), he addresses the oozing sea thus:

> O fair Medea—
> O soft man-eater, furry fine:
> Oh, be thou Jael, be thou Leah—
> Unfathomably shallow!

And then with his intense longing for death, he cries

> The mould thou art of what men be:
> Events are all in thee begun. . . .
>   Undo, undo,
> Prithee undo, and still renew
> The fall forever!

Finally Mortmain dies among the rocks and his body is eaten by vultures and hyenas.

Rolfe is capable of facing such a death as Mortmain's, though "cosmetic-users," as he says, "scarce are bold To face a skull."

Clarel is frightened by Mortmain. And Derwent masks his own emotions by convincing himself that Mortmain "has fits." But even before the death of Mortmain, Clarel has begun to see through Derwent and to decide that even more than Mortmain he "breeds distrust." The separation of Clarel and Derwent comes in a canto significantly called "In Confidence." Derwent, sensing the "fervid earnestness" of Clarel's quest for a "secure retreat," offers Clarel his hand. Calling him "my son," he confesses that he feels "paternal sympathies" for him. Derwent bids the young man be gay and hopeful, exhorting him to shun the "selfish introverted search." "Be not extreme," he says, "midway is best." He warns Clarel not to be like Hamlet, that "perverse" and "indecorous" youth. But here Clarel turns on Derwent in a passion, saying that the next step in such an argument is to denounce Job himself as perverse or immoral. He challenges Derwent to admit that "Doubt bleeds" and that Faith is not "free from pain," and with this outburst terminates his reliance upon Derwent. Clarel finally realizes that to be a "fugitive" from pain, to be too "uninquiring," to "yearn" too much for peace, is to unfit oneself for a world in which to live is to "mix with tempers keen And narrow like the knife." Toward the end of the poem he comes to rely for guidance on the mature, poised mind of Rolfe, though not without uncertainties, misgivings, and sadness.

As the company returns to Jerusalem, Clarel is worried by unhappy presentiments and feelings of guilt because he had left Ruth. Entering the city at night, they see two graves being dug to receive two bodies stretched on the ground. They are the bodies of Ruth and Agar, both dead from the fever. After an outburst of passionate maledictions against God and the universe, Clarel disappears into the fastnesses of the city. We last see him at Easter time, walking with the variegated crowd on the Via Crucis. The poem ends with an epilogue affirming the faith of Rolfe in "the persistent flow" of life's rhythms, according to which "death but routs life into victory."

Clarel is not a supremely contrived poem, but there is a certain order and felicity in the symbols. At the beginning, when Clarel's feeling of frustration and alienation is strongest and when he is trying to make his first explorations of life, we find his state of mind symbolized by blind arches in the walls of Jerusalem, sealed windows, masoned-up gates, and windows so high that Clarel cannot see through them. There are also locked doors; vicariously Clarel suffers through a night during which Celio is locked out of the city. Later in the poem, when Clarel is confused and tentatively afraid, rather than merely frustrated, we find appropriate images: rifted rocks, mountains cloven asunder, a hushed night, and "a pain of troubled wonder." There is a recurring symbolism of stone or dryness and water. The Brook Kedron is continually referred to —as running underground, as drying up, as rushing in torrents, as exemplifying the mystery of the systole and diastole of life:

> All the mountain land
> Disclosed through Kedron far withdrawn,
> Cloven and shattered, hushed and banned,
> Seemed poised as in chaos true,
> Or throe-lock of transitional earth
> When old forms are annulled, and new
> Rebel, and pangs suspend the birth.

Sexual symbolism, intended to refer to Clarel's coming marriage, occurs throughout, as in the rock and sealed-door imagery mentioned above. At one point Clarel sees a kind of tableau, a monk in blue robes surrounded by white doves in the brilliant morning sun; it is a mystic symbol for celibacy which for a moment attracts Clarel. But in the next canto, called "The Recoil," Clarel decides that however many shining masculine or sexless Raphaels or Michaels he may see, Eve cannot be "disengaged" "from sex." At this point the Rose becomes a female sexual symbol and Clarel's symbol of beauty. And it becomes clear that part of Clarel's education consists of learning to accept Ruth as the Rose.

The *Divine Comedy* exerts a distinguishable influence on *Clarel*. We have a hero being conducted through a kind of modern Hell and Purgatory. The long section called "The Wilderness" may be loosely identified as an Inferno; in this section we have the "Sodom Lake" or Dead Sea scenes in which Mortmain defines the graver sins. The section called "Mar Saba" (the name of a monastery on a hilltop) is a kind of Purgatorio, the emphasis being on the milder sins. The return to Jerusalem and Ruth is similar to Dante's journey to Paradise, Ruth symbolizing both Beatrice and the sempiternal Rose of Paradise which Beatrice shows to Dante. Both poems may be said to be based upon the principle of withdrawal and return. As Dante withdraws from the world to undergo an ordeal after which he will be vouchsafed a vision of Paradise, so Clarel withdraws into the wilderness in order to return to Ruth with new knowledge and new strength.

The central symbolic idea in *Clarel* is that in modern times life has become sterile, that life has withdrawn its richness and its ecstasy and is no longer tragic but simply "progressive." Looking about the world, Clarel finds that "all is strange, withdrawn and far." He learns to reject those characters whose spiritual or moral failure disqualifies them from aiding in the "return": Nehemiah, the completely other-worldly man; Vine, the "reverted" man; Derwent, the Laodicean-progressive; and to accept Rolfe, the complete or "central" man with his faith in the "persistent flow" of life. The spiritual example of Rolfe is an affirmative answer to Clarel's question: "Returns each thing that may withdraw?" a positive assertion that,

> The schools of blue-fish years desert
> Our sounds and shores—but they revert;
> The ship returns on her long tack:
> The bones of Theseus are brought back:
> A comet shall resume its path
> Though three millenniums go.

Rolfe is a secular liberal, who, however, has reconciled himself with the claims upon human attention of a Christ, a St. Francis, an Ungar, and a Mortmain.* Rolfe has the temperament of the philosophical naturalist who, while taking account of those extremities of emotion which demand and create absolute values, still insists that the most palpable reality is the "latencies" of circumstance and time which "modify" God and Man. What we may call Rolfe's *sense of circumstance* is Clarel's chief discovery. The purpose of the poem, says Melville, is to plead "Just reason, and appeal for grace." Before Clarel can appeal for grace, he must recognize the fact that reason will not be found in a "secure retreat" but in the struggle of a mind like Rolfe's, which though it finds that "not much is certain," is nevertheless determined to fight its way toward illu-

---

* Rolfe's attitude toward Ungar and Mortmain is a good deal like the attitude a modern liberal might have toward D. H. Lawrence and T. S. Eliot.

mination through the "complex moods" of a paradoxical and diversified world.

Rolfe is Melville's ultimate humanist, the representative figure he had been working toward since he had purged the extremities of his titanism in *Pierre*—the figure, indeed, toward whom the strongest current of Melville's thought had always been flowing. It is Ungar and not Rolfe who is said to be like Ishmael and Ethan Allen. And though Rolfe has strong affinities with the high Promethean hero or Handsome Sailor, he is explicitly dissociated from this ideal figure. Rolfe is a man—human, modified, and limited. He is the human core of the high Promethean hero.

Almost as an act of revulsion or atonement, Melville tried to paint a full-scale portrait of the ideal hero in *Billy Budd*. And *Billy Budd* is a partly unconscious admission that the subtraction of the human core from the demigod had left nothing but a beatified child. Melville the humanist had made his last statement in *Clarel,* and finally the sleeping Christ, like a restive ghost of Pierre, could awaken.

XI

Innocence and Infamy

Melville's last book, a short novel written between 1888 and 1891 and called *Billy Budd, Foretopman,* has generally been praised for qualities it does not possess. It is natural, of course, to wish to see in *Billy Budd* the last ripe word of the aged Melville. And there has been a great temptation, especially on the liberal-religious left, to see in *Billy Budd,* as one writer says, Melville's final "testament of acceptance"—his final acceptance of a "tragic" view of life involving an apotheosis of the common man as Christ and an assertion that what is needed in American life is a leavening of individualism and law by the sympathetic passions of the heart. And *Billy Budd* is said to be Melville's definitive moral statement. But this estimate of *Billy Budd* will do our author no service if, as I think, the moral situation in the book is deeply equivocal.

In Melville's writings there are two basic kinds of hero, both akin, in their several variations, to the central figure of Prometheus. The first kind of hero is the false Prometheus, who in one way or another violates the deep-running, natural, and psychic rhythms of life which are necessary for all creative enterprise. The second kind of hero is the Handsome Sailor: the true hero in whom Prometheus tends to put on the full tragic manhood of Oedipus. This second kind of hero is briefly sketched or symbolized as Marnoo, Jack Chase, Bulkington, and Ethan Allen. In each case, he is a full-statured man, great in body, heart, and intellect, a man with great pain of experience behind him, a young man, but still so fully created a man that, in the case of Jack Chase, Ishmael is moved to call him "sire." At the beginning of *Billy Budd,* the Handsome Sailor is again symbolized, in the following manner:

In the time before steamships, or then more frequently than now, a stroller along the docks of any considerable seaport would occasionally have his attention arrested by a group of bronzed mariners, man-of-war's men or merchant sailors in holiday attire ashore on liberty. In certain instances, they would flank, or, like a bodyguard, quite surround some superior figure of their own class, moving along with them like Aldebaran among the lesser lights of his constellation. That signal object was the "Handsome Sailor" of the less prosaic time, alike of the military and merchant navies. With no perceptible trace of the vain-glorious about him, rather with the off-hand unaffectedness of natural regality, he seemed to accept the spontaneous homage of his shipmates. A somewhat remarkable instance recurs to me. In Liverpool, now half a century ago I saw under the shadow of the great dingy street-wall of Prince's Dock (an obstruction long since removed) a common sailor, so intensely black that he must needs have been a native African of the unadulterate blood of Ham. A symmetric figure, much above the average height. The two ends of a gay silk handkerchief thrown loose about the neck danced upon the displayed ebony of his chest; in his ears were big hoops of gold, and a Scotch Highland bonnet with a tartan band set off his shapely head.

The emblem of Lucy Tartan enlightens the forehead of the Handsome Sailor as he emerges from the depths of Night into the consciousness of Day. He moves as ponderously, but with as much strength and beauty, as Bulkington in *Moby-Dick,* or as revolutionary America itself, setting forth on the path of civilization.

Still, this magnificent and momentous figure does not appear at full scale in any of Melville's books. But Melville made two attempts to portray him fully: one in *Pierre* and one in *Billy Budd.* Not the least part of the wisdom which Melville had achieved at the end of *Pierre* was his realization that he could not portray this heroic figure, except as a perpetual adolescent whose suicide was entirely justified by the fact that he was no match for the realities of the world. At the end of *Pierre,* civilization was shown to be in the hands of conventional society, military power, and Laodicean liberalism. In *Billy Budd* civilization is shown to be in approximately the same hands. And the hero who opposes these forces is no more capable of doing so than Pierre.

Yet *Billy Budd* is a brilliant piece of writing, nicely constructed and balanced between swift, stark action and moral-philosophical comment. Though it falls sadly short of the pure tragedy Melville apparently wanted to write, it is still a moving drama, if a drama only of pathos. And though the portrait of Billy Budd is unacceptable, the other main characters bear the stamp of the author's great intellectual powers as few of his characters do.

As in *Israel Potter,* the scene is the revolutionary days of the late eighteenth century, a period whose still "undetermined momentousness" Melville thought unsurpassed in the whole range of history. This period, as we have noted, seemed to Melville to be America's primeval time, when its first great acts were performed and its best hopes discovered. But the spirit of heroism and liberation could be felt in other nations too, and Billy Budd, though he might as easily have been an American, is in fact an Englishman. He is a youth of twenty-one. His physical strength and beauty no less than his frank simplicity and good will make him a favorite aboard the merchant ship *Rights-of-Man,* where we first discover him. Homeward bound near England, the *Rights-of-Man* is stopped by the outward bound frigate H.M.S. *Indomitable.* The frigate is shorthanded and Billy Budd is impressed aboard and given a post in the foretop. He easily gains the affection and respect of the men and officers—with one exception. The exception is Claggart, the wonderfully conceived and depicted master-at-arms. For no easily determined reason Claggart is "down on" Billy Budd, as an oracular old sailor suggests when Billy comes to him for counsel. With an inhuman cunning Claggart sets his trap for Billy Budd, contriving in various ways to cast suspicion on him. The story takes place shortly after the British Navy has been badly shaken by unprecedented waves of mutiny in the ranks. And so Claggart's best strategy is to involve Billy Budd in a charge of insurrection. He goes to the quarterdeck and tells Captain Vere that Budd is plotting mutiny. The captain, though more suspicious of Claggart than of the accused man, calls them both to his cabin. There Claggart, looking deeply and unflinchingly into Billy Budd's eyes with a kind of savage sharklike hunger and hatred, repeats his charge. Billy Budd has always been handicapped by a stammer which overcomes his power of speech in moments of excitement. He is unable to answer the charge, even though the captain benevolently puts his hand on Billy's shoulder and tells him to take his time. The blocked utterance bursts forth not in the form of speech, but as a tremendous blow on Claggart's forehead from Billy Budd's fist—and the master-at-arms is killed on the spot. A drumhead court is quickly summoned, and though the court and the captain himself are tormented with a deep compunction, they soon sentence Billy Budd to be hanged at dawn—a sentence which is summarily carried out. Billy Budd dies murmuring, "God bless Captain Vere."

It is often said that *Billy Budd* shows Melville's final admission of the tragic necessity of law in human society. The fact of the matter is that Melville had admitted this forty years earlier in *White-Jacket* and had reaffirmed it in *Moby-Dick* by showing that the tragic dilemma of Ahab was in part due to his necessary commitment to the external forms of command. He makes no *discovery* of law in *Billy Budd*; he simply deals with the subject more carefully than he had before. Captain Vere's examination and defense of law in a man-of-war world and his decision that a human life must be sacrificed to this law is impeccable, irrefutable, and fully conscious of the pathetic irony of the situation. The flaw in the book is that Melville does not fully conceive of that which, in a genuine tragedy, has to be opposed to law.

Captain Vere and Claggart are perfectly portrayed. The captain's name—Edward Fairfax Vere—perhaps indicates what he is. He is Man (*vir*), but civilized Man. Though personally superior to the laws of "Cain's City," he nevertheless in all practical matters lives according to these laws. He is a superior type of "citified man." Captain Vere is a bachelor of forty-odd years. He is brave without being foolhardy, a disciplinarian but considerate of the interests of his men. He is inclined to be grave and practical; some of his acquaintances call him humorless and observe a streak of pedantry in his character. Yet he is sometimes given to moments of absent-mindedness, and when he is seen at the ship's rail gazing meditatively into the blankness of space his nickname, Starry Vere, seems especially to fit him. He has no brilliant qualities but is intellectually superior to his associates. He is a reader of books, preferring authors who deal with actual men and events or who philosophize, like Montaigne, in the spirit of common sense. And though his training has made his mind a "dyke" against the spate of revolutionary ideas coming out of France, his arguments against them are reasoned.

Captain Vere is profoundly moved by the plight of Billy Budd, and Melville tells us that the ordeal of the sentence and the hanging was worse for Vere than it was for Billy. Deciding to communicate the decision of the court to Billy in person, he assumes the relationship we have met so often in Melville's books. He becomes a father to a son. The possibility that Vere may in fact be Billy Budd's father is not contradicted by the author; for Billy was a foundling and, as the author suggests, a by-blow of some English nobleman. In *Billy Budd* the father whom the young hero seeks is shown to be purely mundane; he is "citified man" rather than Zeus or Jehovah. Captain Vere's short interview with Billy Budd, the sacred actualities of which Melville only hints at, is a kind of consummation of a quest he has been making all his life. The whole affair has so shaken him that the ship's surgeon suspects a touch of madness, a question which Melville carefully leaves open. Perhaps the captain's touch of madness is only his own terrible consciousness of having finally fulfilled the destiny of "citified man" —to recognize oneself as Caesar and one's son as Christ.

Melville describes Claggart as being about thirty-five. He is spare and tall, with the clean-cut features, except for a disproportionate heaviness of the chin, of a head on a Greek medallion. His hand is rather too small and there is a sort of intellectual pallor on his forehead. He has a trace of a foreign accent and though nothing is known of his origins, he has affinities, perhaps, with some Mediterranean culture. To say that Claggart is a version of the confidence man—the mysterious impostor from the East—may be surprising, but it is true.* Or rather he is the confidence man plus an actively evil nature. The figure in Melville's satire was not the evil man so

---

* The more we look into Melville's works, the more wonderfully complex grows the character of the confidence man. In the chapter on *Israel Potter* we had occasion to note the kinship of the confidence man with Benjamin Franklin and even with such a character as Babbalanja of *Mardi.* The Reverend Mr. Falsgrave and Plinlimmon of *Pierre* and Derwent of *Clarel* are first cousins of the confidence man. So also is the figure of the "master-at-arms," whom we meet as Bland in *White-Jacket* and Claggart in *Billy Budd.* With the confidence man in mind, compare the following phrases used to describe (the appropriately named) Bland:

"There was a fine polish about his whole person, and a pliant, insinuating style in his conversation, that was, socially, quite irresistible. . . ."

"Ashore such a man might have been an irreproachable mercantile swindler, circulating in polite society. . . ."

"I pitied the continual gnawing which, under all his deftly donned disguises, I saw lying at the bottom of his soul."

much as "the moderate man, the inveterate understrapper to the evil man." Claggart is the confidence man invested with a "natural depravity" willed by paranoiac guile and controlled by superior intellect. In his campaign against Billy Budd, he employs all the devices of "confidence." Subtly obsequious, outwardly frank and friendly, he is a "fair-spoken man," speaking in silvery accents with a "confidential" tongue. Conducting himself, as is his wont, with an "uncommon prudence" and speaking with a Pharisaical sense of "retributive righteousness," he sells his case to Captain Vere:

What he said, conveyed in the language of no uneducated man, was to the effect following if not altogether in these words, namely, that . . . he had seen enough to convince him that at least one sailor aboard was a dangerous character in a ship mustering some who not only had taken a guilty part in the late serious trouble, but others also who, like the man in question, had entered His Majesty's service under another form than enlistment.

Contemptuous of this rhetoric, the captain interrupts with: "Be direct, man; say impressed men." But the sweet voice continues, using the confidence trick of misrepresenting the nature of a man. Billy Budd, says Claggart, is a "deep one"; under the fair exterior there is a "man-trap." This is an argument the captain cannot ignore; Claggart has merely to enunciate the charge and his case is won. The full character of Claggart emerges *in spite of* Melville's statement that he is "depraved according to nature." Melville states this, perhaps, because he wishes to oppose two "natural" men— Billy Budd, good by nature, and Claggart, depraved by nature—to "citified man," Captain Vere, who is presumably both good and depraved by nature. But to say that one character is good by nature and another depraved can have only a symbolic value. Claggart becomes evil as a civilized man. He becomes evil in the only way which allows us to understand what evil is: by living in Cain's city and making choices of action. It is, indeed, only his being a certain kind of "citified man" which allows his "natural depravity" or his kinship with the torpedo fish a meaningful symbolic value.

So highly "citified" is Claggart's depraved mind that, like the mind of mankind, it generates a compensatory vision of innocence. And this vision is at the root of his ambivalent feeling toward Billy

Budd, finding its expression to some extent in a homosexual attraction. Billy Budd's "harmlessness" fills Claggart with both longing and revulsion at the same time that Budd's physical beauty attracts him. Like Milton's Satan, thinking of the Garden, Claggart is capable of looking at Billy Budd and weeping "feverish tears." He weeps at being unable to put off the burden of civilization and be "harmless." But in less regressive moments he can feel the active bitterness of the ambiguous attraction-repulsion which Billy rouses in him. "To be nothing more than innocent!" Such a being is in the deepest sense a mutineer, an apostate from Cain's city. It is very difficult not to agree with Claggart.

The weakness of *Billy Budd* is the central character himself. The trouble is that he is not in any meaningful sense what Claggart says he is: "deep" and a "man-trap." He *ought* to be "deep" and in some inescapable human way a "man-trap." Otherwise he cannot function meaningfully in a tragedy which tries to demonstrate the opposition between human nature and the heart on the one hand and law on the other. Otherwise he cannot possibly be the Handsome Sailor. It is surely significant of uncertainty that Melville, though outwardly identifying Billy Budd as the Handsome Sailor, actually hedges. Melville's dedication of his book to Jack Chase inferentially compares Billy Budd with the Handsome Sailor of *White-Jacket*. After describing the Handsome Sailor and symbolizing him as the giant negro, Melville writes: "Such a cynosure, at least in aspect, and something such too in nature, though with important variations made apparent as the story proceeds, was welkin-eyed Billy Budd, or Baby Budd." Melville is determined apparently to have his cake and eat it too when it comes to the question of what manner of man his hero actually is. After thus presenting Billy Budd as a Handsome Sailor "with important variations," Melville goes on to ignore all possible "variations," referring to his hero throughout the rest of the book as the Handsome Sailor. Obviously Jack Chase and Billy Budd have many things in common, but the abyss between them is prodigious. And Melville could not admit this to himself.

Billy Budd is simple, direct, and kindly. He is a sort of Adam, the Adam as yet untainted by the "urbane serpent." He has the "humane look of reposeful good nature" sometimes shown in

statues of Hercules. Lacking powers of reflection, he is a fatalist
as animals are fatalists. He is primeval, unspoiled man wandering,
as if dazed, in Cain's city. In describing Billy, Melville grows hazily
rhetorical: "he possessed that kind and degree of intelligence which
goes along with the unconventional rectitude of a sound human
creature—one to whom not as yet had been proffered the questionable apple of knowledge." He is a "childman." "He had none of
that intuitive knowledge of the bad which in natures not good or
incompletely so, foreruns experience, and therefore may pertain,
as in some instances it too clearly does pertain, even to youth." One
cannot understand the character of Billy Budd except as the final,
and almost the first—first *crucial*—self-indulgence of a great intelligence. Looking backward almost fifty years, trying to convince
himself that such a man might actually have existed, Melville tries
to re-create life on a man-of-war in the image of Eden, insisting
that sailors have a particular kind of "innocence" not found in the
generality of mankind. And while this may be true in a certain
sense—there is no doubt a kind of innocence or at least sexual and
mental juvenility in a sailor's life—we must take *White-Jacket* to
be Melville's clear account of life on a man-of-war; and in that book
he had concluded that man-of-war's men were on the whole less
innocent than the rest of mankind. The character of Billy Budd is
meaningful only as a moving and revealing comment on Melville's
last years.

The author makes an attempt to show that in the course of the
story Billy Budd finds the consummation of his destiny. Having
been sentenced to die by the man who may possibly be his father,
Billy Budd can at last drop the role of Ishmael and become Isaac,
the lawful heir of Abraham. When he first begins to be troubled
by the evidence of a plot against him, Billy Budd seeks advice from
an old sailor described as the mainmastman of the ship. We remember from *White-Jacket* that the patriarchal mainmastman was referred to as an Abraham, and though he is not called that in *Billy
Budd*, the parallel is suggestive. It is this old sailor who has given
Billy the name of Baby Budd; he refuses or is unable to play the
part of Billy's father, as Abraham refuses Ishmael. Later Melville
suggests that Billy finds his atonement with Captain Vere: "The
austere devotee of military duty, letting himself melt back into what

remains primeval in our formalized humanity, may in the end have caught Billy to heart, even as Abraham may have caught young Isaac on the brink of resolutely offering him up in obedience to the exacting behest." This atonement is the logical conclusion to Melville's Ishmael theme, more fully and exactly stated here, in the strict terms of the Ishmael myth, than in *White-Jacket*. In *White-Jacket* the recognition and final meeting of father and son was presented as an act of maturity on the part of the son, a recognition of human depravity, an admission of law, form, and patriarchal majesty, and a consequent liberation of the son's creative energy. In *Billy Budd,* Melville insists on trying to have it both ways: there are suggestions that Billy has experienced a metamorphosis of character through an "agony mainly proceeding from a generous young heart's virgin experience of the diabolical incarnate and effective," and that he is "spiritualized now through late experiences so poignantly profound." The reader accepts this gratefully and with belief. And he reflects that, after all, Melville is going to say that Billy Budd is now the Ishmael who has become Isaac, the harmless Adam who has become the fallen Adam, the foundling of noble antecedents who has become Oedipus the tragic hero. All this would indicate that Billy Budd's agony has made of him a fully tragic, fully suffering, fully knowing man.

But not so. Billy Budd is hanged after sleeping the night out with the serene happy light of babyhood playing over his features. When a man is hanged, certain mechanical-physical spasms take place in his body; his bowels are emptied, his penis erects, and there is an ejaculation of semen. When Billy Budd is hanged, there is a total "absence of spasmodic movement." The tragedy of Melville's heroes had always been that they were "unmanned" by circumstances or the effect of their own moral decisions. Billy Budd was unmanned by Melville himself. There is a hint that the hanging of Billy Budd was a miraculous euthanasia. We recall that in *The Confidence Man* an "invalid Titan" had violently quarreled with the peddler of the Samaritan Pain Dissuader for claiming that his balm was "a certain cure for any pain in the world." In portraying Billy Budd, not as Isaac or the fallen Adam or Oedipus, but as the hermaphrodite Christ who ascends serenely to the yardarm of the *Indomitable,* Melville apparently forgot his "invalid Titan."

2

Billy Budd is a syncretic work of art, and though we must not overemphasize its importance, it is a measure of Melville's final position. It demands to be considered as a "natural" tragedy as the tragedies of Sophocles and Shakespeare are "natural." But it is also a beatific vision, a vision of the hermaphrodite Christ who is mentioned in *Moby-Dick* and who always dimly haunted Melville— that shadowy Christ who, as we have noted, slept restively in Melville's mind after the writing of *Pierre*. If the Rolfe of *Clarel* had appeared in *Billy Budd*, we might have had a fully tragic hero. As it is, we have the Handsome Sailor minus Rolfe, the tragic human core. The residue is something less and more than human, a child or a flower or a radiance. The fall of Simon Magus symbolizes not only the decline of the pagan magic which created *Moby-Dick*; it also symbolizes a reaffirmation of Christianity—more particularly a fresh commitment to the infantile Christ who seeks entrance in *Pierre, Bartleby the Scrivener, Israel Potter, The Confidence Man,* and *Clarel,* and who is finally admitted in *Billy Budd*. It is surely not true, as some writers, including Charles Olson, have alleged, that Melville's weakness for the hermaphrodite Christ is the reason for the disintegration of his art after *Moby-Dick*. For one thing, as I hope I have been able to show, Melville's art did not disintegrate after his best book; it merely changed in various ways, even though these ways were journeys less bracing than the ascent of the magician. Furthermore, in the light of *Billy Budd,* the remarkable thing is that the hermaphrodite Christ appears so little in Melville's other writings; and this is especially remarkable of *Clarel,* the work in which Melville tried most explicitly to deal with moral problems and intellectual positions.

Billy Budd, the "Rose" of Melville's last work, is himself a syncretic conception, the product of nineteenth century nature worship and the image of the divine child-man. Though of all nineteenth century writers Melville is the least open to the charge of entertaining a superficial view of nature (indeed his superiority over Wordsworth and Emerson is his *tragic* view of nature), he nevertheless paid something of the romantic homage to the violet by the mossy stone. The frightening insistence with which, after

Pierre, nature presented itself to him as a stony waste land or a Medean muck, together with his feeling that "Niebuhr & Strauss" had robbed the world of its "bloom," led him to seek for whatever Rose nature in some mysterious or paradoxical way might produce. In the short stories of the 1850's, the Rose, as in *Jimmy Rose,* is a symbol of life reviving triumphantly and with quiet beauty in a hostile environment, a beautiful extrusion from the dark muck and suffering of earth and human life. In "After the Pleasure Party," the Rose is a symbol of sexual fertility and artistic creation. In *Clarel,* as we have seen, the Rose is identified with Ruth, who like Billy Budd himself is both a beautiful product of nature and an angel. In "Weeds and Wildings, with a Rose or Two"—a group of poems written late in life and tenderly dedicated to his wife—Melville uses the Rose as a principle of life which sustains itself though it feeds on nothing but snow or virginity; again the Rose is like the Promethean hearth fire; or it sheds light in a sepulcher, blooming in the very atmosphere of death. The idea that nature, dark and hostile as it may be, paradoxically creates the good and the beautiful is restated in *Billy Budd,* where the young hero is said to embody natural goodness and beauty, a flower of nature, which paradoxically also produces a Claggart. As a social symbol Billy Budd has close affinities with the "natural man" or "noble savage," an idea celebrated by the period in which the story takes place.

But if Billy Budd is natural goodness, he is also divine goodness. He is that peculiarly American god, the beatified boy. His career is like that of Christ; he is persecuted by a satanic Claggart and rebuffed and sacrificed by "citified man." With a loose similarity, Wellingborough Redburn had been persecuted by Jackson and rebuffed by Captain Riga. But Redburn is a creature acting in what Rolfe called "Circumstance" and "Time." At the overt levels of human tragedy, Billy Budd is not a definably human being. The moral content of his character is self-contradictory and obscure. Innocence, Mortmain had said in *Clarel,* is the act of the true heart reflecting upon evil. This is, perhaps, the only kind of innocence we want to take seriously or believe in.

Surely we are not more likely to be moved by *Billy Budd* as beatific vision than by *Billy Budd* as natural tragedy. Yet the story is strangely moving. Let us look below the clutter of its overt levels.

3

At the deep levels of *Billy Budd* there is a massive and terrible image, which, it seems to me, moved the aged Melville so over-poweringly that he was unable to give it direct expression. As Melville says at one point in *Billy Budd*, "every . . . form of life has its secret mines and dubious sides; the side popularly dis-claimed." On the night before Billy Budd's execution, the ship, with its decks, is like the story itself. "The night was luminous on the spar-deck, but otherwise in the cavernous ones below—levels so very like the tiered galleries in a coal-mine."

The real theme of *Billy Budd* is castration and cannibalism, the ritual murder and eating of the Host. During his trial Billy pro-claims his faithfulness to the king and to Captain Vere by saying, "I have eaten the King's bread, and I am true to the King." When, "without remorse," the dying Captain Vere murmurs, "Billy Budd, Billy Budd," he expresses faithfulness, dependence, and longing. He had eaten of the Host, and he was true to the Host. After forty years Melville had returned to the theme of *Typee*. In that book the young hero had extricated himself from the valley by a sudden exchange of passivity for action. Billy Budd is fatally passive, his acts of violence being unconsciously calculated to ensure his final submission. All of Billy's conscious acts are toward passivity, the first one being his quick acquiescence in his impressment, an act which causes the hero-worshiping sailors to regard him with "sur-prise" and "silent reproach." In symbolic language, Billy Budd is seeking his own castration—seeking to yield up his vitality to an authoritative but kindly father, whom he finds in Captain Vere. When anyone else stirs the depths of Billy's longing, threatening to bring his unconscious thoughts to consciousness, he flies into a sud-den rage. When Red-Whiskers, a sailor who had once been a butcher, maliciously digs Billy in the ribs to show him "just whence a sirloin steak was cut," Billy gives him a "terrible drubbing." And when the minion of Claggart approaches Billy on the moonlit deck and, holding out two shining guineas, says, "See, they are yours, Bill," Billy Budd stammeringly threatens to toss him over the rail. The persistent feminine imagery Melville associates with Billy and his statement that "above all" there was "something in the mobile expression, and every chance attitude and movement suggestive of a mother eminently favored by Love and the Graces," indicate that Billy has identified himself with the mother at a pre-Oedipean level and has adopted the attitude of harmlessness and placation toward the father in order to avoid the hard struggle of the Oedipus conflict. The Oedipus conflict entails, of course, the idea of one's incestuous guilt and one's desire to kill one's father. The psychoanalyst might say that Billy Budd has avoided the Oedipus struggle by forming an attachment to the mother at the prephallic level of "oral eroticism" and has allayed his fears of castration by symbolically castrating himself (by being consciously submissive) and by repressing his rage and hostility against the father in order to placate him. That all Billy's rage and hostility against the father are unconscious is symbolized by the fact that whenever it is aroused it cannot find expression in spoken language. Billy can only stutter and use his fists. This is a mechanism for keeping himself from admitting his own guilt and his own destructiveness. For indeed Billy destroys not only Claggart but himself—and even Captain Vere. For a cloud seems to pass over Vere in his last days, and he dies without achieving the rewards his character had seemed to predestine him to achieve; he dies longing for a "child-man" he had once known.

The food symbolism need not be labored. It recurs frequently, and it is the symbolism which takes us down most swiftly into the coherent lower strata of the story, where there is "a subterranean fire . . . eating its way deeper and deeper." Melville even symbolizes moral qualities by their taste, the innocent character having an "untampered-with flavor like that of berries" as against the guilty character, which has the "questionable smack of a compounded wine." Frequently Billy Budd is compared with animals —a heifer, a horse, a dog, a nightingale, a goldfinch. When he is hanged, he ascends to the yardarm like a "singing-bird," watched from below by a "wedged mass of upturned faces"—as if the sailors were birds expecting to be fed. It is said of Billy Budd (the Lamb of God) that the serpent has never bitten him, but after the accusation Claggart is described as a snake.

The idea of Billy as Host is established early in the story. When the lieutenant of the *Indomitable* goes aboard the *Rights-of-Man* in search of new hands and immediately selects Billy Budd, he drinks some of the captain's grog almost as if conscious of performing a ritual. "Lieutenant," says the captain, "you are going to take my best man from me, the jewel of 'em." " 'Yes, I know,' rejoined the other, immediately drawing back the tumbler preliminary to a replenishing; 'yes, I know. Sorry.' " The captain, referring to the pacifying effect Billy has had on his troublesome sailors, then says, "A virtue went out of him, sugaring the sour ones. They took to him like hornets to treacle." Metaphors such as these evoke the primitive rite of slaughtering the young hero in order to eat his flesh and thus obtain his "virtue," his strength, or his heroic quality.

Later in the story Billy Budd spills his soup at mess, and Claggart, happening to pass by at the moment, is inwardly enraged, though outwardly he is only suavely and ambiguously satirical. Melville seems to feel that the enormous eruption of hostile emotion in Claggart may strike the reader as excessive and hence unbelievable. He therefore prefaces one of his comments on the spilled soup with a paragraph which says in effect that the most ordinary event may be a symbolic act which can arouse momentous passions:

Passion, and passion in its profoundest, is not a thing demanding a palatial stage whereupon to play its part. Down among the groundlings, among the beggars and rakers of the garbage, profound passion is enacted. And the circumstances that provoke it, however trivial or mean, are no measure of its power.

The palatial stage is surely the conscious mind or the realm of conscious art, and the abode of beggars and rakers of the garbage is the unconscious mind. There are "beggars" in the unconscious mind, calling the ego back among the rakers of garbage, as Billy Budd calls his own ego back. And is not this whole passage intended as a statement that *Billy Budd* does not present the reader with a "palatial stage" where profoundest passions are enacted but that, instead, these passions are being enacted "down among the groundlings"? This comes close to telling us not only what is wrong with the story—simply that its profound passions do not find adequate objective representation—but also what is wrong with Billy Budd as tragic hero—that there is no "palatial stage" in his personality, no conscious structure, no mind whose disintegration we should watch with pity and terror rather than merely with bewilderment and an obscure sense of loss.

When Claggart spies the spilled soup, it seemed to him "the sly escape of a spontaneous feeling on Billy's part more or less answering to the antipathy on his own." He feels that Billy has insulted him. But what is the nature of the insult? Presumably that, in spilling the soup, Billy has symbolically exposed himself to Claggart as the Host, the vessel from which issues "virtue." ("Handsomely done, my lad!" cries Claggart. "And handsome is as handsome did it, too!") The spilled soup has also exposed Claggart's guilt as an eater of the Host and, furthermore, Claggart's fear of his own unconscious desire to be like Billy; for the psychological content of Claggart's desire to share Billy's innocence is his desire to be the passive Host.

Melville tells us that Claggart's jaw is heavy out of proportion with his otherwise delicately shaped face—Claggart's unconscious motives center upon orality. This occurs to us when, for example, he smiles at Billy Budd with an ambiguously "glittering dental satire." One of Claggart's "cunning corporals" is called Squeak, "so nicknamed by the sailors on account of his squeaky voice and sharp visage ferreting about the dark corners of the lower decks after interlopers, satirically suggesting to them the idea of a rat in a cellar." Squeak spies on Billy Budd and in this capacity is described as the "purveyor" who "feeds Claggart's passions."

I am sure that much of the sacramental symbolism in *Billy Budd* is conscious and intended. But some of it may be less conscious. One cannot be sure how much Melville means by pointing out that two other partisans of Claggart in compromising Billy Budd (two of Claggart's "messmates," they are called) are the Armourer and the Captain of the Hold; but it is a haunting idea that the Armourer represents Teeth and the Captain of the Hold represents Belly. Nor can one say what Thyestean implications there may be in the use of parts of the body in referring to Claggart, whose nickname is Jimmy Legs and whose official title is Master-at-Arms.

As the story concludes, the grim symbolism occurs more frequently and with more intensity. In the captain's cabin Claggart's "mesmeric glance," which Melville compares with "the hungry lurch of the torpedo fish," quickly determines Billy's fate. It is the overt threat of castration which always sets off the explosion of Billy's unconscious fears and resentments. There is a terrible up-welling of his passive emotions, as if in a last attempt to control their aggressive counterparts. Briefly Billy has the expression of "a condemned vestal priestess at the moment of her being buried alive, and in the first struggle against suffocation"—images which convey both the desire for, and the fear of, castration.* But such emotions as these Billy cannot express consciously. He stutters, and strikes Claggart.

Describing the scene in which Vere informs Billy Budd of the sentence, Melville says, "there is no telling the sacrament." There is no telling; but the sacrament can be symbolized. Lying manacled on the deck during the night, Billy is like "a patch of discolored snow . . . lingering at some upland cave's black mouth." His terrible experiences are of the order that "devour our human tis-sues." The skeleton begins to show under Billy's cheek for the first time; he lies between two cannon as if "nipped in the vise of fate." After the hanging of this Lamb of God, after the chaplain has knelt down "on his marrow bones" to pray (as the ballad of "Billy in the Darbies" says), after the night has passed and it is full day, "the fleece of low-hanging vapor had vanished, licked up by the sun that late had so glorified it." The very patriarch of the universe feeds on Billy Budd.

The passage Melville calls a "Digression" is difficult and obscure; but I venture the following account. The purser and the surgeon discuss the absence of spasm in Billy's body. (They are at mess during this discussion: we are continually reminded in *Billy Budd* of the verbal kinship of "mess" with the ritual word "mass.") The purser is "a rather ruddy, rotund person, more accurate as an ac-countant than profound as a philosopher." The surgeon is "spare

* The psychoanalysts tell us that suffocation is sometimes identified in the unconscious with castration. In connection with the cabin scene, the following passage is significant: "Quite often a patient begins to stutter when he is par-ticularly eager to prove a point. Behind his apparent zeal he has concealed a hostile or sadistic tendency to destroy his opponent by means of words, and the stuttering is both a blocking of and a punishment for this tendency. Still more often stuttering is exacerbated by the presence of prominent or authoritative per-sons, that is, of paternal figures against whom the unconscious hostility is most intense." O. Fenichel, *The Psychoanalytic Theory of Neuroses*, pp. 312–313.

and tall" (the same words used to describe Claggart): he is caustic, austere, and something of an intellectual. The two men are opposite types. The purser is the unthinking human animal who kills, vicariously, in order to eat. He is the simple cannibal, as is indicated by his placid rotundity (his being like a purse) and by his crude belief that Billy controlled his spasm by "will power." The surgeon is, like Claggart, a lean, emotionally complex and ambivalent sadist: he is more interested in murder than in food, as may be symbolized by his hastily leaving the mess table to get back to a patient in the sick bay. Thus, this very horrifying passage is not really a digression: it is a brief scene which universalizes the theme of the story by presenting two opposite mythical types of man lingering, as it were, over the body.

As the body of Billy Budd, wrapped in canvas and weighted with cannon balls, slides over the rail, the sailors "who had just beheld the prodigy of repose in the form suspended in air" think of the same form "foundering in the deeps"—an image of the act of eating. Over the spot where Billy has sunk, gaunt sea birds wheel and scream; and though the birds are predictably moved by "mere animal greed for prey," the sight has a surprising effect on the sailors. "An uncertain movement began among them, in which some encroachment was made." It is a brief moment of potentially mutinous commotion, which we can understand by noticing that the captain and his officers are symbolically connected with the birds, a connection the sailors unconsciously make. Immediately after the hanging, there had been a similar murmurous impulse to mutiny among the sailors. But the ship's officers had acted quickly. Their authoritative voice was heard in the whistle of the boatswain and his mates, which was "shrill as the shriek of the sea-hawk," which "pierced the low ominous sound" and "dissipated" it, so that in a moment or two "the throng was thinned by one half."

In a man-of-war world, Melville is saying, law feeds on man, being only a translation into social forms of that "horrible vulturism of earth" of which he had spoken in *Moby-Dick*. And with a complex human vulturism Captain Vere feeds on Billy Budd. Notice the sexual-sacramental character of Vere's reaction to Billy's spontaneous "God bless Captain Vere." At these words, "Captain Vere, either through stoic self-control or a sort of momentary paralysis induced by emotional shock, stood erectly rigid as a musket in the ship-armor's rack." The sexual spasm does not occur in Billy Budd because Billy's vitality or "virtue" has been symbolically transferred to Vere. And yet the transference is ambiguous; paralysis and rigidity suggest death just as surely as erection and the potentiality of the musket suggest life. New vitality has been given to Vere as captain and exponent of martial law (Vere as "musket"), but as man and father he has been stricken.

The intimation of Melville's passages about Lord Nelson is that had Nelson been aboard the *Indomitable* instead of Vere (the two are inferentially compared on several occasions), all this might not have happened, or—and perhaps this is the central point—if it had happened, no subsequent cloud would have passed over Nelson, as it does over Vere. Nelson is the invulnerable and fully mature father, a mythical hero standing behind Captain Vere, a less majestic figure. Nelson already has the qualities of Billy Budd, so that the ritual transference of vitality need not ruin him with its cruel ambiguities. Nelson has the heroic vitality of Billy Budd and the brilliance and audacity of the "jewel" among sailors; it is Nelson's fatherhood which allows him to make "ornate publication" of the very qualities, in sublimated form, which Billy Budd, in the form of infantile rage and hostility, represses. As Melville presents him, Nelson, the "Great Sailor," is the ultimate heroic possibility of the man-of-war world. But he is not of that order of hero represented by Jack Chase; Jack Chase symbolizes a culture beyond the boundaries of Nelson's world. Nelson would never leave his ship to take part in a republican revolution, as Jack Chase did. He is the mythical father whose very presence on board ship, as Melville says, is enough to forestall an incipient mutiny—the uprising, that is, of the sons against the father.

The imposing structure of personality Melville attributes to Nelson is beyond the reach of Captain Vere because Vere's moral stability is not proof against the uprising of the sons. In Claggart he sees his own hostility toward Billy Budd. (The relation of Vere to Claggart and Billy is the relation of a father to his sons, one of whom assumes the aggressive and hostile role of the father and the other of whom assumes the passive role of the mother.) In Billy Budd, Captain Vere sees his own imperfectly redeemed childhood. Vere, imposing and even heroic as he is, must repeatedly return to his own childhood to feed on it and to murder it. For him there is no other way of supporting, of nourishing, the structure of consciousness, order, authority, and legality which constitutes the man-of-war world. The man-of-war world destroys itself by feeding on its own vitality, as the vulture feeds upon Prometheus.

This is in itself a moving idea; and so is the implied identification of Billy Budd with Christ. But is there not still another source of the massive emotion which rests uneasily beneath the imperfect surface of *Billy Budd*? Consider the connections Melville makes between the captains and literature. Nelson's ship is "poetic"; it has "symmetry" and "grand lines." Of Nelson at Trafalgar, Melville writes:

> If under the presentiment of the most magnificent of all victories, to be crowned by his own glorious death, a sort of priestly motive led him to dress his person in the jewelled vouchers of his own shining deeds; if thus to have adorned himself for the altar and the sacrifice were indeed vainglory, then affectation and fustian is each truly heroic line in the great epics and dramas, since in such lines the poet embodies in verse those exaltations of sentiment that a nature like Nelson, the opportunity being given, vitalizes into acts.

Homer is a kind of Nelson. They are the same mythical hero— great captains of the mind, the sea, and the man-of-war world. The author of *Moby-Dick* was such a captain.

Captain Vere "loved books." His name, "Vere," signifies (besides "man") "truth"; he is a speaker of the truth. Both his mien and his interests connect him with different kinds of literature than that associated with Nelson. He likes books "treating of actual men and events, no matter of what era." Such a man of truth is Herman Melville, who writes concerning *Billy Budd*: "The symmetry of form attainable in pure fiction cannot so readily be achieved in a narration essentially having less to do with fable than with fact. Truth uncompromisingly told will always have its ragged edges."

In *Typee*, Melville had already pictured himself as Billy Budd, the youth with the nameless malady who shrank with such inexplicable fear from the tattooing instrument, tipped with a shark's tooth, and who discovered that his elders—the fathers and the warriors of the tribe—were cannibals.

Lord Nelson is not on "the main road"; he is on "a bypath." The central autobiographical figure in *Billy Budd* is Captain Vere. The dark and moving image of the book is Melville as the devourer of his own childhood. An old man with sons of his own,* Melville is overwhelmingly moved with pity for the passive, hermaphrodite youth, an image of himself, who must continuously be killed in the rite of the sacrament if books are to be written or the man-of-war world sustained—or indeed if life is to go on at all.

4

Surely, then—to recall the restrictions on *Billy Budd* which I tried to make in the first sections of this chapter—I contradict myself. Billy Budd *is* a deep one and a man-trap (but if he is, he cannot be "innocent"!). His personality has extensive moral significance and psychological reality. He is highly effective, since he kills Claggart and even Captain Vere. And Captain Vere, not Billy Budd, is the tragic hero of the story.

It seems to me, however, that how one judges *Billy Budd* depends on what level of the story one is talking about. Potentially the story is one of the great tragedies of Western literature. But the upper level, the conscious structure, the "palatial stage" is far too uncreated, self-contradictory, and noncommittal to articulate the underlying images. At the explicit symbolic and dramatic levels of the story Melville draws back in awe from Billy Budd and can speak of him only by painful acts of will which in the very process of becoming articulate cut themselves off from the deepest sources of emotion and thus remain inexpressive. Billy Budd's stammering is Melville's own. When Billy Budd speaks articulately, he misrepresents his own deepest emotions. So does Melville.

* Melville's first son Malcolm shot himself accidentally or on purpose in 1869, when he was twenty and Melville was fifty. The Melville family cherished a phrase spoken by the baby Malcolm in reference to his father: "Where dat old man?"

XII

The Visored Face

This armed man
In corselet showed the dented plate,
And dread streak down the thigh-piece ran;
But the bright helm inviolate
Seemed raised above the battle-zone—
Cherubic with a rare device:
Perch for the bird-of-paradise.
A victor seemed he, without pride
Of victory, or joy in fame;
'Twas reverence and naught beside,
Unless it might that shadow claim
Which comes of trial. Yes, the art
So cunning was, that it in part
By fair expressiveness of grace
Atoned even for the visored face.
                              —*Clarel*

The figure of Ishmael—the outcast seeking his birthright—is implicit in all of Melville's work, from *Typee* to *Billy Budd*. Melville evolved the idea of Ishmael from the complex infantile experience of his own self-mythicized orphanhood, and Ishmael became first the symbol of a generalized orphanhood and then developed into the mask-consciousness which tells the story of *Moby-Dick*. In *Moby-Dick*, Ishmael had become American Man— a possibly heroic personality hidden behind a mask which asked, in effect: What is this man? or What may he become? In each of Melville's novels the masked Ishmael confronts us with this question. Melville's other heroes must be seen as a series of answers to the question. Among these heroes Ishmael seeks his paternity, his mythical connection with society and the order and power of Nature. Melville is primarily concerned with personality and culture rather than with questions of philosophical truth. Nevertheless a basic philosophical theme, the quest of consciousness for reality, runs through his books. Symbolically, this is the quest of Ishmael for either the kind of reality envisioned by a false hero like Paul Jones, who sees a world cleft by "organic disorder" and "derangement," or like the confidence man, who does not see the world at all, or it is a quest for the reality envisioned by a true hero like Bulkington, who sees the world as an organic continuum of suffering and death and regeneration. Looking at Melville's whole work, we see Ishmael, as it were, climbing a tower in the early books, reaching the top in *Moby-Dick*, falling with the ruin of the tower, and then, after *Moby-Dick*, surveying the landscape from lower vantage points. In the early books Ishmael is Human Nature seeking Consciousness; and in the later books he is Consciousness seeking Reality.

In two of the early novels, *Typee* and *White-Jacket*, we have the heroic figures of Marnoo and Jack Chase, brief symbolic portraits of a kind of true hero whom Ishmael admires and in whose image he may make himself as he matures beyond childhood. But the young man of *Typee* cannot become a Marnoo nor can White-Jacket become Jack Chase without great suffering and without overcoming the hazard of false seductive images which seek to "unman" him. *Mardi* represents an important step in Melville's marshaling of the possibilities of Ishmael's character. For in this book the figure of the false Prometheus first emerges. From this time on, Melville showed that Ishmael can become the Handsome Sailor only by coming to terms with the false Prometheus. In the first part of *Mardi* we have the same type of Ishmaelite hero as occurs in the other early books. Then suddenly the whole method and atmosphere of the book changes. The teller of the tale becomes Taji, a titanic figure caught between the extreme absolutes of man's spiritual experience, whose rhythms Melville called withdrawal and return. The creation of Taji, unsatisfactory as it is within the scope of *Mardi*, was one of the decisive acts of objectification which made *Moby-Dick* possible. Taji is also presented as being like Marnoo, but from the drift of the book, especially as seen in the light of *Moby-Dick* and *Pierre*, we surmise that he will turn out to be, not the Handsome Sailor, but the false Prometheus.

Moby-Dick is the only book in which we have a complete pic-

ture of Ishmael and what he may become. Bulkington, that wonderfully concise and tantalizing hero, is what Ishmael may become
if he does not become Ahab. Ahab is a false hero because he
violates the deep-running natural necessity of life's rhythms, "jamming" himself on, smashing recklessly athwart nature's balance of
life and death, performing that huge suicidal act of abstraction
which is the only way he knows of re-allying himself with nature.
In *Moby-Dick* occurs the first portrait of another kind of false
hero—little Pip. If Ahab's fault is that he returns and returns
and returns without ever being able to withdraw, little Pip's fault
is that he withdraws and is never able to return. Bulkington, combining within himself Ahab, the man of power, action, and intelligence, and Pip, the silenced anchorite, is the embodiment of the
rhythms of being and consciousness. He is Man fully formed, fully
human, fully wise.

   Pierre is a legend of narcissism. Melville's main figures are in
the book—Ishmael, the false Prometheus, and the Handsome
Sailor. But they are all Pierre. Pierre will succeed in becoming
Pierre if he escapes the fate of becoming Pierre: this would be a
meaningful psychological problem if the different aspects of Pierre's
personality were clearly conceived. But in this book Melville first
intimates that he is unsure whether the true hero is a man or a
child. In *Moby-Dick* the possibility that Ishmael may become Bulkington is a possibility that he may mature. The horror of reversion
which Ishmael felt on that fateful night when he nearly capsized the
Pequod is the central emotion of *Pierre*. The question the book
asks is, What if the true hero be not ahead of Ishmael but behind
him? Still the book is morally meaningful because it shows, like
Moby-Dick, how a man is unmanned by circumstance and the
force of his own decisions. Melville does not accept Pierre as the
Handsome Sailor. He annihilates him as an imperfect image,
whereas he accords his Handsome Sailors a resurrection and a
future life. In *Pierre* we meet a new false Prometheus for the first
time: Plinlimmon, who (like the Pharisee, Mr. Falsgrave) is the
Laodicean intellectual. (The short stories of the 1850's contain
certain characters who have affinities with characters in the novels
but do not lend themselves readily to schematization. *Bartleby* and
Benito Cereno introduce a new kind of false hero in Bartleby's

employer and Captain Delano, successful Americans who, though good at heart, earnest, and ethical, are morally unintelligent and spiritually obtuse.)

After *Moby-Dick, Israel Potter* contains the completest array of heroes, true and false. Seen in this way, it is a sort of light and playful redaction of *Moby-Dick*, but lacking *Moby-Dick's* terrific energy and vision—though, as we have noticed, the book has its gamesome eruptions from the deep. In this book it is clear that the ideal metamorphosis of Israel Potter is Ethan Allen; and there is no doubt that it is a failure in maturity which makes Israel Potter (the faultful but likable American, compounded of the peddler, the frontiersman, and Brother Jonathan) a "plebeian Lear or Oedipus" rather than a fully developed and unequivocal Lear or Oedipus. For at the end we find him poking around the ruins of the family homestead and muttering, "Father, father." John Paul Jones is the Ahab type and Benjamin Franklin is a metamorphosis of Plinlimmon.

The false hero in *The Confidence Man* has the same faults as Ahab and Pip, though they are represented partly in dialectical-argumentative terms rather than purely in myth and allegory. Like Ahab, the confidence man violates the rhythms of nature, not by willfully smashing through them, but by ignoring and misrepresent-ing them. And his motivations come from those dark, archaic levels where Pip turned to dwell. When we begin to understand *The Confidence Man* in this way, we begin to see how great an imaginative feat was Melville's attack on Laodicean liberalism, how he searched backward into the foundations of human nature for the sources of this apostasy.

Although Clarel is a kind of young Ishmael seeking conscious-ness (Melville may have meant the name "Clarel" to signify "divine light"), the long poem in which he figures exists apart from the heroic hierarchy of the novels. In *Clarel* the characters are secularized and deprived of Promethean-allegorical stature. For though Rolfe has certain affinities with Bulkington and Jack Chase, he is no Handsome Sailor but only a somewhat unhappy reasonable man, a naturalist and a humanist. If, as Melville intimates, the Civil War had confirmed him "in his natural bias for a life with men," Rolfe is his portrait of what he had come to see as purely

human in the Handsome Sailor. Though some readers will feel
that I am making a lamb out of a lion, for all practical purposes
it remains true that Rolfe is Herman Melville, or Herman Melville's ideal of the admirable nineteenth century American. Yet
Billy Budd is the final admission that Melville was disappointed
to find that Rolfe was only Rolfe. For no matter how much Rolfe
might understand and even sympathize with the Ishmaels, St.
Francises, Christs, gods, titans, and children of the world, his
sadness and Melville's sadness over him are the measure of Melville's final disequilibrium. Generally speaking, Melville must be
called philosophically a naturalist, in the sense that he based his
attitude toward life, morals, and art on a broadly conceived idea
of the developing processes of nature. Still he always grasped
beyond nature—or was it still within nature?—for a certain elusive
beatific vision, a certain divine flowering, a shining boyish innocence. The measure of Melville's uncertainty is the fact that finally
he could portray the Handsome Sailor or Promethean-Oedipean
hero only by halves. In Bulkington and Jack Chase and Ethan
Allen he could sketch and symbolize this heroic figure; but beyond
this he could not imagine the figure who would encompass both
Rolfe and Billy Budd. Yet does not this failure point to the short-
comings of American culture as much as to those of Herman
Melville?

2

Writers on Melville have often underestimated him as a thinker
and artist by allowing themselves to be so hypnotized by the myth
of Melville's career that they were unable to read his works. But it is
easy to overestimate Melville; and we must admit finally that his
artistic inadequacies were partly responsible for his gradual sub-
sidence into obscurity after the 1850's.

There was nothing in his intellectual "position" which was necessarily barren ground for the seeds of artistic genius. His opinions
and attitudes can only seem sterile or superficial if we oppose to
them some unverifiable dogma of universal truth. He was a skeptic
who could say with the Rolfe of *Clarel* that "few things are certain"
and who could write (in a letter of 1884) that he was neither

optimist nor pessimist. He was a liberal—a radical democrat of the great ante-bellum type—with a strong conservative streak, a liberal waiting to see what would happen in his time, hoping that men would be left free to accomplish what they could, but a liberal who could denounce and exhort with all the dark gloom of an Old Testament prophet. He wanted a heroic democracy in which man ("Nature's Roman") would be free, frank, and proud but in which standards of manly excellence would be opposed to that modern Diana of ill fame, "unanimous mediocrity." "I am told, my fellow-man, that there is an aristocracy of the brain," Melville wrote to Hawthorne. "At any rate, it is true that there have been those who, while earnest in behalf of political equality, still accept the intellectual estates."

Melville was a humanist—a Promethean humanist—and a naturalist—a Promethean naturalist. And in this Promethean attitude there was less that was vague, utopia-aspiring, and fuzzily ethical than in other nineteenth century Promethean attitudes, for he had a tragic vision of life which hardened him and clarified his vision. He had no consistent belief in God, except as a stern and often absentee Adversary. He thought it the prophetic duty of the moralist and the artist to assert the value of human life against its enemies, whether they were the celestial Adversary or the conventionalists and pharisaical liberals who did his work on earth.

We do not have to deduce all this from Melville's example or from the tendency of his writing: his position is explicit and intellectual. Very great legacies of art have been left us by men whose ideas and attitudes did not in principle differ from Melville's. It is true that Melville did not rest easily in his own position—woe to the man who does! But the explanation of his uneasiness lies less in the flaws of the position itself than in Melville's personal career—in whatever temperamental malaise and illusions of isolation finally extorted his anguished tribute to Billy Budd.

The time is surely behind us when we could think of Melville as no artist at all but only a man with some unaccountable gift of genius whose stirring adventures somehow spilled over into print. He was not a "natural" or "unconscious" artist. (Is not such a phenomenon impossible?) The man who wrote *Typee, Moby-Dick, Bartleby, Benito Cereno, The Encantadas, The Confidence Man,* and *Billy Budd,* the man we see working out different styles suitable to his different purposes, was that conscious and striving creator for whom there is no other word than artist. It is only this fact which can give us an enduring interest in Melville. The "shock of recognition," profound and exhilarating, which comes finally to the student of Melville is not only the recognition that he suffered and failed like a brave, doomed American but that he wrote certain excellent books. We must, of course, see Melville as the stricken Prometheus, the wounded prophet in the wilderness, even (in the words of Ludwig Lewisohn) as the "big bearded violently excited man trying to shout down the whimpering, lonely child in his soul." But what we must come to value most is the continuous act of heroism which made Melville a serious thinker and artist.

When we have recognized the qualities of mind displayed in Melville's books, the imperfections of that mind assume their proper perspective. It was a mind which operated sporadically, impelled by brilliant bursts of energy; a mind which managed a sustained flight only once. Melville was not that supreme kind of novelist who, like Henry James, could prepare himself to write with a perpetual, studious awareness of literary possibilities, with a continual probing and searching and amending. Melville was dedicated to the profession of letters certainly; but he lacked James's power of relentless devotion and his sense of professional purpose. Does not Melville's description of John Paul Jones uncomfortably remind us of Melville the writer:

The career of this stubborn adventurer signally illustrates the idea that since all human affairs are subject to organic disorder, since they are created in and sustained by a sort of half-disciplined chaos, hence he who in great things seeks success must never wait for smooth water, which never was and never will be, but, with what straggling methods he can, dash with all his derangements at his object, leaving the rest to Fortune.

Too much inclined to think of literature as an adventurous invasion into the mysteries of an imperfect world, a wild, exalted, prophetic hunt for an elusive truth, Melville was bound to be too little the continuously professional writer. If, as Alfred Kazin suggests, there was too short a time in American cultural history between Sitting Bull and Henry James, Melville suffered from the shortness of that time, and his work is fractured by the same disjunctions that characterize American literary tradition generally. Fancy "the man who had lived among cannibals" conscientiously studying Matthew Arnold on the influence of literary academies!

Melville was not a supremely inventive writer. He was too little like Daedalus, the continuous contriver, and too much like Prometheus, talking passionately out of his own painful experience. He had experienced too much too early and he wrote too furiously of his adventures, nearly exhausting his early experiences with the completion of *Moby-Dick*, when he was only thirty-two. The writing of his early books left an inner void at which he might be as frightened as he was of the emptiness of space. Even in the early books he was relying on written accounts of South Sea travel, rewriting and adapting long passages from travel books and the accounts of sea captains. *Benito Cereno* and *Israel Potter* were rewritten from subliterary biographies, though Melville wrote so well in these stories that the difference between his versions and the originals is absolute. And of the more purely inventive pieces, *Pierre* remains inchoate and *Clarel* is on the whole prolix and unorganized. As a poet, as Mr. Robert Penn Warren has said, Melville mastered his craft only in two or three poems and in isolated fragments, though, as Mr. Warren suggests, the poetic craft Melville was trying to learn was of a higher type than that "which some of his contemporaries did learn with such glibness of tongue and complacency of spirit."

Despite the distinguished and valuable stylistic achievement which could produce such differing pieces as *Moby-Dick, Benito Cereno, The Confidence Man,* "The Portent," the Supplement to the Civil War poems, and *Billy Budd,* there are frequent failures of language in Melville; some word-besotted rhetorical passage or some awkward posturing of phrase keeps pressing itself upon the attention of the reader—a passage or a phrase which Melville was unable or unwilling to amend. And there is an over-all deficiency in symbolization. The symbols of Movement and Stasis, Light and Dark, Flight and Fall, Space and Time, Mountain and Valley, and so on are often beautiful and sufficient in their context; but they are sometimes crude or vague. And often Melville was unable to refine them and to work out the careful variations upon them which the scope of his work demanded. His symbols lack the subtle quality of grouping themselves into a complex choate relationship which such literary projects as *Pierre* and *Clarel* demand.

3

For two reasons this book has not been primarily a biography. On the one hand, I have thought it the task of Melville criticism at the present time to study Melville's books. On the other hand, even if it were one's purpose and even if one had the vision to write Melville's spiritual biography, there are still too many facts missing, too many gaps, too few letters and documents. No one knew much about Herman Melville after the 1850's; and he himself wrote comparatively little during the last thirty years of his life. Still, one may put together a few scraps and bits of evidence in the hope of doing some service to this great and obscure man.

When Melville moved fom New York to Pittsfield in 1850, he was consciously isolating himself from the American literary culture of the day; this act determined the whole outward course, at least, of his career; over the years his isolation grew gradually complete. The act itself, however, was a positive and productive one. For Melville "withdrew" to Pittsfield in search of the spiritual energy needed for the writing of a great book. His act of isolation was like that of Father Mapple, in *Moby-Dick*, who climbing up into his prowlike pulpit to preach, always pulled his ladder up after him. "There must be some sober reason for this thing," thought Ishmael; "it must symbolize something unseen. Can it be, then, that by that act of physical isolation, he signifies his spiritual withdrawal for the time, from all outward worldly ties and connexions?" Yes, says Ishmael, and what Father Mapple seeks is replenishment "with the meat and wine of the word." As we see from his letters to Hawthorne and from the chapter in *Pierre* called "Young America in Literature," Melville found the literary culture of New York, to which his first books had introduced him, superficial, confining, and devoted to commercial success rather than serious work. Melville had a rather low opinion of his early books (he

called them *Typee, Fiddle-de-dee,* and *Hullabaloo*) and did not
like to think that he would go down in history as "the man who
lived among cannibals." He wanted to write better things, and so
he sought the solitude and open air of Pittsfield. Like Maurice de
Guérin in Paris, he could say to himself when he settled in New
York, "I enter the world with a secret horror";* and like Guérin
he soon found that he must leave the commercial metropolitan
literary scene. One gathers that Melville always wanted fame, that
whatever his love of solitude, whatever his misanthropy, he would
have liked to be a worldly success. "It is not aspiration but ambition that is the mother of misery in man," wrote W. R. Alger in
his *Solitudes of Nature and Man.* To which Melville added (in his
copy of Alger's book) the initials "HM."

But the removal to Pittsfield was not entirely a creative spiritual
act. Melville left New York under a cloud, for he feared that his
literary talent was doomed to an early decline and that this would
bring him some obscure but unavoidable ruination. The familiar
words from a letter of 1851 to Hawthorne seem to indicate this:
"From my twenty-fifth year I date my life. Three weeks have
scarcely passed between then and now that I have not unfolded
within myself. But I feel that I am now come to the inmost leaf
of the bud, and that shortly the flower must fall to the mould."
And consider the strange doomed withdrawal of the "gentleman
madman" in *The Confidence Man*—Charlemont, who "saw ruin
at hand" and mysteriously left St. Louis society, taking the sin of
separation to himself to save his friends from this sin when ruin
should come, fearing that his pride could not sustain the desertion
of his friends. Perhaps as late as 1855–1856, when he wrote *The
Confidence Man*, Melville hoped to "return" to the city, as did
Charlemont, to grow like golden maize "in the encouraging sun of
good opinions." But when he did return ten years later, it was to
the employment in the customhouse, where his solitude seems
to have been as complete as it was in Pittsfield. Did Melville have
an exalted, impossible ideal of friendship, like that of Ishmael and
Queequeg, which made him suspicious of all friendship, which
made him too easily hurt by the tensions and imperfections

* A sentence marked by Melville in his copy of Arnold's *Essays in Criticism,*
probably in 1869.

of human attachments? If so, we must suppose his relation with Hawthorne during the first Pittsfield years, however stimulating and profitable, was in the long run a disillusionment. So ardent was Melville's proffered friendship, so heated and exalted his letters and conversation, so overpowering his epic presence, that Hawthorne was made shy and uneasy. It was an abortive friendship. Years later Melville could surmise (if we may rely on the Clarel-Vine episode of *Clarel*) that as they had talked with each other, Hawthorne had been uncomfortable with a sense of the burdensome psychic demands of an imperfect titan whose sex was somewhat ambiguous. Like Beethoven, Melville could finally say: "I have no friend. I must live with myself alone." *

And so Melville became an American prototype of a special kind of genius: the estranged artist. Seeking his isolation, suffering from it, and still seeking it, he wrote in *Rammon* that "the more spiritual, wide-seeing, conscientious and sympathetic the nature, so much the more is . . . it isolationed, and isolation is the mother of illusion." In the proud, sensitive, and passionate Redburn we can already see the beginnings of Melville's separateness. Redburn, raising his rifle as if in a dream and clicking it at the insolent eye which surveyed his bizarre uncouthness; Redburn, withdrawing into the Ishmaelite wilderness of a private world to protect some inner icon of Being from the marauding and depraved merchantman sailors, was establishing an attitude which could never be abandoned. The proud formality of Redburn's speech, at once embarrassed and embarrassing, designed as it was to protect and assert an impossible aristocracy of the spirit and, as it seemed, to alienate everyone who heard it, this speech became the illusioned rhetoric of Melville's writings, the "nervous lofty speech" to which he refers in *Moby-Dick*. And how much at odds with the world was Redburn's speech! And how obviously it was the mask of one who wanted, nevertheless, to run with the world!

Moby-Dick was Melville's fantasy of attachment, his denial of the isolation which he knew he would both seek and fear as long as he lived. The myth of the book is vast, connective, all-encompassing—reaching out, like the arms of the giant squid, to capture a universe of man and nature in one enduring image and mood.

* Marked in Melville's copy of Alger's *Solitudes*.

Connecting with life, looking for a spiritual life line like the navel
cord of the whale which sometimes got entangled with the harpoons, Ishmael imagined himself in a blissful bed with a cannibal
or strolling through a paradisaical bower with the king of the
Arsacides or looking into the eyes of a fellow sailor as, leaning
together over a bucket, they squeezed lumps of blubber into liquid
sperm and accidentally squeezed each other's hand. Illusions of
isolation, certainly—as much so as the unutterably sweet anguish
of the atonement of Billy Budd and Captain Vere, the lost boy
and the "citified man." But if Redburn's proud, aloof, embarrassed,
opulent speech became the subtle, confluent rhetoric of *Moby-
Dick*, it grew unhappily petulant in *Pierre*. The subject matter of
Pierre and the restless, self-defeating will of the proud rhetorician
drew from him on the one hand a clumsy violence and on the
other a consuming desire to silence his own voice. "All profound
things and emotions of things are preceded and attended by
Silence," writes the author who had unfortunately not preceded
the writing of *Pierre* by silence but by a marvelous utterance.
"Silence is the general consecration of the universe. Silence is the
invisible laying on of the Divine Pontiff's hands upon the world.
. . . Silence . . . is that peculiar mood which prevails at a
solitary traveller's first setting forth on a journey." And silence,
our rhetorician feared, might be his fate. For if he should ruin his
talent by writing like a literary Ahab, violating all the rules of
nature and reason, driven on by some implacable demon, would
he not then be like little Pip, talking to no one in mad grammatical
snatches, declining verbs in a void; like the Spanish sailors on the
San Dominick, signaling distantly, enigmatically, through an impenetrable veil of misunderstanding; like the stunned and appealing
Benito Cereno, who could speak only through the distortion of an
unrelenting censor; like Bartleby, who would say nothing but, "I
would prefer not to," as he receded into the darkness; like Billy
Budd, who could utter strongly felt thoughts only with a stammer?
Would not his rhetoric take on the quality of the bell ringers who
at a distance seemed to be vainly signaling some inscrutable message like a semaphore wigwagging a dead and forgotten language?
And would not the failure of communication react upon the writer
so that he would begin to see the world as a masque of unrealities,

as a tragic "dumb-show seen from a blasted tower," as life looked to Hunilla enduring her long exile in the Encantadas or as it sometimes looked to Melville himself on his Mediterranean travels? For long years of his later career, Melville must have been able to say with Guérin, "I go forward with the isolated feeling of my existence, amidst the inert phantoms of all things." * And he could find solace, or at least kinship of feeling, in Matthew Arnold's statement that "the best are silent now" † and in Guérin's sad praise of the "power and beauty in the well-kept secret of one's self and one's thoughts." ‡ And finally, though he never actually stopped writing, he could say, with Guérin: "The literary career seems to me unreal, both in its essence and in the rewards which one seeks from it, and therefore fatally marred by a secret absurdity." § And to this he could add his own words, " . . . a truth which anyone who thinks in these days must have felt." It would be hard to name a serious American writer who has not been damaged by the haunting sense of the unreality of the literary career. The waste and loss have been incalculable. And so it was with Melville, unsustained by any viable and continuous literary culture, with its cumulative ground swell of common sensibility, its critical give and take, its support and attack. It is strange and pathetic, though surely understandable, to see Melville attentively studying, underlining, and apparently acquiescing in Arnold's essay on the influence of literary academies. Perhaps, in an adequate literary culture, Melville could think, anguished greatness would not be "Railed and hunted from the world." ¶

No temperament could have been less fitted than Melville's to flourish happily in America's Gilded Age. To the old sailors portrayed in the *John Marr* volume of poems (1888), the postwar America seemed a barren world indeed. They lived in the past, finding solace in thoughts of the "Old Order" which prevailed before "tradition was lost and we learned strange ways." The ways of the new era entered upon by America after it had crossed "the bridge of sighs" of the war were the ways of Mammon and the

* Marked by Melville in his copy of *Essays in Criticism.*
† *Ibid.*
‡ *Ibid.*
§ *Ibid.*
¶ Marked in "Empedocles on Etna" in Melville's copy of Arnold's *Poems.*

little foxes, the ways of practical science, money-making, success, and "unanimous mediocrity"—the ways prescribed by that "Pecksniff" who had displaced both Prometheus and Zeus and now "bossed the gods' high mess." The devoted writer and idealist could only "peep about," like Jimmy Rose, "among the marbles and mahoganies" of an alien, opulent, and empty house. It was a lacklustre day, this engineering age, and there could be little gratifying response to a writer, as Melville observed with a wry pun, "mid loud acclaim to Watts his name." Nor could there be much happiness for the reflective man who wished to sit by his companionable chimney and was perforce married to the spirit of a mindless progressivism, an unquiet, baneful spouse who measured all things with her meaningless tape measure and who really wanted to destroy both man and chimney.

What a gulf there had to be between the Gilded Age and this man who wanted his country to worship the Promethean revolutionaries, chieftains, and patriarchs of an earlier day and who had his own roster of saints—great, bluff, pagan gentlemen: the Jack Chases, the Bulkingtons, the Ethan Allens! Melville felt that the country he loved and had tried to exalt and inspirit with his prophetic art had unjustifiably ignored him and beaten him down, though he had tried to speak with a public speech that varied from joyful, epic exhortation to bitter, purifying satire and to grave, moral suasion.

Did Melville grow too unworldly? Was there something a little unbecoming or sentimental in his withdrawn inertness, his attitude of harmlessness, his inability, as Lizzie Melville complained, to keep the family financial accounts? One occasionally feels that there was. He was a little too ready to find a tragedy in the fact that as captain of a ship Ahab had to resort to the "external arts and entrenchments" necessary to the attainment of a "practical, available supremacy over other men." There is more self-indulgence than one likes to think in the "harmlessness" he attributes to Billy Budd. And there is something actively offensive in what he says about Matthew Arnold (from whom he had learned much) in a letter of 1885: that in order to achieve fame a writer must "dilute" his genius "with that prudential worldly element wherewithal Mr. Arnold has conciliated the conventionalists." Reading this, one can only think that Herman Melville might have done better and been happier if he had not shied quite so readily from the ways of the world or had not found such enormous natural supremacy in the "Divine Inert" who shun "the world's hustings." And there may have been a touch of peripheral petulance, of Ishmaelite rancor, of injured self-righteousness, or even of self-pity in his reaction to the words he so vehemently marked in his copy of the New Testament; but were they not, nevertheless, a true and objective criticism?

O Jerusalem, Jerusalem, which killest the prophets, and stonest them that are sent unto thee; how often would I have gathered thy children together, as a hen doth gather her brood under her wings, and ye would not! Behold, your house is left unto you desolate.

In America the best were silent, and American ears were attuned only to the sweet voice of Confidence.

Melville's estrangement from society and his own consciousness of his estrangement have the greatest bearing on our understanding of his personal life. But the note of Ishmaelite self-righteousness which one detects in Melville's attitude toward himself ought to warn us away from a dangerous overemphasis in our study of his books: I mean the overemphasis of the separation between those too easily hypostatized quantities, the artist and society, and its effect on the artist's mind and work. Beginning with the 1920's (to look no further back), the much cherished specter of isolation, as Mr. Quentin Anderson justly complains, has debilitated whole schools of criticism. The isolation of our American artists has been alleged, established, and protected in so many sensitively conceived circles of abstraction that isolation has been made to seem the fundamental and unique quality of the artist's mind. But what does Melville himself say about isolation? First, with the probable suggestion that they may be either good or bad, that isolation creates "illusions." But, second, that the central, motivating quality of the artist's isolation is a denial *of* that isolation; for the isolated mind is the mind which is *more* "spiritual, wide-seeing, conscientious and sympathetic" than other minds. The artist's isolation from society implies, indeed is *caused by*, his superior degree of involvement with it. The artist's withdrawal from society causes his return to it, and vice versa. Melville's greatest book is the one which most profoundly symbolizes this truth. In *Moby-Dick* we have the supreme spectacle of the artist's consciousness, developed to the level of tragic understanding through the tensions of a real and mythicized family history, emerging through the folk myths, or consciousness, of society and transmuting and uttering these myths with an unequaled visionary exactitude. If some inscrutable fate should condemn all but two of Melville's books to oblivion, we should want to save *Moby-Dick* and *The Confidence Man,* because these are the two books which tell us most about Melville's mind. And in these books we preeminently see the artist's consciousness ("Ishmael") returning through the consciousness of the culture in which and out of which it lived. This return of the artist's consciousness is the defining act of his moral assertion, and it is no accident that *Moby-Dick* and *The Confidence Man*—encompassing a· whole culture, exempting no man from responsibility, as Billy Budd is exempted—are Melville's two preeminent moral statements. All men are estranged, but those who are *only* estranged cannot be called artists.

We cannot, of course, understand even the personal life of Melville by speaking only of his relation to society. He himself knew that there were other considerations:

> 'Tis not the times, 'tis not the sophists vex him.
> There is some root of suffering in himself,
> Some secret and unfollowed vein of woe.*

Melville was subject to attacks of nervous disorder; Dr. Holmes was called in by the family to see if Herman, who had not been well during and after the writing of *Pierre,* was going the way of his father; and there is a letter dated 1876 (when *Clarel* was being published) in which Lizzie Melville asks a relative not to visit just now and admits that her husband's nervous condition frightens her. These were presumably nervous attacks consequent upon Melville's obscure, abiding neurosis. Melville knew that he was in some way like Ahab, "a pedlar with a crushing pack," like his own invalid Titans and Maimed Men in the Glen, like his own "Pierre Glendinning." Where did Melville get that terrible sense of

---

* From "Empedocles," marked by Melville.

disaster, which made Redburn want to smash the glass ship, the cherished family art piece, and made the author of *Moby-Dick* destroy the *Pequod* with such a supernatural transfixion and apocalypse? And where did he get that lyrical sense of fear—that fascination with the huge mindless motions of matter: the machine-like man-of-war, the whale, the paper mill, the slow shuffling of the tortoise among rocks, the silent swaying of John Brown's body; that fear of space, unmeasured, featureless, instinct with appalling power; that fear of whiteness; that terror of the annihilating god; that hypnotic spell with which he beholds the Medean mother-principle of the world and shudders at the awful guilty sensation of stasis and petrifaction? Did it begin in some dimly imagined or remembered family vision of plunder and mutilation? Melville had a fear of robbery, as we gather fom the recurring image of the secret crypt which is alternately plundered, renounced, or protected and from that pure white jacket whose pockets the young hero had to sew up to foil the thieving sailors, who seemed to regard them as "closets, crypts, and cabinets" containing valuables. This primitive fear always remained with Melville and one may guess that with growing insistence it influenced him to write less and less, making him fear that to put himself into his writing was to allow himself to be "unmanned" like Ahab and Pierre and Billy Budd.

Herman Melville may have had more than ordinary reason to berate the Anarch (as he does in "After the Pleasure Party") who made two separate sexes. As has often been said, there are no real women in his books: Fayaway is only a lovely wraith from the childish springtime of the world; Yillah and Lucy—despite her symbolically willed completeness—are insubstantial radiances; Hautia and Isabel are vortexes which threaten to mutilate and engulf the unwary; Mary Glendinning is a Semiramian monster. Always in Melville's writings the female body—that Tartarus of Maids—revives some primitive fear, some dark ambiguous awe, some sick revulsion, some guilty, stonelike paralysis; always it assumes an image like the abstract albino skin of Yillah, the Medusa face, the "soft man eater, furry fine," that terrible man-trap crouching in the last recesses of inward vision. Female beauty —tender, erotic, and joy-giving—he could see only in men: in the beautiful youth Antinoüs; in that Ishmael who knew such bliss with Queequeg; in Pierre, the girlish Prometheus; in Billy Budd, the girlish Christ. In *Redburn* there were two images of the author: Redburn himself, who would survive and mature, and Harry Bolton, the homosexual youth who was doomed. But Harry Bolton lived on in Melville.

Melville's strain of homosexualism was entirely inward and subdued. He was a devoted family man, despite the periodic overseas trips he made (the last of these was a voyage to San Francisco on his brother's clipper in 1860), despite the eccentric demands of his genius, and despite his inability or disinclination to make money. A letter of 1860 to his little daughter Bessie, datelined "Pacific Ocean" and printed with large comic strokes of the pen, is gay and gently affectionate. His severe but gentle letter of the same period to his son Malcolm, lecturing him on "poor shabby fellows" who worry and disobey their mothers, is faithfully paternal. And there seems no reason to question one's impression that his marriage was in the long run devoted and affectionate on both sides. Melville's Lizzie, one concludes, must have had rare strength and womanly understanding. There can have been little enough in her upbringing among the Massachusetts Shaws to prepare her for a lifetime with a man who could not help thinking of himself as an "invalid Titan" and who in his books loved men better than women and signified this fact with his homoerotic fantasies—fantasies that surpassed life in their poignant tenderness and in their titanic primeval surging.

As "After the Pleasure Party" says in effect, Melville suffered bitterly from his inevitable sense of being celibate, the more so because he was apparently a man of powerful erotic drives. The waste and the pain of this half-celibacy, one gathers, were harder and harder to bear when he found that he could never write again as he had in *Moby-Dick*. He had fallen once more, like Simon Magus, like Urania, and every fall exacted its penalty. Can anything exceed the suffering implied by the cruel little phallic masque Melville jotted down in his *Journal* after seeing a Temple of Venus near Naples? "*Temple of Venus*. Round. Summit wavy with verdure—corpses dressed for a ball."

In his copy of Arnold's *Essays*, Melville marked the following sentence (Arnold is speaking of Keats and Guérin): "The temperament, the talent itself, is deeply influenced by their mysterious malady; the temperament is *devouring*; it uses vital power too hard and too fast, paying the penalty in long hours of unutterable exhaustion and in premature death." And to these words Melville added: "So is everyone influenced—the robust, the weak. . . . We are what we were made." It is certain, as we have noticed, that Melville feared an early doom. When he spoke in 1851 of the bud that was about to fall to the mold, he was merely setting down one image of his central myth about himself: the myth of the Fall. From the earliest period of his mythicized orphanhood, when his father failed in business and died and the family was forced to get along at a lower level of existence, he looked back to felicity and forward to disaster. The fall of the Melvilles and the author's exile from his family were to find many symbolic metamorphoses: the fall from heaven of the nimble god Roo, the fall of Enceladus and all the Titans, the fall from innocence of White-Jacket, the fall of Simon Magus, the perpetual fall of all mankind, and the fall of the United States from the "Founders' Dream." Pascal had thought of man as a "ruined archangel," as Melville noted; and there is no doubt that this is the way Melville thought of himself.

The search of Ishmael, fallen from felicity, was for his father; and the search took two directions: either it was a growing, creative search for form and guidance and power and authority or (as in *Israel Potter*) it was a defeated poking about among the ruins of the family house for the lost one. In *Moby-Dick* a surging, growing man has found the paternal principles of art and life for which he sought in the earlier books. The towering ego of the writer is in full possession of consciousness and the world and is in harmony with whatever divinity may reside in "the now egotistical sky." But what has happened to *Pierre*, despite the beauties of the book? A spiritual disaster has overtaken the writer, an apocalyptic shattering of the tower, a disintegration and a relapse which longed for its own lovely image and was filled with unimaginable horror. *Moby-Dick* was an overextension which Melville could never again quite approximate and from which he could never quite recover. Having gained that bright, ill founded eminence, he must creep back perilously into the recesses of the past and his childhood, turning back like Orpheus into the darkness. He must dream that wish-dream of reversion which Ishmael barely escaped in *Moby-Dick*. And the dream of Ishmael is the immaculate marble pillar—static and pure—which represents Death. With horror and longing, the author of *Pierre* turned back, like Mortmain, to the Medean muck and "mould . . . of what men be," and beholding the godlike frame of the author of *Moby-Dick*, he cried, "Undo, undo,"

> Prithee undo, and still renew
> The fall forever!

The shining tower collapsed on its own infirm foundations, and Melville sank back to earth and into her caverns. Enraged, violent, petulant, he sank down like Simon Magus out of space. Was he ready, like Mortmain, to die? Once, he wrote to his brother in 1862, he "cherished a loose sort of notion that I did not care to live very long. But I will frankly own that I have now no serious, no insuperable objections to a respectable longevity." In 1867 he marked these words of Beethoven in his copy of Alger's *Solitudes*: "I was nigh taking my life with my own hands. But Art held me back. I could not leave the world until I had revealed what lay within me." And Melville went on, whatever the pain of exile and disappointment, to think, to change, to grow in wisdom, to humanize the ruined archangel as much as he could.

And indeed the archangel did grow human. Alienated and stricken though Melville may have been, his personal myth came to include, after the early 1850's, the figure of the Anglo-Saxon gentleman: the lawyer in *Bartleby the Scrivener*, Captain Delano in *Benito Cereno*, and Captain Vere in *Billy Budd*.*

Captain the Honorable Edward Fairfax Vere—a man of aristocratic connections; a man committed to the ways of the world and aware of the tragic implications of the commitment; a captain who wielded authority and knew the social necessity of "forms"; a man compassionate and honest but vulnerable to the wounds of pathetic passion, which he lacked the brilliance to defend himself against; a man of common sense, a realist, but with a vein of fantasy which

---

* Melville's elder brother Thomas was a sea captain. And *Billy Budd* seems to have been originally suggested by an episode in the life of one of Melville's cousins, also a captain.

made the name of Starry Vere appropriate; a respectable man and, in his fundamentally second-rate way, successful until in his late years a cloud passed over his life—such was this "speaker of truth" with whom Melville identified himself in his fiction.

Captain Vere is the image of strength and integrity which Melville kept before him in the years of sickness and confusion during the 1850's. A man who feared that his fate might be that of Bartleby or Benito Cereno or Billy Budd needed in the interests of personal sanity to mythicize another part of his character. It may be that Melville's ability to offset the Billy Budd image of himself with the Vere image is what enabled him to pass through the period when he "did not care to live very long" and what finally removed all "insuperable objections to a respectable longevity." Yet Captain Vere is inextricably and even fatally involved with the regressive and doomed son. And he died a middle-aged man.

The central figure of the final passages of the Melville myth is the Old Sailor, a man who has some of the worldly characteristics of Captain Vere but who has a deeper vein of mystery because of certain dark events in his past. He is not so much overshadowed as branded. He is Ishmael grown old. The Ishmaelite intransigence, setting him apart from every man, still persists, though Ishmael now grows mellow and sometimes cannot quite remember the circumstances of his youthful wanderings. Like Captain Vere, the Old Sailor is depicted in *Billy Budd*: he is the mainmastman, the "old Dansker" who calls Billy "Baby Budd." Or rather he is the old Dansker mythicized and renamed "Daniel Orme," as we discover in a prose sketch which Melville labeled "omitted of Billy Budd." I take the Daniel Orme fragment to be very much a self-portrait. It begins by warning the would-be biographer that the face of Daniel Orme is stubbornly visored.

We try to ascertain from somebody the career and experience of the man, or may seek to obtain this information from himself. But what we hear from others may prove but unreliable gossip, and he himself, if approached, prove fastidiously uncommunicative. In short, in most instances he turns out to be like a meteoric stone in a field. There it is. The neighbors have their say about it, and an odd enough say it may prove: but what is it? whence did it come?

Like a falling meteoric stone, Daniel Orme, once captain of the top on a man-of-war, had descended to a station at the foot of the mast as he grew older, and finally, as a "septuagenarian," had "slipped into obscure moorings ashore." Always somewhat distant and unlike his fellows, he at last was "specially noted" for his unsociability. As if haunted by the dark memory of certain tragic events in his early life, he was moody and spent much time muttering to himself. As his heroic mien gradually gave way to the attrition of the years, he lost some of his old aloofness and gruffness. Now

a stranger accosting him sunning himself upon some old spar on the strand, and kindly saluting him there, would receive no surly response, and if more than mere salutations were exchanged, would probably go away with the impression that he had been talking with an interesting oddity, a salt philosopher, not lacking in a sort of grim common sense.

The Old Sailor had the curious habit of turning back his frock to contemplate a mark on his body and would growl his resentment at anyone who surprised him in the act. His friends put a drug in his tea, and while he slept, they examined the mark. It was a crucifix tattooed in indigo and vermilion over his heart and gashed across with a thin white scar. Usually, Melville says, sailors wear the cross tattooed on their forearms. For Daniel Orme, Christianity was not externalized and active, but a thing of the heart—massive, intimate, hidden, and because of its inwardness Orme's Christianity was canceled out or emasculated. The scar was the mark of the man-of-war world, a saber cut Orme had sustained in protecting his ship against the boarding enemy.

The gossips of Daniel Orme's lodging place reported to the landlady that Orme was a "*man forbid*, a man branded by the Evil Spirit," and they intimated that "it would be well to get rid of him." But "the good woman . . . was a sensible lady" and "she turned a deaf ear to all solicitations against him." God bless Lizzie Melville!

Rumors about Daniel Orme's supposedly criminal or satanic career persisted: one of them alleged that he had been a "buccaneer." Far more than he ever knew, such underhand slanders had accompanied Orme throughout his life. In his days at sea he had kept apart from his fellows; "there was a quite leonine droop about the angles of his mouth that said—*hands off*." And now in

his obscure land moorings he grew somewhat hazy about his surroundings and "pursued his solitary way with not much from without to disturb him." In his retirement

the superannuated giant begins to mellow down into a sort of animal
decay. In hard, rude natures, especially such as have passed their lives
among the elements, farmers or sailors, the animal decay mostly affects
the memory by casting a haze over it; not seldom, it softens the heart
as well, besides more or less, perhaps, drowsing the conscience, innocent
or otherwise.

Was not the author of *Billy Budd* such a man, not always knowing
whether he remembered or forgot and somewhat drowsy over the
question of the innocent or the otherwise?

And the drowsiness became darkness. On Easter Day, Orme
was discovered alone and dead on a windswept height overlooking
the sea. Sitting on the ground, leaning back on a battery of obsolete
and rusty cannon, he had smoked his clay pipe to the bottom of the
bowl. His eyes were still open, fixed with a "vital glance" on the
hazy outlet to the ocean. Perhaps after all there was no truth in
the rumors about the criminal past of Daniel Orme. Perhaps his
moodiness and his strange starts and grimaces could not be attributed to his being pursued by avenging furies. Were not these
freaks and grimaces only the to-be-expected grotesque "wens and
knobs and distortions of the bark of an old chance apple-tree in an
inclement upland, not only beaten by many storms, but also obstructed in its natural development by the chance of its having
first sprouted among hard-packed rock?" Life had been hard for
Herman Melville, whose profession was art and the seed of whose
genius had been dropped as if by chance among rocks and had
somehow flourished in the inclement environment. But his development had been natural, though so adamantly obstructed. One need
imagine no avenging furies, no hidden guilt beyond the burden
of every man, to account for the outward scars and distortions of
mind and body. The knobs and wens of an apple tree, the small
organic madnesses of a man, were the inevitable marks of the
suffering which gives life, the scars of birth. In a society that
wanted to see a kinship between the artist and the criminal, one's
continuing sanity depended upon knowing that it did so and upon
going one's own way.

Daniel Orme "lies buried among other sailors, for whom also strangers performed the last rites in a lonely plot overgrown with wild eglantine uncared for by man." Melville died on September 28, 1891. His wife and two daughters and a small group of family friends accompanied the body to Woodlawn Cemetery. Only one newspaper carried an obituary notice. But now strangers have begun to perform the rites which are due him. No doubt we shall never know exactly how Melville lived or how he died. For there are many ways to live and die: the way of Ahab or Pierre or Benito Cereno or Billy Budd or Captain Vere or Daniel Orme—or the way of a respectable citizen and retired customs inspector who died quietly in New York City. To perform the rites is to remain the stranger. That is our American plight. Yet it may be that we begin to accept the conditions of love, to connect and to identify ourselves with one another—with those younger, with those older, with the future, with the past and the past's great dead. It would be foolish to crow that at last America has come of age; but it would be more so to suppose that this can never happen. When our maturity does come, it will be because we recognize and accept our "kindness"—our human love and our identicalness of "kind." Such was the thought that once moved Ishmael to exclaim:

Oh! my dear fellow beings, why should we longer cherish any social acerbities, or know the slightest ill-humor or envy! Come; let us squeeze hands all round; nay, let us all squeeze ourselves into each other; let us squeeze ourselves universally into the very milk and sperm of kindness.

A high culture cannot be pervasively riven with inner estrangements. And neither can the citizen of a high culture. This simple truth, exemplified in every natural organism, our liberal democratic thought has often failed to honor. We do not accept; we reject. We do not connect; we sever. We do not identify; we puff our inner righteousness into an image of the universe and annihilate every other image. To be sure, we must reject, sever, and annihilate everything that denies our ultimate freedoms. But the error of our liberal thought, the question of freedom apart, is that it longs to be in love with estrangement: with the divorce of parts, the interstices and loopholes, the disjunctions and the blank spaces, the hiatus between the sexes, the abyss that separates generations, the enmity between the terrified ego and the unconscious, between action and motive, between reason and myth, between father and son. And the icon of the liberal mind in love with estrangement has been the hooded phantom, the white mask, the common man without features, mind, or sex. If we are really, like Ahab, the votaries of the white icon, we shall continue our murderous lopping and cutting and severing of the great body of Leviathan until all of life is hacked out. But if we are Ishmael, we may live to love Leviathan, who is the mythical body of the world, of our culture, and of ourselves.

Index

303